A Quest for Time

A Quest for Time

The Reduction of Work in
Britain and France, 1840–1940

Gary Cross

UNIVERSITY OF CALIFORNIA PRESS

Berkeley / Los Angeles / London

University of California Press
Berkeley and Los Angeles, California

University of California Press, Ltd.
London, England

Library of Congress Cataloging-in-Publication Data

Cross, Gary S.
  A quest for time.

Includes index.
    1. Hours of labor—Great Britain—History.   2. Hours
of labor—France—History.   I. Title.
HD5165.C76   1989   331.25'72'0941   88-27839
ISBN 0-520-06532-8 (alk. paper)

Printed in the United States of America

Acknowledgments of passages published elsewhere:
"The Quest for Leisure: Reassessing the Eight-Hour Day in France,"
Journal of Social History 18 (Winter 1984): 195–216. Revised.
Reprinted by permission.
"Les Trois Huit: International Reform, Labor Movements, and the
Eight-Hour Day, 1919–1924," *French Historical Studies* 14 (Fall
1985): 240–68. Reprinted by permission.
"Worktime in International Discontinuity, 1886–1940," in *Worktime
and Industrialization: An International History,* ed. Gary Cross
(Philadelphia, 1988), pp. 155–81, © 1988 by Temple University.
Reprinted by permission.

Contents

Preface

Like many novice labor historians during the early 1970s, I was intrigued by the origins and fate of politically conscious labor in the upheaval of nineteenth-century industrialization. Perhaps a majority of my peers focused on the formation of industrial working classes up to World War I. I was one of those who looked for an explanation of why and how these labor movements changed—especially by an apparent narrowing of perspective—in response to the rationalized economies of the twentieth century. The result was a seminar paper, and the research on that project was the beginning of this book.

In my paper, I attempted to address an old question—the decline of the ideals of workers' control in France after 1914. After finding the political and ideological approaches of institutional histories insufficient, I shifted to the presumably firmer ground of technological change to explain the decline of revolutionary labor and came to a rather conventional conclusion: in the face of managerial and mechanical assaults on skill-based work, French labor had little choice but to embrace the corporatist formulas of reformism or the bread-and-butter economism of communism. Soon I dropped the topic to pursue the same general problem from a different angle—the impact of immigration on the shifting of the French working class in a conservative direction.

Yet I never was satisfied with this approach. After about ten years of tilling on the margins of the field in immigration history, I decided to give my first topic a second look. I had been dissatisfied for some time with several dominant trends in labor history: the search for autono-

mous working-class cultures at the price of neglecting the political contest and the tendency to view twentieth-century labor reformism as an
inevitable product of modernization or of false consciousness and un-
heroic compromise. As the Western nations drifted toward the Right in
the 1970s, the key historical question appeared less the fate of revolutionary challenges to capitalism than when and how democratic reforms
could penetrate the social order.

I also came to see that my earlier approach neglected the significance
of life beyond the workplace. The new history of gender, family, and
even leisure, which surely has put traditional labor history in a shadow
since the mid-1970s, seemed to offer fresh approaches to the labor
question. I might have undertaken a community historical study, an approach that has served well to elucidate the full dimensions of class and
culture. But I remained convinced that questions of class in relationship
to the state had yet to be fully explored and that these issues required a
national—and, indeed, international—perspective. It was clear, however, that work was an insufficient unit of analysis and that reform had
to be understood in the broad context of leisure and family as well.

In particular, reflecting on my early work, I was struck by the almost
obsessive interest that labor had in the interwar period with the reform
of worktime—especially the eight-hour day and the claim to it as a
right of citizenship. I found in this concern with working hours a new
significance. It was not a consolation prize in a lost contest over the
character of industrial society but an expression of a far deeper quest for
time. The eight-hour day was surely central to the postwar debate over
the shape of the French economy and society. It occurred to me that an
investigation of worktime might serve as a prism through which to look
at this critical transformation of labor in a new light. The issue was not
merely the reduction of working hours but the reallocation of time, a
shift that affected life beyond employment as much as the experience of
work. I hoped to find in this quest for time a way of linking the radicalism of labor history before World War I with the reformism that followed and of relating changes in work with shifting attitudes toward
family and leisure.

I stirred up more dust than I could realistically settle in one book,
but it seemed worthwhile to press on. The fact that a movement for
shorter working hours was one of few fresh fronts on which European
labor moved in the late 1970s and 1980s made the historical experience
of this movement even more significant. And because of the difficulties
that these struggles have encountered, a long view of the problems of
reform became all the more useful.

I dug at the stump of this old tree, uncovering roots that were rather deeper and more extensive than at first expected. Perhaps most important, I found that an investigation of the French short-hours movement was insufficient. Not only was the quest for time an international movement at almost every stage, but its transnational character was essential for its success. Moreover, by looking in detail at another country, I could break out of the ghetto of national (and particularly French) labor history and address a wider audience. I chose Britain because it was arguably the birthplace of the short-hours movement and provided its most important literature until at least the early 1890s.

The result is this book. Its occasional polemical bark is as much directed toward the ghost of my earlier thoughts as it is toward those of contemporary scholars. I hope readers will find that this work grows from the concerns of the last generation of labor history and is not merely a reaction to them. The book focuses on the politics of worktime, and only secondarily on its culture or economics. Still by "politics" I mean more than a study of labor legislation and collective bargaining—although these areas are important and far too long neglected by social and labor historians. The question of worktime reform is unanswerable without analysis of the ideological struggle over the political economy of time, changing attitudes toward work and leisure, and the broad economic context.

I owe a great deal to many who broadened my perspective on this topic. Among the people who gave me their time and ideas are Clive Behagg, Julian Jackson, Karl Hinrichs, Teresa Murphy, David Roediger, Kathryn Kish Sklar, Irmgard Steinisch, and Robert Sykes. Each of these people share with me an interest in the historical problem of worktime and have made important contributions to this question. Conversation and correspondence with them has sharpened my focus and extended my view. Other scholars, who for the most part also have done work in this field, have also critically read parts or all of the text. They gave me a hand when I was skating on thin ice. These include David Brody, Gerald Eggert, Steve Fraser, John Horner, Benjamin Hunnicutt, Lucien Karstens, Wassily Leontief, Wayne Lewchuk, Anson Rabinbach, Martha Shields, Dan Silverman, Carmen Sirianni, Stewart Weaver, and Lee Shai Weisbach.

I owe much to Harvey Goldberg, who seventeen years ago led that seminar that set me on the track of this subject; despite the likelihood that he might well have disagreed with a good deal of my argument, I think he would have seen some of himself in the results. James E. Cronin not only gave generously of his time in assuaging my various anxieties but also offered invaluable aid to this French historian trying to find his way into the thicket of British social history. The financial support of the National Endowment for the Humanities and the Institute for the Arts and Humanistic Studies at the Pennsylvania State University was much appreciated. Finally, Maru Cross has contributed more to this project than I can express.

Abbreviations

ASE	Amalgamated Society of Engineers
BPP	*British Parliamentary Papers*
ChDoc	Chambre des Députés, *Annales, Documents parlementaires*
ChDeb	Chambre des Députés, *Annales, Débats parlementaires*
CGT	Confédération Générale du Travail
CGTU	Confédération Générale du Travail Unitaire
ECA	Early Closing Association
EEF	Engineering Employers' Federation
F^{22}, F^7, F^{14}	Series in Archives Nationales de la France
HMWC	Health of Munition Workers' Committee
IALL	International Association for Labor Legislation
ILO	International Labor Office
ISTC	Iron and Steel Trades Confederation
LSE	London School of Economics and Political Science
ML	Ministry of Labour
MRC	Modern Records Centre (University of Warwick)
PP	Archives de la Prefecture de Police (Paris)
PRO	Public Records Office (London)
RCL	Royal Commission on Labour (1892–1894)
SDeb	Senat, *Annales, Débats parlementaires*
SDoc	Senat, *Annales, Documents parlementaires*
TUC	Trades Union Congress

1

A Question of Time

For historians, time is an objective fact, a yardstick that allows them to lord over those who "merely" lived in the past. Yet, for the living individual, time is the scarcest of resources. It is involuntarily consumed and, despite our wishful thinking, it cannot be "saved." For preindustrial and religious peoples, scarcity of time generally meant the brevity of physical life; and many sought to suppress the "terror of time" in an unending cycle of religious rites of "eternal" beginnings. Most modern people face this frustration differently. We attempt to anticipate the future in the present. Society no longer seeks to suppress time; rather the object is to "gain" and "save" it by more efficiently consuming it.[1] We seek also to allocate our time. For most of us, the central issue is the portion of life necessary for work and the periods free from it.[2]

We have resolved the dilemma of scarcity by creating neat packages of time: regular eight-hour workdays interrupted by the weekend, annual summer vacation, and retirement. What may appear to most of us as a natural allocation of time is, of course, unique to twentieth-century industrial democracies.

The modern distribution of time has important normative implications: some may believe it came at the price of the intensification of the pace of life and the unnatural segmentation of time into moments of work, play, and family activity; for others, the modern solution to the time problem has produced an extension of personal freedom and a rational and efficient demarcation between the temporal realms of social necessity and individual liberty. In any case, there is no obvious reason why any work and leisure package should be understood as normal or natural. Indeed, one might assume that a portion of increased productivity would be distributed as leisure. Yet, despite steady economic growth since World War II, there has been little change in working hours in recent years; in fact, the eight-hour day has been the norm for seventy years. Shifts in the allocation of time in the nineteenth century were similarly discontinuous.

Just when and why has this meaning and distribution of time changed in the modern world? Most historians have provided technological or economic answers to this question. For example, Jacques Attali has structured a global history of time around the development of the tools of its measurement and the elites that controlled its use. His work neatly summarizes a common and attractive technological determinism.[3]

It is almost a truism that the key to the industrial era was not the steam engine but the modern clock. Its capacity to measure minutes and later seconds allowed a new intensification of the tempo of life. Time, which had once been organized by the clergy according to the season and week, had become in the late eighteenth century a tool of industrialists to regulate the minute flow of production.[4] Work for the first time could be precisely regulated and even intensified. Unlike the calendar, which allowed for the play of irregular labor, the clock became a weapon used by employers to eliminate the gaps in the traditional day of work; it assured a continuity and uniformity of output even without the benefit of the machine. Clock time—unlike the broad durations of the past—became a means of quantifying the economic value of labor. Along with the division of labor and the mechanization of work, clock time made possible the treatment of labor power as a commodity, as so many units of time. The value of a product or service was now measured by the time necessary to produce it. Time had become money.[5]

This analysis, of course, helps explain two basic realities of the industrial age: the devaluation of leisure and other nonwork activities by the owning classes and the persistent attempt of workers to raise the price of their labor time by making it scarce through the reduction of hours. To be sure, in the long run, leisure regains value. But economic historians tend to understand this in narrowly monetary terms: with rising incomes, workers may choose to "buy" leisure—that is, forgo additional income for free time. But leisure is perceived primarily as consumption time, periods in which domestic and pleasure purchases can be made.[6]

This line of argument has the virtue of coherence and explanatory power. It links technology with a new economic hegemonic elite. Josiah Wedgewood with his set factory hours, Frederick Taylor and his stop watch, and Charles Bedaux with his "B" units that claimed to apportion both worktime and rest time—all capitalized on the power of the clock to regularize and intensify the pace of work.[7] This theory helps to separate us clearly from our premodern ancestors who gave time other meanings than money and who melded work and leisure time.

Although this is surely a necessary explanation, it neglects the complexity of change and the input of noneconomic factors in the redistribution of time. In particular, an economic-technological explanation fails to account for the discontinuities and conflicts that accompanied the historic changes in the allocation of time. It does not explain when working hours were reduced. Often this approach contains at least an implicit judgment that clock time has been accompanied by the cultural hegemony of entrepreneurs who have succeeded in crowding out traditional values and imposing their "commoditized" notions of time upon the workers.

This view is surely incomplete, because it leaves out politics and that complex phenomenon of popular pressure and intellectual leadership that shaped the destiny of modern liberal democratic societies. Most simply, the economic-technological argument ignores the factor of reform. When and why working hours were reduced and a new labor standard achieved are questions that must address the problem of discontinuity and the complexities of motive and power. Although this issue was born in the workplace, it is resolved only in the political arena, and often in an international context.

I do not propose here to offer a narrative history of the legislation and collective bargaining relating to worktime. That would be as onesided as economic-technological determinism. I choose to write neither a political nor an economic and social history. Rather I attempt to forge a link between these approaches. I give primacy to politics, but will also attempt to root reform in at least the topsoil of social and labor history.

The overriding theme of a generation of modern labor historians, inspired by scholars like E. P. Thompson and Michelle Perrot, has been to explain the rise and decline of social conflict and class consciousness within workplaces and communities. This concern has produced an extraordinary number of local and trade studies that have enriched our understanding of the experience and values of ordinary people. Yet for most of these historians labor reform is basically unproblematic. Reform seems remote to the experiences of workers, only marginal to more essential social change, or even as mere marks of bourgeois hegemony. Labeling this tradition as history with the politics left out is unfair for these workplace and community studies have sought to explain broad political change; moreover, British social historian G. Stedman Jones has recently argued for turning from the workplace and community to the arena of political discourse in order to resolve outstanding historical questions. The problem, I think, is less the lack of a political perspective than a narrow one. The focus has varied from country to country. In Britain, the critical period was probably the rise and decline of Chartism; in France, the revolutionary episodes that culminated in the growth and collapse of syndicalism. In both cases the primary concern has been to explain the rise and fall of systemic challenges to the social order and less the conditions that make for subtle but significant shifts in the terms of the social contest.[8]

Contemporary historians of reform have sought to explain the roles of intellectual and political elites in the origins of the welfare state and the domestication of class conflict. Sanford Elwitt and Judith Stone have provided us with fresh views of the elite agenda in the late nineteenth century to recast French capitalism. And new accounts of the history of the British Factory Acts of the 1830s and 1840s have clarified the role of reforming elites in this critical period. But these histories usually ignore the role of popular forces in the transformation of law; they often presume that social control is the principal objective of reform. Recently, however, Robert Sykes and Stewart Weaver, for example, suggest more complex social origins and purposes to early Victorian British factory reform.[9]

There are some hopeful signs of the relinkage of political and social history. Still, it is an imposing prospect to attempt to break subdisciplinary barriers. Moreover, pervasive and persuasive interpretative traditions continue to blind us to a full exploitation of this partnership. I label these perspectives the "time as money" theory and the "modernization of labor" interpretation. Together these views impede an appreciation of the role of time reform, especially between 1890 and 1940 when the eight-hour day and other modern divisions of time were introduced.

Time, Money, and Industrial Labor in the Nineteenth Century

A fundamental distinction between preindustrial and industrial meanings of time is basic to most histories of the reduction of working hours. This perspective has been nurtured both by the image of prefactory worktime constructed by nineteenth-century "hour" reformers and by recent historians of early industrialization. According to a popular perception, preindustrial artisans worked intermittently and, when incomes rose, they labored fewer days; in general, because there was no rigorous distinction between work and nonwork, these craftsmen were not conscious of time. Gradually, however, the modern calculating spirit, first developed by early industrial entrepreneurs, also spread to workers. While employers learned to measure labor value in terms of time and sought to maximize this value by extending hours, laborers also slowly "learned the rules of the game."[10] They evidently discovered the relationship between productivity, pay, and worktime. When employers found ways of increasing hourly output, workers demanded a monetary share of increased productivity and insisted that worktime beyond a standard period of production be paid a premium or abolished. Time has become a "currency," says E. P. Thompson, "not passed but spent." Thompson summarizes the industrial history of labor and worktime:

The first generation of factory workers were taught by their masters the importance of time; the second generation formed their short-time committees in the ten hour movement; the third generation struck for overtime and time-and-a-half. They had accepted the categories of their employers and learned to fight back with them. They had learned their lesson, that time is money, only too well.[11]

According to this view, not only had time become commoditized but "natural" work rhythms had been abolished. Employers gradually undermined the "task-oriented" behavior of the artisan with his irregular work calendar and his "polychronic" behavior in mixing work and play.

When work was centralized in the factory and labor lost control over tools, methods, and pace of production, the wage earner adapted to "time-oriented" work. Life became segmented between hours of intense labor and periods of rest. Only the homemaker and mother with her relative isolation from the social division of labor ultimately retained preindustrial notions of time and work. Thus, industrial work discipline, E. P. Thompson claims, changed "the inward notation of time" and distorted human needs. He concludes that "we must learn to break down barriers between work and life."[12]

Despite the usefulness of these analyses of the origins of "time as money," increasingly these images of early industrial worktime (admittedly oversimplified here) have been challenged. The common claim of nineteenth-century reformers that the eighteenth-century workday was short and relatively autonomous has been qualified.[13] The ten-hour day was closer to the standard in eighteenth-century England than the eight-hour day of the mythical "free-born Englishman." Twelve hours generally prevailed in France. More important, for many journeymen, apprentices, domestics, and farm servants, all of the laborers' time was at the disposal of the master during the work contract. The actual length of each day varied with the vicissitudes of nature, the market, and employer needs. While the merchant-manufacturer may have had no direct control over artisans who worked by the piece, Michael Harrison has recently found that their working week in England was far more regular than previously supposed.[14]

The number of holidays—up to 164 days in seventeenth-century France—has been cited as evidence of a more relaxed attitude toward worktime. Yet these holidays were usually related to the enforced leisure of the "dead season" in the agricultural or artisan production cycle. They were far from the modern paid vacations for they neither allowed individualized leisure nor provided the income necessary to enjoy this "free time." These holidays were mostly lost days of income that would have to be made up in long workweeks to follow.[15]

Moreover, recent historians note that the struggle over the allocation of time was hardly an invention of the nineteenth-century short-hours movements. Although few workers directly challenged the "traditional" workday, the numbers of days that artisans and even servants were willing to work varied with the season and wage levels. As Michael Sonenscher suggests for eighteenth-century France, artisans usually viewed wage work as a supplement to other sources of income (e.g., farming). Employers' demands on labor time correlated less to the dictates of the sun (as "preindustrial" theory would have it) than to the costs of maintaining inventories and interest charges on raw materials. Masters often had an incentive to increase the workday during rush periods to get the goods out and then to lay off labor or reduce hours in the dead season. An attempt to put the time of journeymen at the disposal of employers was behind the labor passport or *livret* and the legal obligation to work in Old Regime France.[16]

The campaign to force artisans to reallocate their time toward work, especially wage labor, took many forms. Economists frequently advocated artificially low wages and high prices as an inducement to force workers to extend their hours of wage work.[17] Another vehicle for breaking old work habits was the campaign to reduce the number of holidays. For example, in France during the Revolution, the Le Chapelier Law granted employers unlimited power to regulate employment, including worktime, eliminating the controls of guilds and municipal authorities.[18] In Britain, numerous efforts of gentry, publicists, and committees for the suppression of vice to reduce holiday periods in the eighteenth century have been well documented.[19]

Specialists in the history of early industrialization have long stressed the importance of the centralized workplace in the imposition of work discipline and the lengthening of the working day. Not only did the factory make regular working hours a condition for employment, but new managerial techniques enhanced the ability of the employer to intensify worktime. Mechanization, especially in steam-driven textile mills, provided incentives to raise working hours. Efforts to amortize costly equipment over a shorter period, attempts to reduce costs as competition increased and prices dropped, and hopes of taking advantage of new gas lighting all encouraged the lengthening of working hours.[20]

Historians, however, have increasingly questioned the impact of the factory on enforcing time discipline. As Duncan Bythell and James Schmiechen have recently documented, the unmechanized, subcontracted work of the sweating system had surely played a greater role in the intensification of work.[21] Moreover, the victory of commoditized time was hardly complete even by the mid-nineteenth century. The traditional holiday of Saint Monday survived in well-paid tailoring and other trades until the 1860s in Britain and France.[22] Increased demand for output led often not to mechanization but to the expansion of the work force. In the mid-nineteenth century, only where women and children worked did employers impose more than an effective three-day week upon Birmingham and Black country metalworkers. British miners may have seen an increase in the workday in the 1840s, but the practice of Saint Monday, summer short-time work, and early quitting on Saturdays in summer remained. English construction workers in the 1830s successfully resisted attempts to raise the ten-hour day. The real lengthening of the workday in nineteenth-century Britain took place mostly among workers in mechanized textile mills and other trades competing against machines and overcrowding.[23]

These revisions of the history of "time as money" are helpful. But perhaps most important, this interpretation of the history of worktime generally ignores the positive role of reform. As Thompson suggests, by about 1850 British workers had "learned their lesson, that time is money, only too well." Efforts to shorten hours, then, have been understood as economism and adaptations to the imperatives of a triumphal capitalism.

Yet the nineteenth century brought less the victory of economic time than new and often contrasting attitudes toward the allocation of time. A bourgeois leisure (as well as work) ethic emerged. The goal of economic accumulators to "save" time meant not only to increase the productivity of working hours but also to defer leisure to a later period. Note the life of the apostle of economic time, Benjamin Franklin. His *Autobiography* reveals not a man of endless hours of work but rather a person who carefully planned or rationalized his workday, insuring highly productive hours of work but also long blocks of time in the evening and at midday for reading, diversions, and conversation. He claimed to work an eight-hour day. Even more important, his youthful years of economic time provided him the opportunity for an early retirement from business at the age of forty-two, whereupon he devoted the rest of his long life to a variety of self-directed activities that might well be called leisure. The nineteenth-century European and even American bourgeoisie adopted essentially the same strategy: long hours of work in youth were "invested" in middle-age leisure and long holidays.[24]

In contrast, workers built their reformed leisure strategy around weekly days free from work and a reduction of daily hours. Because the wage earner lacked the opportunity to forgo income for an extended period, the laborer was unable to imitate the merchant, lawyer, and politician on the August vacation. With insufficient resources to "save" time (in reality, income), the worker sought to "spend" free time in frequent, regular, and necessarily short doses. Saint Monday was to the worker of the mid-nineteenth century, says the British artisan Thomas Wright, what the vacation was to the bourgeois. Part of the middle-class resentment of the workers' inconstancy and presumed lack of time thrift may reflect different strategies for distributing life time.[25]

Gradually, however, a new work and leisure ethic emerged in the late nineteenth century for all classes. The ideal increasingly became that of uniform durations of work, compressed into as few hours as necessary in order to maintain production and income; at the same time, leisure time was radically segmented from work and packaged into predictable, long blocks of personally disposable periods, distributed in doses over the day, week, year, and life-span. This new approach to time contrasted with the traditional pattern of irregularity and the melding of work and leisure.

Of course, one might argue that this change of strategy was in part an accommodation to the exigencies of industrial capitalism. Workers were certainly obliged to adapt to the reality of the segmentation of life, because industrial capitalism separated work and home and made necessary a synchronizing of interpersonal activities. Indeed, the compression of work into an 8:00 A.M. to 5:00 P.M. schedule, five days a week, is one of the most rational ways of solving these problems. This changing time economy may also reflect an instrumentalist attitude toward work, as a mere economic means to the only remaining arena of personal freedom—leisure time.[26]

These new approaches may also signify the trickle down of the bourgeois ideal of "saving time"—forbearance of leisure until it could be coupled with income. Workers may well have found a linkage between accumulating savings and a different, perhaps more satisfying, allocation of time free from wage work. This included not only vacations long enough to allow workers extended periods away from the industrial environment, but also years of a work-free childhood and a retirement before ill-health reduced the value of "free time."

The provenance of new attitudes toward work and leisure is a most complex issue. We must await the new research of nineteenth-century specialists to understand more fully these changing values during early industrialization. As the innovative essays in Patrick Joyce's recent collection reveal, meanings of time to the nineteenth-century worker were far more complex than the formulas of social theorists.[27] Surely we can agree that the worker's time economy in the industrial era went well beyond the sociologists' notions of adaptation or social convergence.

This claim can perhaps most clearly be defended by investigating the dynamics of hours reform in the nineteenth century. These movements suggest motives that go beyond accommodation to the "time-as-money"

ethic and also reveal significant differences—along with points of convergence—between elite and popular motives.

First, time reform was rooted in values that challenged the "severely
workful" obsessions of Europe's Coketown entrepreneurs. An important literature of the history of leisure documents important counter-
cultures that rejected commoditized time. Of course, the rich continued
their leisure traditions. But more significant, bourgeois reformers sought
not the mere repression of working-class leisure but its transformation.
In place of the boisterous and often violent seasonal outbursts of wakes
weeks and races or the daily visit to the tavern, advocates of rational
recreation proposed the wholesome leisure of family walks, uplifting
reading and education, and organized sport. For some historians these
efforts represent a new form of class struggle as elites attempted to
make leisure conform to new standards of rationalized worktime. Still,
there is much evidence that many workers also supported these expressions of leisure. Wage earners as well as middle-class reformers in Britain sought to restore the Saturday half-holiday from the 1840s as essential to the enjoyment of rational recreation. Later, French Catholics
(and retail clerks) challenged the poor enforcement of the Sunday closing principle.[28]

Second, concern that the working-class family was incapable of enforcing social discipline and of reproducing itself led even laissez-faire
liberals to advocate regulation of factory worktime. Relatively early, the
intelligentsia in England and France reached near consensus over the
need to release time for married working women to reverse the apparent disintegration of the family and to provide a domestic alternative to
the male drinking culture. Still earlier, an awareness of the fragility of
childhood and the political and economic need for mass education led
elites to insist that youths be withdrawn from the workforce, at least
part of the day. As a means of "saving" the family, reformers gradually
convinced politicians of the social necessity of a shorter workday, a
regular weekly day of rest, and eventually the paid vacation.[29]

The working classes did not fully embrace this approach to reform.
In the first place, the divergence of time strategies between classes was
surprisingly persistent. The regular and frequent hours of rest time promoted in the ten-hour and eventually eight-hour movements captured
the imagination of workers long before vacations, retirement, or even
an extended childhood. Moreover, the gradual change in the time strategy of workers may be linked less to *embourgeoisement* than to the interaction of different working-class communities. Perhaps the nineteenth-

century factory worker, as Bienefeld claims, had a particular interest in reducing the daily doses of labor due to the fatiguing regularity of mechanized work; by contrast, the artisan accustomed to a seasonal and irregular job flow preferred to hang on to Saint Monday and holidays. Significantly, both ideals were beginning to merge by the end of the century.[30]

In addition, for workers liberating time from labor went beyond the question of rational recreation and family stability. Free time meant liberty, not only from the constraints and alienation of an industrial work environment, but from authoritarian relationships. For example, the shopworker or office worker sought to limit the employer's access to his and her time; in seeking to end the "living-in" system, these workers attempted to create a clear separation between the masters' time and their own. The intermingling of work and life for many dependent workers—in shops, farms, or domestic service—was not an ideal to be defended but a curse to be overcome.[31]

In many subtle ways workers recognized in "free time" a concrete expression of personal liberty and the opportunity of leisure. It was a right of citizenship. In the 1830s long factory hours in Britain were frequently and often unfavorably compared with New World slavery. The American short-hours movement in the 1860s borrowed freely from the discourse of the abolitionists. And the American slogan "eight hours for what we will" perfectly expressed the quest for autonomous time, without any attempt to justify the social or economic utility of leisure. Increasingly in the nineteenth century, popular short-hours advocates argued for a "normal workday," based not on the calculus of productivity, fatigue, or social stability, but simply on the right to equality of leisure.[32]

Finally workers accepted segmented time not merely as a necessary adaptation to the separation of home and work but as a positive quest for family life. Although this claim is hard to prove, it seems that the ideal became not merely shorter workdays but synchronized blocks of domestic time. Workers repeatedly resisted multiple-shift work, sex- and age-based variations in working hours, and even staggered vacations in this quest for family time. With the increase in income, not only did time become more precious but leisure became more than periods of physical restoration or consumption. Free time became social time. People began to demand that working hours accommodate social as well as economic needs. Workers who sought overtime rates were not merely trying to turn time into money. They sought to give some measure of value to their deprivation of social time—those hours of "common enjoyment."[33]

These challenges to the time-as-money thesis suggest an alternative way of understanding the question of worktime during the early phases of industrialization. The dichotomy of preindustrial and industrial attitudes toward time is inadequate, and hour reform cannot be understood within the limited categories of "economism," "adaptation," and "convergence." Time reform was a complex blend of motives and agencies that fits poorly into any theories of social control. Rather these movements were largely protracted struggles that fundamentally challenged liberal political economy and culture. And they extended far beyond the defeat of the revolutionary alternatives to capitalism and into the twentieth century.

Modernization, Industrial Conflict, and Reform, 1880–1940

A second impediment to a wider view of time reform is the theory of the "modernization" of labor. To simplify, the argument, applied to worktime, runs as follows: during industrialization, workers learned to adapt to factory discipline, developed an instrumental attitude toward their jobs, and abandoned traditional leisure patterns. Wage earners relinquished their preindustrial preference to work only so long as necessary to maintain customary living standards. Instead, workers became willing to abandon leisure when the availability of consumer goods stimulated the desire to work longer to gain additional income. The laborer eventually became an "economic man" and the traditional problem that improvement in productivity only led to decreased working hours was finally overcome. This laid the groundwork for industrial modernization: the reduction of worktime could be stabilized at an optimal level of labor efficiency while productivity could rise indefinitely; leisure could become not a threat to economic growth but a stimulant to consumer demand and thus create an incentive to steady work; and labor then could finally become a partner with capital, accepting managerial control over work in exchange for growing levels of consumption and time to enjoy it.[34]

Modernization theory is largely based on a particular reading of American industrial history, extended to western Europe. It is sanctified by the industrial relations school of Clark Kerr and John Dunlop, who in their primer, *Industrialism and Industrial Man,* assert that after a "century of experience . . . the choices for workers are seen to be more limited; how to accommodate, to participate in the industrial order, and to share in the gains." Industrial rationalization, while limiting autonomy at work, allows freedom to consume in leisure time. This perspective has often been embraced by students of the "affluent worker" as well as by many Marxist social scientists.[35]

The upshot of this analysis is that with industrialization workers accepted a trade-off: abdication of control over the pace and use of worktime in exchange for expanded access to nonworktime and increased income. This trade-off may be associated with the emergence of "corporatism," "consumer society," or "Fordism." James Burnham and Reinhard Bendix, for example, claim that between 1890 and 1940 leading employers in the Western world (or, at least, in the United States) abandoned an entrepreneurial code of behavior for a corporatist approach to decision making. While this new manager sought to deprive labor of control over worktime in order to increase productivity, he presumably also stressed cooperation with workers. The manager offered an exchange of more intense and less autonomous work for reduced hours and more pay. When workers abandoned the traditional attempt of artisans to control the work process, they adopted a corporatist solution—a demand for leisure and income tied directly to increased labor productivity.[36]

Accordingly, over the long run, a consumer society emerged in which leisure time coincided rather than conflicted with the imperatives of market expansion. Stuart Ewig argues that in the precocious America of the 1920s, "shorter hours and more pay" were accepted by employers in order to "habituate a national population to the exigencies of mass production," giving the masses time (and income) to develop the "civilizing" taste for consumer goods necessary for the survival of capitalism.[37]

Of course, this view applies best to the American context, at least before the post–World War II period when "Fordism" spread to western Europe. Still, both American and European critics of contemporary industrial culture ranging from Sebastian de Grazia to Jürgen Habermas have argued that time liberated from work was appropriated by consumption, with depoliticizing and culturally narrowing results. As a variation of this theme, Georges Friedmann and other students of the "degradation of work" in the early twentieth century see modern leisure as primarily an escape from meaningless work. Workers became integrated into a culture manipulated by advertising and scientific management.[38]

Like the time-as-money argument, modernization explains much about the contemporary world—the apparent decline of an autonomous labor culture with the creation of new forms of bourgeois hegemony and the popular acceptance of a segmented world of work and leisure.

Yet this analysis poses problems. First, there is little historical evidence of a "trade-off," certainly before 1945 when real incomes began to rise sharply. Rather the impetus for the reduction of worktime preceded mass consumption and very few European (or American) employers conceded time as a means of expanding markets even in the era of Fordism in the 1920s. Moreover, the historic relationship between leisure and consumerism was far more tenuous than suggested in this analysis. Neither employers nor workers thought predominantly in terms of consumption when the eight-hour day was won in 1919. Nineteenth-century ideas survived long into the twentieth: even in the 1920s, the argument was over the issue of whether additional free time promised rational recreation, the expansion of workers' culture, or debauchery. A relative minority conceived of the leisure question in consumer terms. Control over the content of leisure concerned few in western Europe. Throughout the interwar years, the issue remained what it had been in the nineteenth century—a conflict over the availability rather than the uses of leisure time.

The reduction of worktime was far more problematic than modernization theories suggest. It was not a simple corollary of industrial maturation but a product of prolonged and intense industrial and political conflict. Hours reform was neither a consequence of industrial rationalization nor a capitulation to bourgeois hegemony. It was a capsulation of industrial conflict at a critical stage of modern liberal capitalism.

Free Time and the Biases against It

Clearly the reallocation of time away from work was not simply a fruit of improved productivity nor was it directly related to increased income. Technological gains were much more likely to be expressed as either increased profit (and investment) or consumption than increased leisure: few workers were able to make the economists' theoretical choice of buying time as incomes rose.

Economic historians sometimes argue that the demand for leisure was pent up as incomes increased, only to be released in spurts when wage rates were sufficient to support leisure activities. However, this assumes that workers were in a position to choose between time or money. Rather, although employers resisted granting concessions in both areas, generally they were far more hesitant to tolerate reductions in working hours. Shorter hours disrupted scheduling, raised unit costs, increased the expense of training labor, and limited the ability of business to respond quickly to orders without the expense of maintaining inventories or making capital improvements. Moreover, businesses could adjust to changing markets less easily with a diminution in hours than wage increases. If a firm maintained an official long day, it could still reduce worktime in slack periods; and during a rise in demand it could insist on the full workday without costly overtime. A shorter "normal day" was necessarily more expensive. In contrast, until after World War I, wages were easily raised or lowered with the market. Nineteenth-century employers feared that reduced hours would intensify competition, require compensatory innovations, and ultimately raise wage costs. Fewer hours seemed to place a ceiling on output, profit, and growth.[39]

Not only were employers biased against worktime reductions but often workers' interests frustrated the choice of time over income: when economic conditions were bad, workers had a *collective interest* in sharing (and thus reducing personal) hours, but they lacked organizational power to win this goal. This was in part because the *individual* had an incentive to work as much time as possible, especially if wages or rates had been cut. At the same time, when trade was brisk, and market conditions were ripe for reducing hours, many workers chose to recover wages lost in the last recession by laboring long hours.

Moreover, opposition to shifting time from production had roots far deeper than wage costs. Although economic and political elites gradually agreed that society required free time for mothers and children, this concession was rarely granted to men. When the nineteenth-century labor intelligentsia defined leisure as a right of citizenship, they challenged classical liberal doctrines—the legal extraterritoriality of the workplace and the free labor contract. Even more deeply, this idea conflicted with a long-lasting fear of male working-class sociability. Elites associated male leisure with disorder, imprudent consumption, and ideological insubordination. Their refusal to guarantee men a minimum of leisure reflected a gender culture that neglected noneconomic male roles, especially in the family.

Finally and probably most important, economic competition impeded the reduction of working hours. Businesses, threatened by the cheap goods of others who continued a long workday, would not risk a reduction of hours. In the 1830s, this dissuaded individual factories from abandoning the thirteen- and fourteen-hour day despite obvious social disutility and questionable economic advantage. The same fear of competition was the principal obstacle to reducing worktime in the 1890s: the increase in international competition prompted even the British (who earlier had led in shortening worktime) to hold fast to, at least, a nine-hour workday. The economic nationalism of the 1920s similarly threatened the eight-hour day. These were powerful biases against the redistribution of time even when productivity increases made it possible.

Shorter hours often had a more radical economic impact than did wage increases; thus, reductions in worktime were far more discontinuous. Diminutions in working hours often coincided with peaks in the economic cycle—that is, when employment rates were high, when "markets [were] soft," and when the "institutional pressures" of organized labor were the greatest. Success in shortening worktime among the strongest sectors of labor might, through the principle of "price leadership," be spread to less organized sectors; this, for example, happened in the early 1870s in Britain.[40]

Nevertheless, the discontinuity in the diminution of the "normal workday" (from ten to eight hours, for example) did not fit any particular economic configuration. Reductions in the periods 1847–1850, 1869–1873, 1906–1908, 1919–1920, 1936–1938, and 1945–1947 did not share common economic determinants (such as employment, or wage and price trends). For the most part, they were periods of democratic mobilizations and popular challenges to political elites. They often took place on an *international* scale and followed long periods of debate over the question of worktime. In most cases, laws or multi-sector collective bargaining produced these changes. In other words, worktime reductions usually were political.[41]

The roadblocks to the redistribution of time were not easily broken at the level of the firm; only slowly and sporadically were they penetrated by the state; ultimately they were unstopped by the simultaneous action of several competing countries.

Only by the end of the nineteenth century were the classical liberal prejudices against the public policing of time effectively challenged. Economic theory played an important role in undermining liberal doctrine. Theorists and production-minded employers increasingly recognized that only *efficient* time was money, whereas merely long working hours were costly. The progressive belief that social stability required time free from work gradually extended from women and children to men. By the 1890s, fears that fatigue would produce a race of morally truncated and unproductive workers initiated a more positive theory of leisure, even for men. These ideas gained scientific legitimacy through the efficiency movement in the generation before World War I. Elites began to rethink their attitude toward working-class leisure: an expanded family life might well create a more stable and even a more conservative labor force.

Yet the change was not merely a reflection of a "softened" bourgeois opinion or an attempt to integrate labor into a conservative consumer economy. The trend toward shorter hours was also a product of new workers' attitudes, especially a preference for family time over the solidarities of the work group. Implicit in the demand for the eight-hour day was a complex of values about social time that sometimes paralleled the views of reformers and, as often, took different tracks.

These two forces came together often in the political arena—both to overcome employer and conservative resistance to hour diminutions and to reduce the stumbling block of competition. As the market widened and international competition limited the freedom of the nation state to regulate the conditions of its own work force, labor and elite reformers favored economic disarmament through a simultaneous reduction of worktime across frontiers. Yet, despite the dreams of the First and Second Socialist Internationals and the plans of liberal advocates of transnational labor legislation, the sharpest decreases in worktime occurred only in periods of international political discontinuity. The two best examples of this phenomenon were the periods 1847–1850 and 1919–1920 when the social order was challenged on an international scale.

An International Approach: British and French Worktime

However valuable national labor and policy histories may be for identifying trends in industrial relations and politics, they

neglect the broader arena that contenders also played in. Labor and reform movements operated in an international framework long before
they were effective at a national or often local level. More important,
the world market had a deep impact on reform agendas. It is not just
the contemporary worker whose labor standard is dependent upon the
international economy. This was also true of the early Victorian textile
worker, and it became increasingly more significant to other trades as
the nineteenth century wore on. Most important, reductions of worktime came usually in periods of international discontinuity—especially
the late 1840s and late 1910s—when the rules of the market were
suspended.

An international approach should also be complemented by a comparative one. Despite the temptation to generalize from the experience
of one area or trade, historians generally recognize that cultures took
different paths toward the reduction of worktime. Recent investigations
into the meanings of time by David Brody for early industrial America
and by Thomas Smith for seventeenth-century Japan remind us of the
futility of simplistic universal modernization models.[42] However, comparative historical studies are still extremely rare.

This book will make a modest attempt to correct the one-sidedness
of the national (or local) history by focusing on two states, Britain and
France. In one sense this book will be a history of Western industrial
approaches to worktime, which should provide interesting points of
comparison with historians working on this theme for the United
States and elsewhere. By studying two countries, I avoid the temptation
to generalize from one nation state or to write exclusively for specialists.
I chose these two countries because they experienced relatively early industrialization and political liberalization. Yet, because these processes
took quite different forms in Britain and France, these nations took di-
vergent paths toward the reallocation of time.

As outlined in the appendix, the key contrast was that throughout
the century French working hours were considerably longer in most
trades than were the British. A combination of factors—inefficiency, a
more traditional work culture, and the survival of a seasonal pattern of
production—all contributed to the relatively long workday in France
and the slow pace of worktime reduction. An equally important factor
may explain the difference in worktime—the relatively slow rate of liberal reform in France. Throughout the nineteenth century, the French
state was consistently behind the British in regulating working hours.
Whereas the British in 1847 instituted a ten-hour day in textile factories, the French in 1848 settled for a twelve-hour maximum. The in-

spectorate was also much slower to develop in France, which not only assured that less-efficient firms were protected from competition by their ability to extend worktime, but also encouraged all firms in a region to adopt the hours of the factory with the longest workday.[43] The relatively early and large-scale organization of British labor as compared with the late and rather ineffective consolidation of French unions played a major role. As a result, in the twentieth century collective bargaining dominated the process in Britain, whereas the state mediated the reduction of hours in France. Gradually, however, the two nations converged even if they followed different paths to the liberation of time from work.

Worktime and Reform

The struggle over time has been as basic to industrialization as the contest over space and social output. Yet the era when the greatest temporal shifts in Europe occurred was roughly in the century after 1840. Since that time, the industrial workyear has fallen from a high of 3,000 to 3,600 hours to the contemporary standard of 1,650 to 2,000 hours.[44] Moreover, during this century emerged the ideas of the eight-hour day, the weekend, the paid vacation, and regular retirement—all characteristically modern solutions to the conflict between time and money, leisure and work.

The remainder of this book will attempt to offer a broad explanation of the origins of these "temporal institutions." Because these doses of time appeared in national, indeed international, contexts, I have chosen not to produce a local study. Rather I have undertaken a comparative, parallel history of worktime in Britain and France and stress the essentially international character of the quest for time.

A book that promises to cover such a wide range of issues must necessarily also seek limits. This will not be a history of leisure, even though the appearance of new leisure forms will be noted. It will not be an economic history of worktime, although I will consider the economic consequences of the reduction of labor time as it affected the movements for shorter hours. Finally, this book cannot do justice to the full range of issues that I have introduced here. I was obliged to focus on what, I will argue, was the most important phase in the reallocation of personal time—the struggle for the eight-hour day. Still, I will raise a number of related issues—the intellectual and political problem of policing time in the nineteenth century, the movement for weekly rest and the Saturday half-holiday as a prelude to the weekend, and the origins of the paid summer vacation. My objective throughout will be to shed light on the redistribution of time and the many factors that made these changes possible.

Those who lament the apparent passing of a trained leisure class may be right that time liberated by the hour or day from work can never be true leisure.[45] Yet we live in a world that has democratized labor—at least in the sense that almost all are expected to contribute to society. Thus, a central moral and political question remains. How do we allocate time between the dictates of economic obligation and the freedom of personal fulfillment?[46] This has always been a political problem. Changes in the distribution of time have never been merely a function of technological and economic change. Rather temporal reallocations have been a product of conflict and debate, the fruits of ideology, persuasion, and power. It was a century of contest that produced the norms of the eight-hour day, weekend, and annual vacation.

Contemporary industrial society has solved the problem of the distribution of time in terms of regular doses of leisure that break the flow of worktime. To be sure, the cadence of labor may have increased since the advent of the factory; and economic values have "polluted" leisure time. Still, a fundamental characteristic of twentieth-century society has been the quantity, and perhaps even the quality, of time away from work. This reflects not merely the necessity of rest from the stressful pace of modern work (which in many cases is a relatively happy substitute for the exhaustion of physical labor); nor does it simply attest to the economic necessity of time to consume and to nurture future workers. Rather this redistribution of time toward leisure represents a concrete reduction of authority and compulsion, a personal realization of liberty, and even a democratization of opportunity for personal choice.

This may appear to some to be an overly optimistic view of modern industrial society. It may well underestimate the survival of the values of economic time and overestimate the leisure gains of labor. These points may be argued. Yet I insist that social reforms like the eight-hour day have made a positive difference. Indeed, this book is largely based on this supposition. In an age when reform has largely vanished from the political agenda, it is perhaps the duty of the historian to display the liberty of the past.

2

Policing Time: The Nineteenth-Century State and Working Hours

One defining feature of the nineteenth-century liberal state was a basic reluctance to regulate the labor contract. Midcentury revolutionary pressures to guarantee work, assure minimum-wage standards, or regulate hours of employment for adults were resisted in the name of freedom to work and the extraterritoriality of the workplace. Although commodity markets might be accorded public attention, the factory, like the domestic workroom, was viewed as private space, the realm of personal liberty. Yet from the beginnings of the century, these liberal dogmas met opposition. While social conservatives questioned free market ideas and broad interpretations of privacy, by midcentury bourgeois reformers also had begun to modify their faith in unrestrained liberalism. One area where consensus was reached early was in the regulation of working hours in industry.

Numerous studies that concern this period of liberal reform largely focus on the British Factory Acts up to 1847.[1] These works often ignore, however, the wider and longer record of liberal state intervention in worktime. Moreover, they generally stress the successes rather than reveal the ambiguities and failures of hours reform. Some scholars emphasize the paternalistic roots of reform that attempts to use regulation to check the power of industry and reduce economic competition;[2]

others stress the impetus of bourgeois welfare and economic rationalization,[3] or the attempt to foster social stability through reform[4] or
more subtly to create a modern division of labor and time through limiting the hours of women and children.[5] Yet few of these works clarify
the theoretical roots of the short-hours question in the history of political economy. Perhaps ultimately most important, these studies have
often ignored the objectives of workers in the short-hours debate and
underestimated the degree to which time reform was a compensation,
granted in the midst of broad popular pressures.

Our task in this chapter is not to provide a detailed, much less definitive, exposition of the question of nineteenth-century regulation of
worktime in Britain and France. Others have thoroughly mined sources
and are presently reinterpreting the Factory Acts.[6] This chapter certainly cannot provide a labor history of worktime prior to the 1880s.
Rather the purpose here is to offer a broad context for the understanding of the relationship between the liberal state and the policing of time
and thus provide a useful backdrop for an understanding of a second
and more aggressive stage of hours reform that emerged in the 1880s.

Worktime and Political Economy

The roots of the problem between liberalism and work-
time may be found in the history of political economy, especially in the
understanding of the relationship between time and productivity. Adam
Smith challenged the mercantilist doctrine that long hours of work and
low wages were required for high rates of daily output. In the *Wealth of
Nations* he recognized that shorter hours and higher wages could enhance the incentive to produce and improve the physical capacity to
work.[7] Yet most of Smith's successors either ignored the question of
worktime or claimed a direct equivalency between hours and output.
Even the obvious relationship between mechanization and increased
productivity did not convince economic theorists that shorter worktime was an appropriate means of distributing the fruits of economic
growth. This theoretical backsliding may reflect the class biases of classical political economy. It certainly evaded the question of how the
benefits of improved productivity should be divided between investment, consumption, and free time. Even the marginalist school of
William Stanley Jevons ignored the relationship between time and pro-

ductivity: Jevons explained the late nineteenth-century movement for shorter hours as the propensity of workers to seek free time when real income rose. The impetus toward shorter hours was then part of a consumer's choice between goods and leisure. Significantly, this analysis entirely ignored the relationship between work intensification and the demand potential for decreased worktime. Instead, marginalists claimed that increased productivity was incompatible with reduced hours.[8]

Marx, of course, was an exception. One of the themes of his chapter on "The Work Day" in *Capital* is the reciprocal linkage between worktime and the intensity and productivity of work. Mechanization and the division of labor created a more dense, more fatiguing workday, which in turn prompted the demand for shorter hours. Reduced worktime in turn only induced employers to replace the "extensive" workday with a more intensive one through mechanization. The reduction of worktime was the key to the struggle between employer and worker over the extraction of surplus value; yet it was also the driving force in economic development. These relationships at the point of production were ignored by most economists in the nineteenth century. Thus, like the question of wages, worktime was conveniently excluded from playing a positive role in the laudable goal of economic progress. The key to growth, so self-serving of capital, remained investment.[9]

The failure, however, of economic theory went further. The unwillingness to investigate the question of worktime revealed also a refusal to "cost out" the price of social reproduction. Marx stressed that mechanization and competition uncorked customary and natural limits on the workday. Longer hours reduced the time available for bodily restoration and family life. Insofar as the limits of daylight were surmounted by gas lamps and expensive machinery increased competitive pressures to extend the workday, social time was compressed into increasingly inadequate length. Marx argued that a shorter workday then was the *sine qua non* for the reproduction of the work force. This replication, of course, was a basic need of capital, but one that the market system had no means of providing. Indeed, competition directly frustrated the long-term interests of capital by encouraging the deterioration of human resources. The solution, noted Marx, was a legal limit on social exploitation, a goal that benefited capital as a class but frustrated individual capitalists.

Marx's analysis was not developed in isolation. He closely followed the investigations and conclusions of Robert Horner, chief factory inspector during the debates and aftermath of the 1847 Ten Hour Act in Britain. Moreover, his linking worktime both to productivity and to social reproduction were common themes in the debates over the Factory Acts and subsequent movements for shorter hours.

Yet there were important ideological membranes that impeded the permeation of these ideas into liberal thinking. First, the cost of replacing extensive with intensive work methods—especially in the context of short-run competitiveness and profitability—limited the receptivity to a short-time political economy. When Liberal governments policed worktime, they did so primarily to prevent enterprises from gaining an unfair advantage over the competition by operating their works longer than the norm. Some capitalists favored hours regulations in order to reduce the possibility of undercapitalized or inefficient firms from competing by utilizing long hours. Hours reform was also an indirect form of reducing production and thus diminishing price-cutting pressures. These motives, rather than the desire to encourage economic efficiencies, made laws setting maximum hours acceptable to midcentury Liberal parliaments.

Second, while ten-hour proponents linked short hours to improved labor efficiency,[10] the main argument was not couched in the language of political economy but in that of social reform. Moreover, this liberal social economy of time was gender and age biased. The necessity of social time for children and, later, for women may have been widely recognized by midcentury. But male leisure or even family time seldom was identified as a public concern. This attitude may be simply explained as a product of liberal "free-agent" doctrine, yet it also reflected a phobia of male working-class leisure, as well as opposition to the "republican" implications of working-class males with time for politics. Perhaps even more important, this view represented an unwillingness to recognize male roles in the family. The restriction of maximum-hours laws to "minors" was a clear expression of an age- and gender-based division of labor. It presumed a public interest only in the training and cultural formation of youth, the primacy of female responsibility in the work of reproduction, and male status as the primary breadwinner—without the corresponding right of participation in public affairs. Neil Smelser may be correct in proposing that worktime laws advanced the increasing specialization and temporal segmentation of social functions, and that this process may be associated with "modernization." Yet these laws also reflected deeply ideological biases, consistent with liberal political and family doctrine. Moreover, far from signifying an inevitable modernization of time and thus a narrowing of cultural options, these biases were challenged by workers and some reformers.

Sharp discontinuities in nineteenth-century hours reform were inevitable. The factory movement culminated in the systemic crisis of midcentury in both France and Britain. Nevertheless, the scope of the first short-hours movement was limited: like the revolution of 1848, it was a midcourse correction in competitive capitalism, hardly the expression of the "political economy of the working class" as Marx had hoped. Efforts to extend the policing of time in the second half of the century were as halting as were electoral and other reforms.

Boundaries of the British Short-Hours Movement, 1816–1850

Britain was the pioneer in the modern policing of time. British legislation in 1819 demanded a twelve-hour daily maximum for children in cotton textile factories; in 1833, children's hours were reduced to eight (with provisions for education); and, in 1847, the working hours of women as well as children were restricted to ten. These laws at first only applied to textile factories. Yet they would gradually be extended to a variety of trades; and, although they excluded men, the close relationship between male and female (and child) labor often led to the same reduced hours for men. At a slower pace, the French imitated the British. The British act of 1833 was copied in 1841 and modified in 1848, reducing worktime in mechanized plants to twelve hours. However, the French would achieve the British legal standard of a ten-hour day for factory women and children only in 1900. French law was more than a shadow of British legislation; it reflected a different constellation of social and political discourses. Still, the British example warrants the more extensive treatment.

Despite the onslaught of laissez-faire ideology in Britain in the late eighteenth century, many had misgivings about the propriety of an unregulated labor market. Traditional municipal regulation of apprentices was gradually extended to worktime. From the 1780s, Manchester officials on the advice of physicians advocated a ten-hour day, longer midday breaks, and improved education for poor youths apprenticed under the Poor Law. These concerns became law in an 1802 law that restricted hours of parish apprentices to twelve per day.[11]

However, by 1815 the urbanization of the textile industry had reduced the problem of apprentices who had formerly been sent to a distant rural factory by parents. In its place rose the issue of the child laborer who often worked with the parent. Although factory work of ten
and a half to fourteen and a half hours per day was often no longer than
labor in cottage industry or agriculture, it was more visible. Factory
work also was confined in a closed environment and, unlike farm or
handicraft labor, was not relieved by informal rest breaks. Moreover,
reformers increasingly believed that these hours of factory labor were
not controlled by the parent but dominated by the logic of competition
and machine production. The paternalism that had formerly applied to
parish apprentices now seemed appropriate to children still under the
nominal care of their parents. The cotton merchants, Robert Peel and
Robert Owen, introduced legislation for eliminating factory work for
children under ten years of age and a ten-hour day for children up to
sixteen years of age. Medical experts claimed that factory work threatened the physical development of children. Moreover, John Doherty's
Manchester Cotton Spinners Association agitated for a ten-hour bill.
Employer opposition, however, led to a compromise law in 1819 that
provided only a twelve-hour day for children nine to sixteen years old
and was restricted to cotton textile workers. The absence of an independent inspectorate made the law a dead letter when employers spread out
the twelve-hour schedules of children in split shifts and when parents
lied about ages of their children.[12]

The ten-hour movement was revived in 1831 in tandem with electoral and corn law reforms. It attracted an extraordinary political and
social mix. Older histories stress the anti-industrialist ideology of Tory
radicals like Richard Oastler, Lord Ashley, the Reverend G. S. Bull, and
Michael Sadler. Some entered the movement via their opposition to
black slavery. Oastler condemned the "Yorkshire slavery" of factory
operatives who were "compelled to work as long as the necessity of
[their] needy parents may require or the cold-blooded avarice of your
worse than barbarian masters may demand."[13]

Since Marx, observers have argued that Tories, taking vengeance on
Liberal industrialists for the revocation of the Corn Laws, were responsible for the Ten Hour Act in 1847.[14] Yet recent scholarship has stressed
that many manufacturers accepted hours laws as a way of forcing their
own liberal hours practices (grounded in economic efficiency as much
as humanitarianism) on their less enlightened competitors. These same
authors, however, emphasize that the issue of worktime was not a crea-
ture of party politics or the conflict between agrarianism and liberal in-

dustrialism.[15] The short-hours movement was a complex mélange of overlapping and partially conflicting discourses.[16]

Until recently, the popular radical voice in the factory movement has been too often seen as a mouthpiece of liberal or conservative manipulators who silenced working-class dissent with well-timed reform in 1847. This stress on elites not only obscures the political objectives of popular short-hours movements but misinterprets the different social objectives of popular and elite advocates of reduced factory hours. As E. P. Thompson noted, "the Factory Movement represented less a growth of middle-class humanitarianism than an affirmation of human rights by the workers themselves." During every period of legislative debate over working hours, from 1819 through 1847, workers' short-time committees appeared. They were especially prevalent in spinning regions of Yorkshire and Lancashire.[17]

The sociologist Neil Smelser provides a social context for an understanding of the short-hours movements of the 1830s and 1840s. Smelser argues that the principal impetus for short hours was the attempt to restore the "technological basis of the existing family structure," which had been destroyed in the movement of production from the domestic economy to the factory economy. Mule spinning broke up the working arrangement between father and child when the male spinner required more children helpers than he had in his family. The development of power looms eliminated the need for men and created a new group of female and child loom tenders hired directly by an employer. Such changes, argues Smelser, frustrated male roles as organizers of domestic production and, as Engels complained, "unsexe[d]" the man and took "from the women all womanliness." Attempts to control hours, according to Smelser, were but one means of delaying the process of sex and age differentiation in capitalist production. Like the strikes against machines that preceded the hours movement and attempts to exclude women from spinners' unions and to restrict spinning jobs to male relatives, the short-time movement was an effort to preserve the patriarchy of the domestic economy in the factory context. By reducing adult hours (under the cover of restrictions on the labor time of children), skilled work would be spread among male heads of households and the demand for children unrelated to male adults would decrease.[18]

These concerns of workers were, of course, embraced by their elite patrons like Lord Ashley, who saw the factory as a threat to the domestic unit. Even Engels argued that "when women work in factories, the most important result is the dissolution of family ties."[19]

Yet the eight-hour law in 1833 affected only children from nine to thirteen years of age but not the hours of machines or of parents. There-after, factory owners were able to double the number of child laborers while obliging adults to work against two shifts of child helpers for fourteen or more hours. Smelser argues that this law only exacerbated the problem of the family economy. Thus, textile workers were willing to extend the hours of children to ten per day in order to reduce the number of unrelated child workers and to coordinate the schedules of parent and offspring. Concern that children would be left unsupervised to wander the streets was a basic element in arguments by spinners that working hours should be synchronized. The 1833 law also gave rise to the brief demand of the National Regeneration Society for an eight-hour day for all workers.[20]

Smelser dismisses this eight-hour movement as a "disturbance" that would be "handled" or channeled later by middle-class reformers and more sober workers into ten-hour legislation that was consistent with economic reality. By the 1840s, workers had abandoned their efforts to restrain the functional differentiation inherent in factory production and had conceded age and gender specialization: they traded the father-child work unit for laws regulating and even freeing early childhood from factory work and embraced the bourgeois doctrine of separate spheres. Thus, through Factory Acts, the education of the young could be assumed by the state; women could increasingly concentrate on do-mestic and childrearing functions, and men, on breadwinning. The Fac-tory Acts also helped employers adapt production to the efficiencies of "an evolving capitalist economy."[21]

Smelser's effort to focus on the social and especially family dimen-sions of the short-hours question is most useful. Yet he obscures several important differences between middle-class and popular social and eco-nomic objectives. To be sure, workers sought to use the shortening of worktime to put a brake on the evolution of competitive industrial capi-talism; but the objective was not simply to rein in the inevitable trend toward social differentiation. Rather the idea was to demand a distri-bution of the benefits of technology. This implied several distinct chal-lenges to Victorian political economy.

In 1842, the Yorkshire Short Hours Committee noted that the self-acting mule greatly enhanced the productivity of the spinner. Under unlimited working hours this naturally led to unemployment. The problem then was a "superabundance of the means for producing wealth." The partial solution was to restrict the growth of foreign mar-kets (which would only lead to further speculative industrialization) and to encourage "home colonization." A corollary was to reduce work-time, which would "increase the value of labour in the exact proportion of its diminished quantity." Wages would increase, gradually "get[ting] at the innumerable and immense masses of wealth . . . and imperceptibly scatter them again among the community." The objective was both to end "gluts and panics" caused by overproduction and to redistribute wealth by reducing the power of capital to expropriate value that the overworked wage earner created.[22] This view, of course, was shared by the advocates of machine taxation and "spade socialism"— "disturbances" in Smelser's view or a misdirection of economic theory in Neil Thompson's.[23]

Yet the ten-hour day was not only to redistribute income but to reallocate time. More important, this did not necessarily imply a rejection of mechanization. Popular proponents recognized that shorter hours would both produce efficiencies in the use of labor time as well as shift "wasted" hours of work to the free use of individual laborers. "Let us have shorter time and invention will soon stimulate a sufficient supply for our wants. The toils of the poor will be diminished and relaxation, health, and contentment will predominate," said William Kenworthy in 1842. The reformer John Fielden, generally a good spokesman of the spinners, argued in 1833 that, because of mechanization, eight hours was the equivalent of twelve hours of work twenty years earlier. "Eight hours of confinement and labour in factories per day are enough for either adult or child of 13."[24] This was hardly a rejection of mechanization but an insistence that the fruits of mechanization be shared by all workers in the form of free time. As important, this argument was made entirely apart from the question of sex or age. The ambiguity over mechanization would remain, however, and reappear in each of the short-hours movements (see chapter 3).

Nostalgia for the "traditional" family work unit may have been central to the short-hours movement in the 1830s. Yet what spinners were trying to "preserve" was family time apart from factory work. The problem was not merely the introduction of other people's children to the workplace but the lack of time with one's own children. This is the point where the 1833 law was most onerous because it reduced the number of those hours and made problematic the supervision of children "excluded" from the factory for all but eight hours while the parent's working hours may well have increased. One solution was to increase parent-child contact within the factory. An even better solution to factory hands was to increase it outside of work. This was clear in that the immediate response of the spinners to the 1833 law was a demand for an eight-hour day for all.

To be sure, workers embraced the ideology of gender time. Fielden argued, for example, that an eight-hour day provided "sufficient time . . . for education, recreation and sleep" for all; moreover, he had specific objectives for each sex. Free time would allow men "to produce the best of every article in the shortest time, at those branches of industry, they are, or may wish to be, engaged." In the rhetoric of the artisan, free time was to affirm the skills of the male producer. By contrast, Fielden argued that shorter worktime would allow women "to wash, bake, make and mend clothes and stockings and all other domestic duties appertaining to cottage economy in which knowledge a large majority of females in the manufacturing districts are now so lamentably deficient."[25] John Doherty, a short-hours activist, denounced the increased role of women in industry. He insisted on shorter hours for men in order that women and children might be protected by their husbands and fathers.[26] The Yorkshire Ten Hours Committee in the 1840s demanded the gradual withdrawal of women from factories; and others insisted that women with nonworking children should be fired. Clearly these male-dominated workers' movements thoroughly embraced the ideal of the women's domestic sphere. At the same time, they used this ideology against the hypocrisy of employers who insisted that women workers be obliged to work twelve-hour workdays outside the home. It was not only conservatives like Ashley who lamented the "savagery" of wage-earning women but working people who shared these views that long working hours deprived wage-earning families of proper diets, adequate child care, and domestic comfort.[27]

Yet these movements went beyond bourgeois gender ideology. Fielden argued for free time to teach both sexes to be sober, avoid debt, and to be "good fathers and mothers, good husbands and wives." The idea was not merely to drive women from the factory and into the kitchen, but to restore, or more accurately, to create time for the family as a moral or social complex. The Ten Hour Act in 1847 may have been sold under the cover of rescuing women for domesticity; however, it was supported by male spinners as a means of increasing their own leisure (as Fielden admitted). For many it was probably also a means of realizing family time apart from work where, even in the cottage industry of nostalgia, opportunities for being "good fathers and mothers" were few.[28]

This suggests some subtle distinctions between the social views of reformers and those of wage earners toward worktime. Reformers were often more concerned with the apparent inadequacy of working-class childrearing than they were with enhancing the proletarian family. A growing "children's concern"[29] surely was reflected in the witnesses before the Sadler committee of 1832. They focused on the need to free children from "over-exertion and long confinement" in the factory for the "improvement of their minds, the preservation of their morals and the maintenance of their health." Medical advisers like Dr. C. T. Thackrah of Leeds stressed that with long factory hours "human beings . . . decay before they arrive at the term of maturity." Rough discipline and moral environments that reminded observers of "brothels" were other arguments for restricting children's hours. Moreover, the reduction of hours in 1833 was intended to be linked with the introduction of two hours of formal education at the factory.[30]

What is striking about the 1833 law is both its paternalism toward working-class children and its disregard for the proletarian family. It reflected a presumption that parents had lost their rights to regulate the time of their children and that the state had become the tutelary parent. This attitude had provided the rationale for parish apprenticeship laws and was almost without reflection adapted after 1815 to laws that protected children under the formal care of parents. Reformers doubted that workers were capable of raising their own offspring. It was then in the interest of society as well as the children that the state assume partial responsibility for their socialization. Children's time in service to the family economy should be limited—even if, as many pointed out, parents objected.[31]

Low income and large families prevented workers from withdrawing their children from the labor force. These parents believed that child labor was a necessary form of discipline and training. Thus, in 1833 parents opposed the eight-hour law for children because adults were unable to supervise their offspring outside of work; some even tried to get their teenage children jobs in unregulated trades like collieries. Superficially at least, laborers and their employers sometimes shared an interest in child labor.

Yet again the response of operatives was ambiguous. Their frustration with the 1833 law was not merely that it limited the number of hours that their children could contribute to the family wage economy. Some workers went further to assert their rights as parents to retain control over their children—not just in the factory but in time away from the control of employer or schoolmaster. In demanding a uniform workday, they were seeking the right to participate in childrearing; indirectly they challenged the paternalism of middle-class child welfare advocates.[32]

Worktime was not only the site of family ideology; for both middle-class and popular advocates, it also had broader political meanings. Yet again differences can be seen. In the context of liberal rationalism, a shorter factory workday was both a principle of natural equity and a biological necessity. Sadler in 1832 argued that a workday of ten hours or less prevailed in almost all occupations (even in agriculture as a yearly mean); night work was prohibited in the Bible and even prisoners and slaves (according to British code) were worked only ten hours, exclusive of meals. "This natural regulation prevails everywhere, and has been observed in all ages."[33]

To violate the natural law of a ten-hour maximum was also to court biological disaster. Reformers made debaters' points when they identified lower life expectancies in manufacturing districts as compared with rates in rural parishes. They found that work in factories had intensified, compounding the problem of "unnatural" hours of work.[34] This thinking, although founded on new statistical science and biological principles, was still unsubstantiated by modern physiology and often remained couched in moralistic terms.[35] These ideas were developed in the late nineteenth century in work and fatigue science, which played an important role in the later short-hours movement (see chapter 5).

More important here, these arguments for equality in worktime were rooted as much in the idea of natural equity (or at least the traditions of "free-born Englishmen") as they were in the welfare language of fatigue science. Not only were the short-hours reformers linked to the egalitarian impetus of the antislavery movements but at least some were associated with electoral reform.

However, middle-class reformers were inconsistent in applying these notions of natural time limits to men or even women. The political meaning of short hours was severely restricted in that it was denied as a right of citizenship. Instead, the biological costs of overwork were applied primarily to children. Ashley observed "the gentleman will not ride his hunter before he is full grown." Yet the factory owner exploits the child worker. The twelve-hour day, he noted in 1844, began for the girl at age thirteen, "the tenderest period of female life." For the sake of the race, this practice must be abandoned. Leonard Horner, the influential factory inspector, held in 1837 that the eight-hour day for nine- to twelve-year-olds was appropriate. However, restriction on the hours of those over twelve—"above the age of childhood"—was a violation of workers' rights as "free agents." The radical political dimensions of the biological argument were thus channeled into the terms acceptable both to liberal free-agency theory and educational paternalism.[36]

Elite reformers of whatever political stripe obviously remained within the constraints of liberal ideology. Their reluctance to go beyond the scope of such protective legislation was rooted in their unwillingness to enter the realm of work and economics in explaining the social crisis of industrial labor.[37] For example, the Statistical Society of London in the 1830s was keenly aware of deteriorating social conditions in the factory districts but it stressed the social rather than work environment as the source of the problem. Inadequate housing, illiteracy, absence of religious influences, and intemperance caused poverty, not low pay, job competition, and long hours. This meant that free time, far from affording adult male workers with the opportunity for social betterment, actually undermined social discipline and the management of scarce household resources. Free time meant debauchery, at least until the social environment of male workers could be moralized.[38]

Of course, laissez-faire opponents systematically refuted the claim that unusually long hours of unstinted and confined labor was a physical hazard to workers. Alexander Ure in a famous passage in his *Philosophy of Manufactures* in 1835 asserted that children took "pleasure in the light play of their muscles" in their work as piecers in textile factories. And Nassau Senior noted the "extraordinary lightness of the labour, if labour it can be called," which made long hours perfectly acceptable.[39] Yet between 1831 and 1850, political economists gradually yielded on the question of regulating child labor; they abandoned the argument that such restrictions violated parental rights, impoverished working families, and threatened to leave children alone in "fireless homes in ignorance." By 1837, even Senior agreed that children needed the substitutionary parental protection of the state until they reached sixteen, the age at which parental obligations ended.[40] Thus a consensus emerged and the discourse of free agency merged with that of paternalism.

Yet, despite the arguments of those seeking to create working-class domesticity and protect "motherhood," laissez-faire liberals were more reluctant to grant worktime restrictions to women. Although women were largely treated as minors in the law, liberals saw this protection as a violation of women's liberty. Behind this hypocrisy was the recognition that women's labor was more important than that of children under thirteen. In 1837 Robert H. Greg argued that shorter hours would ruin the British textile trade. When cheap cotton in America and low wages on the continent were combined with newly imported machinery, the British textile trade would lose its dominant position. Although Richard Torrens by 1844 had no ideological objection to a ten-hour law, he claimed that such a reduction was an attempt to do the impossible—to raise wages above the maximum determined by land and the productivity of work. Senior, in his famous "Letter on the Factory Acts," claimed that shorter hours would destroy all profit, the key to future prosperity, for profit was made in the last hour of work.[41] The ideology of domesticity was subordinated to that of the "wage fund" and competition.

Finally, early Victorians saw in the short-hours movement a political threat, a fear that drew even middle-class proponents of hours reform away from the egalitarian conclusions of their own naturalistic arguments. The political implications were clearly expressed by the radical John Doherty, who linked shorter hours to the rights of "free-born Englishmen" and rejected the liberal claim that worktime was outside public scrutiny: "Is the personal liberty, or the actual imprisonment, of a very large portion of the king's subjects, *a mere matter of private business.*" Nonworking time was equated with personal freedom and a right to be protected by society.[42] John Fielden wrote to William Cobbett in 1833 that the recent hours legislation was inadequate and that the "unions amongst themselves [must] MAKE A SHORT TIME BILL FOR THEMSELVES."[43]

As Stewart Weaver has noted, the popular factory movement was largely indistinguishable from the democratic cause of Chartism. Moreover, opponents viewed short time as a "republican notion of controlling the labour market." George S. Bull, a Tory radical preacher noted for his support of the reduction of children's hours, opposed Fielden's movement for a universal eight-hour day as too "republican." Weaver argues that "shorter time was a variation upon a traditional demand for political citizenship—a breach in the walls not of *laissez-faire* but of corruption, tyranny, and oligarchy."[44]

In what ways was the short-hours movement political? First, a reduction of worktime for men as well as children and women would redefine the market, improving not only the economic share of labor but shifting *power* between the classes at the point of production. It would also eliminate the ability of employers to coerce workers into an unlimited surrender of their freedom (in time) for the means of subsistence. Indeed, many workers believed that if the iron law of wages prevented any permanent improvement in material standards, shorter hours could at least liberate another scarce resource—time. An hours law, like the repeal of the Poor Act of 1834, was to be a means of removing "slavery in every form."[45]

Finally, worktime legislation was a key to fulfilling the formal political right, as yet not won, of manhood suffrage. It was not merely the need of bodily restoration or of limiting fatigue that was the purpose of the popular short-hours cause, but autonomous time for self-education and participation in public life. The same people who opposed manhood suffrage often opposed the liberation of time for men. Even Parson Bull shared this distrust of male free time. In an open letter to the National Regeneration Society he wrote, "There are many of you that would not give up one hour's occupation, one hour's comfort, or the price of one glass of ale, to save *your own class* from distress and ruin. . . . Now, therefore, do exercise a little forbearance and keep your little political playthings still and quiet, when great practical questions are under discussion."[46] Men with such views may have found palatable the "liberation" of children from work (if that would provide time away from immorality and for the inculcation of middle-class values in schools); even free time for women was a virtue, for no one expected them to be diverted from their many domestic tasks to muddle in politics. Not so for working-class men. Shorter worktime meant autonomy and this undermined the political order.

Both middle- and working-class views of short hours were cast in narrow terms. The relationship between worktime and productivity, ignored in liberal political economy, played only a minor role in radical and working-class theory. While popular proponents of shorter worktime had alternative economic interpretations, they were contradictory, divided as they would be for the remainder of the century, between what appeared to be backward- and forward-looking visions of a mechanized world. Instead, social and moral arguments dominated short-hours discourse. This language fit the growing public focus on the child and the moral rhetoric of the separate spheres. This social economy of time offered a common ground for both middle-class reformers and working-class beneficiaries of regulation. Yet their objectives did not coincide: the paternalism of the reformers blinded them to the quest for autonomy of working-class parents and the objective of autonomous time. Ultimately the political implications of the general right to short hours divided the movement.

French Variations, 1828–1847

The French experience largely paralleled the British. Still they followed their own path in the quest for time. In the reactionary era of Restoration France, there was little opportunity for popular expressions of short-hours ideas and reform was even more narrowly cast than in Britain. In fact, the impetus for worktime reform came from progressive industrialists from eastern France.

As early as 1827 the Mulhouse textile manufacturer, J. J. Bourcart argued that the fifteen-hour day in French mills was less productive than the twelve-hour day that prevailed in Britain; he claimed also that long hours for children were producing a generation of moral and physical degenerates. In 1835 Mulhouse manufacturers agreed to restrict the working hours of children and in 1837 they petitioned the Parliament for legislation. This new attitude was perhaps partially the result of the success of the statistical economist Louis Villermé in convincing employers of the costly impact of long hours on the future work force. Like his British counterparts, Villermé stressed the physical deterioration of factory children as compared with that of rural youth. Moreover, at least a few industrialists realized that only government intervention would save factory children from the evils of overwork: voluntary reductions in working hours were frustrated by cutthroat competition.[47]

The issue of child labor became a point of convergence, uniting otherwise disparate economic schools. French social Catholics shared with Tory radicals an antipathy to mechanization. Eugène Buret was apprehensive that the new factory system was destroying family enterprise, leading to deep trade cycles, and disrupting class harmony. And the Baron de Morogues attacked the "yoke of industry for killing the joys, gaiety, and freedom" of children. Yet even "liberal" economists like Adolphe Blanqui agreed that "both their bodies and their souls are ruined" by long hours.[48]

What held both groups together was the conviction that working-class parents had ceded their rights over children by their "immoderate thirst for money," which led them to drag their little ones to the mill. Even those skeptical of hours laws were supporters of obligatory education. The 1833 law that obliged communes to establish primary schools led naturally to the plan in the late 1830s to abbreviate the working hours of children under twelve years of age. In 1838 an advanced thinker, Daniel Légrand, advocated maximum hours for working mothers so that they might carry out their "sacred duties as wife and mother and to rehabilitate the working class." Yet the French elite was even less willing than the British to compromise economic advantage of a ready supply of female hands for the virtues of working-class domesticity.[49] French advocates of a sexual division of labor organized around gender-differentiated worktime were rarely heard until the 1860s.

Even more unusual in France were appeals for the right of male leisure or even of family time. In part this may have been because French labor—the natural source of these ideals—was less organized and less visible than was its British counterpart during this period. To be sure, some skilled workers in 1840 struck for a ten-hour day in construction, tailoring, and metals in St. Denis; and in 1843 typographers peacefully won the ten-hour day in Paris. Yet these movements were quite rare in the authoritarian climate of France after the repression of Republican and labor movements in 1832 and 1833. In contrast to Britain, they were practically absent from the mechanized textile industry.[50]

The failure to develop a fuller social economy of time in France had other roots. An important factor was the focus of elite reformers on the moral environment rather than the time poverty of French labor. Both "Christian economists" like Louis Reybaud and H. -A. Fregier and liberals like Blanqui shared a common discourse: access to alcohol, tobacco, and other "temptations" of the urban environment not only produced debauchery but excessively raised household budgets. Low rates of productivity were caused by early morning drinking and the allure of "cheap amusements"—not the organization of worktime. These writers frequently condemned the moral environment of workers but usually had no solutions other than Christian "circles," authoritarian housing projects, or advice that employers build factories in rural districts. Overwork of adults was seldom considered as a cause of alleged moral degeneracy. On the contrary, it was the *irregularity* of work, "all the short work breaks," that produced moral failing. Villermé noted that piece workers began and quit at will, worked hard for three to four days and then "deliver[ed] themselves to excess the rest of the week." Blanqui found that the "sterile leisure of the working populations has only profited the bars and clubs resulting in their physical and moral intemperance." They ignored the social impact of work intensity or fatigue and found incomprehensible the view that time was necessary for the cultivation of moral autonomy among workers.[51]

Also a factor in forming the French social economy of time was the uncompromising commitment of the Orleanist Parliament to laissez-faire. Whereas British political economy in the 1830s was beginning to concede the utilitarian principle of state regulation of worktime, French liberals held fast to the doctrine of privacy: Gay Lussac of the Paris Chamber of Commerce in 1840 denounced all protective legislation because the manufacturer "is sovereign in his own house." This view prevailed in 1841 when the French Parliament excluded workshops employing under twenty workers from regulation on the grounds that this would be an invasion of the "privacy of the home."[52] In the name of the "family economy," the petty workshop was to be protected from restrictive legislation. Although British hours laws were first applied only to textile factories, they were extended to small-scale industries from the 1860s.

Even more than in Britain, when the French decided to police factory time they did so primarily to control economic competition. Reduced hours would diminish output and thus "reestablish an equilibrium between supply and demand," as Blanqui noted. This, of course, had been a concern of the Mulhouse textile group as early as 1827. The objective was not to "rationalize" French industry by forcing firms to increase efficiency or to drive out marginal units that could not compete without extensive working hours. Rather it was to protect industry collectively from "destructive competition." This approach was typical of the well-known conservativism of nineteenth-century French textile entrepreneurs.[53]

So central was this economic objective that it conflicted with the other major goal of regulation—to educate and facilitate the physical maturation of the future work force. By 1840 consensus had been reached in the Orleanist Parliament over the need to regulate child labor. Still, divisions remained as to how to implement this policy. The legislative debates revealed the new childrearing discourse that had taken form in Britain nearly a decade earlier: when the parent "traffics in his children . . . society has the right to say to him: this child no longer has a father. It is I who must protect him," declared Hyacinthe Corne. In language reminiscent of Rousseau, Corne argued that children under eight not only lacked the physical capacity for factory work but required "pure air, gaiety, and free movements" for normal development.[54] Minister of Public Education Villemain argued that a restriction of worktime for eight- to twelve-year-old children to eight hours was essential for the success of primary education. He revealed the nub of the issue when he claimed that for "commercial interests" the question of children's education was secondary to their goal of controlling competition and overproduction.[55]

Sigismond-Jacques Dietrich, deputy from Lille and textile manufacturer, represented these commercial interests. He advocated not an eight-hour day for children ages eight to twelve but a twelve-hour day for all factory workers over the age of ten (excluding from work anyone beneath that age.) His arguments were uncharacteristically "modern": Dietrich claimed that reduced worktime meant efficiency. A twelve-hour system would create a more regular work schedule, end extremes of overtime and short time, and thus enable workers to turn "to the life of the family and the comforts of the home from the life of the cabaret." The key to his proposal, however, was that ten- to twelve-year-olds were the "vast majority of children in the best factories" and that to impose an eight-hour day on this age group would disorganize production. A twelve-hour day for everyone from the age of ten (the age of entry into the workforce) would end wild trade swings because the pressure to operate thirteen or more hours to undercut market prices or gain a larger market share would vanish.[56]

The minister of public education, of course, objected to this proposal for it would end education at the critical age of ten. Dietrich's amendment was defeated; the 1841 law allowed children from the age of eight to work in mechanized workshops (employing at least twenty laborers) but restricted hours to eight until the age of twelve whereupon a twelve-hour day was admissible. Children were supposed to be in school half the day until reaching the age of twelve. Dietrich's fears, however, were borne out. Manufacturers found it difficult to organize eight-hour relays for children when the adult workday was twelve to fourteen hours; moreover, there was a shortage of schools. Finally, because there was no paid inspectorate (chambers of commerce were expected to regulate themselves), the law was a dead letter.[57]

In response, the royal government in 1847 proposed to extend the law to all industry and to adopt Dietrich's proposal by imposing a twelve-hour day from the age of ten. However, Charles Dupin radically transformed this plan in the House of Peers. As a sop to small "family" shops, his proposal abandoned all regulation in workplaces containing less than ten laborers; but he retained the short day for eight- to twelve-year-olds. In the interest of promoting domesticity, the proposal extended to women a limit of a twelve-hour day. It also provided for a paid inspectorate. This proposal reflected a coalition of educational paternalists and small producers. The rationalizing interests of the Mulhouse capitalists (albeit also "Malthusian" in their desire to limit production) were defeated. Still the issue was unresolved when the Revolution of 1848 broke out.[58]

The policing of worktime in the liberal states of Britain and France in the second quarter of the nineteenth century surely reveals the ambiguities of reforming interests. The failure of economists to deal directly with the relationship between worktime and productivity (an omission that favored dominant economic forces) assured that the question of worktime would be expressed primarily in social terms. Ambiguous social models—lack of consistent commitment to the ideal of domesticity, the separate spheres, or male moralization—meant that political consensus could only be reached around child-labor reform. Yet even the virtue of allowing time for the reproduction of the work force was not universally embraced. The dictates of production, still organized around the symbiosis of adult and child labor, conflicted with the goals of educational time. The confusion within elites in both countries assured that the midcentury resolution of the crisis of time would take place in the context of political upheaval.

The Midcentury Crisis

The late 1840s are well known for Chartism in Britain and the Republican revolution in France. Significantly, elites responded to these pressures by passing legislation that placed a ceiling on the competitive pressures to extend worktime.[59]

As early as the fall of 1841 in Britain, the hours issue was revived. The West Riding Short Time Committee proposed to the home secretary a ten-hour day for women as well as children through sixteen years of age. They proclaimed their intention of seeing the "gradual withdrawal of all women from the factories," maintaining that "home, its cares and its employments, is woman's true sphere." The Peel government responded over a year later with a bill that limited young child labor to a half-day (six and a half hours). This legislation was designed to correct the unworkable character of the eight-hour provisions of the

1833 law. Still, reformers did not relent, and by 1846 they again rallied around a ten-hour bill that was passed in 1847. Some Tories supported the bill to get revenge from Liberal industrialists for the repeal of the Corn Laws in 1846. Still 922 textile employers had signed petitions favoring the ten-hour day and political factions were divided over the bill.[60] The threat of Chartism and the pressure of the short-hours movements in the textile districts surely played a decisive role in winning this concession in 1847. It was hardly granted as a palliative to pacify British labor or merely an early step in the creation of the welfare state. Rather even a revolutionary like Marx could claim that "the political economy of the middle class [had] succumbed to the political economy of the working class."[61]

The 1847 law was, however, flawed. It limited the hours of children and women to fifty-eight hours of work per week but allowed them to be employed anytime between 5:30 A.M. and 8:00 P.M. This led to the widespread use of relays as squads of women and children were released from work at various hours in the day; this scheme assured formal adherence to the law and allowed employers to operate factories for twelve or more hours per day; but it disrupted the lives of working families. Moreover, tensions ran high as employers challenged the law in court. Instead of class war, a compromise was reached in August 1850 that gave employers a ten-and-a-half hour weekday and a seven and a half hour Saturday (sixty hours) in exchange for the abolition of relays.[62]

To be sure, this regulation was applied only to the minority of workers employed in the manufacture of cotton textiles. It excluded cottage trades where even longer hours prevailed and merely legalized the hours standards of the more efficient firms. Yet the ten-hour day was roughly two hours below the standard on the continent. Moreover, it confirmed not only the principle of government intervention but established a workable inspectorate. It had the effect of containing the pressures of competitive capital to extend worktime beyond the extreme acceptable for the reproduction of the labor force. It probably led to a more efficient work force as Marx and others had predicted.

At the same time, the midcentury reform maintained the myth of protecting only minors. It probably contributed to the gradual elimination of child labor; but it denied a maximum workday as a right of citizenship. Moreover, it was clearly a victory for the competent bourgeoisie, whose efficiency was rewarded by driving out the less productive employer who was denied an unlimited use of manpower. Yet, the ten-hour day was also a positive gain for British labor.[63]

The midcentury social crisis in France also coalesced around worktime. The February revolution gave expression to popular feelings about hours that had been muffled in the repressive years of Louis Philippe. If the last item on the agenda of the Orleanist Parliament was the hours of work, the new provisional government on February 28, 1848, immediately was obliged to promise public-works jobs for the unemployed of Paris and the convocation of a labor commission. Two days after the first meeting of that commission, the revolutionary government issued a decree stating that because "manual labor that is too long not only ruins the health of the worker, but prevents him from cultivating his intelligence and thereby threatens the dignity of man," the hours of work were to be lowered by one hour. The next day, after complaints from workers that daily hours in Paris varied from eleven to twelve hours, the commission decreed that Paris hours would be set at ten and provincial worktime at eleven.[64]

The leftist deputy from Elbeuf, Michel Alcan, claimed that the March 2 decree was greeted with "an extreme joy, with a delirium in the manufacturing centers. It was a true deliverance." The liberal economist Adolphe Blanqui agreed that worktime was the "most widespread" issue of 1848 and "has excited the highest degree of general emotion." In August 1848, despite the climate of disillusionment with the revolution, the leftist deputy M. Carbon could still argue in the Assembly that the state had the duty to eliminate "incessant work [which] only enervates man, makes him a candidate for drunkenness . . . [and] destroys the family."[65]

Yet what impact did this decree have upon the Second Republic? Adolphe Blanqui claimed that the decree was a mere formality; 42 percent of cotton textile workers in the important center of Lille were unemployed by July 1848 and 41 percent worked only six hours per day.[66] Still Albert Blanc of the Labor Commission insisted that the decree be enforced for both men and women, and another decree in April imposed a fifty to one hundred franc fine on first violators. The historian William Reddy finds evidence of enforcement in the textile regions. Contemporaries noted that workers fought among themselves as the more needy demanded the old working hours when employers closed or laid off workers rather than accept the government's decree.[67]

This hardly suggests that the question of worktime was a nonissue. Indeed the March 2 decree was one of the reforms that the Assembly attacked after the repression of the June Days uprising in Paris, which effectively ended the Revolution of 1848. There was substantial support in the Assembly in August for a simple revocation of the March 2 decree. By a vote of 67 to 342 the Assembly opposed continuation of the decree. Deputy M. Duffet favored revocation in the name of the "right to work." Léon Faucher felt that any hours law would lead to wage and price controls, restore *Colbertisme,* and drive workers from factories (which would be inspected) to domestic workshops (where no controls were possible); worktime control would hurt seasonal industries and in general undermine the law of supply and demand. This mix of laissez-faire dogma and appeals to special interests corresponds to Reddy's recent analysis of the French textile employer.[68]

However, this apparently reactionary assembly did not simply abrogate the policing of worktime. Rather it adopted Dietrich's proposal, offered first in 1840 and supported by the Orleanist government in 1847—a twelve-hour limit for all workers in factories and mechanized workshops. Minister of Interior Senard piously defended the right of the state to protect even the adult worker from unhealthy conditions, claiming that society cannot tolerate conditions that "compromise the present and even future humanity." Pascal Duprat proposed a twelve-hour standard as a balance between the need for business growth and the health of workers. More revealing, he noted that most manufacturers agreed that this figure was reasonable. Moreover, Charles Dupin defended (as he had in the previous regime) the interests of small business by advocating and eventually winning wide exceptions to the twelve-hour rule and defeating Catholic proposals that workers be guaranteed Sunday rest.[69]

Unlike the British, the French seemed willing to abandon liberal doctrine and to regulate adult worktime. This difference is less significant when we note that the British limitation of protection to women and children was a smokescreen for a universal reduction of worktime in protected trades. Another distinction was that the French law applied to all *usines* and *manufactures,* not just textiles. Yet again, in characteristic French fashion, administrative decrees followed that radically narrowed the range of regulated industries—exempting in particular small "family" industries. As important, the French had no effective inspectorate until the mid-1870s. Finally the French law tolerated two more hours of daily work than did the British, a clear indicator of the relative backwardness of both the French economy and its reforming drive.[70]

Political upheaval was necessary in France, even more than in Britain, to induce the state to police worktime. Yet in both cases the regulation produced not a sharp decline in worktime but rather the legal sanctioning of norms accepted by the majority of employers. In this sense both laws represented a means of enabling industry to control competition and eliminate marginal producers. They also reflected a growing if still feeble recognition of the social costs of endless work. This view was surely expressed in the political discontinuity of the late 1840s, which led to the temporary coalescence of reform and labor that produced the British Factory Act of 1847 and the French decree of March 2, 1848. The ensuing reaction led to the conservative revisions of August 1850 and September 1848. Still, in neither country was there a return to the status quo ante. Yet the limits of the liberal social economy of time were revealed in the slow pace of reform after the crisis of midcentury.

Elaborating Liberal Principles: Policing Time, 1850–1914

The general contours of the midcentury Factory Acts prevailed in the following seventy-five years of liberal predominance in western European political life. Hesitancies gradually were overcome in the application of hours law; French legislation slowly caught up to British standards as the English ceased to take initiatives. The contradiction, however, between market and family discourse remained. This situation impeded not only the reduction of worktime but, especially in France, created laws that were unenforced and even unenforceable.

The British side of the story can be told relatively briefly. Patrick Joyce and others have found that the Factory Acts were widely accepted in the cotton textile industry by 1859 when employers recognized the inevitable decline of child labor even though the numbers of female workers increased. The discontent of the 1830s and 1840s largely disappeared after 1850 when employer paternalism, worker deference, and interclass regional solidarity often supplanted earlier conflict.[71]

From 1860 to 1878 the Ten Hour Act was gradually extended to most branches of manufacturing. Little change occurred until 1902 when an amended Factory Act further restricted the hours of children (extending the half-shift system to thirteen- and fourteen-year-olds). None of these laws offered protection to men (although they almost always were applied to them).[72]

This hardly suggests that worktime had become completely rationalized. The old tactic of cheating on the clock (time cribbing) still was practiced in Oldham in 1913. And the Factory Law did not apply to the sweaters in the East London tailoring trades. As late as 1913, the Nottingham lace industry continued to require its employees to do after-hours work at home. Most significant, these legal restrictions did not apply to retail trade, transportation, or agricultural workers.[73]

Factory Laws policed industrial competition on the outside margins of socially acceptable working hours. When reformers attempted to apply the nine-hour standard that had been won by organized engineers and builders in the early 1870s to "protected workers," Parliament refused to cooperate. In general, Factory Acts were extended to new industries only after a majority of firms had already reduced hours to the sixty-hour standard or even less. To be sure, hours legislation guarded women and children from night work, insured regular meal breaks, and limited the hours of unrelieved labor (to four and a half hours by the 1870s). In these ways they fulfilled the liberal mission of protecting the "family." Yet the upshot of legislation was primarily to discipline the minority of firms who sought a competitive advantage by extending worktime beyond industrial norms. Finally, as the century wore on, British legislation grew increasingly cautious. By 1914, British hours law was scarcely more generous than in France.

Slow Liberalization in France, 1850–1913

Louis Bonaparte's Second Empire not only demobilized French labor but signaled the further advance of laissez-faire. Not only was the labor inspectorate inadequate,[74] but a leading opponent of adult hours regulation, Léon Faucher, became minister of commerce in May 1851. Within a month he had "freed" a number of industries from the twelve-hour rule and exempted all "simple workshops" including any with less than ten workers. This change excluded all but about nine thousand workplaces in France. To the textile industry Faucher granted overtime for cleaning machines and seasonal rushes, moves that made the law a farce. Employers in sugar refining, chemicals, and flour mills (who claimed the need for seasonal overtime) were exempted. Because the September 1848 law provided for no control over relays, mills often used these split shifts to keep machines operating fourteen or more hours per day. And, of course, nonmechanized work sites (like construction) had no regulations.[75] Ironically a survey of chambers of commerce in 1850 revealed that most members in industrialized departments supported the twelve-hour law of 1848 as a means of controlling over-production. Still, the Second Empire was an era of dogmatic laissez-faire and of special interests.[76]

Only during the tentative early years of the Third Republic was the question of worktime reform again reconsidered. It reappeared in the political vacuum created by the repression that followed the Paris Commune of 1871. Eugène Tallon, for example, took up the question of reform where it left off in the last years of the Orleanist regime. He was skeptical that the working classes were ready for social betterment. Before employers should increase wages above subsistence levels, Tallon argued, they must also "raise the worker's intelligence, morality, develop his attachment to his family and teach him the love of saving." His remedy was classic bourgeois familialism: encourage male working-class stability in marriage and family life, and support the gradual withdrawal of the wife to the home to create a well-managed and economical household and to foster an atmosphere of "peace, good harmony, and prosperity in the family."[77] Jules Simon promoted a similar familial image: nostalgia for family cottage work, and the superiority of southern and rural work to the antiutopia of Lille and Roubaix factory towns. The presence of women in the factory not only threatened male economic predominance and undermined a moral bond between the husband and wife but resulted in the "semisavagery" of children. Still, Simon was not optimistic that women could be withdrawn from wage work, despite the economic advantages of dividing production and consumption functions between men and women. His solution was to encourage a wider range of domestic-based employments for women—working as seamstresses, for example—where the traditional domestic economy and the modern idea of "home economics" could be spatially and temporally linked.[78]

Beyond this unrealistic combination of nostalgia for cottage labor and the modern notion of housewifery, Simon and Tallon could only offer a reform of the 1841 law. Their proposal, modeled after the 1844 half-day system of the British, included a six-hour shift for children under twelve and a sixty-nine-hour week (eleven-hour day) for twelve- to sixteen-year-olds. This would assure a half-day of education for the younger set and an hour of schooling for the older group.

In effect, despite the rhetoric of maternal domesticity, the imperatives of French industry required a continuation of a twelve-hour day for women (and thus all industry). Even the idea of a sixty-nine-hour week for teenagers was rejected in the law that was passed in 1874. And, in the name of parental authority, it did not apply to fathers who directly employed their children. These men, of course, could be expected to carry out their "sacred duty" to protect their own offspring.[79]

Only in 1879 were legislators willing to consider extending the policing of time below twelve hours for workers more than twelve years old. In the 1870s, textile workers from Rouen and Reims had repeatedly petitioned the government for a new hours law. A trade union congress in 1876 channeled these demands into a call for a ten-hour day for both women and children—modeled after the British law of 1847. Martin Nadaud was their spokesman in Parliament.[80]

In 1881 Richard Waddington presented a favorable committee report to the Chamber; a government survey of unions found a vast majority in support of the bill, a sentiment confirmed by continued agitation for a ten-hour day among the textile workers of Lyon. Yet the bill got nowhere. Between 1881 and 1892, various worktime proposals were shunted between the Chamber and the Senate six times. Probably the biggest impediment was Senate opposition to including women as "minors" requiring protection.[81]

Parliamentary debates in March 1881 and February 1882 reveal alternative discourses and a context for understanding the liberal constraints on the political language of free time. Waddington voiced traditional Republican rhetoric in defending government intervention: the "more a state is civilized, the more it extends its action." Martin Nadaud and the aged Louis Blanc associated the hours movement with each phase of the saga of French democratization and with the "general will" as expressed in the petition movement of workers.[82] In this debate, however, reformers were obliged to go beyond their traditional Jacobinism, respond to right-wing objections, and identify the unique character of factory work.

The laissez-faire Right insisted that hours legislation for adults would be an "exceptional law," made in the special interest of factory workers and that the twelve-hour law of 1848 was acceptable only because it regulated "dangerous" employment. Deputy Marcel Barthe argued that thirteen or more hours of work represented "unhealthy and dangerous" working conditions, which society was obliged to police. He further claimed that the twelve-hour factory day, presumably established in 1848, was a "universal norm" and insisted that factory work had become more healthful and less dangerous since midcentury. Regulation was justified only in the rather narrow exercise of police powers, not for social engineering and, most certainly, not to create a new social right to free time.[83]

The response of reformers demonstrates how this political language dominated the terms of debate. Advocates of hours regulation argued that machinery may have reduced physical fatigue but factory work had introduced regularity and discipline, and deprived wage earners of "pure air."[84] Reformers were almost obliged to overstress the harmful and involuntary character of mechanized work—that the pace of the machine and the logic of capitalist competition rather than the workers' self-interest controlled his pace and length of work. For some this removed factory workers from the ranks of "free adults" and made them subject to the protection of minors in "dangerous trades." Yet the framing of the debate in terms of the factory—and distinguishing it from "open air" or unmechanized occupations—deflected the argument away from the citizen's right to a shorter workday. Rather the reduction of labor time was a physiological need for the exceptional factory worker.[85]

Moreover, the reformers' riposte to laissez-faire liberalism fell into the familiar familial language of Tallon and Simon—without perhaps the overbearing paternalism.[86] Family-saving rhetoric was the best retort to the conservative Senate's insistence on the free agency of women in 1882. Senator Alexandre Oudet argued that only in the family where the wife has time to create a comfortable home will the male worker not be "led astray on the dangerous path of utopia," a theme repeated by social Catholics like Albert de Mun.[87]

Despite the convergence of radical, moderate republican, and Catholic ideologies around the themes of factory fatigue and social time, the Chamber added an hour to Nadaud's bill in 1881. The next year the Senate rejected by a three-to-two margin even this modest eleven-hour limit for women and children. Everyone, of course, recognized that an eleven-hour law for women would be also applied to men. Again, French elites were unwilling to compromise economic interests—really a problem of industrial inefficiency—for the sake of stabilizing or moralizing the French working-class family.[88]

Five years later, following the Senate's rejection of a similar eleven-hour bill, the Chamber responded by passing a ten-hour bill for women and children. By 1890, even textile industrialists from Roubaix petitioned the government to ban night work for women as an antidote to moral perversion and the destruction of family life.[89]

Only in 1892 was a law finally passed. It raised the age of entry into the factory to thirteen years, and for women and children guaranteed a six-day workweek and prohibited night work; the law limited the hours of thirteen- to sixteen-year-olds to ten and restricted the hours of sixteen- to eighteen-year-olds and adult women to eleven.[90]

This tiered system was an awkward compromise of conflicting social and market ideologies. Indeed, it was an administrative and social nightmare that made little business sense and disrupted workers' families. Although supporters anticipated that the ten-hour rule for twelve- to sixteen-year-olds would set the factory schedule for all, inventive employers found ways of staggering the hours of "protected workers" to enable factories to operate twelve hours per day. Inspectors were faced with three different hours systems and a complex of relays that could not easily be regulated. One Lille cotton spinning company used twenty relays and another used eighty. Fathers complained to the Superior Labor Commission in 1893 that their teenage children "have a free hour to spend without supervision on the streets in the company of a band of other children. We fear the lessons and adventures to which they are exposed." Inspectors noted that relays resulted in "unhealthful meal breaks" and disrupted the "family table." Prominent cotton textile employers, long the ally of the inspectors in enforcing the hours laws against wildcat competitors, petitioned the government to legislate a uniform hours system.[91]

The legislative response was predictable. As early as 1894, Senator Lecomte proposed a bill limiting the workday to eleven hours for all, including men, in factories that employed protected workers. This measure would have simplified enforcement and eliminated some of the problems with relays. Yet Chamber bills insisted on a ten-hour standard, rejecting the prospect of raising hours for children. The compromise adopted in 1900 was a progressive decrease in the hours for men who worked in the same location as women and children from eleven in 1900 to ten by 1904. Relay work for women and children was abolished.[92] Finally, the French had reached the standard initiated by the British over fifty years earlier.

This hardly ended the problems of policing French worktime. In 1900 some thirty strikes were reported in Paris, Cherbourg, and Tourcoing against wage cuts resulting from the decrease to an eleven-hour day. Likewise largely successful strikes by workers in textiles and the metal trades followed the reduction to ten hours in 1904.[93] Moreover, French courts in 1901 allowed employers to separate men from women in the same building and thus avoid the limit on male worktime. The law's vague decree powers allowed a recorded level of six million hours of overtime in 1905.[94] Marginal businesses sometimes fired apprentices to evade the law. A trade unionist from Moulins protested "our children are excluded from the shop at the moment when they ought to learn a trade; the workers' children, thanks to a poorly designed law, have . . . only the school of the street, the school of vice."[95]

In the long run, however, these tactics proved not to be cost-effective. By 1907 inspectors found that employers were adjusting to the new regime. Production losses were absorbed by further mechanization and more regular work. In Lille, for example, the factory inspector was proud to announce that the introduction of the ten-hour day had led to the elimination of two short breaks that had previously "allowed workers more numerous visits to the cabaret." The initial fear that the law would destroy the apprenticeship system (part of a general concern over the erosion of skilled training) proved to be unfounded as the proportion of youthful workers rose in 1910. The law had no effect on female employment in its first decade. And the number of reported violations of the law quickly declined.[96]

Still the lack of uniformity between those workers exempted from all controls, those under the twelve-hour system dating from 1848, and those regulated by the ten-hour law of 1900 continued to frustrate the inspectorate. Again, division between the two houses prevented the adaptation of a Chamber proposal for a uniform ten-hour day for all industry.[97]

Why a country with such apparently advanced political ideas could be so laggard in carrying out social policy has attracted the attention of many historians. This complex and little-known history of the French policing of worktime is an excellent illustration of the problem. Although it can be exaggerated, French bourgeois ideology throughout the century reflected a nostalgia for the rural domestic economy, forms of which survived even in textile factories. At the same time, modernizing French legislators wanted to encourage gender and age differentiation in ways that did not always conform to the still prevailing "family" organization of work. The result was an exceedingly slow adaptation of British legislative standards, frequent compromise of worktime gradations legally distinguishing different age and gender classes, and considerable administrative confusion. The goal of liberating child time for the sake of moralizing the future worker contradicted the immediate needs of employers. The objective of freeing mothers' time for housewifery was a modern idea—although couched often in reactionary garb; yet it likewise required an economy more advanced than the French elite wanted or had really created.

Like the British reformers' use of the hours language in the 1840s,

French advocates of regulating worktime could not embrace the idea of uniform hours. Even though this was practical to both the substantial industrialist and factory inspector, it violated the atavistic economic individualism of the French bourgeoisie for whom any government control was unacceptable; uniform hours also violated the special interests of the petty, but politically influential, firm. Equality of worktime also undermined the very notion of a "protected class" and the claim that children because of their immaturity required the aid of the state-parent or that women, as vulnerable vehicles of the womb and as invaluable vessels of France's demographic future, needed special treatment. Finally, uniformity implied that the privilege of short hours was a right of citizenship. Despite the precedent of the twelve-hour law of 1848, the idea of the progressive reduction of the workday for all was politically impossible in liberal France.

Nevertheless, the difference between the "backward" French and "advanced" British can be drawn too sharply. Both countries conducted extraordinarily similar debates over worktime. Moreover, by 1900, at least in regard to legislation, the two countries were largely comparable insofar as the British leadership in social legislation had come to an end.

Political elites in both countries had reached an impasse. They were unwilling to abandon the notion of "protective legislation." By 1892, both countries had finally embraced the ideology of maternal domesticity by granting women shorter hours. Yet neither would concede this right to men as men. The "universal" twelve-hour law of 1848 in France applied only to factories (necessarily "dangerous" and thus requiring police protection) and was supported by industry to control competition among employers. And the nineteenth-century British state never violated the free-agency doctrine.

The most advanced argument of reformers in both countries was that factory (and mine) work—as distinct from the freedom of labor in the open air—deserved special protection. Yet to have gone further and proposed a universal standard of worktime would have extended the rights of citizenship beyond civil and political liberties to that of a right to autonomous time. This would have suggested that a share of the increase in social product should be by right distributed as leisure. Such a notion was a fundamental affront to the bourgeois understanding of work and compensation. Yet it is precisely over such ideological terrain that a revived short-hours movement in the 1880s would begin to challenge the liberal limits to the policing of time.

3

Challenging the Liberal Economy of Time, 1886–1912

For almost seventy years the eight-hour workday has been the norm in industrial societies. This modern standard for the allocation of personal time emerged between 1885 and 1920, becoming the nearly universal means of dividing daily economic obligation from personal freedom. Although increased productivity provided a necessary backdrop for this reallocation of time, the actual eight-hour standard was a fruit of an intellectual and political struggle over work and leisure. In a complex debate, which ranged throughout the industrial world in the late 1880s, the terms of the twentieth-century conflicts over worktime were set.

In 1894, the French Marxist Jules Guesde declared, "the eight-hour day is the most important reform that can be realized under capitalism."[1] Unlike the ten-hour question in Britain in the 1830s and 1840s, the eight-hour day was essentially an *offensive* struggle, an attempt to lower hours below the contemporary standard rather than merely an effort to contain the erosion of customary working time. In contrast to the nine-hour movement of the 1860s and 1870s in Britain, it was a demand for a universal standard, neither linked to the productivity of any industry nor isolated to a particularly well-organized trade. Finally, unlike the parliamentary battle for a ten-hour day in France in the 1880s and 1890s, the eight-hour movement went substantially beyond a middle-class elite; rather, it had broad roots in labor and the Left. It won the enthusiasm of both conservative trade unionists and socialists on both sides of the channel.

Still the reason why workers embraced maximum-hours legislation is not at all obvious. Specialists in nineteenth-century labor history have often identified time concerns of workers with attempts to preserve traditional work patterns. Richard Price, D. A. Reid, and Clive Behagg, for example, stress the tenacity with which British construction and other skilled workers clung to their informal work breaks and traditional Monday holidays. Such people were not likely participants in short-hours movements. One might argue that maximum hours appealed primarily to factory workers. Yet William Reddy finds that French textile workers in the mid-nineteenth century protested not wages and hours but the "decline of the multiplicity of purposes that work fulfilled."[2]

At least implied in these analyses is the supposition that many types of workers were slow to focus on labor time because they did not see themselves as being within a wage market system. Long clinging to the categories of the cottage worker and independent artisan, even clearly industrial workers sought to retain control over the process of work, including the use of time within the workday, rather than to modify the length of that day. Only when the employer had reduced the wage to a measure of worktime (by reducing the role of skill) did workers try to regulate daily output by reducing hours; by restricting the supply, they could raise the price of their product—labor time. Put another way, in the face of the employer's growing influence over the content and value of the labor day, workers sought control over the length of that day. By the "external" means of reducing hours, the unemployed could be absorbed, workers' bargaining positions could be strengthened, and wages could be raised. For these reasons, according to this view, skilled British workers in the late 1860s sought a nine-hour maximum.[3]

Thus, short-hours movements have often been identified with a growing economistic outlook—the reduction of labor's struggle to the goal of maximizing pay at the price of control over the methods, pace, and social organization of work. Growth of interest in worktime, then, meant abdication of any claim of labor for organizing society in its own image. Some labor historians have argued that hours demands were little more than "circuitous means of getting a raise." Although trade union leaders might have spoken in lofty terms of liberating workers for self-improvement or family life or claimed that worktime strikes were offensive demands, many observers have disregarded these words. Historians have seen these ideas as merely expressions of bourgeois reformist ideology or a rhetoric that superficially unified a labor movement that otherwise was riddled with divisions.[4]

There is, of course, much truth to this line of thought (as we shall see in this chapter). Still, the linkage of short hours to economism is one-sided and blinds us to important dimensions of the meaning of time in late nineteenth-century industry. The labor historians' stress on the integration of workers into bargaining structures—especially in Britain—obscures the nonmonetary elements of the hours question.

Alternatively, by focusing on the persistence of workers' control we may avoid the errors of imposing a theoretical world of the marketplace on the reality of work life or of mistaking the programs of leaders for the views of the rank and file. But we also risk misreading changing attitudes about work. Traditional family solidarities built around work doubtless survived the onslaught of the market, but laborers often wanted a new kind of familialism. After all, the pooled family wage economy was founded on low individual wages and a lack of time for childhood development and domestic life. If it was ever an ideal, and not merely an adaptation to necessity, the fact that workers embraced wage and hours reform points to a new family strategy. Individual workers sought a "family wage"—income sufficient for the adult worker (usually narrowly identified as the father) to support a family and thus to free its members for domestic life. Moreover, workers greeted the passing of the old long but "porous" workday with ambiguity. Despite the loss of a sociable work culture, in the long run workers demanded a reduction of worktime to enhance the opportunity of social relationships *off* rather than on the job. Whether for good or ill to the labor movement, workers accepted the demarcation of time and thus the separation of family and society from work.

By investigating the quest for a new "normal day," we may find a somewhat different perspective from which to interpret working-class culture and labor history. At the same time, we will focus on the point where work and culture intersect—the allocation of time.

Also important to a fresh perspective on late nineteenth-century labor is a new assessment of the role of politics. New unionism in Britain and Marxist syndicalism in France have long been understood as part of a rising tide of political class consciousness in the late 1880s. Yet labor historians have interpreted both the growth of collective bargaining and working-class political participation as symptoms of the integration of workers into the bourgeois order. In this context, the movement for an eight-hour law was merely a component of a reformist program of protective labor legislation—and a goal greeted with equivocation by individualistic members of the working classes.[5]

Yet there is much evidence to argue that it was the political impotence of the British (and even more so of the French) unions rather than their ambiguity toward or integration into the capitalist polity that was the problem.[6] More important here, worktime demands were not simply imposed on workers by leaders imbued with bourgeois reformist ideology. They were easily the most difficult concessions to win on the shop floor and thus they required the intervention of the wider society.[7] Moreover, while workers had vastly different reasons for seeking shorter hours that sprang from the diversity of their work, the key fact is that workers coalesced (if imperfectly) around the eight-hour idea. This suggests a common appeal to time *outside* of work that overrode the diverse circumstances of work and points to the idea of the "right" to leisure time. The attraction of the eight-hour day had as much to do with the political demand for the equality of free time as it did with conditions on the shop floor. This blind spot to the relevance of politics is an understandable lapse in a literature that seeks to understand the social dynamics of industrialization. Yet, by obscuring the radical significance of protective labor legislation to workers, these historians miss the centrality of the growing quest for time away from work.

A study of the discourse of the short-hours movement from the 1880s to 1914 may shed new light on these issues. Essential to this ideological debate was the formation of an economic theory of nonworktime. These ideas focused on the work rather than the family-leisure issue. As such, they challenged some of the foundations of liberal political economy. At the same time, they reflected new attitudes toward leisure as well as work that, far from being antithetical or irrelevant to the aspirations of workers, often coincided with them.

The Emerging Debate over Worktime, 1880–1891

In the 1880s the eight-hour day was a reform that fundamentally challenged the industrial regimes in France and Britain. Not only did it threaten capital accumulation, but it raised the specter of a legal entitlement for all workers. It was resisted by employers and only slowly accepted by many workers and union leaders.

In Britain, despite an increase of 34 percent in real wages in the 1880s, no appreciable reduction in hours occurred.[8] To be sure beginning in 1859, struggles within construction and engineering trades eventually produced the nine-hour day during the boom of 1866–1873.[9] Female-dominated industries gained legal hour parity with the cotton textile industry by the mid-1870s. During the stagnant period that followed, few gains were won. Most workers labored ten hours and some, like railway employees and retail clerks, worked twelve and more.[10]

In the 1860s, the eight-hour day was the dream of the visionaries of the First International; in the 1880s it was revived by a small and divided group of London socialists. However, although Chartists had supported hours laws, the British Trades Union Congress (TUC) throughout the 1880s had rejected such bills as "grandmotherly legislation"—a threat to trade union voluntarism.[11]

New conditions produced new strategies in Britain. The Great Depression of the 1880s led to unemployment rates of 10 to 12 percent in organized trades and resulted in declining prices and thus wages. In response, organized labor turned to a shorter workday in order to spread work (e.g., in construction) or to reduce output and thus raise prices and wages (e.g., in mining). Reform-minded economists like Thomas Brassley found maldistribution of income to be the cause of the stagnation.[12] Reduced hours would reverse this shift of income toward capital. Further, the inability of craft unions to control the spread of "systematic overtime"—despite the nominal advantage of a nine-hour day—led these trades to the camp of worktime reform in order to stem unemployment and lower wages. Skilled operators of blast furnaces favored a legal shortening of worktime as an alternative to the "evils of strikes" and as a means of protecting the majority who desired to work less time from the minority who sought to maximize earnings.[13]

The emergence of new general unions after 1886 increased the demand for a legal eight-hour day. Convinced that "general" or unskilled workers lacked the resources to withstand long strikes, new unionists advocated legal protection. Hours demands in Britain stimulated unionization drives among coal gas workers, railroad employees, tramway staff, bakers, and dockers in the active years of 1888 to 1891.[14]

In the 1880s, the workday in France was even longer than it was in Britain: only 40 percent worked as little as eleven hours, while the rest labored twelve or more hours. French textile workers had followed the British in the upsurge of short-hours strikes in 1871–1872 (mostly seeking a ten- instead of a nine-hour day). In the reactionary period following the Paris Commune, however, they were easily defeated. Whereas British factory legislation expanded in 1874 and 1878, parallel French parliamentary drives were blocked by conservative majorities.[15]

By 1880, the socialist and labor Left had begun to recover from the catastrophic defeat of the Commune. Labor law was liberalized in 1884; a trade union federation was organized in 1886; and the Parti Ouvrier Français (POF) was founded in 1880. Yet practical efforts for the reduction of worktime were largely limited to skilled trades that suffered from technological changes and a lengthy parliamentary battle to win a legal ten-hour day for women and children. From 1880, the POF used the ten-hour debate in the Chamber to make ritual appeals for an eight-hour day, a goal that was obviously most distant in the future.[16]

In Britain, between 1886 and 1891, an unprecedented wave of writing on the eight-hour day flooded the press. In 1889, Sidney Webb, the academic and generally cautious Fabian socialist, declared that the eight-hour day would be the "inevitable result of an age of democracy, the fruit of the next election."[17]

One serious obstacle was the opposition to hours legislation that was still strong within the British TUC. Old-line craft union leaders like Henry Broadhurst feared that a legal maximum would sap union initiative, be too rigid for seasonal skilled building trades, and would lead to wage controls.[18] In France, relatively powerful anarchosyndicalists in the unions challenged the "statists" with their call for shorter days through direct action.[19]

Yet the problem ran deeper than tactics. British advocates sometimes blamed the attitudes of a "labor aristocracy" who feared that "permanently raised wages (always the consequence of reduced hours) of unskilled labor would . . . lower their own wages." A minority of coal hewers, mostly from Durham and Northumberland, opposed an eight-hour law (although they worked even fewer hours): it would eliminate the ten-hour system of their boy helpers and impose a hated three-shift system upon adults. Finally, many contemporaries noted the opposition of the leaders of workers in many building trades and textiles, as well as the foot dragging of the TUC's Parliament Committee. J. Mawdsley of the Cotton Spinners held that an eight-hour law was "socialistic" and the work of "driving ignorant mobs."[20]

Yet the opposition went beyond the selfish skilled minority or the laissez-faire old guard. British unions in export industries feared competition with long-hours regions. One textile union official declared in 1890 that he would support the eight-hour day "only after India gets it." Wage earners in low-wage industries (e.g., female clothing workers or tramwaymen) anticipated reduced incomes if hours were legally reduced. Workers in task-organized occupations like building, skilled metals trades, and house painting found the eight-hour proposal to be too inflexible: it would leave work unfinished and likely cause tensions with second-shift workers. Some blast-furnace men opposed eight hours even though they worked up to twelve hours because it would mean the end to traditional rest breaks and might lead to an unbearable intensification of work.[21]

In France, conservative trades like printing shared with their British counterparts the fear that output and wages would suffer with a sharp diminution of worktime. Also anarchists declared that an eight-hour day would only lead to further mechanization and an "aggravation of misery in real society."[22]

This ambivalent response of workers toward legal hour reductions was magnified many fold in both parliaments and among employers. Employers, of course, held that hours legislation violated the tenets of classical liberalism—the free labor contract and the disutility of social legislation. By seeking a legal time limit, said William J. Shaxby, labor desired "aristocratic power"; workers hoped to "make capital subservient to labour, instead of allowing each side concerned to exercise the rights of a party to a strictly business contract." This proposal was only a Trojan horse, a popular means of imposing "wholesale state regulation of wages" and socialism. In France, Yves Guyot and Guy de Molly spoke essentially the same language. Numerous reports from French chambers of commerce revealed unwavering opposition to all controls over worktime. Robert Giffen, the statistician of the British Board of Trade, simply argued that worktime reductions were the natural and inevitable by-product of increased productivity. This process was distorted by premature legal action, which would do little more than produce labor shortages, lower wages, and capital flight. Charles Bradlaugh, a prominent British Radical, found an hours law as "weakening to, if not destructive of the self-reliance for which this country has been famous." Workers unable to win shorter hours through collective bargaining "do not deserve statutory aid, nor will it really help them." It would reduce output and thus income even if the wage fund was shared by a larger group of workers.[23]

This view was based on the assumption that, as John Hobson put it, an "industrial law . . . forbids any possibility of a general rise of wages . . . excepting in accordance with the slow operation of the motive to save." A reduction of hours, agreed the French politician M. Donnat, would lower profits, savings, and investment, and thus the wage fund. British employers had long lost confidence that they could compete against longer-hours nations. And the French press somewhat later referred to hours laws as the "commercial Sedan," which threatened to bring economic defeat to France in the face of the rising new industries of Germany, the United States, and Japan.[24]

Finally, employers had no faith that mechanization or a more rested worker would be able to compensate for reduced hours. Textile employers claimed that production decreases would be proportional to the diminution of worktime because machinery rather than effort determined the rate of output. But even managers of gas works with practically no machinery doubted that the manual laborer could intensify his hourly output in a shorter day. Few employers were willing or able to replace long workdays with doubtful experiments in increasing productivity on the shop floor. Probably even fewer employers believed that it was possible to regulate leisure in order to improve productivity. Not many would imitate Henry Ford in the 1910s in Detroit.[25]

To be sure, a small number of highly placed conservatives like Randolph Churchill or Albert de Mun advocated reduced hours to improve the family life of workers. Cardinal Manning declared that "on the domestic life of the people, the whole political order of human society reposes." However, such paternalism was surely a dying force by the 1880s. It was nearly swamped by the classical economic theory of the wage fund and the fear of international competition.[26]

Two Apologetics for Time

It is within the constraints of labor ambivalence and employer opposition that we can understand the apparently economistic framework of eight-hour discourse. Advocates sought to eliminate structural and cyclical unemployment and to push up wages. The noneconomic goals of leisure time to empower the working classes with intellectual and physical culture or to enable laborers to enjoy family life—themes that had often been central to the short-hours movements of the 1830s and 1840s—were much less evident by the 1880s. Paul Lafargue's *Le Droit à la paresse*, with its mocking of the bourgeois obsession with work and its praise of "laziness" or leisure, was published in 1880. But it was a seldom acknowledged embarrassment to pragmatic advocates of the eight-hour day. Sidney Webb's *The Eight Hours Day*— doubtless the most thorough of discussions on the worktime question—devoted only 6 of its 249 pages to the moral and social benefits of reduced working hours.[27]

However, this is not proof of Webb's disinterest in leisure for self-improvement or family life. It reflects the view that the benefits of free time were self-evident.[28] The campaign focused on strategy and the economic effects of the eight-hour day. These were themes of an *apologetic* rather than *utopian* discourse. Advocates did not simply abandon the moral vision of Owen's eight-hour day for "economism" or "reformism" but advanced to the practical question of winning labor and public support for a radical reform within the context of capitalist democracy in the 1880s. At the same time, leisure objectives were implied in this economic apologetic—goals largely consistent with the attitudes of the rank and file.

The first task was to persuade a skeptical labor movement and dominant liberal public of the utility of legislation. To an audience of organized labor, British advocates of an eight-hour law stressed that a legal hours standard eliminated the need for costly strikes, insured hours gains during economic downswings, and created jobs for unemployed union members and thus preserved union jobless benefits. This strategy appealed to organized workers who had recently failed to win worktime decreases through bargaining (e.g., joiners and railwaymen), whose contractual nine-hour day had been defeated by "systematic overtime" (e.g., engineers), and whose experience with sliding-scale contracts and arbitration had not produced high wages (e.g., coal miners).[29]

On the other hand, New Union activist Tom Mann argued that the "organization of workers . . . will come after, not before, a great reduction in working hours" and that this required a "compulsory eight hour day." The old union claim that "every man has the right to earn a living" was frustrated by the "greed" of some workers. Especially dock and tramway unions sought a legal eight hours as a way of creating sufficient work for a permanent body of laborers to support families and to shift the large numbers of casual workers into other jobs.[30]

More broadly, the legal eight hours promised to create a new labor standard. H. M. Hyndman found Bradlaugh's argument that worktime should be consistent with the profitability of each enterprise to be an invitation to exploitation. Webb and many others defended the history of British Factory Laws as a peaceful means of diminishing economic competition. Mann and Webb argued that the legal eight-hour day would not disarm Britain in the global economic war, but would allow it to jettison marginal industries that relied on sweated labor. "England could do without her farthing toys and penny puzzles," Webb declared. Moreover, a higher labor standard did not undermine the ability of the British to compete because short-hours countries were always the most efficient.[31]

Yet the threat of competition drove labor—especially in export-sensitive sectors like textiles—to seek "legislative enactment at one and the same time" in all industrial countries.[32] This approach would amount to an economic disarmament treaty. By 1889 British, French, and most other European and American labor movements advocated this simultaneous reduction of hours on an international scale.

An even more urgent problem was to demonstrate that the eight-hour day would not lower living standards. This led to the postulating of two rather distinct theories, drawn from differing economic assumptions and, more important, contrasting apologetic objectives. Yet these views never crystallized into opposing theoretical schools and they were even held jointly by the same eight-hour propagandists.

One theory, which may be called "redistributionism," argued that fewer hours would shift wealth from capital to labor. It was tailored to counter the claim that shorter hours meant lower wages and to appeal to the worker who feared unemployment. This argument was a rejection of the traditional wage fund theory, which claimed that job sharing schemes would only reduce individual salaries. In England, H. M. Hyndman, Sidney Webb, and George Bernard Shaw argued that reduced hours would raise wages: workers' pay was not the product of output divided by the labor supply but was determined by the demand for labor. Reduced hours would force employers to hire additional workers (and thus raise wages); lower profit, interest, and rental income would follow. Prices would not necessarily increase even if labor costs rose because demand rather than costs determined prices. Instead there would be a shift of investment away from luxury goods to the (now) more profitable mass markets. This apologetic, drawing selectively from the theories of J. S. Mill and even Henry George, held that shorter hours would weaken the economic power of the parasitical landlord and rentier while, at the same time, assuring full employment.[33]

Among French Marxists similar assumptions led to economic "neo-Malthusian" conclusions. Paul Lafargue claimed that shorter hours would eliminate overproduction and thus the imperialist drive for new markets; a reduced workday would also reduce the throngs of servants and bureaucrats that lived like parasites on the overwork of the laborers. Jules Guesde likewise stressed that shorter hours meant the end to excess output, which, in turn, had led to periodic unemployment and low wages.[34] Moreover, Louis Niel during agitation for an eight-hour day in 1905 argued that with hours reduction there would be no compensatory increase in hourly production, nor should there be. The essential purpose of shorter worktime was to absorb the jobless, created by the "incessant development of machinery," to reduce the army of the unemployed, and thus to raise wages.[35]

This redistributionist position assumed essentially a no-growth economy and ignored the impact of hours reductions on productivity and technology. At base, a worktime reduction would spread employment without lowering living standards. Its appeal was to an uncertain worker who feared that the living standard would drop with decreased hours.[36] It was effective in periods of widespread unemployment like that of the 1880s. Similar arguments reappeared in the 1930s and 1980s in somewhat parallel economic conditions.

A second and in the long run more important theory of the impact of shorter hours on the economy may be called "productionism." This line of thought answered the charge that shorter hours would lead to economic stagnation and reduce competitiveness with long-hours nations. According to this view, hours reductions would not necessarily create jobs but would increase productivity and eventually stimulate technological innovation. French socialist Jean Longuet claimed that "when one reduces the daily workday to a normal length [eight hours], one augments, at the same time, the intensity and productivity of labor." For, as Paul Boilley claimed, "if one prolongs the time of work beyond eight hours per day, the intensity of work decreases proportionately with the lengthening." In effect the eight-hour day meant a "maximum of productivity in a minimum of time without a threat to health."[37] This assumed a fixed physical capacity of labor to produce— that it could be "inefficiently" spread out in ten or twelve hours or more effectively concentrated in eight. This view reflected the new discipline of work science (see chapter 5).

Shorter hours would also encourage mechanization insofar as employers were forced to improve productivity to compensate for reduced labor time. Technology was not a threat to labor autonomy but a means of freeing the worker from "the brutal yoke of manual labor." This surprisingly optimistic French view of technology remained a major theme among syndicalists, despite the continued defense of artisan values.[38]

This linkage of the shorter workday with technological innovation was rooted in the socialist's association of French capitalism with "routine" and technological backwardness. Lack of innovation, in turn, was responsible not only for low living standards but also for long hours. Rather ironically, many French socialists held an image of the American economy as a model for France. This appeal to the American future was, of course, a well-established French utopia encouraged by French visits to American exhibitions from 1876, after which delegates reported the wonders of American productivity to intrigued French audiences. Boilley claimed, for example, that American workers produced three times as much while working one-quarter less time than the French. Boilley argued that the eight-hour day would lead to economic concentration; this trend could only "facilitate the infinite perfection of industry [which will] become . . . the ideal structure for the collectivity to come." The identification of short hours with American technology and a gradualist path to socialism influenced French socialist thinking until the 1930s. This view was, of course, consistent with economic conditions in France—its relative economic backwardness and the seeming unwillingness of French capital to innovate.[39]

Yet even Tom Mann, the radical British trade unionist, made similar arguments: reduced hours would lead to a more efficient, concentrated economy. Marginal firms, relying on sweated labor, would no longer compete with capital-intensive firms. Mann's thinking was not only shared by Marx but was probably derived from him. Yet it was held by a broad non-Marxist group of socialists and reformists, including Sidney Webb.[40]

Shorter hours also meant consumption. A corollary to productionist theory was that increased leisure would make workers into consumers and thereby stimulate growth and employment from the demand side. Webb and Cox argued that leisure created wants that increased markets for popular services and goods. Henry H. Champion held that the eight-hour day would "excite a desire for additional means of recreation, amusement, and cultivation." And Tom Mann claimed that leisure provided workers "with the desire for the products of manufacture."[41]

Even the "revolutionary" French unions of 1906 claimed that short hours created more "needs" not only for "intellectual improvement" but "increased consumption." Union leader Victor Griffuelhes argued in 1904 that "leisure leads the worker to desire to consume more, will increase his needs, and will lead to the proportionate increase of production."[42]

These ideas (in Britain especially) paralleled the view of the American economist and friend of the American Federation of Labor, George Gunton. In his book, *Wealth and Progress,* Gunton developed a "demand-side" theory of economic growth that reversed classical economic theory; its central tenet was that capital accumulation was dependent on wages and working-class consumption, rather than investment. Wage levels, in turn, correlated with the "social opportunities" of the "most expensive" workers. These "opportunities" for consumption could be realized only with additional leisure time. "The development of labor's capacity to consume wealth is as important economically . . . as it is to increase his power to produce," Gunton declared. At the same time, consumer needs encouraged productivity. Gunton found that improvements in the "standard of living" drove workers into having "such a conscious need for an object that its absence will cause sufficient pain to induce the effort and sacrifice necessary to its attainment." This view paralleled that of the influential European economist and later advocate of the eight-hour day, Lujo Brentano. Employers, he claimed, no longer needed to maintain long hours or low pay to assure a profitable output—a view long held by many economists and employers. Rather advanced consumer needs, developed in leisure time, would stimulate individual productivity. The "leisure pole" then posed no threat to the "work pole" because both complemented each other on the balance beam of consumption.[43]

From the productionist perspective, growth rather than redistribution would be the consequence of shorter hours. The eight-hour day would not spread work or reduce unemployment directly; but, by broadening the mass market, it would create jobs. This theory did not assume a stagnant economy; rather it held that increased leisure would stimulate technology and enhance the motivation of a consumption-oriented worker to increase his daily output despite reduced hours. These views would eventually prevail over the themes of redistributionism because they seemed to both Marxists and reformists to be consistent with economic trends.

Meanings of the Eight Hours to Workers

These positive assessments of work intensification and increased consumption may appear to conform to the values of the "economic man," which, according to modernization theory, had emerged among workers by the late nineteenth century. Yet these views were part of an apologetic agenda. Most important, beneath these purely economic rationales was an outline of a modern work and leisure ethic that hardly conforms to the image of the "economic man." And these views of work and freedom from labor leaders were often shared by the rank and file.

For advocates of redistributionism, for example, the objective was not merely a reallocation of income and work but also of time. They sought to eliminate the seasonal irregularities of employment that were common in a wide array of industries. Annual fluctuations were the result of climatic factors affecting production; yet these variations also reflected seasonal markets, which led employers to intensify output only in response to an immediate demand in order to reduce overhead costs. Because of seasonal production, many workers seldom had a "normal" day—even of ten or twelve hours; rather, laborers worked overtime during "rush" periods and then suffered economically and psychologically during the under- or unemployment of the "dead season." Forced idleness, as Guesde pointed out, was the opposite of leisure. The latter required economic and psychological security. A normal workday of eight hours, by contrast, would oblige employers (and consumers) to alter the structure of their business (and demand) in order to distribute work evenly throughout the year.[44]

Thus, British house painters complained that public unwillingness to hire in winter led to overtime in the summer and created annual cycles of indebtedness alternating with feverish overwork. A regular work year would guarantee income for a permanent core of British dockers, unionists argued, and reduce the competition of casual labor.[45] A shorter and thus more regular workday would eliminate the seasonal pattern in French clothing and hat trades, an irregularity that had been intensified by mechanization.[46] In Britain, miners complained that the nine- or ten-hour day assured long hours in winter but short-time work in summer, when men got two or three days of employment per week. An eight-hour day "would equalize things a little," argued one miner in the 1890s.[47] The desire for an eight-hour day reflected a quest for a predictable allocation of personal time and the goal of wedding income to leisure time.

This was particularly evident in attempts of trades to restrict overtime. In 1891, the British Bookbinders Union sought overtime rates to be applied after forty-eight hours in order to discourage "systematic overtime." In 1897, British engineers demanded not only a normal eight-hour day but a ceiling of eighteen hours of overtime per month.[48] These facts discount the claim that workers sought shorter hours simply in order to earn overtime rates at an earlier hour. This hours strategy may reflect the urbanization and increasingly sedentary life of the European worker. No longer was it common for industrial workers to alternate seasonal periods of wage work with agricultural self-employment or to "tramp" from job to job. Thus, the seasonal job meant not the "tour" but the intolerable regularity of unemployment. Further, these views reflect a change in values: workers increasingly sought daily leisure in a stable job to seasonal "playing" or frequent job changes.

Even the productionist ideology suggested elements of an emerging leisure ethic. For example, Brissac found in the intensification of work a way of "freeing man for intellectual joys." He placed no value on the integration of work and life; rather Brissac desired the liberation of life from work.[49]

This idea was echoed widely by trade unionists in the 1890s and later. The support of unions for technical progress was not simply a public relations effort. Rather it was a practical means of compressing the workday and liberating time for leisure. Some trades like mining required unproductive time on the job because of insufficient machinery. For example, British miners claimed that inadequate supplies of ore cars and inefficient winding equipment greatly slowed the process of removing coal from mines. Improved machinery would not merely or even necessarily increase output; but it would reduce the time necessary for the miner to be in the pit. Metalworkers also complained of time wasted in the delivery of materials, which had to be made up later in more hours on the job. British chemical workers demanded that rest breaks during their twelve-hour days should count as work because the laborer "is constantly there, and he must not leave [the job] even to go away for his meals." The problem was less the character of the work than the sacrifice of time.[50]

Other trades, dependent upon the vagaries of consumption, expressed a similar desire for a more compressed day. Railroad and tramway workers denounced the two- or three-hour midday break, which extended the time workers were at the employer's disposal; British carmen complained of the practice of stretching deliveries to 11:00 P.M. or midnight for the convenience of customers. A similar issue was raised among Paris seamstresses whose "watch" at the dress shop often extended for several hours following theater performances in order to accommodate wealthy American tourists.[51]

Resistance to early morning work had long been evident among the British. The requirement of the 1864 Factory Act that work begin at 6:00 A.M. was impractical because the early start frustrated the family duties of women garment workers. But even male workers in Birmingham and the Black country in the 1870s did not arrive at work until 8:00 A.M., a pattern also common among commuters in London, especially in the dark mornings of winter. Victorians pitied the Lancashire textile worker, who was obliged to be awakened by the "knocher-up," who at 5:30 A.M. rapped on the worker's bedroom window with his long pole and attached umbrella wire.[52]

The preference for a more compressed workday is evident in the desire of wage earners for more compact blocks of labor time, even if this meant sacrificing traditional work breaks like the *casse-croûte* in France. In Britain, the eight-hour day often eliminated the breakfast break (usually taken at 8:00 or 8:30 A.M.), which traditionally had been necessary because work commenced at 6:00 A.M. Several progressive engineering firms that introduced the eight-hour day in 1891 eliminated the unproductive first "quarter" by starting work at 8:00 A.M., presumably after workers had completed breakfast and when supervisors had finally appeared on the work site. By 1897, British engineers campaigned for the eight-hour day with the argument that starting work at 6:00 A.M. before breakfast was wasteful and that it made workers "stale." By shortening breaks—as well as worktime—the hours consumed by a job could be reduced from twelve for the ten-hour workday to nine for an eight-hour day. This would liberate time for the family. Workers' evenings could be extended, and they could enjoy breakfast with their family if they did not have to arrive at work until 8:00 A.M.[53]

French propaganda was even more focused on the reconstitution of family life. Time was necessary for the "joy of family" and to partake of the "intimate embraces of the home." Shorter days would allow wage earners to "work in their gardens or attend their vineyards." Michelle Perrot stresses how the iconography of the Confédération Générale du Travail (CGT) emphasized family togetherness. A common picture was the worker's family gathered around a table with steaming soup, representing a "nostalgia of peasant life." In contrast to the trend toward compact workdays, some French wanted longer time for the midday meal and the right of wives to leave the factory at 11:15 A.M. in order to prepare it. In 1881, miners in the Gard struck against the suppression of the lunch at home, chanting in a demonstration, "down with the lunch buckets." Yet this variation only confirms the centrality of the goal of family time. An 1893 French survey revealed that textile workers and masons were willing to accept lower pay in exchange for shorter hours. A Paris construction worker claimed "we prefer 8 francs for 8 hours to 12 francs for 12 hours"—although this was hardly universal.[54]

Wage earners frequently conceived of worktime as not merely hours at the point of production but as time at the disposal of the employer or minutes consumed by work-related activities. This was certainly the view of European miners who struggled for a generation over the concept of an eight-hour day, "bank to bank" (from entry into the pit until exit)—even though an hour or more might be consumed getting to the coal face and a half-hour used in food breaks. Militant workers even argued that all the time lost "in service to industry" from "rising to clothes changed" at the end of the day was worktime.[55]

The long day especially affected women. Amie Hicks of the London Rope Makers stressed that her household tasks were never done before midnight and that a ten-hour day required that she rise at 5:00 A.M. In the needle trades, women with "double duties" sacrificed high piece-rate earnings by arriving only at 9:00 A.M. and occasionally made up work in the evenings.[56]

Of course, the increasing intensity of work, partially the result of technological change, was surely at the heart of the quest for short hours. Webb and the Frenchman Charles Coriolon argued that long, increasingly arduous hours simply shortened life; in effect, a producer only had so many working hours per life and that this time could be humanely distributed over a long existence or concentrated in a short, unhealthful life. French food workers linked long hours with tuberculosis and an early death: "We have had enough. We want to live."[57]

The same concern with work intensity animated British engineers who resisted the introduction of the "one-break system" without decreasing daily hours. This meant a later quitting time or a shorter lunch break. Engineers argued that a longer afternoon stint made workers "prematurely old." The question of the length of a continuous work period—which dominated discussion over the factory laws for women—became also a central concern for male industrial workers as the intensity of work increased and as leisure was gradually purged from the workplace.[58]

Still the quest for shorter hours was hardly a negative desire for release from exhausting labor; reduced worktime was to assure the "full utilisation of [workers'] evenings." After-work hours were necessary for the "satisfactory training of [workers'] families" and in order that workers would no longer be "strangers to the pleasures of home and domestic comforts."[59] This new interest in the evening hours for leisure—as opposed to the traditional mixing of relaxation and work during the daylight hours—reflects rising domestic opportunities (e.g., through the use of artificial light), probably a growing interest of men in home life, and also the widely perceived responsibility of women for improving domestic and child-care standards.

Moreover, this trend corresponds to a shift in the spatial relationship between wage work and family-leisure activities. Industrialization not only increased productivity, making a reduction of labor time feasible, but physically separated productive from "reproductive" or family activities. In Britain, engineers and printworkers in the 1890s insisted on the eight-hour day in order to compensate for the increased time lost to commuting. Especially in London, central residential neighborhoods were converted to businesses, and, at the same time, new living standards and new tram routes encouraged suburban migration. As a result, skilled workers began to lose considerable time in commuting. The engineers' leader, George Barnes, claimed in 1897 that members from London had to rise at 4:30 A.M. and rush to work to be at the job at 6:00 A.M.[60]

This expulsion of leisure from the workplace and the spatial division of home and work required an equally sharp temporal demarcation. The quest for reduced working hours in part can be seen as the only practical means of recovering in "blocks" of family-leisure time the "bits" of that time lost in industrialization. As the historian G. Stedman Jones notes, with suburbanization, working-class men abandoned the pub of their workmates for the neighborhood bar, which they increasingly visited with their wives. Long evenings began to count more than long work breaks.[61] The movement for the Saturday half-holiday reflected a similar interest in uninterrupted periods of family-leisure time (see chapter 4).

Beyond all of these diverse motives for shorter worktime was a common political objective. Widely disparate groups of workers sought an eight-hour standard in the early 1890s. These included unskilled, migratory coal stokers in the British gas works who labored seventy-two to eighty-four hours weekly as well as skilled, permanently employed craftsmen who worked merely fifty-two or fifty-four hours per week. Labor leaders repeatedly rejected the employers' claim that labor time should vary with the intensity of work and that those with light or intermittent jobs should work more hours than wage earners whose labor was heavy and constant. Instead labor witnesses before the Royal Commission of Labour asserted a universal human right to a minimum of leisure time quite apart from the question of fatigue. The French slogan *les trois huits* asserted the right to as much time for leisure and rest as time for work. A British blast-furnace operator stated the matter simply: "I cannot understand either a ton of coal or a ton of bread being so valuable as a man's Sunday to him." Further, an eight-hour day would allow the poor to "buy their own," observed British Hosiery Federation leader S. Bower, and not to live off the rate payers. The drive for shorter hours was a practical realization of the formal political idea of liberty. Tom Mann claimed an eight-hour day would render superfluous the "upper class patronage of semi-pauperised workers' children," for a shorter workday would give economic stability and time for poor parents to raise their own families independently.[62]

The identification of time with liberty was often expressed by the French during the agitation of 1904 to 1906. "We need liberty like we need bread." And time from work would make the laborer more "conscious" of what liberty is. Mechanization should not only provide increased material goods but free man from "slavery" to learn a new "duty" in life, "to enjoy oneself." And, having learned "diversions," the worker "will dream of other conquests."[63]

In fact, T. Steel of the Tyneside General Labour Union refused to apologize for common workers' leisure. When asked before the Royal Commission of Labour what a laborer could do after finishing a 4:00 A.M. to 12:00 P.M. shift, he simply replied:

They please themselves; they have got their time to themselves . . . if there is a dog fight on or some other attraction, they will go out to that in the afternoon. . . . I may say that dog fights are very nice things.[64]

Ultimately the often observed expansion of leisure opportunities in the 1880s made short hours attractive. We have not the space to enter the rich field of popular culture in the late Victorian period. We need only to note the growth of the music hall, cheap rail excursions, and other forms of popular recreation in both France and Britain to make our case. The quest for time was more than an attempt to raise wages, reduce unemployment, or enhance workers' control over output and process. Time transcended work as people of vastly different occupations sought the same opportunity for *social* time.[65]

The late nineteenth-century political economy of short hours, however, was not always consistent with a positive assessment of leisure time. Productionists, in particular, uncritically embraced the "efficiency" movements in the 1890s and 1900s; in so doing, they underestimated the psychological costs of work intensification and its impact on the utilization of nonworktime. Moreover, their casting of leisure in consumerist terms may have deprived labor of a leisure theory based on self-improvement.[66]

Yet these issues should not obscure the fact that short-hours movements contributed to a shift from a traditional to a modern leisure ethic. For many, the eight-hour day meant not merely increased disposable time but uniform worktime, compressed into as few hours as necessary to maintain production and income and separated from predictable, long blocks of time available for family and leisure. This relatively new approach to the allocation of time stands in contrast to a traditional pattern of irregularity and the melding of time for work, family, and leisure.

The Politics of Eight Hours, 1887–1892

Between 1887 and 1892, the call for eight-hour legislation dominated debate in both British and French labor circles. Indeed, it was probably the leading issue at the international level and was a major purpose of the Second International in 1889 and the first May Day demonstrations the following year. International support for the eight-hour day was, however, tentative. Support, while widening in Britain, was soft; and French adherence to the legal eight-hour day was tempered by suspicion of the parliamentary path and the institutional fragility of unions and the Left.

Proposals for eight-hour legislation were defeated by a vote of 29 to 79 at the British Trades Union Congress of 1887. Yet, by 1889, the power of the old guard had begun to wane in the midst of new unionist successes in organizing London dockers and orchestrating an eight-hour day for coal gas producers and female matchworkers. A successful eight-hour resolution for miners at the TUC in 1889 was followed in 1890 by a proposal for the legal eight hours for all workers. This measure was narrowly passed by a vote of 181 to 173. Despite this weak approval, support among skilled trades was not reflected in the negative votes of their leaders; even major opponents like Broadhurst and the Cotton Spinners reversed themselves by 1892.[67]

The infant French Workers Party of Jules Guesde had supported a legal eight-hour day in 1880 and four years later adopted a German proposal calling for an international effort to win legislation. Guesde's trade union federation, organized in 1886, followed suit although its strength was largely limited to the textile and mining regions of the north and east.[68]

The idea of an international eight-hour day was, of course, hardly new. It had been a major theme at the First International Workingman's Association in 1866.[69] At international trade union conferences held in Paris in 1886 and in London in 1888, Caesar de Paepe of Belgium attempted to revive the ideal of the defunct First International. Yet in both cases British delegates opposed international hours resolutions.[70]

British antipathy was broader than a preference for voluntarism. It was also rooted in a well-known English mistrust of international labor action. The British government refused to join a Swiss parliamentary call for an international conference on labor legislation. Leaders of the TUC honored the request of their prime minister, Lord Salisbury, that they not vote in favor of hours legislation at a Paris meeting in July 1889 that led to the founding of the Second International.[71]

The inaugural Congress of the Second International, however, embraced the plan of the American Federation of Labor; national unions organized simultaneous demonstrations on May 1, 1890, in favor of a legal eight-hour day. The goal was "the reducing of toil for those working too hard [and] providing jobs for those who have none." Shorter hours would bring "leisure, that is, life, liberty and action for the working class." Only if hours were reduced in unison across frontiers could the new labor standard be assured of success. While socialist delegates, of course, insisted that labor laws were insufficient, they argued that a reduction of work would "arrest the gradual degeneration of our race [and] aid the development and fitness of humanity for higher forms of society."[72] These sentiments, following the tradition of workers' self-emancipation, dominated the language of eight-hour proponents into the 1920s.

Not since 1848 had protest been on such an international scale as in May 1890. In preparation for May Day, a special journal, *The International Eight-Hours Day,* was published in Basel with American and European contributors. In France, meetings beginning in March 1890 were widely held. The eight-hour propaganda sparked a strike among the coal miners of Westphalia. And one-day strikes and mass demonstrations took place on Thursday, May 1, in Vienna, Berlin, Rome, and Paris. Parades delivering petitions for the eight-hour day were held in hundreds of mining and manufacturing towns in Europe.[73]

In Paris, the police formally prohibited street demonstrations; 500 soldiers were posted at the Place de la Concorde. While Guesde expected 200,000 to rally before the Palais Bourbon, *Le Figaro* claimed that only 50,000 joined the one-day strike. Paul Lafargue announced that May Day had become the "festival of the proletariat of the Two Worlds"—that America and Australia, who had been pioneers in the eight-hour movement, had joined the Old World in a global struggle for free time. Petition drives organized by socialist unions demanded not only eight-hour legislation, but the end to night work, a minimum wage, and other issues. The anarchosyndicalist press, however, denounced this appeal to the bourgeois state, offering instead the formula that May Day should be the "first act of a war" between the classes. Still, the idea of the *trois huits* had wide appeal.[74]

The more practical British decided to wait until Sunday, May 4, when a large crowd could be assured without the risk of a one-day strike. Although there were two processions, one led by the London Trades Council and the other by the Bloomsbury Socialist Society, *The Labour Tribune* claimed that 250,000 participated. Skilled tradesmen in top hats and kid gloves walked among the roughly dressed dockers and women ropemakers and matchworkers. The parade took two hours to pass before Hyde Park corner; there were fifteen platforms for the speakers from the leading lights of the British Left and labor. The aged Friedrich Engels expressed the optimism of the moment: "The English proletariat, newly awakened from its forty years' winter sleep, again enter[s] the movement of its class. . . . The grandchildren of the old Chartists are entering the line of battle."[75]

The eight-hour day was a powerful unifier for it promised something for nearly everybody. It would solve the problems of low wages, unemployment, the unpredictable work year, and the miseries of overwork. In many ways, the eight-hour day was a panacea—a quick, relatively painless way of overcoming the weaknesses of labor, of catapulting it into a new stage of growth, and, for some, of accelerating the pace toward social revolution. Yet it was more than a fig leaf to disguise divisions. The eight-hour day expressed a nearly universal desire for free time that transcended the growing conflicts in that age of chauvinism.

The Collapse and Significance of the Hours Movement, 1891–1912

Implacable divisions within the labor movements and, even more important, the tenacious opposition of business and politicians made an international hours standard an unrealistic objective in the 1890s. The dreams of May Day 1890 became merely a pious list to be dredged up each year in ever more formal and futile propaganda efforts.

Bills for the eight-hour day in 1890 and 1891 failed to get beyond preliminary parliamentary stages in either country. In France, an hours bill was passed in 1892, which merely provided a ten-hour day for children and an eleven-hour day for women in industry. In part as a result of the hours agitation, the British government decided early in 1891 to convene a Royal Commission on Labour. After lengthy testimony, completed in 1894, the majority report rejected significant state intervention to regulate worktime and only confirmed the vague powers of the Board of Trade to pressure employers in dangerous trades to reduce excessive worktime and to publish hours data.[76]

An effective political alliance never formed. Only a portion of the British Liberal party joined the eight-hour cause while leaders such as A. J. Mundella and William Gladstone opposed it on classical liberal and economic principles.[77] Potential allies among religious conservatives, who advocated a universal Sunday holiday, restricted shop hours, and reduced worktime for women and children, had little in common with secular male trade unionists. The unions remained divided as to strategy despite the headway made by advocates of a legal eight hours. In France, the split between the Guesdist unions who favored parliamentary action and those anarchosyndicalists who gathered around the *bourses du travail* obviously weakened an already tiny trade union movement. Divisions and confusions between redistributionism and productionism surely threatened the intellectual coherence of the movement.[78]

Still political action was not an unqualified failure in Britain. Refusal of "Lib-Lab" members of Parliament in 1891 to support eight-hour bills helped spark the formation of a Labour Representation Committee in the London Trades Council and the Independent Labour party. And, by 1894, TUC pressure obliged the Liberal government to grant eight-hour days in the government arsenal at Woolwich and later in other public facilities. The French followed suit after the election of a Radical government in 1899.[79] In Britain, skilled trades like the bookbinders and builders struck for a forty-eight-hour week, settling for compromises. Most of the 58,800 nongovernment British workers who had the eight-hour day in the 1890s were employed in firms whose owners voluntarily granted shorter workdays (e.g., some gasworks or progressive engineering firms). In France, however, even these small gains were nonexistent.[80]

Clearly in both countries, neither a political nor an industrial strategy was successful. The optimism of the period between 1886 and 1892 had faded in the midst of political impotence and internal divisions. The depression of 1892–1895 only further deflated the short-hours movement. The universalist goals of the legal eight hours seemed to narrow into demands for particularist legislation—weak eight-hour laws for coal miners (in 1905 in France and 1908 in Britain)—or capitulation to the old bourgeois notions of advancing protective labor legislation for the salvation of women and children. Religious and philanthropic reformers played decisive roles in promoting the weekly rest law in France and early-shop-closing legislation in Britain. As in the past, these laws were sold to the public as a means of preserving the family and of protecting women (see chapter 4).

Some historians argue that the quest for a shorter worktime was always ambiguous. The British TUC only lamely endorsed an hours law, and although the logic and justice of a universal standard was apparent to many leaders, workers rejected the statist solutions of the socialists, really preferring to "be left alone."[81] In France, the annual May Day ritual declined after the disheartening massacre at Fourmies in 1891. Worktime played a relatively small role in strikes: in the twenty years before the war only 15.5 percent of work stoppages involved stated hours grievances compared with the 63 percent concerned with wages. It is easy to understand why most labor historians have ignored worktime in the generation before 1914.[82]

Still, it would be an exaggeration to assert that labor movements ceded the hours issue to middle- or upper-class reformers or that there was a decline of an autonomous working-class worktime movement. Unions independently sought early shop closings, weekly rest days, and the Saturday half-holiday as we shall demonstrate in the next chapter. The political effectiveness of labor everywhere was in its infancy. This impotence explains the conservative tactics of the union leaders. Clearly, the internationalism of the period between 1886 and 1892 proved also to be ephemeral. Not only was the Second International incapable of exercising any influence on national affairs, but it could not discipline national labor movements (especially in Britain and the United States). Most important, the general abandonment of the universal eight-hour day after the early 1890s reflects not ideological retrogression but the enormity of business opposition.

The short-hours issue reappeared only at the crest of strike waves and was undertaken mostly by the best-situated unions. Surely the most important examples were the British engineers' strike of 1897–1898 and general strikes in France in 1906. Numerous studies of the British engineering strike have emphasized union efforts to maintain control over work rules and machinery and the attempt of the newly organized Engineering Employers' Federation to break or reduce union power.[83] Yet the strike of 1897–1898 began in London over efforts of engineers in private firms to share in the forty-eight-hour norm of government arms works. It was the Employers' Federation that claimed that the strike was nothing but an attempt of the union to restrict the use of machinery and to preserve the privileges of the declining craft worker. The lockout ended in January 1898 after almost all firms rescinded the eight-hour day. The Engineering Employers' Federation held fast to a fifty-four-hour week for its members until after World War I.[84]

Throughout the strike the issue of worktime and its relationship with mechanization was clear. Union president George Barnes argued that a share of the increase in productivity should go to additional leisure time: "vast improvements in machinery," he argued, had not been paralleled by wage increases and the "margin of leisure has been diminished." At the same time, Barnes added, "workmen are ever getting more conscious of new and laudable desires." The only permanent way of enjoying the benefits of this increased productivity was not in higher wages, which "tend to melt away, as the unemployed roll grows larger with each recurring depression . . . [but] in shortening hours of labour." Barnes attacked as diversionary disputes over machine use. The central issue was the economic possibility of the eight-hour day, already successful in progressive and government engineering firms.[85]

The Engineering Employers' Federation replied that the worker was fully compensated for mechanical improvements through wage increases and lower prices. What the workers were really demanding was "six weeks' additional holiday every year." The issue was not merely control over the work process or the preservation of skills, but the share-out and allocation of the fruits of increased productivity.[86]

In France, the CGT revived the short-hours cause in 1904 as it dramatically prepared to implement the slogan, "after May 1, 1906, we will no longer work more than eight hours per day." Interest grew in 1899 after the introduction of the eight-hour day in post-office industries and in 1902 following the vote in the Chamber for an eight-hour day for coal miners.[87] In 1904, the CGT formed a special committee for organizing propaganda. Hundreds of meetings in the trades and thousands of brochures, leaflets, and posters were published appealing to the cultural as well as economic advantages of the eight-hour day. Agitators like Emile Pouget, editor of the *Voix du Peuple*, saw the eight-hour issue as a "springboard" for activism. Indeed, in 1906, the year of the height of hours agitation, 64 percent of the recorded strikes in France at least partially were concerned with hours (compared with 14 percent in 1904).[88]

Whereas metal and construction workers in Paris and some dockers supported this campaign, moderate printers' unions opted for a negotiated nine-hour day and socialist parliamentarians rejected the appeal to direct action.[89] Enthusiasm had disappeared one month before May 1, 1906. Perhaps no more than 115,000 participated in ninety-three strikes for the eight-hour day. Few concrete gains were made in these nineteen months of campaigning for shorter hours. The inability of the CGT syndicalists to achieve a wider success probably contributed to the decline of the ideology of direct action after 1906.[90]

This failure, like that of the British engineers in 1898, should not be attributed to workers' disinterest in worktime but to the enormous resistance of employers to this threat to their "freedom to manage." In 1906, French employers ignored the eight-hour demand and attempted to divert attention to the international linkages of the CGT and the syndicalist threat to the social order.

In Britain there were numerous uphill battles for short hours in the two decades before the war. In 1894 blast-furnace operators attempted to replace the onerous system of two twelve-hour shifts with three daily stints of eight hours. Although this effort succeeded in only a few firms, this campaign was revived in 1905 and continued until the war. Locomotive operators repeatedly lobbied the Board of Trade to pressure railroads into lowering hours. By 1912, both railway workers and engineers revived the eight-hour demand, again with no success.[91] In 1911, the British printers' unions demanded forty-eight hours just as they had in 1891 and 1900 only to meet employer intransigence. The underlying issue was the preservation of jobs, but like the agitation against the premium bonus system in the engineering trade, it was also a protest against the intensification of work.[92]

Surely the most important example in Britain of the difficult task of negotiating worktime reductions was the struggle for a miners' eight-hour day. It was first proposed in Parliament in 1890 and was repeatedly frustrated by the resistance of the Northumberland and Durham miners; in 1906 the Liberal government finally supported an eight-hour bill and a select committee supported legislation. Still it was only in 1908, after two years of unrelenting lobbying by the Mining Association, that an eight-hour law was passed.[93]

The eight-hour day came for most workers only in the aftermath of

World War I, some thirty-three years after it was first seriously proposed. Only then was the political and ideological opposition to the eight-hour day overcome. First, improvements in productivity from increased mechanization and scientific management proved that reduced hours did not necessarily mean less production or lower wages. Second, a non-socialist international movement for labor legislation, which emerged between 1890 and 1919, legitimized the radical idea that a simultaneous reduction of working hours could prevent any nation from gaining a competitive advantage. Third, policy makers began to realize that increased leisure would be used in family life and consumption rather than destabilizing forms of free time (like alcohol abuse or radical agitation).

Winning the eight-hour day required the mobilization not only of organized labor but of an interclass political coalition. Ultimately it needed an international network. In the context of the increasing international struggle for markets, the eight-hour movement of the late nineteenth century lacked sufficient ideological clarity and, more important, political cohesiveness. Only after another generation of agitation and persuasion, and of coalition building, could the eight-hour day erupt on the industrial scene. It is to this history that the next two chapters are devoted.

4

Family Time and Consumption Time: Shop Hours and the Origins of the Weekend

The modern conflicts between family and production have concerned social theorists and reformers since industrialization began to undercut the domestic economy and to separate work from family life. Attempts to liberate domestic and leisure time from the market were central to the Factory Acts and short-hours movements. Perhaps even more important were the parallel efforts to free continuous blocks of time from market labor. Nineteenth-century reformers insisted that a period of uninterrupted freedom from wage work—first a full day and then a day and a half per week—was essential to the restoration of traditional values. It meant the "reunion" of family, the cultivation of religious values, escape from urban work environments, and the development of "rational recreation." Unlike the short-hours struggles, movements for the "weekend" (and also the annual vacation) were often orchestrated by social and religious conservatives. Against the demands of the market, these conservatives proclaimed the right to, and indeed necessity of, leisure as an antidote to the social divisiveness of economic competition and as a means of preserving cultural values.

At the same time, one of the principal purposes of "free time" was to consume. As industrialization deprived domestic units of their productive function, "family time" was increasingly devoted to shopping. And as the free time of industrial workers increased so did their demand for recreational facilities. Both trends conflicted with the autonomous time of workers in the distribution and leisure industries. Where production workers experienced long hours and full six-day workweeks, retail and leisure trades had little choice but to keep even later and often Sunday hours. Competition for customers often frustrated the collective interest of shopkeepers in restricting hours and in "efficiently" concentrating consumption time. Finally, conflicts arose over what types of services were to be available during the free hours of workers. Must bars and music halls as well as excursion trains and pharmacies be kept open late and on Sunday? Was it acceptable to sacrifice the free time of any particular group of service workers for the "general" good?

These issues often separated production workers from distribution and leisure workers; they sometimes also divided labor from conservative advocates of leisure time. These contradictions appeared most clearly in the problems of the early-shop-closing movements in Britain and the Sunday Rest campaigns in France.

Both of these movements, whose roots were in the early nineteenth century, reached their climax in the generation before World War I. They were largely championed by social and religious conservatives. Their patronizing goal of "restoring" traditional values and advocacy of the interests of shopkeepers did not always coincide with the time interests of the production workers who dominated the unions.

Yet we cannot identify the quest for the weekend and shop closing with "reactionary" elites. Production workers had their own agenda for pursuing weekend time (although they were slow to develop this goal) and commercial employees were capable of independent action in defense of free time. Labor historians have often neglected this problem between work and family (leisure) and have sometimes overemphasized working people's concerns with economic issues and the workplace. Those intellectual and political historians who have addressed this problem have generally posed it in terms of the cultural agendas of conservative elites and their attempts to impose these values on the working classes. As a result, they have largely ignored the desire of labor for leisure and family time.

This chapter will attempt to fill these gaps by addressing the cultural content of the movements for weekly rest and early shop closing. By leaving to others the complex (and interesting) political history of these movements, I will focus on the ideal of continuous free time, conflicts between distribution and production workers in the pursuit of that goal, and the relationship between elite norms and working-class values in the quest for leisure and family time.

Shop Time and Rest Days: British and French Patterns, 1800–1880

The traditional drabness of British nightlife and Sundays in contrast to French "gaiety"—at least in Paris—is a common stereotype.[1] Beyond this tourist perception was, however, a measurable difference in attitudes toward continuous leisure and, especially, consumption time. British Sabbatarian traditions dating from the seventeenth century were revived in the 1830s. By contrast, in France the observance of Sunday shop and workplace closure was never strong before the Revolution; and in the nineteenth century, despite the Restoration's Sabbath law of 1814, not only French markets and entertainments remained open on Sundays but so did a wide variety of other retail businesses and even some industries. British Sabbatarian societies were influential fifty years before and were more successful than similar organizations in France. Whereas British merchants were able to restrict business hours in the early twentieth century, their French counterparts never made a similar effort.

British Sabbatarianism, at times linked to temperance, was revived in 1831 with the Lord's Day Observation Society. This and similar groups organized to enforce powerful Sunday closing laws. They pushed for parliamentary commissions in 1832, 1847, and 1850 to control residual Sunday trading without success. Major campaigns were waged against Sunday railroad, canal, and mail services. Competition for sales among retailers and resistance of consumers, especially in working-class districts, frustrated Sabbatarian zeal. A working-class demonstration in Hyde Park in June 1855 against efforts of London merchants to limit Sunday markets further culminated mounting displeasure over a law passed in 1854 that closed pubs on Sunday afternoons.[2] Up to 150,000 workmen barricaded nervous wealthy promenaders in the park and shouted at them, "Go to church!" Soon thereafter pubs were reopened most of Sunday afternoon. This boisterous rally, which shocked many in the post-Chartist lull of labor activity, was proof of the distance between the church-sponsored Sabbatarian campaign and the aspirations of workers for unrestrained leisure on Sundays.[3]

Still, English Sabbatarians won a prohibition against brass bands in the parks on Sundays, saw the withholding of some music hall licenses in the 1880s, and managed to block the Sunday opening of the British Museum and National Gallery until 1896. Despite the fact that Sunday was the only day in the week available for amusement, for the rigorous English Christian the Sabbath should be spent in church and in religious study; and those not sharing this ideal should not be allowed to flaunt their impiety in public. The various Lord's Day committees were composed mostly of rather inflexible and perhaps insecure members of the influential commercial and gentry classes; they saw respect of God's law as a barrier against general subversion of authority.[4]

The founding in 1855 of the National Sunday League reflected a different approach to Sunday leisure: the league rejected the dogmatism and negativity of the Sabbatarians and encouraged wholesome "rational" recreation such as brass band concerts in parks and the opening of museums and galleries on Sunday as alternatives to "degrading amusements." In 1858, the London-based Sunday Rest Association was formed to encourage the closure of shops in poor districts. It attempted to broaden its appeal beyond the pious to include "all philanthropists." This association stressed not worship but the therapeutic and social benefits of a "day of rest throughout the year." Sunday freedom from work and shopping would bring peace to the home by ending the hectic "turmoil" of the Sunday market. The image of Sunday as a day for the restoration of moral as well as physical faculties became a commonplace.[5]

These campaigns in Britain for Sunday rest were not entirely successful: as late as 1890, seasonal and continuous process trades (like brickmaking and metallurgy) remained seven-day jobs; and Sunday employment on the railroads was common despite periodic Sabbatarian pressure since the 1830s. Moreover, after 1871, the Lord's Day Acts were relaxed for a variety of convenience shops, including tobacconists, newsagents, and confectioners. Still, for the vast majority, Sunday was a day of rest—if not excitement. In the twentieth century, the British continued to argue against the propriety of popular entertainment and even (into the 1930s) of showing films on the Sabbath. The most common diversions on Sunday were focused on the pub (despite its limited hours), rail excursions, and the ritual reading of two or more newspapers.[6]

The French Sabbatarian movement was a pale shadow of the British. France had perhaps the least regulated labor market and the longest worktime of any industrial nation in the late nineteenth century. Workdays of twelve hours (often seven days a week) were common during rush seasons in steelmaking, construction, and food processing. Glass and paper makers, construction workers, railroad guards, distillery laborers, and the vast numbers of bakers, butchers, waiters, and store clerks labored seven days a week. In some continuous process industries, the costs of a weekly shutdown meant that these plants operated every day.[7]

The seasonal and petty businesses that predominated in French cities and towns were ill-adapted even to a weekly closure of business. Pressures for rapid fulfillment of contracts led industries dependent upon weather (like construction) or annual market changes (like the garment industries) to work continuously except in the "dead season." Many retailers felt obliged to open on Sunday (at least until noon) in order to accommodate the consumer needs of the laborer and farmer whose workweek extended until 6:00 P.M. or later on Saturday. Even small clothing stores, especially those in working-class districts, opened on Sunday. Only on the Sabbath did they have a competitive advantage over the new city-center department stores, which were closed that day. To retain customers, these small businesses had little to offer the buyer but the convenience of long hours of service.[8]

These factors militated against a universal weekly rest in all industrializing countries. Yet they were more extreme in the French case, especially in comparison with the Anglo-American world. In France, the influence of a militant anti-Catholicism was clear in the 1880 repeal of the Sunday closing law of 1814. Surely more important was the fact that the long workweek of industrial wage earners in France required an even longer workweek for commercial workers in order to accommodate the consumption needs of blue-collar workers. Because there was a larger percentage of employed married women in France than in Britain (56 percent in France in 1906—20 percent excluding farm workers— compared with 9 percent in Britain in 1911), working-class shopping and services had to be concentrated in hours after work. French women—expected to shop and maintain house, as well as to earn wages—required late and Sunday shop hours.[9] Far more than the French love of "gaiety" went into the furor of French Sundays.

A custom closely related to the Sabbath was the Saturday half-holiday. This medieval practice was associated with the preparation for Sunday (or other holy days) and, in the cottage economy, with the "handing in" of work on Saturday mornings. By the eighteenth century, however, the Saturday half-holiday had largely disappeared except in schools, parliaments, and courts. It sometimes competed with another form of half-holiday, Saint Monday. In England, a Monday vacation was common among engineers and some other skilled trades as at least a partial day of leisure following the Saturday pay day; sometimes it was necessitated by the late arrival of work materials to start the new week. It survived into the 1860s and in parts of the Midlands into the 1880s.[10]

In Britain, beginning in the 1830s, skilled building trades began to negotiate for shorter Saturdays. Moreover, in the 1840s, workers in shops and offices with the aid of their employers insisted on an early Saturday closing (at 4:00 P.M. and later 2:00 P.M.). In the 1850 Factory Act, women and children were granted a 2:00 P.M. Saturday finish (following the custom of releasing child textile workers early on Saturday). As the provisions of the Factory Act were broadened to include other industries, the Saturday half-holiday was not only granted to a wide assortment of "protected" workers, but also to men who often could not work without the collaboration of women and children.[11]

It has been sometimes claimed that skilled male workers were coerced into trading the hallowed tradition of Saint Monday for the presumably less threatening practice of the Saturday half-holiday. This may have been true in the engineering trades of Coventry or Manchester when increased mechanization and work discipline obliged punctuality on Monday morning and forced workers to abandon an irregular work-week. Yet these cases are surely the exception. Instead, a combination of trade union pressure, middle-class paternalism, and the Factory Acts made the Saturday early quitting time nearly universal in British employment by the 1890s.[12]

In contrast, the "*Saint Lundi*" of French workers from the mid-nineteenth century gradually disappeared without the compensatory free afternoon on Saturday. In practically no industries was Saturday a shorter workday. The Saturday half-holiday was so rare that it was known in France as the *semaine anglaise*. This only made more pressing the need for Sunday trading to accommodate the shopping of these workers.[13]

The French practice of *Saint Lundi*, common in relatively well-paid and male-dominated industries (like tailoring and construction), declined by the 1870s; yet absenteeism on Monday continued to run high and French workers showed a late and ambiguous support for the *semaine anglaise*. Moreover, in some textile houses, employers granted women workers an early quitting time on Monday evening in order to facilitate shopping. In any case the business week in many trades (e.g., laundry, food-processing) culminated only on Saturday, while Monday and even Tuesday were relatively slack workdays. This traditional rhythm of the workweek was slow to die in France despite the widespread propaganda against Saint Monday.[14]

By the 1850s, in Britain the Saturday half-holiday had become an important symbol of family life and of the therapeutic value of leisure. Reformers argued that not only were Saturday afternoons to be used to improve physical conditioning of young men (for voluntary military service), but to provide fathers with the opportunity to spend time with their children. Saturday afternoons would give man the leisure to develop "a power over his [childrens'] minds, and to exercise a more genial and trustworthy authority than that which would be merely granted to his position as a parent." Not only a change of attitude but real time was necessary for the new "democratic" style of childrearing.[15] Saturday half-holiday alone would bring physical and mental restoration. This language reflects the erosion of the old religious ideas of Sabbatarianism and their replacement by the rhetoric of biological equilibrium: weekly exertion and care was to be balanced by weekend rest and reflection.[16]

More concretely, reformers argued that Saturday afternoons should be utilized for shopping and male recreation so that Sunday could be more fully devoted to rest, worship, and family togetherness. The Early Closing Association (ECA) in the 1850s advocated a Saturday half-holiday in combination with early payment on Friday (instead of Saturday evenings) as an antidote to late Saturday or Sunday shopping. If industrial workers devoted Saturday afternoon to shopping, this would liberate the Saturday nights and Sundays of distribution workers.[17]

In both Britain and France the idea of weekly rest had subtly shifted from the mere defense of the religious calendar to the notion that time away from economic competition and industrial toil was a biological and social necessity. Increasingly the self-discipline of the work ethic was challenged by the morality of rational recreation. For various reasons this shift was sited at the sales counter rather than at the workbench. Not only did sales clerks (and sometimes office personnel) work longer hours than did production workers—extending their service through the weekend—but many came from (or aspired to) the middle class and thus were appropriate targets for the middle-class reform of rational recreation. Although both weekly rest and early shop closing

were closely related ideas, because of the early success of British Sabbatarianism, the British were able to move on to the second goal long
before the French.

Early Closing in Britain, 1842–1928

When a group of London drapery shopworkers orga-
nized the ECA in 1842, retail stores expected their clerks to work from
8:00 A.M. to 9:00 P.M. Grocers and pharmacies remained open 7:00 A.M.
to 10:00 or even 11:00 P.M. Saturday hours often extended to 11:00 or
12:00 P.M. with cleanup following to 1:00 A.M.[18]

Late Saturday hours prevailed especially in working-class residential
neighborhoods. There, shopping was a form of Saturday night family
entertainment when the lights and shop wares attracted thousands
along the otherwise drab city streets. Working-class families commonly
did their grocery shopping late on Saturday night, sometimes after the
pubs closed at 11:00 P.M. or following music hall performances. Some
grocers reopened on Sunday morning to accommodate late-hour workers. As late as 1890, early-closing advocate Thomas Sutherst estimated
that 25 percent of shopworkers labored ninety hours per week, and
50 percent worked eighty hours. Perhaps an eighty-five-hour week was
the norm.[19]

The ECA was the most important organization that attempted to
challenge these hours. From the beginning it favored voluntarism and
appeals to the Christian consciences of well-to-do customers. For example, in July 1857, the ECA organized meetings of dressmakers' assistants and milliners to hear a speech by the bishop of Oxford; he not
only blamed long hours on the "selfishness and monopolizing spirit of
certain employers" but he called on the ladies of London to allow reasonable time for dressmaking. The ECA, however, was primarily concerned with the hours of young (often middle-class) *male* white-collar
employees. In February 1856, ECA leader James Duke called on Lord
Campbell, justice at the Court of the Queen's Bench, to finish business
at 2:00 P.M. on Saturday, a successful effort at freeing young legal Bob
Cratchits for an "extended weekend." This gesture was gradually followed by other courts. In May 1857, leading Tory churchmen pressed
officials to close government offices, dockyards, and arsenals at 2:00 P.M.
on Saturdays as an example to private business. The closure of the Stock

Exchanges at 2:00 P.M. on Saturday in 1855 rapidly led banking, insurance, and wholesale houses to follow suit.[20] These were relatively easy victories for they were as beneficial to judges, lawyers, and bankers as to their junior clerks.

A more formidable task was to obtain the earlier closure of London stores. By 1853, the ECA was divided into twelve London districts that, with the assistance of Anglican rectors and Ladies Auxiliary Committees, sought agreements between merchants to close daily at 8:00 P.M. Shop assistants and owners joined together to eliminate an hour at the counter. At first such pledges were successful only in central London. Drapers were obviously more responsive than were grocers. By 1858, the most common tactic was to employ volunteer canvassers to persuade shopkeepers to close at 7:00 P.M., at least in the winter. The ECA or similar organizations were also active outside London, again led by clergy and "influential men." In Bradford, for example, as early as 1849 most dry goods merchants agreed to close at 7:00 P.M. in winter. Because retail shops did most of their business Saturday afternoon and evening, the pragmatic ECAs persuaded shops to close early on one weekday in compensation for a long Saturday.[21]

The ECA was closely linked to the rational recreation movement. The ECA at first appealed directly to merchants, asking them to aid the physical and moral development of their young male assistants. In 1843, a prize essay (awarded by the Drapers' Association) stressed the physiological consequences of long shop hours: "The human body stands in certain established relationships to the external world and is placed in an economy of fixed organic laws, upon the strict observance of which, under God, its well-being depends." Long shop working hours necessarily violated these laws. Store workers lacked sufficient "pure air." They were deprived of daily contact with plants and were subject to the stale atmosphere of the closed shop (which grew worse in the evenings because gas lighting competed with humans for oxygen). Physical exhaustion was less a problem than improper use of muscles: shop assistants were "all day on the move, yet never in exercise."[22]

Still it was the moral consequences of long hours for male clerks that were the most forcefully opposed. The language was vintage rational recreation. Only by releasing these employees earlier could they cultivate "rational enjoyments." Instead, practically the only amusements available after 9:00 P.M. when they closed shop were the vices offered by the pub and the street. In 1843, Thomas Honibone argued that "confinement so long . . . produces a morbid state of feeling," and that for relief shop assistants needed "outdoor exercise." He even claimed that their fifteen-hour workdays developed in them an "excessive faith in wealth, extremely prejudicial to the growth of moral affections." Finally, these early advocates of early shop closing stressed that a reduction of store hours was in the owners' interest: early closing would decrease gas and coal consumption; and because the "public would be compelled to purchase what they required at much shorter intervals, business throughout the day would be more brisk, and time enjoyed for profitable purposes."[23]

The ECA went beyond the negativity of the early temperance and Sabbatarian movements for a more positive view of leisure. Free time was a "growing necessity for relaxation from the pressure of business." The increasing problem of drink was the result of employees "too much exhausted to find [enjoyment] in natural rest." Saturday afternoon was an opportunity for "employers extending to those in their service increased facilities for moral improvement and healthful recreation." The half-holiday would provide "innocent relaxation . . . [and] remove the present temptations to misspend Sunday."[24]

This stress upon the moral betterment of young male clerks and retail assistants gradually gave way to a somewhat different focus: the self-interest of shopkeepers for freedom from the confines of the counter and secondarily the needs of a growing group of female shopworkers. Although prominent Lords continued to patronize this movement, by 1870 the ECA had become the agency of shopkeepers.

At the same time, the inability of owners to reduce shop hours without legal constraints became increasingly obvious. While the ECA held fast to the voluntarism of the 1850s, Tory member of Parliament John Lubbock proposed legislation in 1873 to restrict the hours of young women and children who served as shop assistants. In the same year, a "Traders' Committee" in London proposed a bill to enforce shop closing at 8:00 P.M. Only in 1886 did the rising tide of "statism" overwhelm the ECA: Lubbock was elected to the board of the ECA, which, in turn, narrowly voted for legal action. Because of the inability of the more substantial shopkeepers to oblige stores in the "poorest localities of the great cities" to close earlier, legal action seemed inevitable.[25]

Despite the public support of parliamentary leaders like Lord Salisbury, Joseph Chamberlain, and Herbert Gladstone, legislation was painfully slow and inadequate.[26] An 1887 law only provided a seventy-four-hour limit on the workweeks of women and children up to eighteen years of age. It failed to address the problem of the competition of family businesses where no worktime controls were imposed. Women trade unionists viewed this law as discriminatory—a threat to women's jobs.[27]

Again, in 1901, when another select committee studied shop hours, 290 trade associations formally supported an optional two-thirds majority closure by local governmental "order." Although in 1904 this modest proposal became law, by 1909 only fifteen thousand shops were covered by these local "orders" and many allowed shops to remain open as late as 11:00 P.M. In 1903, Charles Dilke proposed a complex shop closing bill along with a maximum workweek of sixty hours for employees. Although Home Minister Herbert Gladstone supported this bill in 1909, shopkeepers were skeptical that a uniform shop closure act would pass. Indeed, Gladstone soon abandoned this concept, relying instead on the voluntary option provisions of the 1904 act. This, of course, placed all of the burden on stores with employees (whose hours were to be restricted to sixty per week). This gave small family shops a competitive advantage. As a result, tradesmen's organizations abandoned the proposal; and the new law, marshaled through Parliament by the young Winston Churchill in 1912, did no more than grant shop assistants freedom one weekday at 1:30 P.M.[28]

At first glance this mediocre record is surprising. The only organized opponents of early closing in the 1901 hearings were pawnbrokers and liquor store owners whose business was often concentrated between 8:00 and 11:00 P.M. Yet tradesmen in poor districts as well as those in middle-class neighborhoods supported legislation. This proposal was clearly directed against the marginal family shops on the "side streets" in an effort to oblige them to conform to the hours standard of the more substantial stores. Only a law would prevent the competitive pressure of creeping hours.[29]

Small but growing organizations of shop assistants also supported early closing in the 1890s. Even the trade unions were not hostile to early shop closure. For example, in 1901 the Glasgow United Trades Council affirmed that most male workers or their wives shopped either immediately after work (between 5:30 and 6:00 P.M.) or right after dinner. These workers admitted that, although they might well shop later if stores remained open, there surely was no need for it.[30]

How then do we explain the difficulty in passing legislation? Michael Winstanley, a historian of early shop closing, argues that the liberal ideological scruples of the politicians impeded early-closing legislation. While it was acceptable to "protect" minors from unhealthful periods of labor, it was hardly admissible to constrain free enterprise (especially when it did not clearly serve the public interest) by obliging entrepreneurs to close shop early. Parliament could compromise by tolerating such controls if they were voluntary and were set at the local level. The alternative solution within this ideological framework was to have limited the hours of employees; this, however, placed family shops at a distinct advantage. The idea of using shift workers to accommodate both public convenience and the leisure of distribution staffs and owners was either not considered or it was clearly rejected (e.g., in the 1920s) as a threat to family and social time.[31]

Another impediment to regulation involved divisions within the ranks of British shopkeepers. Although repeated surveys by the ECA found a majority of store owners supporting early closing, substantial minorities "refused to reply." In an ECA survey in London in 1900, only 53 percent of the shops supported early-closing legislation while most of the rest "could not be reached." Small shops with little stock and with insufficient turnover to discount prices had nothing to offer consumers but the convenience of long hours. This was even truer with costermongers and street market sellers. Some 30 of the roughly 120 London street markets regularly opened on Sunday morning. None of these groups, although unorganized, would support early-closing laws.[32]

Divisions between shopkeepers and their assistants also impeded early shop closing. In 1881, a London lawyer, Thomas Sutherst, organized the Shop Hours' Labor League, which pressed for a legislative alternative to the voluntarism of the ECA. Sutherst condemned the ECA as indifferent to workers' conditions and essentially an employer-run organization. Although at first Sutherst wanted the Factory Acts to be applied to all white-collar workers, by 1886 he more pragmatically endorsed the idea of early closing.[33]

By 1889, the league was transformed into the National Union of Shop Assistants. This group long remained a tiny enclave of mostly male employees; by 1910 perhaps twenty thousand belonged. Although over one million shop employees were enumerated in 1910, they were dispersed in 460,000 shops. Despite the impotence of the Shop Assistants, hostility between them and the ECA grew in the 1890s: individual retail workers ceased to support the ECA and the Shop Assistants increasingly saw the ECA as powerless (outside of London) and as a competitor with trade unionism.[34]

British retail clerks were an independent force for reduced shop hours and they had their own agenda: they opposed the lack of regular and sufficient lunch and tea breaks and the custom of working an hour or more after the shop closed for "straightened up stock." Shop assistants also protested the old practice of "living in," especially for adult workers.[35] Anxiety of shop employees for their future animated this movement. One member from Liverpool claimed that 50 percent of the male assistants ended up on the docks after they lost their "young and smart appearance." Because few shopworkers became owners, few were willing to sacrifice the present for an unlikely future. Instead of expecting the independence of the entrepreneur, shop assistants increasingly demanded the freedoms of labor—time at their disposal in exchange for wage work.[36]

Although shop assistant organizations shared with their employers a desire to reduce store hours, the ECA remained primarily a front for retail trade associations with close links to the aristocracy and the Tories. Although the 1912 Shop Closing Act was a failure, the ECA finally succeeded during the war. In January 1915, under the pretense of conserving fuel, the ECA petitioned the government to order shops to close at 7:00 P.M. on most weekdays and 9:00 P.M. on Saturdays. By October, the ECA convinced the government to adopt its proposal under emergency war powers. But again a surprise parliamentary maneuver in the Commons led the home secretary to replace a closing hour of 7:00 P.M. with a more modest 8:00 P.M.[37]

For ten years after the war, the ECA was able to extend the wartime hours rules even though they encountered persistent opposition. In March 1919, the ECA formally endorsed the goal of shop assistants for a forty-eight-hour week as necessary for the "nation's health and strength." Both groups rejected the idea of shift work. Yet the shop assistants' unions remained unreliable soldiers for the ECA. Class and cultural chasms were not so easily bridged. Moreover, the TUC was lukewarm to the early-closing program. For example, in 1918, unions supported the government when it tolerated shops that remained open until 10:00 P.M. in east London. The eight-hour day allowed a 5:00 P.M. quitting time for most production workers, which justified the closure of shops at 7:00 instead of 8:00 P.M. Yet few workers were willing to give up the convenience of an additional hour of consumption time. And only half of the confectioners, chemists, newsagents, and second-hand clothing dealers favored early closing; majorities of shopkeepers in working-class London districts opposed controls.[38]

However, it was not merely the ECA's conflict with labor and petty tradesmen that was the problem. Consumers of all classes—and through them, the pressure of competition—frustrated the leisure goals of the shopkeepers and their workers. Even the ECA admitted that the "resistance of consumers" frustrated the proposal of the London Suburban Drapery Trades for a general lockup on Saturday afternoon. Moreover, in 1921 the government passed new regulations of shop hours that allowed confectioners and newsagents to remain open until 9:30 P.M. This rule benefited consumers more than business. In the 1927 hearings on shop hours, newsagents' trade associations asked not to be exempt from the shop closing rules. In some areas confectioners desired a special "order" for an 8:00 P.M. closing but lacked resources to win it. The committee rejected these appeals in the name of public convenience.[39]

The result of these conflicting forces was the 1928 Shop Closing Act. It essentially endorsed the status quo. To be sure, stores in central business districts increasingly closed at 7:00 P.M. Still, lockup at 8:00 P.M. remained legal. The 1928 law was designed for the shopkeepers, not their employees, who could be obliged to work after closure. The only restriction on employees' worktime was the 1887 law that limited the labor of children to seventy-four hours per week. The Shop Assistants Union from 1919 had continuously pressed for a forty-eight-hour maximum, which was won for minors only in the 1930s.[40]

The ECA, throughout the 1920s, remained a powerful "vigilance committee" guaranteeing the enforcement of early closing as well as sponsoring middle-class leisure. The association in London organized weekend excursions to romantic castles; and the group was a principal supporter of daylight savings time as a means of extending after-hours outdoor recreation.[41]

Despite their limited victory, the ECA provided a clear expression of the leisure objectives of British commerce. Their French counterparts, by contrast, lacked the cohesion and single-mindedness to achieve parallel goals. Instead, French moralists and retail workers struggled for the more modest goal—a leisure minimum of a Sunday holiday.

Sunday Rest in France, 1889–1910

The movement for a weekly day of rest in France was more impassioned and met more resistance than similar efforts elsewhere. Its beginnings in 1853, when R. P. Picard founded the French Association for Rest and the Sanctification of Sunday, were hardly promising. Picard, a former president of the Society of St. Vincent, with links to Catholic royalist philanthropy, never was able to make this group anything but a pale reflection of British and American Sabbatarian organizations. It limped along with perhaps three thousand members by 1889. In response to years of effort, a few lightly traveled train stations were closed Sunday mornings and some pharmacies in provincial towns agreed to open only on alternative Sundays. Yet most store-keepers would do no more than offer their employees the "equivalent" of a Sunday rest in two half-days off or a two-week "vacation" during seasonal business lulls. When Sabbatarians won voluntary shop closings in some Catholic centers (e.g., Dijon and Le Havre), soon violators caused nearly universal return to the seven-day week.[42]

European and American Sabbatarians convened at the Paris Exhibition in 1889 in an International Congress for Weekly Rest. Like the ECA (and the Second International, which was founded at the same time and place), these Sabbatarians concluded that the only solution to the problem of economic individualism was legislation. French Catholic promoters of the "Lord's Day" had finally concluded that this very concept met with intractable opposition from strong anticlerical elements within the Chamber of Deputies. As one delegate put it, "Pharisaic Sunday Laws had failed to protect the Church." Not only must Catholics cease opposing "modern ways," but they must stop seeking special laws for religion; instead they should promote "social laws" in coalition with "philanthropists."[43]

These early advocates of a social *Ralliement* of Catholics to the Republic went in two ideological directions. First, they clothed Sabbatarian piety in the language of physiological necessity. An emerging school of hygienists and public health physicians were enlisted to argue that weekly rest lengthened life (by seven years according to one estimate); Sunday rest raised the oxygen levels of workers and improved circulation necessary to avoid various diseases, from tuberculosis to hemorrhoids. Others claimed that a free day would reduce the fatigue that currently tempted the worker to "restore the inadequacy of his intellectual and physical forces with alcohol." Harmful "stimulation" rather than beneficial recreation were the fruit of unrelieved toil. Sunday rest was in the national interest, Catholics asserted; it was a means of restoring health to the fatigued masses and thus of guaranteeing a refreshed "race" and higher rates of fertility. These ideas, so similar to the British language of rational recreation, could win a wide audience in this nation that was losing the demographic battle with the enemy, *outre-Rhine*.[44]

Still probably more important was the second approach—the claim that Sunday rest would restore family life: all work should cease one day a week ("habitually" on Sunday) as a guarantee that family roles could be fully played. If the day of rest were rotated between different groups of workers, the degradation of shiftless leisure would be perpetuated; each working morning would be a *Saint Lundi* for those who had wasted their day off the night before. By contrast, a universal day of leisure would assure the "intimacy of the couple and link . . . them to their family, encouraging the moral union of the household and the education of the children."[45]

This shift from "communion with God" to the "sweetness of the foyer" represents a fundamental shift in the discourse of the conservative struggle against the Time-Moloch of industrial and commercial society. This ideology was hardly new in the movement for a weekly rest. Still, it reveals an important model for the use of nonworktime more in tune with a mobile and individualistic society. Late nineteenth-century Sabbatarianism represented a basic shift from the seasonal Catholic calendar built around priest and parish to a calendar grounded in the regularity of weekly time spent developing the essential "moral cell of society"—the nuclear family.

This ideology also "gendered" free time. Sunday rest was to provide males with the wholesome influence of family life. It was to enable women to become part-time housewives—to have time for domestic chores and influence. A Sunday holiday would help realize the nineteenth-century dream of a moralized working-class family where the foyer, dominated by the mother and wife, would overcome the allure of the street and cabaret to the father and son.

The implications of this familial ideology for women were made clear in the quest for the *semaine anglaise*. From 1889, advanced leaders of the weekly rest or *repos hebdomadaire* in France advocated a Saturday half-holiday as a guarantor of the "sanctity" of the Sunday rest. Without an early closing at least of factories and wholesale commerce on Saturday afternoon, working women would be obliged to shop on Sunday morning. Accordingly, their Sunday afternoons would be consumed with housework. When industrial workers had to work a normal ten or more hours on Saturday, millions of retail employees were deprived of the benefits of Sunday leisure for they had to return to the counters on Sunday to serve the industrial work force. To be sure, the argument continued, men and boys might be tempted to waste their Saturday afternoons in bars and unsupervised play (and thus men probably "needed" the *semaine anglaise* less urgently than did working mothers).

Still, men had domestic tasks that they should be able to complete before the Sunday rest—home improvements, some shopping, and the "guidance" of their children.[46]

In some ways, this analysis of the ideology of the weekly rest confirms the argument of the Foucault school of cultural history, especially as expressed by Donzelot in his *Policing of Families*. The apparent goal of advocates of Sunday rest was to domesticate the working-class family. It was to replace the now weakened social controls of community, church, and clan with a set of internal constraints engendered through an expansion of domestic space and the moral impact of the parent over the children. Only by providing time for these family functions to develop could there be an acceptable alternative to state intervention in the growing problem of social reproduction. Also by increasing the male's duties in the family and especially by enhancing the presumably conservative role of women, the temptation of radical male solidarities (like trade unions and socialist parties) could be effectively countered.[47]

One might extend Donzelot's argument: in France, with its "problem" of the employed mother, the conservative family had hardly an opportunity to develop. If the French working class had to be deprived of the full-time housewife of the bourgeoisie, something nearly everyone deplored, it should at least have a part-time "housewife" on the weekend. By contrast, patriarchy was to be expressed in worktime more than family time. This ideology offered a gender-based ideal for "leisure" time that was a necessary corollary to the sexual division of labor time. Sabbatarian ideology shared much with the rationale for granting women a shorter workday than men (see chapter 2).

Yet this line of reasoning is not entirely satisfactory. The logical effect of Sabbatarianism may have been the adaptation of the working-class family to industrial capitalism. Yet many, especially Catholic apologists, had essentially reactionary goals—to restore religious influence through the Trojan horse of the family. More important, the *repos hebdomadaire* was not the exclusive goal of patronizing social elites but the desire of workers who had an autonomous agenda and expressed it in a hostile political climate.

These points become plain when we survey the history of the origins of the French weekly rest law and the movement for the Saturday half-holiday. After 1892, when the weekly holiday became obligatory for women and children in industry, there were repeated proposals to extend this right to all workers. French shopkeepers and some industrialists were divided over a weekly rest law. In response to a Senate debate over the Chambers' weekly rest bill in 1904–1905, ten of twenty-eight local chambers of commerce formally rejected any law. Opponents included not only Angers, Grenoble, and Marseille, but, notably, Paris. Five others, however, perhaps influenced by the Church, favored a Sunday holiday with the balance supporting a weekly rest law with no fixed day off. Employer organizations were similarly divided. The Federation of Industries and Commerce of France and textile and clothing employers favored it, whereas bread, butcher, and pastry industries stood adamantly in opposition. The Merchants Association of Toulouse in 1904 demanded a weekly rest law because competition prevented shopkeepers from getting the day off, which they needed "as much as workers." The Chamber of Commerce of Cambrai rejected exemptions from the law for family-operated enterprises or small marginal businesses, for this would give them a competitive edge.[48]

Yet the powerful Federation of Retail Merchants, composed of roughly 550 associations (centered in Paris), was largely founded to combat the *repos hebdomadaire*.[49] Ideological commitments to laissez-faire liberalism doubtless motivated some of the opposition. Especially given the "familial" character of many of these retailers, the federation interpreted legal regulation as an intrusion into private life. Other opponents of a law claimed that consumer needs had to be accommodated: food stores complained that even a noon closure on Sundays would not work because customers only arrived at that hour. Because large central urban stores often supported legislation, marginal neighborhood shopkeepers feared that the weekly rest law was a conspiracy to drive them out of business. Some shopkeepers complained that one-third or more of their business was conducted on Sunday. Bakers were adamant that French customers would not tolerate stale bread (something that their British counterparts had less fear of). Butchers and other food retailers insisted on remaining open Sunday morning because consumers lacked iceboxes. Competition between small neighborhood bakers and larger more mechanized bakeries made the petty producer extremely sensitive to local clienteles and unwilling to hire additional help to replace staff on a day off. Seasonal industries (e.g., women's tailoring, the canning of fruit preserves, baking, running hotels and resorts, and even automobile manufacture) insisted on continuing the practice of yearly "vacations"—mostly unpaid leaves during periodic lulls in demand—in place of weekly rest.[50]

In contrast to the ambiguities of the shopkeepers, French retail clerks strongly supported weekly rest. After 1902, local unions of white-collar and service workers repeatedly petitioned, demonstrated, and even struck for the *repos hebdomadaire*. Retail clerks throughout France were particularly active; so were butchers, breadmakers, restaurant workers, postal clerks, barbers, and even laundresses.[51]

While agitation for the weekly rest was strong among affiliates of the CGT, independent or Catholic-related societies of retail clerks and white collar employees joined the cause. At the national level, the CGT gave only slight attention to the *repos hebdomadaire*, emphasizing instead the eight-hour day. Yet service and white-collar workers, who generally were quiescent, were passionate about the Sunday holiday. One union of food-service workers in the Gironde complained that without weekly rest, they were the "pariahs of the laboring world." The Federation of Clerical Employees declared that the "prejudice between the *veston* and the *blouse*" has made the industrial worker ignorant of the overwork of the white-collar employee.[52]

Support for a collective day of rest (almost always Sunday and generally not for religious reasons) was widespread. A few groups, like bakers and restaurant workers, accepted a rotating or "weekday" holiday. But most did not. Workers were adamant about the need for a full day of rest: by 1905, some advocated a guarantee of thirty-six hours of continuous freedom from work—especially in those trades where late Saturday night work was common. Employer proposals for two half-days or even a few weeks of annual "vacation" as alternatives to the *repos hebdomadaire* were vigorously rejected. These alternatives to the weekly holiday of course often accommodated the flow of business: small retailers, bakeries, and restaurants might well be able to do without workers on a slow business day like Monday, in the off-season, or when the working employer went on vacation. Consumer habits and the rush season made a regular full day of weekly rest costly for such businesses. In effect, by insisting on Sunday rest, these workers challenged the seasonality of many trades and the extreme lengths to which businessmen sacrificed the personal needs of employees to the desires of a few customers. Workers sought simultaneous, continuous, and regular blocks of time released from work in order to protect family time or "social time."[53]

Surprisingly few unions insisted on guarantees that weekly pay levels be maintained. Many white-collar clerks, of course, were paid by the week and thus the *repos hebdomadaire* would have little monetary effect on them. Yet many workers and employers assumed that even if current weekly wages were not guaranteed in a holiday law, employers could not reduce salaries, which for workers were already at subsistence levels. Employers who tried to decrease daily wages after the ten-hour day became law only provoked largely successful strikes. Finally, even in seasonal trades like construction there were signs that workers were willing to forgo the traditionally erratic cycle of work and rest for a more regular pattern of work, pay, and rest. Under some circumstances, they were willing to trade wages for time.[54]

What became the weekly rest law in July 1906, however, responded more to the lobbying efforts of commercial interests than to the proposals of French labor. Although all workers were guaranteed twenty-four hours of free time per week, both the proposal of thirty-six continuous hours of rest and the guarantee of a universal Sunday holiday were defeated. The law provided an amazing number of exceptions for various trades, which compromised the social function of weekly rest. These included a weekday instead of Sunday holiday, a rest period of twenty-four hours from Sunday noon to Monday noon, and a half-day Sunday combined with a full day of rest once in fourteen days. Most common was a rotating holiday once per week (e.g., in food service, leisure industries, public works, hospitals). Workplaces with less than five workers were obliged only to give two half-day rest periods. The law was suspended for fifteen Sundays per year in "open air" industries. Special "derogations" were also allowed upon the petition of the prefect. Moreover, workers found that the government was reluctant to enforce the law vigorously in the face of organized small-business opposition.[55]

Despite these astonishing accommodations, both bakers and restaurant owners objected to the cost of additional personnel made necessary by the rotating employee holiday. Retailers petitioned for derogations on Sundays prior to holidays; seasonal industries repeatedly claimed exceptional status. In the Chamber, Deputy Georges Berry proposed revisions of the law to save commerce in the outlying areas of Paris from "nomads . . . clandestine sellers who will go into workers homes to the detriment of the real merchants who pay taxes." Berry favored the mere requirement of a half-day rest period per week with the other half-day being made up in "vacation" or any other arrangement.[56]

Until the war, the issue of the *repos hebdomadaire* continued to fester. Immediately after the promulgation of the law in September 1906, up to two thousand Parisian retail clerks formed pickets each Sunday to protest against businesses that (because of their size) could remain open. Demonstrators, mostly from the downtown department stores, were convinced that only if the small "peripheral" stores (e.g., near the Bastille or République) were forced to close on Sundays would the weekly rest survive for any retail clerks. These almost weekly confrontations between the French petty bourgeoisie and the white-collar worker continued until the winter cold and discouraging results quieted them in January 1907. These militant store workers were joined in an interunion committee of action by tramway, postal, butcher, barber, and food service unions.[57] Bartenders and bakers petitioned government and promised strikes if their employers carried out their threats to close on Sundays as a protest against the holiday law.[58]

This quest for time was hardly a goal imposed on workers by the machinations of a reformist bourgeoisie. There was widespread support for an integral *repos hebdomadaire:* by 1905, about one-third of the locally elected *conseils départementaux* petitioned for a weekly holiday law. Still, the bakers, clerks, and the legions of other workers who were denied regular rest largely stood alone against the small-business interests that succeeded in frustrating the ideal of an integral and collective day of leisure.[59]

A second step in the origin of the weekend, the Saturday half-holiday, also became a rallying point for the entitlement to leisure in France before the war. To be sure unions were often suspicious of the *semaine anglaise* especially after it was proposed by conservatives in the Senate in 1902 as an alternative to the legal ten-hour day.[60] The *semaine anglaise* also seemed to threaten the tradition of the *Saint Lundi,* which was still practiced in some male-dominated trades. Yet, in 1905, after one automobile plant granted its workers a Saturday half-holiday, other plants struck unsuccessfully for the same privilege. In 1906, the socialist Edouard Vaillant proposed the *semaine anglaise* in the Chamber and increasingly thereafter unions paired the *semaine anglaise* with the eight-hour day. In 1907, in the midst of the struggle for the weekly holiday law, textile workers in Lyon struck successfully for the Saturday half-holiday in the summer months.[61]

The concept had gained sufficient legitimacy by 1912 for the government to conduct a survey of 1,288 unions, chambers of commerce, and various other local public bodies concerning their views on the introduction of the Saturday half-holiday in France. Of the 641 union respondents, 556 favored the Saturday half-holiday, at least for women. The responses of this broad sampling of articulate labor provide an unusual picture of worker opinion on the value and use of leisure. Supporters' rationales were often similar to those economic arguments made for the eight-hour day: the *semaine anglaise* would reduce unemployment and create "regular periods of work and rest, [which would] lead to a reduction of alcohol abuse" and allow workers to become more healthy and better prepared for the duties of citizenship.[62]

We also hear the desire for family time in terms at least superficially similar to those raised by the Catholic and "philanthropic" reformers: a Saturday early closing would assure an "integral weekly rest," especially for women whose shopping and housework could be finished in time for a Sunday of family activities. It would enable male workers "to help their wives in the cares of housework and to attend the meetings of friends or organizations"; and for children, Saturday afternoons could be used for "exercise" and vocational education.[63]

Does this suggest that these workers had been indoctrinated by the cultural standard of economically dominant classes? Perhaps, but one could equally argue that these sentiments reflect the public relations efforts of unions (especially after the failure of the confrontational approach of the anarchosyndicalists in 1906).[64]

More important, a close reading of labor's approach to the *semaine anglaise* often suggests an agenda rather different from that of bourgeois and Catholic reformers. For example, the Bourse du travail of Seine-sur-Mer favored the Saturday half-holiday to end the tendency of employers to take advantage of the "greedy" wage earner who willingly accepted overtime. The leather workers' union of Perigueux expressed disgust with the "irresponsible worker" who "toiled overtime Friday and Saturday and often on Sunday for more money and then drank from exhaustion, often being unable to return to work until Tuesday or Wednesday." The Saturday half-holiday would oblige this individual to adopt a more regular and healthful work pace. More important, it would eliminate the pressures placed on the responsible worker to conform to this harmful cycle of labor and rest. This was surely the code for the older "family man" who naturally objected to a chaotic pace that was perhaps more tolerable to the less mature worker. These union members insisted that the *semaine anglaise* would force these careless wage earners to return to the "family hearth, and there to rediscover a love for one's home, which so many workers forget because of the brutalization of continuous toil."[65]

These views were expressed by some "independent" (Catholic or otherwise anti-CGT) local unions. Yet, they were also voiced by so-called revolutionary federations of the CGT. Note the propaganda of the construction union, whose advocacy of shorter workdays and the *semaine anglaise* was linked to the creation of a new standard of order, comfort, cleanliness, and sobriety in the working-class home. Perhaps, most interesting, the *semaine anglaise* produced images in its propaganda of the rested male worker surrounded by a loving family, a decorated kitchen, and bountiful dinner table.[66]

These views went beyond the idea of the part-time housewife to include expectations of male family roles. They closely paralleled the increasing concern of union leaders with alcohol abuse in the working class, with juvenile delinquency among poorly supervised children of working parents, and with interest in providing physical education and recreation for youth. Although more research is needed in this area, the Saturday half-holiday surely reflected a growing sensitivity of workers to the apparent declining influence of fathers over the training and vocational fate of their sons. The notion of the "irresponsible worker" and the desire to revise work schedules to eliminate Saint Monday went beyond the conservative (Catholic) laborer; it expressed more than the intent of the union leader to force the common wage earner to abandon his "irrational" irregularity. Rather it reflected a familial propaganda embraced by a wide range of labor activists. As Lenard Berlanstein shows in his study of the Paris working class in this period, these values were embraced by a portion of the rank and file.[67]

In the nineteenth century, the challenges to the tyranny of unlimited worktime went beyond production workers and their economic interests. They were shared also by the commercial work force and expressed religious and family values. Just as production workers gained access to increased leisure, the labor force in the distribution trades embraced a new ideal of personal time. Traditional Sabbatarianism was secularized: the apologetic for weekly rest was increasingly grounded in biological imperatives. More important, domestic roles were situated in the temporal frame of the weekly rest and Saturday half-holiday.

Yet these movements often faced insuperable contradictions. Reformers, retail clerks, and, especially in Britain, shopkeepers made often heroic efforts to create blocks of free time for those behind the counter; yet commercial competition and ultimately the public's convenience meant limited success. The individualism of the French shopkeepers in a relatively unrestrained commercial culture and the long workweek of French production workers made even the Sunday rest an impossible standard before the war. Their English commercial counterparts were, of course, more successful. Yet, despite their superior organization and strong Sabbatarian traditions, competition also frustrated the British early shop closers. At the root of the problem was that the "weekend" of the production worker deprived the commercial and entertainment worker of the same privilege. Until the development of shift work in the twentieth century, the pleasures of the many required the unceasing toil of the service worker.

Although the weekly rest and early-shop-closing movements had links with conservative elites and petty tradesmen, commercial workers also embraced these causes. These movements represented another example of the quest for a social minimum of time liberated from work. Even more clearly than the eight-hour movement of production workers, weekly rest and early shop closing were distinct from the economic and work-related concerns of employees.

These retail employees developed a consensus over a new allocation of "leisure time." They expressed a quest for more regular, simultaneous blocks of time free from work. To be sure, the ideal of the weekly rest was hardly invented by the commercial trades. Nevertheless, by the 1890s, the goal of the weekly holiday had lost its Sabbatarian roots: its value was expressed through the religion of the family. Competitive pressures and the unwillingness of the majority to do without the convenience of shopping "at all hours" frustrated this goal. Yet this struggle was the site of the origins of one of the most characteristic features of contemporary industrial culture—the weekend.

Finally, despite the social and cultural fissures that frustrated these reformers, they did share a common language with the eight-hour advocates in industry—that of efficiency and fatigue. As chapter 5 will show, a new science of work justified the state's intervention to protect the citizen from the toll of overwork.

5

Efficiency and Reform: Work Science, the State, and Time, 1890–1918

The ideological contest between labor and property had surely reached an impasse by the last two decades of the nineteenth century. Increasingly both the language of "association" and the appeals to laissez-faire were inadequate in the era of the second industrialization and liberal democracy. The demand of labor to control the work process as well as the employer's claim to unrestricted use of hired labor time had insufficient appeal. This was true in spite of the survival and even flourishing of the traditionalist discourses of syndicalism in France or the Property and Liberty League in England.[1] A labor doctrine of expropriation or redistribution failed clearly to address the vexing problems of technological growth, the world market, and mass production. An employer ideology of "freedom to manage" hardly answered the problems of the increasingly complex character of the workplace and the threat of rising industrial powers like the United States and Germany to national economies. It also ran against a growing popular resistance to industrial authoritarianism.[2]

In the 1890s rather different languages emerged based on direct appeals neither to work nor to property but on the concepts of socioeconomic efficiency and integral progress. These ideologies were buttressed by the scientific measurement of the biological and engineering potentials of labor productivity. The efficiency movement took two rather distinct forms: a science of work, arising out of the medical laboratory; and scientific management, emerging from the growing and increasingly independent profession of the industrial engineer. In the early stages, the science of work was theoretical and focused on the potential of the human "motor"; however, scientific management was always more practical, concentrating on the organization of the workplace and the pecuniary incentives necessary to increase productivity.[3]

Still, both movements shared common values and, as the war approached, they became increasingly similar. Moreover, they were linked to a broad network of international reformers drawn from a wide variety of professions—law, politics, the new ministries of labor, the church, and even trade union bureaucracies and progressive business circles. Both work scientists and scientific managers shared a common strategic ambiguity regarding the industrial contest. Although both groups accepted existing property relations, they often rejected the extreme property claims of the traditionalist entrepreneur. For them, the workplace was to be governed not by the sovereign owner but by the universal standard of science. Some even supported labor legislation and state inspection based on their discoveries and claims. They generally accepted the inevitability and even desirability of the market's role in allocating status, power, and wealth. Yet these reformers usually rejected the unrestrained competition that created short-term profit at the price of long-term deterioration of human capital. They opposed competition that drove down the labor standard; instead they advocated legislation to maintain a level of living and working conditions and approved the use of technology to improve these standards. Most of all, many advocates of industrial science believed that they were above the conflicts of management and labor. Their mission was to promote reforms that would not only increase productivity but improve social efficiency. Yet they inevitably "leaned" toward either capital or labor while producing ideas that were serviceable to both sides.

One could argue that the scientism of the efficiency movement was a response to pressures to create a new "age of labor discipline"—to find a new rationale for industrial authority after traditional paternalism and the "driving" methods of the past had proved to be inadequate.[4] A new "scientific" wage and social hierarchy in the factory built around the engineer could replace the increasingly challenged authority of the owner and foreman. By promising to increase man-hour output, the efficiency movement could also compensate employers for hour and wage concessions that increasingly pressed on profit.

Yet industrial science could also be adapted to labor. It offered an apologetic essential in the democratic forum of public opinion, state-mediated collective bargaining, and parliamentary politics; it provided labor with its own definition of the "national interest." The language of industrial science became, like earlier discourses of "republicanism" and the "free-born Englishman," a rhetorical form that served both business and labor. Nowhere is this made clearer than in the uses of the science of work and scientific management in the ongoing debate over worktime. In France, the ideology of scientific management (although tempered by the ideas of fatigue research) dominated, whereas in Britain the work science movement played a greater role.

Scientific Management and Worktime in France, 1890–1918

Taylorism as an ideology and tool of management is well known. Students of the "work process" have long debated the impact of scientific management on the creation of the mass-production worker and its challenge to skilled workers' control of the workplace. As an American movement of professionally trained engineers, the success (and, more often, failure) of European disciples to spread the news of Taylorism to Europe has been well documented.[5] Historians have noted that trade unions, especially after World War I, generally accepted and even embraced Taylorism. This trend is often presented in terms of the victory of reformism and class collaboration.[6]

In fact, Taylorism as it would often be perceived in Europe—as a broad ideology of productivism—had been long a central theme of trade unionism and not just of the "reformist" stripe. As we have seen in chapter 3, it played a vital role in an evolving apologetic for short hours in the ideological whirlwind between 1888 and 1891. Not only could mechanization and improved work methods compensate for hours reductions but shorter worktime was the only way of forcing employers to make labor time more efficient. From at least the 1880s, British and French socialists and trade unionists looked longingly to an American package of short hours and high wages tied with the bow of enhanced labor productivity. Although this American utopia may have been a myth, it was serviceable. The European Left found in America "proof" that a short-hours, high-wage work force—rather than capital accumulation—was the driving wedge of economic progress. The "American standard" and the "American system of manufacturing" were sticks to beat the European employer whose refusal to modernize his plant and business methods had blocked social and economic progress. Neither labor movement had to be sold on productivism—a form of demand-side economics. Especially for the French, an American cast to productivism was positively attractive.[7]

At first glance, Taylorism seems hardly the ideal foundation of a labor ideology. As is well known, Frederick Taylor attacked wage earners for "soldiering"—working at the pace of the slowest producer. He attempted to gain knowledge of the potential pace and methods of the individual worker and then to win control over output and skill from the work group. A web of innovations from functional foremen, to time and motion studies, bonus payment plans, and new work routing systems focused on increasing managerial control of the shop floor. Taylor's practices not only denied value to skilled work but his wage policy was a pure form of pecuniary behaviorism, an obvious threat to work group solidarities, seniority systems, and traditional norms of effort and paced expenditure of energy. In a word, for many workers Taylorism was often little more than a speedup veiled in the language of science.[8]

Taylor's ideas for enhancing managerial control over production were hardly new to France, and thus he found there, as early as 1900 at least, a small audience among employers.[9] By 1907, not only had Taylor been translated and popularized by the engineer Henri Le Châtelier, but Louis Renault had hired a Taylorite engineer to introduce time and motion study. This experiment and a subsequent strike in 1913 at Renault's automobile plant provoked a wide and bitter attack on Taylorism in the trade union press.[10] Emile Pouget's book, *L'Organisation du surmenage* (1913) claimed that motion studies "stifled the ingenuity of the worker" and placed a premium on brute strength and manual dexterity rather than intelligence. Taylor's claim to know the "one best way" of work and his assumption that the "best mechanic is incapable of working efficiently without the daily aid of his instructor" was an insult to the workers' dignity. Alphonse Merrheim declared that Taylorism reduced the worker to "an automaton ruled by the automatic movements of the machine" and weakened the "market value" of professional and skilled workers.[11]

The Renault strike became a lockout, and ended in a management victory. No longer was there any effective resistance to the transformation of the French automobile industry into a mass-production industry. Moreover, after the failures of the general strikes of 1906, the CGT was unable to expand its base beyond a core of intellectuals and the shifting sand of conflicting and transient union members in mostly skilled and public service trades. Renault's easy victory only confirmed this trend.[12]

Leaders of the CGT clearly recognized their organizational impasse; they realized the inevitability of economic rationalization and the decline of the skilled mechanic. Moreover, many French trade unionists were keenly aware of the backwardness of French industry and began to see innovation as the only means of raising living standards. In 1911 and 1913, CGT chief Léon Jouhaux blamed long working hours and low wages on the industrialists' failure to modernize.[13]

In this context, it is not surprising that a "revised edition" of Taylorism was greeted with greater labor interest. In response to opposition in American shipyards to his methods in 1912, Taylor defended his innovations before a well-known congressional investigation of scientific management. Far from being antilabor, he claimed, his system would usher in a "mental revolution," ending class conflict in the factory. Taylorism benefited both sides, providing short hours as well as high wages for the worker and increased output for the employer. Moreover, the worker as consumer would get a more plentiful supply of cheaper goods. As an alternative to fighting over the share of the pie, scientific management would increase "the size of the surplus until the surplus became so large that it was unnecessary to quarrel over how it should be divided." Even management's control over work methods had its redeeming aspect: at least this control was to be based on scientific principles rather than the arbitrary will of the boss.[14]

Taylor's "mental revolution" offered little more than management's promise of higher wages and shorter hours in exchange for labor's ceding control over production. Yet by shifting the focus of Taylorism from the microcosm of conflict between the stopwatch man and the worker and toward the macrolevel of economic progress, Taylor diffused his reputation as an enemy of labor. He also provided a serviceable ideological framework for French labor.

As early as 1913, French socialist Ervin Szabo argued that scientific management could replace the "bourgeois lord" with the "producer" who had learned the "scientific knowledge of efficient production." Taylorism would also destroy the old skill-based fragmentation of French workers and (despite the growth of big capital) assure the increasing dominance of a united class of producers. This obvious Saint-Simonian interpretation of scientific management, in spite of the naiveté of its sociology, had a wide resonance among working-class intellectuals. One year after his 1913 condemnation of Taylorism at Renault, A. Merrheim of the metalworkers conceded that "new methods are required in a new industrial stage." Taylorism could increase the standard of living of workers and consumers, and could be equitably applied. Most important, the CGT used these ideas in its attack on the noninnovating French *patronat* whom the unions blamed for France's poverty and the country's increasingly noncompetitive position in the world market.[15]

Moreover, even the early opposition to Taylorism was not clearly based on a rear-guard reaction to economic rationalization but rather on the nonparticipation of labor in the process of increasing productivity. During the Renault strike, Merrheim indicated the direction the CGT would increasingly take:

A rational organization of work is absolutely necessary for the progress of industry. . . . As for me I think that the Taylor system adapted to the French mentality will be introduced more and more in industry. . . . The interest of workers is to supervise this process and to favor all those efforts in the degree that they do not harm their moral, economic, or physical interests.[16]

This was not merely a grudging acceptance of a fait accompli. After all, only a handful of French factories had adopted any aspect of Taylorism. Rather, it was an outline of a new concept of workers' control. The craft tradition was abandoned; now, labor was to "supervise" innovation in the struggle for the benefits of increased productivity.

This goal proved to run far ahead of reality. In the aftermath of the failure at Renault, the majority in the metalworkers' union favored the organizing of the new unskilled laborers. Yet the historic weakness of French unions in the proletarianized sector and their inability to expand beyond local municipal coalitions and to organize national industries greatly limited their effectiveness.[17]

It is not surprising then that the leadership sought allies among scientific reformers. For example, as early as 1907, Jean-Marie Lahy and his Laboratoire central de psychologie expérimentale des hautes-études had gained the support of printworkers in his study of work methods. Lahy, along with Jules Amar and Armand Ibert, proposed not only improved labor productivity but also, through studies of the physiology of work, a reduction in fatigue and nervous exhaustion. This group also favored giving workers consultative rights in decisions regarding industrial innovation.[18] These signs of a cooperation between labor and science, along with a more conciliatory Taylorism, made the scientific management movement more palatable to French labor.

Most important, scientific management was a tool in the short-hours movement. Innovations that enhanced labor productivity made the eight-hour day economically feasible. Taylorism gave objective validity to the claims made by the productivists between 1886 and 1892. This use of Taylorism became even more clear during World War I.

The war provided French engineers, the CGT, and even a portion of business with a unique opportunity to rally around the flag of Taylorism as well as the tricolor. Engineers like Emile Nussbaumer, Bertrand Thompson, and Charles de Freminville made well-publicized experiments in Taylorizing French munitions plants.[19] French trade unionists embraced Taylorism at the same time as they collaborated in the war mobilization. As "delegates of the nation," Jouhaux and Merrheim joined a number of commissions that provided manpower for the war economy and "encouraged all necessary modifications of work and facilitated the rapid adoption of new work methods."[20]

The CGT found allies who shared its commitment to the modernization of postwar France. Albert Thomas, a right-wing socialist deputy, embraced Taylorism when he became undersecretary of state for munitions in 1915. He not only favored bonus piece-rate systems but also motion studies, vocational selection, and increased division of labor. He opposed lengthy overtime and Sunday work for a more compressed workday.[21] In April 1917, in his *Bulletin des usines de guerre*, Thomas summarized his position on Taylorism:

No longer will the worker be content with fixed salaries that he gains for a week of nonstrenuous work. No longer will the employer be happy with the careless methods of the past. The employer now wants a greater productivity; the worker wants the highest salary; and they give each other perfect satisfaction when they reach their goals by a method of payment for work based on results.[22]

Thomas echoed Taylor's "mental revolution" and provided a concrete prescription for class cooperation after the war.

Yet, despite the support for Taylorism by key munitions makers like Renault and André Citroën, application of these ideas during the war was limited even in progressive capitalist circles. Louis Renault exemplified the traditional paternalism of the nineteenth-century French *patronat*—favoring workers' gardens and city services to improve the moral environment of labor—while believing that substantial social reforms, including a shorter workday, were to follow, not parallel, increases in productivity. The progressive bourgeoisie thus shared with Thomas and the CGT little beyond a willingness to improve management and to mechanize. And even these goals were held only by a small group of large employers.[23]

Although the CGT had worked with business representatives during the war, it would be incorrect simply to label their behavior as reformist. The CGT's Minimum Programme adopted one week after the armistice was certainly opposed to prewar syndicalism; but it went far beyond business plans for enlightened, paternalistic capitalism. Its opening sentence was "We must direct ourselves to take control of production." As a first step, it advocated the preservation of the organizations "installed in the course of the war," in order to forestall a revival of the "Oligarchy" whose private interests had been "strangling industry and consumers." A program of "incessant progress of production" and developing "all new inventions and discoveries" was to make possible a number of social reforms—social insurance, education, and especially the eight-hour day. These reforms were to prepare the worker for the "ultimate goal of emancipation."[24]

This formula was in many ways a modernization of the traditional ideology of workers' self-emancipation, while attempting to expand trade union support beyond production workers. Leaders were more interested in reaching out to consumers and the new working class of technicians than to the employer class. Like Thomas, Jouhaux embraced the incentive wage; but he saw it not as a trade-off between business and labor but as a means to "link the interests of the producers to those of the consumer." Between 1918 and 1921, the CGT leadership attempted to create alliances between consumers, technicians, and labor groups. For example, the CGT organized a short-lived National Council of Labor (1919–1921) and collaborated with technicians in journals like *Information sociale et ouvrière* and *L'Atelier*. This coalition was to be based on a creed that combined productivism with a dramatically improved labor standard. As Jouhaux declared at the 1918 Congress of the CGT, "We must strive to realize this formula, the maximum production in the minimum of time, for the maximum salary with the general increase in the buying power for all."[25]

The CGT found in Taylorism a method and even more an ideology that seemed to break their impasse: enhanced productivity created by an alliance of workers and technicians would free the labor movement from its particularist fetters and provide it with an effective rationale for a reallocation of time.

The Science of Work: Efficiency and the Necessity of Rest

For the generation before World War I, the idea of fatigue was a preoccupying concern. Scientists measured the capacity of the human body for work and calculated the economic and biological costs of exceeding its optimal use. To be sure, the emergence of a science of fatigue, or ergonomics, preceded the intensification of work during the second industrialization. As Anson Rabinbach and Georges Ribeill have shown, the science of work emerged from a new corporal physics first developed by Hermann von Helmholtz in the 1860s. His conception of the body as a motor that transformed matter into motion gradually replaced the early notion of the body as an externally directed or motivated machine. This image of the worker as a "human motor" undermined traditional paternalism: appeals to the worker's conscience and attempts to create a regulated moral environment in a company town lost validity. The psychology behind close supervision, detailed regulations, the "driving" practices of industrial authoritarianism, or even the pecuniary incentives of Taylorism now was invalid. Instead output became a function of the largely "internal" capacity of the human engine.[26]

Thus, work was "cleansed" of any normative significance and became the object of physiological study. Its investigation, according to one of the most influential scientists of work, Angelo Mosso (1891), should be made by "independent men . . . free from all preconceptions." These investigators could then raise the question of output above the conflict between management and labor—beyond claims of the laziness of the worker or the exploitativeness of the employer. Productivity was then reduced to a physiological dimension, the proper concern only of scientists.[27]

These scientists of work objectified the production process into the measurement of the motion and optimal speed of muscles. By eliminating wasted movement, they attempted to reduce strain and the consumption of energy. The ideal was to assure optimal output over relatively *long* work periods rather than realize short-term maximum production at the price of long-term labor fatigue and deterioration. Work scientists viewed fatigue as the equivalent of the governor on a steam engine—a "psychic factor which regulates the expenditure of energy of the human motor, so as to ensure its most economic working." While advocating rest and warning against fatigue, they stressed the need for "scientific" determination of optimal repose rather than irregular voluntary rest breaks. Although they deemed repose as essential, most work physiologists (especially in Germany, where much of the laboratory work was done) pointedly abstained from taking stands on the issue of worktime. The French scientist Jules Amar declared that the eight-hour movement was a "heresy," and claimed that daily worktime should vary with the character of work and the sex and age of the human motor. The labor ideal of a right to a daily maximum of work was "unscientific."[28]

All of this suggests that the science of work was far more amenable to management than to labor. Indeed, it was a tool of an enlightened employer, intent upon optimizing output rather than wasting labor by failing to "husband" and maintain properly his "human capital."

Yet the discourse of work science was also serviceable to the cause of labor and social reform. Especially in France, a second generation of efficiency scientists who emerged about 1905 established links to organized labor. Armand Imbert at Montpellier encouraged CGT participation in scientific meetings concerned with occupational accidents. He developed statistics proving a correlation between duration of labor and accidents. Jean-Marie Lahy, who in 1907 had won the cooperation of skilled workers in his investigations of fatigue, later advocated that wage earners participate in determining changes in work methods.[29] Ilia Sachnine and Marc Pierrot applied the findings of work science to polemical attacks on overwork. This scholarship was utilized in Edouard Vaillant's bill for an eight-hour law in 1898 and especially 1906.[30]

Somewhat later in Britain, a similar group, including N. A. Brisco, Arthur Shadwell, P. Sargant Florence, Charles Myers, and H. M. Vernon, advocated that scientists cooperate with trade unions. They favored measures that would enhance "ease of work" rather than merely "speed of work."[31] Moreover, members of the work science group were critical of scientific management: instead of Taylor's appeal to the workers' pecuniary interest, they stressed the mental and physical conditions of work; instead of Taylor's desire to select only the most capable workers, work scientists sought merely to eliminate the incapable.[32] Mosso advocated banning night work for women. Amar, Lahy, and Imbert openly favored shorter workdays and the *repos hebdomadaire*. The book *Fatigue and Efficiency*, written by the American Josephine Goldmark, was a popularization of European work science and was widely read in Britain. Its primary purpose was to defend an eight-hour day for women.[33]

The impact of fatigue on human capital was an imporant theme in the British Inter-Departmental Committee on Physical Deterioration (1904), created after the revelation that 28 percent of British recruits for the Boer War were physically unfit. The impact of long hours on health and output was also analyzed in the official reports of the labor inspectors in Britain. In 1913, the British Home Office commissioned Professor A. F. Stanley Kent to conduct research into the impact of industrial fatigue on output.[34]

Fatigue, it was argued, not only affected output but reduced the value of human capital. Exhaustion reduced longevity; decreased fertility of women; stunted growth of youth; produced insomnia and liver and digestive disorders; and, in general, increased morbidity. Fatigue was associated with nervous disorders; Sachnine even concluded that long working hours contributed to the relatively poor mental health of workers. Of course, the length of worktime was also held responsible for alcoholism. Pierrot argued that laziness was not the cause of listless work or absenteeism; rather overwork created this lack of motivation.[35]

Physical fatigue caused an accumulation of waste products in the muscles, excessive carbon dioxide in the blood, and deterioration of the heart and other vital organs. Work scientists argued that eight hours of uninterrupted rest and a full day of weekly repose were physical, not merely moral, necessities. Time was needed to clean out the system and Sunday walks were required to replenish the blood's oxygen supply. Jules Amar referred to the *repos hebdomadaire* as a "sovereign necessity."[36]

Yet most authors held that nervous fatigue was even more dangerous than physical exhaustion. Close monotonous work, even in clean factories and with a minimum of physical energy, argued Goldmark and Sachnine, was at least as fatiguing as heavy work. Atrophy of muscle groups and overwork of eyes and fingers had to be reversed in rest and recreative exercise. Overstimulation and lack of aeration in the long hours of retail work caught the attention of the international consumer's league movement. Pierrot concluded that "labor ought to be reduced to no more than a minimum portion of daily activity of man." Neither the machine nor the division of labor should be abandoned but time at work should be reduced to allow for biological recovery and "happiness" outside of work.[37]

Fatigue science obviously was applicable to the short-hours movement. The definition of fatigue as the diminished capacity to produce and the claim that fatigue varied directly with duration of work made worktime the key to optimizing output. Accordingly, the limiting factor in production was not motivation (or, negatively, laziness), which had traditionally justified long hours in order to win a reasonable output from intractable labor. Rather the horizon of production was biological capacity. Rest was not a mere negation of productive time but an "active" phase in the restoration of muscles, nerves, and vital organs. Moreover, the time required for the muscles to recover from fatigue increased with the duration of work. Thus, an overly long work period was self-defeating. It inevitably was followed by absenteeism (or sickness) proportionate with the excess over optimal worktime.

Because the goal was to discover the "optimum" duration of work, consistent with high sustainable levels of output, investigators focused increasingly on discovering those hours of work that were the most productive. This led to the discovery that early morning output (before the traditional 8:00 A.M. breakfast break) hardly justified fixed capital expenditures. The same was true of work on Saturday afternoon. In Britain, a Ministry of Labour survey in 1913 found that the length of the workday had surprisingly little impact on productivity. In one study women pieceworkers produced almost all of their daily output between 10:00 A.M. and 4:00 P.M. despite the fact that the workday may have extended from 8:45 A.M. to 7:45 P.M. Women garment makers seldom produced more in a week that included overtime than in a "normal week." Of the 185 firms in the Ministry of Labour investigation that had reduced hours below industrial norms, only 6 complained that hours reductions led to diminished output.[38]

These facts might be explained in a number of ways: first, women pieceworkers had relatively fixed or customary expectations of income; thus they worked only to the point of reaching that traditional wage level—no matter how long they were on the job. Yet the fact that output did not drop with worktime reductions suggests that these workers had a reserve of energy sufficient to maintain output in order to preserve income levels. Less fatigued workers, because of a reduced duration of work, reached optimal output. Having eliminated the least productive early and late hours, the employer found no appreciable impact on daily production; and workers compensated for any losses with increased effort in the most productive hours.[39]

One might argue that the work efficiency movement was in reality a rationale for the increasing resistance of labor to "overwork." Fatigue could be measured not only chemically (e.g., increase of toxins in the blood) but behaviorally in reduced output, spoiled work, increased accidents, and even absenteeism. Workers were fatigued and thus overworked because they would not perform at 6:00 A.M. or after 7:00 P.M. or on Saturday afternoon and Sunday. As observers had noticed by 1900, wage earners increasingly were sensitive to overwork. This was doubtless due in part to the greater speed and intensity of work—a theme that increasingly absorbed TUC discussion in the decade before World War I. Moreover, British factory inspectors noted increased complaints over working hours on the eve of the war. Significantly, many of these complaints referred to practices that were legal but that laborers assumed were violations of law.[40] Surely labor's threshold of tolerance for long stints of work (or labor at "unsociable hours") had declined. In some measure, the age of fatigue science was a reflection of this lowered willingness to sacrifice time for output.

The sophistication of fatigue science grew during World War I, providing a powerful support for the reduction of worktime after the conflict. This was particularly true in Britain where significant field (as opposed to laboratory) research in efficiency science was done. In August 1914, Britain, facing an enormous labor shortage, suspended the Factory Laws. Even "protected" workers were allowed to labor from 6:00 A.M. to 9:00 P.M. Sunday overtime was a commonplace in munitions plants. The Board of Trade abandoned all efforts to regulate worktime on the railroads where ninety- to one-hundred-hour workweeks were not unusual. And skilled work in toolrooms was extended daily from 7:00 A.M. to 9:00 P.M. with a "short" shift of 7:00 A.M. to 4:00 P.M. on Sunday.

In spite of patriotic appeals, however, productivity soon dropped off. As early as February 1915, tardiness and absenteeism ("bad time-keeping") had become a major concern of the British government. Official reports confirmed that iron, electrical, and shipbuilding trades lost significant time due to voluntary absences. One report (1915) claimed up to 44 percent of shipyard workers were tardy, blaming it on the fact that bars were allowed to be open before 6:00 A.M. The old complaint reappeared that overly liberal laws regulating pub hours allowed the bar to compete with overtime and the punctual onset of work. This had led in the opening months of the war to new regulations allowing judges to close bars at 9:00 P.M. rather than 11:00 P.M. or later.[41]

By August 1916, the government held hearings regarding the need for holidays for munitions workers. Witnesses reported that output had decreased significantly during the previous Christmas, Easter, and the "holiday which was supposed not to be a holiday" (Whitsuntide). Even a war could not overcome the rhythms of the seasonal festivals. Allen Smith of the Engineering Employers' Federation complained that ship riveters "go away for weekends" and if the government granted them a holiday, the problem with bad timekeeping would only be accentuated. Moreover, employer witnesses firmly opposed giving a holiday to workers in "relays" for that would only have meant that a "holiday spirit prevails for a month." As Richard Croucher has shown for the munitions industry during World War II, neither patriotism nor the suspension of trade union power was able to reverse work and leisure habits. Still the Glasgow and West Scotland Armament Committee in May 1915 required that employers identify and fine persistent bad timekeepers; as late as January 1918, the government removed draft exemptions from flagrantly bad timekeepers.[42]

There were, however, alternatives to these conservative solutions to poor work habits. In September 1915, a lobby of health and fatigue specialists convinced Lloyd George to create the Health of Munitions Workers' Committee (HMWC). The HMWC exercised considerable influence over the hours of work in munitions factories through the Welfare Department for war factories, which from January 1916 inspected plants for violations of health regulations. The committee expressed perfectly the ideology of work science. A 1918 summary of the HMWC's work declared:

It is [the worker's] individual health, mental development, and moral well-being which is the guarantee of effective labour. . . . [The] human being is a finely adjusted physiological instrument not to be wasted. . . . Fatigue is the sum of the results of activity which show themselves in a diminished capacity for doing work. . . . If industrial rhythms are faster than the natural rhythms of the body, they must produce accumulated fatigue.

This report even went on to claim:

In so far as hours of work in excess of those suitable for maximal efficiency have been imposed during the last two or three generations of modern industry upon the workers, a tradition of slowed labour must necessarily have arisen, probably in large part automatically, as a kind of physiological self-protection. . . . [Without this] unconscious slackening of effort, output might have been even more unfavourable than it is known to have been for the hours of work consumed.

This extraordinary statement is a clear expression of the doctrine that biology determines output and is a ringing denunciation of excessive hours.[43]

While embracing the physiological model, the HMWC echoed the now common moral argument in favor of women's rest: free time was necessary for "creating and maintaining a wholesome family life, and secondly of developing the higher influences of social life." Moreover, all workers needed an "opportunity for recreation, exercise, and the discharge of ordinary duties of citizenship and domestic life"—even in war. Finally, the committee recognized that the long hours worked under the pressures of military mobilization could not be expected with the peace. Moreover, the Commission of Enquiry into Industrial Unrest of 1917 echoed these ideas when it claimed that fatigue and the consequent "nervousness" of workers was in large part responsible for the rank-and-file labor unrest of 1917.[44]

It should not be surprising that the HMWC found wanting the traditional punitive solutions to bad timekeeping. An HMWC survey of absenteeism and tardiness in February 1916 discovered that while on average workers lost only 1.74 hours per week, shipbuilders lost 4.24 hours. The most obvious explanation was that shipbuilders worked the most overtime of any group studied (7.05 hours compared with an average of 5.23 hours). Lost hours more than erased the relative gains in overtime. As late as October 1917, women workers also lost more time to absenteeism and tardiness than they made up in overtime.[45] Insofar as bad timekeeping and thus reduced output were linked to fatigue, the only solution was reduced worktime.[46]

Soon HMWC investigators were analyzing the impact of shorter hours, rest breaks, and even holidays on output. In 1916–1917, H. M. Vernon conducted careful studies of shell production of women under different work schedules. Compared with a 74.8-hour week, *hourly* output was 34 percent higher with a nominal workweek of 61.5 hours and 58 percent higher with 54.8 hours; even *weekly* output was 11 percent higher in a 61.5-hour week and 9 percent greater in a 54.8-hour week. Moreover, output per hour rose with hour diminutions only gradually over a four-month period. This confirmed the doctrine that workers did not simply raise output to recover lost piece-rate income. Rather, "a worker, [found] unconsciously and gradually by experience that he could work more strenuously and quickly for a short-hour week than for a long-hour week." By eliminating Sunday work, which had produced "six days of work in seven days," output also improved.[47]

By January 1916, Vernon had concluded that men and boys should not work more than sixty-five to sixty-seven hours and women only sixty hours per week, with Sunday rest for all. By mid-1917, he revised those figures downward to sixty hours for men and fifty to fifty-five for women. More efficient work movements, more prompt starts, and regular daily and weekly rest with a minimum of overtime would, according to Vernon, easily recuperate lost worktime.[48]

Researchers for the HMWC embraced many worktime reforms; they found that the "one-break system" increased output and advocated replacing overtime with a two-shift schedule. These schedules would maximize the use of machines without damaging "human capital."[49] The HMWC also favored regularly spaced short rest breaks and holidays. Investigators found that the five-hour "stint" allowed under the Factory Act was too long. They favored the use of regular ten to fifteen minute tea breaks, which "should be compulsory and rest pauses at other times be checked as far as possible." Vernon found also that output rose dramatically after and before holidays. These rests were more efficacious than mere reductions of daily worktime because they facilitated plant repair and allowed rest for management who could not take the "odd day off like the ordinary worker." In August 1916, Dr. George Newman, chairman of the HMWC, testified before a special Holidays in Relay Committee that at least 30 percent of munitions workers were in great need of a holiday for "jollification." They needed "physiological rest" and even more a "change of thought and of experience." He advocated short trips from Arsenal to Blackpool. Newman preferred a brief holiday of two to three days for "the average worker does not know how to spend a holiday."[50] Even these modernizers were hardly free of traditional employer paternalism.

The recommendations of the Health of Munitions Workers' Committee did not go unheeded. As early as May 1916 the Munitions Ministry Committee on the Hours of Labour (led by B. Seebohm Rowntree) recommended the elimination of Sunday work, a sixty-five-hour maximum workweek for youths under eighteen, and a twelve-hour daily maximum for women. These rather modest requests were mostly implemented by November 1916. Moreover, Munitions Tribunals refused to insist that men work Sundays. In any case, by the end of 1916 most employers realized that Sunday work was unprofitable.[51] By July 1917, the Munitions Ministry required employers to adhere to a sixty-three-hour maximum for all workers. And, in November 1917, the Minister of Munitions, Winston Churchill, believing that bad timekeeping was "entirely due to long hours and overwork," ordered fifteen national munitions factories to reduce hours from sixty to fifty per week, despite the opposition of management. Churchill's action prompted a committee of the Engineering Employers' Federation to study reduced worktime.[52]

The Home Office conditionally supported a two-shift system even for women (divided between 6:00 A.M. to 2:00 P.M. and 2:00 P.M. to 10:00 P.M.). Employers of women textile workers, especially in northern England and Scotland, increasingly adopted the one-break system after 1917, starting work at 8:00 A.M. Both winter darkness and the problems of long journeys to work and family duties made arrival at work at 6:00 A.M. very difficult. This reform often meant a reduction from fifty-four hours to fifty hours. Employers attempted to recover part of the lost ninety minutes of morning work in a lengthened afternoon stint. This led workers to demand an eight-hour day ending at 5:00 P.M.[53]

All of this activity points to the "technical" support for labor's postwar bid for reduced worktime. The one-break system and the two-shift scheme became openings for an eight-hour day. Fatigue science gave legitimacy to short hours and provided a scientific rationale for granting it to a work force that, even during the war, was unwilling and probably unable to sustain unstinted labor.[54]

This function of work science as a vehicle for an improved labor standard and social peace was most clearly revealed in Lord Leverhulme's *The Six Hour Day*. This book, published in 1918 by a member of the well-known Lever Brothers, painted a postwar picture of "progressive democracy" as an alternative to "the slough of socialism and anarchy." His vision of "a symmetrically and proportionately increased" economic pie eschewed both the "magic of the 'perpetual motion' fetish of long hours of toil with low wages and the 'philosophers' stone' of 'ca'canny.'" A key to the solution to social conflict was a six-hour day in two or three shifts, a scheme that would both eliminate fatigue (and increase leisure) as well as maximize the use of machines. As the "dull monotonous grind" of long hours would end, the principal cause of "labour unrest"—"nervousness"—would be eliminated. Output levels would be maintained by the introduction of occupational screening, improved work methods, better tools, and electrification. This would be "no loafers' paradise" but a time-efficient economy, where there would be no place for the "idle rich or ca'canny poor." Higher wages would result and, with shorter hours, new markets for consumer goods would be generated. At the same time, a new economy would emerge, characterized by increased output facilitated by the shift system. Finally, with increased leisure, Britain could build an "improved race," create garden suburbs, and, by extending the school-leaving age, develop an educated citizenry.[55]

Leverhulme's book, cited both by the HMWC and by labor intellectuals, expressed a material utopia that had wide appeal. Carter Goodrich, in his study of workers' control movements after the war, noted the willingness of British (like French) labor to accept piece rates and bonus systems (when they were negotiated) and to cooperate with mechanization (when higher wages and reduced worktime were part of the package). This achievement required less a technical solution than a political one, a fact that had been obvious to reformers since the 1890s upsurge of interest in the eight-hour day. It led to an important but ultimately fragile movement for interclass cooperation. It attempted to redirect the old contest over work and property, hours and output, toward the productive but also socially liberating solution of a time-efficient economy.[56]

Corporatism and International Reform, 1890–1918

Work science and Taylorism had obvious policy implications. The reformist wing of these movements sought allies within the state bureaucracies and political networks. A reform coalition emerged in Britain and France that employed the language of industrial science to fashion a politics of interclass cooperation. In the 1890s, this group was roughly associated with solidaritism of the Radical party in France and the left wing of Liberalism and Fabian Socialism in Britain. Although this network had few successes before World War I, it emerged during and briefly after the war as a principal contender for shaping early twentieth-century capitalist democracy. Perhaps its most important contribution was in helping to win an international eight-hour day in 1919.

At base this network hoped to create "social peace" by attaching the working classes to the established order. This would be accomplished by alleviating economic inequities and insecurities through the progressive income tax, social insurance, workplace regulation, and job-finding agencies. To reduce industrial conflict, many reformers also favored collective bargaining and, when necessary, public mediation and arbitration.[57]

Yet members of the reform network went beyond the question of "social peace." A more positive theme was an efficient social economy. The state should recognize the social as well as the productive components of the economy. Through regulation, especially of worktime, the work force would be more effective both on the job and in society.

These themes were hardly new to the 1890s. They underlay the debates over the British Ten Hour Act of 1847 and the liberal discourse on worktime in the nineteenth century. Yet they were applied with new vigor and greater authority in this progressive age of scientism. This group rejected the old distinction between the "free" adult male worker, whose "rights" were violated when the state intervened in the job contract, and the dependency of female and child labor. Insofar as the ideal was an improved social economy and thus the reduction of the pathologies of an "unscientific" allocation of time, this classical liberal distinction made little sense.

The new reformers also rejected the traditional "moral" analysis of social diseases (alcoholism, labor unrest, and poverty). Using recently developed sociological and economic analysis, they increasingly linked these "moral" failings to economic insecurity and overwork, rather than to inadequate "social controls." Theories of fatigue science were especially important in this context. Reformers also tended to reject economic individualism and the worship of "market forces," so dear to the classical liberals. This made them more amenable to the technological approach of the Taylorites to solving the problems of distributing wealth and time. Indeed, technology rather than minimum wages or even worktime regulation was their favored solution to the social problem of economic insecurity and overwork. Their critique of classical economics led them to conclude that unrestricted competition could lower rather than raise the material and moral standards of working-class families. Finally, by establishing wider organizations—both corporatist and international—the reform network created new vehicles for change.

In France and Britain, these movements took forms that reflected their somewhat different systems of industrial relations. I will briefly identify major organizations and trends separately for each country. Yet the reader should notice that the similarities outweigh the differences.

In the 1890s in France, an extraordinary coterie of law and economics professors, allied with a small core of government officials, and Radical and moderate socialist deputies formed a network committed to state intervention in labor relations. This group centered around Paul Cauwès's *Revue d'économie politique* (from 1886). Prominent activists included the legal experts Raoul Jay and Charles Rist, the economists Paul Pic and Charles Gide, the bureaucrats Arthur Fontaine and Charles Picquenard, and the politicians Justin Godart (a Radical) and Alexandre Millerand (an independent socialist). Educators in this group trained students who produced many of the studies cited in this volume.[58]

From 1899, Fontaine, director of the Office du Travail, assured increasingly sophisticated collection of data on worktime and other conditions of employment essential for legislation. He helped to establish a tradition of openness to reform within, and introduced a generation of functionaries to, what became after 1906 the Ministry of Labor. Despite their often antirepublican politics, Albert du Mun and other Social Catholics proposed a legislative agenda and an interventionist and corporatist ideology that was quite similar to the secular Radicals and moderate socialists. Even the Marxist Paul Lafargue, in December 1891, briefly advocated a legislative alliance with Social Catholic deputies. Alexandre Millerand, as minister of commerce (1900–1902), introduced experimental eight- and nine-hour workdays in various government establishments.[59]

Most reformers preferred a system of workers' cooperatives and collective bargaining to state regulation. Yet organized French labor remained weak: only 180,000 workers were members of unions in 1890 and, although this number rose rapidly after 1900 reaching nearly 1 million by 1913, this represented only 12 percent of the industrial work force. Moreover, multiclass institutions (e.g., the *prud'hommes* and the *conseils du travail*) palled into insignificance when compared with interclass German social insurance committees or wage boards in Britain. Government conciliation during strikes was confined to the ad hoc mediation of prefects. Therefore, a program of labor legislation was a necessary substitute for weak collective bargaining.[60]

Labor legislation was not only to even the playing field, but to contribute to technological modernization and gradually to improve wages. Drawing on comparative wage data, Jay, Waxweiler, and others noted correlations between short hours, high wages, and high productivity. Thus, legislation for shorter workdays, far from undermining business competitiveness, was to create conditions encouraging innovation and subsequent improved productivity.[61]

This shift of the short-hours debate from the protection of women to the creation of a more efficient economy removed one of the principal obstacles to the advocacy of short hours for men. Charles Rist's study of the regulation of the workday for men found meaningless the classic distinction between the "free" adult male and the "dependent" female and child worker. By 1899, Parliament apparently agreed when it regulated the hours of men on the railroads and, by 1905, in the coal mines.[62]

In Britain, a similar network of reformers emerged in the 1890s. It was based in the Webbs and their Fabian associates who had much influence in the academic community. In the early 1890s, liberal academics like John Rae, Thomas Munro, Thorold Rogers, Victorine Jeans, and Stanley Jevons all favored some form of hours regulation. With access to a number of journals, including *Contemporary Review, The Nineteenth Century,* and *National Review,* as well as the eclectic but scholarly *Economic Journal* and even the *Journal of the Royal Statistical Society,* this group was hardly isolated.[63]

Between 1892 and 1894, the Royal Commission on Labour gave a full, if not largely favorable, airing of proposals for labor legislation. The result in 1893 was the creation of the Labour Department within the Board of Trade. It published the *Labour Gazette,* a compendium of data and information regarding labor relations and legislation. The Labour Department, first headed by A. J. Mundella (a prominent Liberal member of Parliament and president of the Board of Trade) was largely staffed with people sympathetic to unionization. They included, for example, H. L. Smith of Toynbee Hall and John Burnett, former Amalgamated Society of Engineers' official and one-time leader of the nine-hour movement. The Labour Department was charged with facilitating joint boards for collective bargaining; only as a last resort did it provide mediation. The number of joint boards, representing regional associations of employers and trade unions, increased from 64 in 1894 to 325 in 1913—although many were ephemeral. As early as 1892, centralized national bargaining took place in coal and cotton textiles. And in 1906, with the victory of the Liberals, a number of items on the reform coalition's agenda became law: that year the Trade Disputes Act was passed, which protected trade union funds in strikes; in 1908 the Miners' Eight

Hour Act became law; and in 1909 the Trade Boards' Act established committees to set minimum wages in sweated trades.[64]

Like the French, British reformers favored a system of collective bargaining to assure "social peace." Yet they were far more successful than the French. Britain had a far larger and more cohesive trade union movement—organizing over twice the percentage of the work force on the eve of the war. Moreover, British employers were much more willing than their French counterparts to join associations for the purpose of collective bargaining.

The principle of "home rule for industry" reduced the demand for a legal reduction of worktime for males in Britain. Yet although Liberal and Labour party members continued to petition for general eight-hour legislation, powerful employer organizations like the Engineering Employers' Federation successfully resisted hour reductions. And, also like the French, the British government in 1891 introduced the eight-hour day in state-owned shipyards and armories. Still, in Britain hours reform was primarily channeled through a superior trades organization infrastructure. In contrast, French reform was focused on legislation.[65]

Despite these national differences, in both countries the reform network adopted international strategies. These groups had long recognized that the market tended to depress the labor standard even as it contributed to economic efficiency. This, of course, had been a principal rationale for national legislation since the 1840s in both countries. Yet, by the 1890s it was becoming obvious to reformers that the problem of competition was international. In 1870 and 1871, British engineers succeeded in winning a nine-hour day, despite the fact that in the short run it raised costs. In the 1890s, however, employers stoutly resisted the eight-hour movement, noting the declining dominance of British machinery in the world market. Technology and capital had become increasingly mobile and labor productivity less advantageous to the British. Thus, in contrast to the 1840s or 1870s, the refusal of English business in the 1890s to lead Europe in raising the labor standard met with parliamentary approval.[66]

From the standpoint of reform, the solution was to create an international labor standard undergirded by conventions or treaties that assured rough uniformity across industrial frontiers. This alone would prevent international competition from undermining the advanced hour (or other labor) standard of any country.

Robert Owen was the first to advocate international labor legislation in a letter to the Congress of Vienna in 1815. If this proposal was curtly dismissed by conservative diplomats, the concept hardly died; in 1880, an international conference on public hygiene in Brussels called for a common set of labor standards (weekly rest, prohibition of night work for women, a "normal" workday, etc.). German economists of the "historical school," including Lujo Brentano and Gustav Smoller, as well as Social Catholics like Wilhelm Von Kettler, supported international labor standards.[67] In 1881, a group of Swiss textile manufacturers and reformers, concerned with cutthroat competition, asked the Swiss Federal Council to call an international conference for setting labor norms. The logic of the transnational labor standard was also clear to the founders of the Second International in 1889 in Paris, who made an international eight-hour day their leading demand.[68]

In an effort to formulate a conservative alternative to the program of international socialism, William II abandoned Bismarck's cautious position of nonintervention in the labor contract. He coopted the Swiss plan for an international labor conference, when he convened his own meeting in Berlin in March 1890. After fifteen days of discussion, delegates from Britain and most western European countries published the following recommendations: raising the age of entry into mines and factories to fourteen and twelve years in northern Europe and to twelve and ten years in the south; for women, an eleven-hour maximum workday, pregnancy leave, and prohibition of night work; and for all "dependents," the "desirability of a day of weekly rest." These most mild proposals pointedly excluded regulating the worktime of men, which Jules Simon, the elder representative of France, declared was contrary to "liberty." It did, however, establish the precedent of international labor conferences and legitimized international regulation.[69]

In 1897, another group met in Brussels. It was composed not of diplomats but of savants, many of whom were schooled in the new theories of work science. They ranged from Ernest Mahaim of Belgium, and Lujo Brentano of Germany, to Paul Pic of France. In 1900, this group founded the International Association for Labor Legislation (IALL). A French section was formed in 1901. Its directing committee in its first decade represented a curious ideological mix: it included not only the reform network (e.g., Cauwès, Fontaine, Pic, Millerand, and Jay), but Hubert Lagardelle (editor of *Mouvement Socialiste*), moderate trade unionists Edmond Briat and August Keufer, and even the "Blanquist" socialist Edouard Vaillant, Social Catholic Albert de Mun, and Christian Democrat Abbé Lemire. The British section, founded in 1905, included the academic Thomas Oliver as chairman, with Sidney Webb and the Lord Bishop of Oxford as vice-chairmen. Committee members included a galaxy of "Lib-Lab" figures: A. H. Crosfield, J. W. Hill, Alfred Monds, Sophy Sanger, and the trade unionist Arthur Henderson. The IALL recognized fifteen sections: perhaps the French and German were the strongest. It served as a vehicle not only for international communication on labor legislation (through its International Labor Office in Basel) but provided labor with ties to influential reformist elites.[70]

The IALL's achievements, however, were few. At international conferences held in 1906 and 1912, the IALL promoted two international conventions over which there was wide consensus—the prohibition of white phosphorus in the manufacture of matches and night work for women. By 1914, sixteen states had ratified the former and fourteen, the latter convention. In 1910, the IALL initiated a campaign for international conventions to eliminate night work for boys under eighteen and a ten-hour day for women and children.[71]

These measures hardly seriously challenged the code of nineteenth-century liberalism. Yet the idea of extending the concept of the treaty from the traditional arenas of diplomacy, war, and commerce to the "domestic" realm of the workplace was a radical idea. It threatened the extraterritoriality of productive property and asserted the universal right of workers to a minimum labor standard in spite of the "laws of the market." By 1912, the IALL went further by supporting a system of three shifts of eight hours in continuous-process industries (steel, chemicals, glass, etc.) in place of the traditional schedule of two twelve-hour stints. Although without success, this campaign was a breakthrough. Not only did it go beyond the taboo on regulating adult male labor, but it drew heavily on the literature of fatigue science.[72]

The moderation of the IALL may be interpreted in part as strategy. In seeking to win a general acceptance of the principle of an international labor standard, this organization was careful to propose the most widely accepted norms. Yet there were also sharp divisions within the international reform network as to what not only could but should be done. For example, in 1892, L. Brentano, an important theorist of a high-wage and short-hours economy, rejected the possibility of a universal hours standard: given the wide differences between the productivity rates of different economies and work cultures, such a standard would be "unscientific" and impede the development of poorer regions. Moreover, in the French section, while Vaillant had argued for an eight-hour law for twenty years before the war, de Mun stressed mostly the *repos hebdomadaire*. Paul Pic and Alexandre Millerand increasingly took a cautious stance on hours reform and, after the war, attacked the eight-hour law. Yet the IALL became the core of an international network of labor reformers whose members founded the International Labor Organization in 1919 and, on a much larger scale, attempted to create an international labor standard. They played a vital role in the coming of the eight-hour day.[73]

Reform and World War I

During the last year of World War I, it had become apparent that many of the traditional constraints against reduction of the workday had broken down in France and Britain. Faith that technology and new work methods could overcome lost labor time was widespread in French reformist circles; efficiency science had won advocates in the British government. In France, the Ministry of Labor supported the claims of Thomas's Ministry of Munitions that industrial innovation was the key to social reform. In Britain in 1918, the Industrial Fatigue Research Board institutionalized the work of the Health of Munitions Workers' Committee. These bodies provided data in support of the claim that efficiencies could be won with reduced durations of work.

Yet there remained strong opposition to the principle of a normal workday. In 1918, the British Munitions Ministry met stiff opposition from employers who were convinced that the pace of work in a shorter day would remain the same if not worse than in a longer day. In December 1918, railroad employer Lord Bessborough claimed that an eight-hour day would "wipe out all margin of profit" and textile employers denied that short hours could recover production standards without the addition of expensive new machinery. Despite the appeals of the one-break system and shift work, management feared that workers would resist these innovations as disruptive to family life. Moreover, even Minister of Labour Robert Horne, as late as January 1919, opposed a general workday. Although he accepted the notion of linking worktime to fatigue, Horne argued that hours should be set according to the "nature and conditions of work" and not standardized at eight hours as a social entitlement. He favored no more than collective bargaining to bring a reduction of worktime—not legislation.[74]

In January 1919, French labor inspectors reported only modest revision of prewar hostility to shorter hours among employers. Whereas the idea of a *semaine anglaise* for women and youth was widely accepted, the eight-hour day was not. Although these labor inspectors had embraced the rhetoric of the conservation of "human capital," traditional fears of mass leisure and the ideology of *liberté du travail* still prevailed. The increasing importance of France's "competitive position" played a predominant role in inspectors' skepticism regarding an eight-hour standard. In addition, small businesses continued to reject any efforts to compress worktime as threats to their labor-intensive businesses.[75]

The ideology of industrial science and the reform network went far toward legitimizing the social and economic utility of a short workday. Yet the principle of the *trois huits,* as labor standard and a right of citizenship, was far from being established. The impetus for a successful movement would come from the war itself. Mass discontent emerged among workers and returning veterans who sought a release from the fatigue of the war factories and expected that real change would be the reward for their four years of sacrifice.

6

Labor Insurgency, International Reform, and the Origins of the Eight-Hour Day, 1917–1924

The "three eights," the equal distribution of the day between work, rest, and leisure, had been a slogan for a generation of May Days since 1890. It became a reality for many only with the eight-hour movements of 1917–1919. While Lenin's dream of world revolution failed, the eight-hour day swept across Europe as governments and employers conceded this major reform to exhausted and sometimes militant people.

The movement for the eight-hour day spanned the prewar and postwar periods. It was an expression of a growing popular desire for time liberated from work and available for new leisure opportunities and emerging family-centered values. Its radical demand for a reduction from a nine-, ten-, or even twelve-hour workday challenged, as could no wage increase, the economic and cultural status quo. Not only had the eight-hour day been a symbol of the Second International, but it had been a transnational goal of labor and reformers in a developing world economy where competition blocked improvements in the labor standard at the national level.

The eight-hour day was also a linchpin in a broad economic and social program: it promised not only to reduce unemployment and raise wages, but also to rationalize and intensify production, and to rejuvenate family and cultural life. It was to create a new social economy of time. Moreover, these objectives bridged class lines, drawing both the support of organized labor and a network of professional reformers. A loose interclass coalition emerged briefly in 1919, winning in principle an international eight-hour day while other reforms and revolutionary goals failed.

Labor and social historians of the prewar generation, however, have largely ignored the hours issue, relegating it to the minor status of a wage-related matter or seeing it as a diversion from revolutionary projects.[1] Yet the goal of reduced worktime was more than an economic issue. The eight-hour movement expressed a new leisure ethic—the desire for regular continuous blocks of time free from the work environment. Further, employers traditionally resisted worktime reductions much more intensely than wage increases. The British engineers' strike of 1897 and even more the French general strike of May 1906 for the eight-hour day appeared only at the apogee of union expansion; yet unbending employer opposition guaranteed that they achieved little. The eight-hour day was a radical objective that could be won widely only at the national level and, without a revolutionary upheaval, only with the assistance of well-placed political mediators.[2] Most of all, it required the context of both an international insurgency and a political network—a period of social discontinuity and restructuring. Ultimately, the significance of the eight-hour day became clear only after World War I when these conditions emerged.

Thus, an insurgency that spread across Europe between 1917 and 1920 issued an eight-hour day as its first and most permanent fruit. Although this reform played an important role in the Versailles Treaty and became a goal of the International Labor Organization, social historians of the postwar period have fixed their attention on the insurgency. While this emphasis has helped to explain the origins of the split of the European Left, it also has obscured the interaction between insurgency and reformism in the coming of the eight-hour day.[3] A neglect of politics—both at the national and international level—has left social history without an explanation of how these socially significant reforms were won.

International historians, traditionally focusing on the postwar balance of power and ideology, and more recently on the economic consequences of the war, have neglected this attempt to create a national and, indeed, international labor standard based on the eight-hour day. Of course, postwar reformism centered also on questions of national planning, workers' control, and nationalization—all products of wartime mobilization. Yet the hours question became a particularly sensitive barometer of the power of labor after 1918; it played a central role in the ongoing struggle between advocates of reform and restoration, between proponents of international economic "disarmament" and nationalist market competition.[4]

This chapter analyzes the coming of the eight-hour day (or the forty-eight-hour week) to Britain and France in 1919. It explains how contrasting political structures and labor relations systems produced differing paths to this new leisure standard in these two nations; it illustrates the continuing impact of national institutional and cultural factors on an important trend in industrial societies. Yet even more, this chapter analyzes how the postwar period opened up a unique opportunity for an international labor standard—a goal that has eluded and, in fact, has been largely abandoned by twentieth-century reformers after the mid-1920s. The debates over the eight-hour day crystallized a new discourse for both labor and management and helped to set the terms of the modern social contest.

War, Insurgency, and Reform

In the six months after the armistice, the demand for the eight-hour day became irresistible. In Britain, from December 1918 to March 1919, major industries rapidly conceded reductions in worktime, the government promised an eight-hour law, and a wave of strikes swept the land for even more advanced demands for free time. In France, on April 23, 1919, the new Parliament approved an enabling act for an eight-hour day and a six-day week. In contrast to the ten-hour law, which was debated from 1892 to 1904 before it was implemented and still excluded many men, this act was passed with extraordinary speed, taking merely eight days from Chamber debate to enactment, and it "only" excluded farmworkers.[5]

These dramatic reversals of a generation of business and government hostility to eight-hour reform were not merely rewards for sacrifices made during the war. As noted in chapter 5, officials in both France and Britain resisted the eight-hour trend. As late as July 1916, the allied unions at Leeds demanded no more than a postwar eight-hour day for men in continuous-process industries (e.g., metallurgy and chemicals).[6]

This breakthrough can only be explained in the context of insurgency and a reform coalition that emerged in the last two years of the war; in turn, these forces drew on a generation of campaigning for shorter labor time. Eight-hour agitation had hardly been shelved for the war. In Britain, a threatened strike of railroad workers forced the Board of Trade into promising, in August 1917, a "favourable attitude" toward the reduction of worktime after the war. And British engineering unions had merely postponed their demand for a forty-seven-hour week for the duration. As early as June 1918, unions as diverse as iron molders and textile workers sought negotiations for the eight-hour day. In July, miners proposed a six-hour day.[7] Moreover, in France the emerging militancy of women munitions workers produced strikes in 1917 that forced the government to concede the ten-hour day with a Saturday half-holiday (the *semaine anglaise*)—a demand that for a generation had animated women workers.[8]

In the fall of 1918, both the TUC and the CGT had raised the eight-hour banner for postwar social reconstruction. Appeals were clearly linked to prewar hours apologetics. On January 28, 1919, the French socialists submitted a bill for the eight-hour day for all employees. The socialist proposal recalled the old arguments that the Chamber of Deputies had so often heard from Jules Guesde and Edouard Vaillant before the war.[9] A reduced workday would alleviate unemployment (expected after the demobilization), diminish the psychological and physical costs of increasingly mechanized work, and insure more time for family life and self-education.[10]

Yet, by 1919 proponents of the eight-hour day focused primarily on political and efficiency themes. First, both labor movements stressed that increased leisure was a just reward for the "working masses" for their "sacrifices" during the war and a proper expression of a new postwar world "fit for heroes"—regardless of the immediate economic costs. A common workday, despite traditions of sharp differences in labor duration, was to be a social right. A second and even stronger theme was to relate short hours to economic innovation. British trade unionists stressed the economic payoff of a briefer, more efficient workday with lessened fatigue; the French emphasized that the eight-hour day would lead to a "better regulated and more intense production," insofar as employers were forced to compensate for reduced worktime by introducing more productive methods.[11] Both British fatigue science and French Saint-Simonianism were commonplace themes in prewar socialist and labor theory, even if they were not always embraced by trade unionists.[12] Third, the postwar short-hours movement could claim to be international. Although the eight-hour day had been a demand of the two Socialist Internationals, only in 1919 had the dream of international labor legislation become a possibility in that brief and dramatic restructuring of interstate relations.

These three appeals became the basis of a loose coalition encompassing not only the socialist and labor Left, but an important network of middle-class reformers in both countries. As described in chapter 5, the gap between labor and industrial reformers decreased in the generation before and during the war. In Britain, work efficiency experts gained significant influence over working hours through the Health of Munitions Workers Committee. They successfully promoted the ideas of the efficiency of a compressed workday, the one-break system, shift work, and the regular but regulated holiday. These investigators were concerned not only about output but were convinced that long fatiguing hours contributed to workers' unrest.[13] Important sectors of British industry—especially the engineering employers—had been prepared for a major reduction in hours during the war.[14] Finally, the Whitley Report of March 1917 was the culmination of years of effort by the British government to encourage collective bargaining as a means of setting industrywide labor standards. The Joint Industrial (or Whitley) Councils created a somewhat important instrument for postwar industrial hours agreements in less organized trades.[15]

In France, the war also created a loose coalition between organized labor and socially influential reformers. Advocates of coupling innovation with shorter hours embraced scientific management as a way of reducing hours while raising output and wages. The socialist head of the Munitions Ministry, Albert Thomas, encouraged the use of piece rates, mechanization, and factory reorganization. This dovetailed with the CGT's own idea (developed as early as 1916) that industrial innovation could pave the way for postwar social reforms. On November 7, 1918, the CGT leadership looked forward to the introduction of new technologies that would force management into consulting "our technical and administrative staff" who "will be ready to organize a new society" based on the "law of progress." To be sure, Thomas and his successor in 1917, Louis Loucheur, were far less daring than the British Ministry of Munitions in experimenting with short hours; still, after the war, they were leading advocates of reduced worktime as a necessary component of a package of industrial modernization in France.[16]

The integration of the CGT and the Left into the *Union Sacrée* government in August 1914 seemed to create the possibility of a new system of industrial relations patterned after the English. Yet, despite the creation of multiclass manpower commissions, factory delegates, and arbitration in the war factories, nothing like the British shop stewards or the Whitley Councils and works committees emerged in France. Thomas and other bureaucrats tended to deal directly with employers and workers' delegates rather than mixed committees (and then most often on terms favorable to employers). The legacy of weak trade union organization and relatively intransigent employers was an institutional corporatism that was far less developed in France than in Britain.[17]

Indeed, especially after the collapse of the *Union Sacrée* in September 1917, a substantial opposition to these tripartite bodies emerged in metal goods, railways, and construction led by Pierre Monatte, Gaston Monmousseau, and Raymond Pericat. By the spring of 1918 these *minoritaires* led antiwar strikes and, in emulation of Lenin's Bolsheviks, hoped to smash the French state and create soviets out of French unions. Responding to the Bolshevik challenge, an official of the metalworkers, Alphonse Merrheim, denounced "catastrophic" political revolution. Whereas Bolshevism was "incomplete," merely a destruction of the bourgeois state, Merrheim proposed an "economic revolution." It would emerge from a new type of reformism involving labor's direct participation in economic planning, a new and popular form of corporatism. The sharp division on the Left over postwar strategy not only intensified the ideological debate but weakened the bargaining position of French labor. The result was that the movement for worktime reductions in France focused on the state rather than on the negotiating table; moreover, the dependence of labor reformers on middle-class political allies was more pronounced than in Britain.[18]

The International Eight-Hour Day

Still no coalition would have been possible without the international crisis of 1917–1920. What had happened between the modest demands of the Leeds Conference in July 1916 and January 1919 was an international movement for the eight-hour day. Eighthour proclamations began in the Bolshevik Revolution of 1917 and then spread in 1918 to Finland and Norway, and to Germany in the wake of the November Revolution. By mid-December, the movement then passed to the new states of Poland, Czechoslovakia, and Austria.

From the revolutionary regimes of eastern and central Europe, it spread to Switzerland, where up to four hundred thousand struck for the eight-hour day in December 1918. In February the movement reached to Italy in a wave of shutdowns that first affected the metals industry and then spread to textiles, chemicals, and even agriculture. This insurgency produced eight-hour laws in Spain, Portugal, and Switzerland by June and in the Netherlands and Sweden by November 1919.[19] That workers in so many differing regions used this unique opportunity for reform to reduce working hours is powerful evidence of the near universality of the appeal of increased leisure.

International pressure from below for reduced worktime was paralleled by hopes that the eight-hour day would become international law. Committed to this goal was a transnational network of reformers often rather erroneously labeled "Wilsonians." Many in these group were linked to the IALL. Key British actors were George Barnes, a moderate former leader of the Amalgamated Society of Engineers (ASE) and active in the eight-hour movement since 1897, and Malcolm Delevigne, a Home Office bureaucrat and frequent delegate to international labor legislation conferences.[20] In 1919, important French leaders were Justin Godart, a radical deputy and chairman of the Chamber's Labor Commission, and Albert Thomas, from 1919 director of the new International Labor Office in Geneva (ILO). As an alternative to cutthroat competition and class conflict, this group advocated international and interclass cooperation. The association had long supported worktime reductions (although, only in 1919, the universal eight-hour day). Increasingly this group shared the perspectives of the reformist wing of the Second International, whose program they largely adopted.[21]

This reformist network cooperated to incorporate this program in the peace treaty. George Barnes declared that the war had been a "great leveler," that the advanced countries had now to establish an "international standard" for labor because "capital has no country." In particular, the labor standards of poor countries must be raised: "to safeguard Dundee [we must] raise Calcutta." Justin Godart wrote in more idealistic terms: because the World War "was a war of peoples, not of the mercenary," the treaty, "in place of the classic articles devoted to the prerogatives of dynasties or of the alliances of kings," would have to be "concerned with human interests." A treaty that included labor statutes not only would produce a more lasting peace, but would assure an international labor standard by eliminating competitive pressures.[22] This linkage between national labor reform and the creation of an international labor standard won French parliamentary recognition. On November 26, 1918, Godart gained Chamber support for negotiations on a series of international conventions, which included worktime reductions.[23]

The scheme for an industrial peace treaty was not isolated to the liberal-left establishment. On January 25, 1919, Georges Clemenceau persuaded the Preliminary Peace Conference to create a Commission for International Labor Legislation. This commission provided an alternative to the appeal of Bolshevism and the socialist's Berne Congress for the attention of European labor. It was a perfect expression of the internationalism and corporatism of the IALL: American labor leader Samuel Gompers, who represented President Wilson, was its chairman, and the CGT's Léon Jouhaux served as "technical assistant" to businessman and minister Louis Loucheur. British interests were represented by Barnes and Delevigne.

The Commission for International Labor Legislation embraced a moderate British proposal of creating a permanent international labor office that, through annual international labor conferences composed of tripartite national delegations, would write international labor conventions. Agreeing that international action was needed in the face of "the nervousness of workers' opinion," the commission recommended on March 19 that an "Eight-Hour Convention" be drafted in Washington in October at the first International Labour Conference. These ideas were enshrined in the Peace of 1919 (part XIII): "peace can be founded only on the base of social justice," which in part required the "application of the principle of the eight-hour day or 48-hour week." Despite this rather ambiguous commitment, workers and even employers believed that the eight-hour day had international legal sanction in the spring of 1919.[24]

British Unions and the Concession of Time

Both international insurgency and diplomacy were necessary backdrops to the eight-hour day in Britain and France. With the peace came an explosion of trade union negotiation for increased leisure. British union officials in heavy industry negotiated at the national level for an immediate forty-seven- or forty-eight-hour week. Still long before the armistice, British militants in coal mining and engineering were mobilizing for workweeks below the forty-eight-hour level.[25]

By February 2, 1919, because of rapid demobilization, the Ministry of Labour warned the War Cabinet of the threat of unemployment. As early as December 1918, in response to fears of layoffs, radical shop stewards in munitions works near Newcastle, Coventry, and Glasgow agitated for forty-four-, forty-, and even thirty-six-hour workweeks. Even Robert Horne, a stern Tory minister of labor, recognized that "the question of working hours" had become "acute and pressing and that workers were unwilling to submit to long negotiations after four and one half years of hard routine." Horne recognized that the postwar labor unrest was different from the past: not only had union officials lost control over some of the rank and file, but a tight labor market and expectation of government intervention on the workers' side might well require "general reform." Moreover, the government generally accepted the equity of workers' claims for decreased worktime. As Lloyd George admitted one week after the armistice: "It is not a question of whether the men can stand the strain of a longer day, but that the working class is entitled to the same sort of leisure as the middle class."[26]

The most powerful British unions were quick to lay claim to that leisure. The National Union of Railwaymen redeemed the government's pledge of shorter hours on December 6, 1918, in an agreement with the Board of Trade. The owners were not even a part of the negotiations. The engineers and related unions met with the Engineering and Shipbuilding employers in September and, although union leaders were expected to insist on a forty-four-hour week, they settled on November 31 for a forty-seven-hour week. These agreements opened up the sluices for a gush of worktime agitation that played a dominant role in the unsettled season following the war. While major industries, especially coal mining and dockyards negotiated for a workweek less than forty-eight hours, a series of unauthorized local strikes burst out in January and early February.[27]

Workers in engineering and shipbuilding were the most militant. One-third of the engineers had voted against the forty-seven-hour "sellout." Wildcat strikes broke out in response to employer interpretations of the national hours agreements. Although most of these grievances were quickly resolved, the union leadership was forced to return to the bargaining table with the demand for a forty-four-hour week.[28]

Even more dramatic were the Glasgow and Belfast strikes of late January. The forty-hour movement had been brewing on the Clyde since the fall of 1917. Indeed, the forty-hour goal was the moderate position accepted by the institutional Left. Some engineering shop stewards had pressed for thirty-five or even thirty hours. Hoping to undercut these advanced demands, an amalgamated committee in Glasgow voted narrowly for a strike for January 27.[29] This job action was strongest among munitions engineers and shipbuilders, but it also gained support among municipal workers. Although a demonstration on January 29 produced clashes between police and strikers, Andrew Bonar-Law, a leading Conservative Cabinet member, refused to talk to a delegation from Glasgow. The strike died out within two weeks after dockworkers refused to join and efforts to link up with militant ASE members and electrical workers in London had failed.[30]

These bursts of rank-and-file militancy hardly died in February. They continued sporadically through the summer of 1919. It is likely that they forced government officials to make rapid and largely favorable settlements with coal miners and dockworkers. Moreover, although the Glasgow municipal "general" strike failed miserably, the more effective organizational model of the Triple Alliance did not. Composed of coal miners, railwaymen, and unions representing transport and dockworkers, the Triple Alliance threatened massive industrial action. In March this powerful coalition won favorable government intervention: the railwaymen finally obtained a complex forty-eight-hour agreement. The dockers and other transport workers went further and won a forty-four-hour week of "effective" work. The miners had demanded a six-hour day. After threatening a strike, the government, which still controlled the mines, awarded them a seven-hour day based on a hastily convened Coal Mines (Sankey) Commission.[31]

These victories in the key sectors of heavy industry prompted a diverse movement for worktime reductions elsewhere. As railworker official J. N. Clynes pointed out, "we could not detach any one great trade from the rest of the business." The example of the engineers in machine shops of the textile industry and in iron and steel mills was followed by others in these works. Some campaigns grew out of prewar hours struggles: for example, blast-furnace men won a fifty-six-hour week—for many, a reduction from a twelve-hour day, seventy-two-hour workweek. Construction workers gradually gained a forty-four-hour workweek while textile workers settled on a forty-eight-hour week.[32] Even the poorly organized bakers and retail clerks demanded shorter hours. In the spring the Joint Industrial Councils settled mostly on the forty-eight-hour standard in numerous small trades.[33]

The eight-hour day had been won in Britain largely through crisis bargaining activated by an emboldened trade union movement and supported by the state. Behind both forces stood the threat of industrial action. In the end, Parliament and national politics played only a minor role. On February 4, 1919, the Federation of British Industry called for a joint conference of industry and organized labor to deal with the "grave conditions of industrial unrest." In response, on February 27 key representatives of organized business and labor met in an industrial conference.[34] In April, the conference drafted a forty-eight-hour bill at the very time when the French were preparing similar legislation. The purpose was to generalize the worktime reductions gained by the most powerful unions. Only domestic workers, seamen, and later farmworkers were to be exempt. The liberal opposition to regulating adult male worktime and setting a national hours standard appeared broken.[35]

Yet neither politicians nor apparently organized labor showed much inclination to rush an act through Parliament. Outside of complaints from the weak farmworkers' unions and seamen, organized labor scarcely noticed the bill in 1919. Voluntary Whitley committees, trade boards, and, most often, national negotiation committees achieved a basic forty-eight-hour standard without legislation. The result was an "industrial devolution." Parliamentary action could only play the role of guaranteeing the new hours standard and of assuring its generalization to the weakest, least organized trades. In 1919, at least, organized workers apparently felt strong enough not to insist on this guarantee.[36]

Insurgency and Politics: The French Eight-Hour Victory

In France, the relationship between insurgency, organized trades, and politics was quite different. The French produced few strikes for worktime reductions in the first quarter of 1919. Indeed, even though the French were slow to show signs of an hours movement, this was doubtless the result of much weaker unions and a more repressive war economy than disinterest in the international movement. Still, by March 1919 French metalworkers, dockers, miners, and textile workers had demanded an eight-hour day. An alarmed Ministry of Interior reported CGT growth especially in the white-collar sectors. Layoffs in war industries had stimulated eight-hour agitation. Moreover "the fever of enjoyment and pleasure" often expressed in a "frenetic epidemic of dancing" could not be contained after more than four years of sacrifice. A reduced workday surely had an enormous appeal in 1919. Indeed, police favored increased leisure as a means of "relaxing instincts too long suppressed."[37]

The CGT leadership eagerly exploited this situation. In early March, Jouhaux warned that "France is now on a volcano" and that he "declined all responsibility," if, by May Day, the Parliament had not voted for an eight-hour bill. As early as November 24, 1918, a CGT mass meeting called for an eight-hour day for all workers—just days after the revolutionary regime in Germany had conceded this demand. The eight-hour day headed the list of reforms in the CGT Minimum Program of December 15 and in January 1919 Jouhaux won from the government a vague promise for worktime legislation.[38]

Despite the CGT's threats of mass action, the reformist leaders were not sanguine that a political strike for the eight-hour day would succeed and were, of course, afraid of unleashing the Bolshevik bogey on themselves.[39] They supplemented the threat of insurgency with the Interfederal Cartel, probably inspired by the British Triple Alliance. In March, the CGT formed this cartel from its strongest unions (transport, maritime, mines, metal, and construction) in order to coordinate bargaining for the eight-hour day and to enforce a May 1 deadline. After ten days of negotiation, the metalworkers won a national contract on April 17. In the face of strike threats for May Day and the growing movement for a forty-four-hour week, employers conceded a workday of eight hours (forty-eight hours per week). Similar negotiations in the rail and construction industries produced contracts by the first week of May.[40] In this context, the generalized threat of an unleashed insurgency and the rallying around the workers' May Pole were effective weapons to mobilize the traditionally languid Parliament to take action.

The CGT leadership also found temporary allies in the government, which was determined to contain labor militancy. In January 1919, Georges Clemenceau, famous for breaking the 1906 eight-hour strikes, asked Louis Loucheur to convene what was significantly called the Interministerial Commission on International Labor Treaties to draft an hours law. After meeting merely five times between March 15 and April 7, the commission of notables from Parliament, labor, and management submitted a bill to the Chamber.[41]

Business representatives on the Loucheur Commission were often unwilling participants. They argued in a "minority report" that if an eight-hour day became law, production would decrease, labor shortages would emerge, and transportation and other costs would rise. It "will change victory into defeat," placing France in a disadvantageous market position.[42]

Despite business opposition, Loucheur informed his friends in management that "in this difficult hour no party could decline all responsibility." Even Louis Guerin, the hard-line representative of French textiles, recognized that this was "not the time to be opposed in principle to the progressive reduction of the workday" and that "if the majority of states adopt the principle of the eight-hour day . . . in spite of [our] apprehensions, France cannot oppose it." Both the urgency of mounting militancy and the legitimacy of the eight-hour day in the international legal arena forced employers to accept a law.[43]

Defenders of the eight-hour bill, like Godart and Thomas, argued that the CGT had accepted mechanization as the price of reduced hours; an international eight-hour standard was inevitable; and this new standard would prove to the soldiers that "something had changed."[44] The law was a compromise, incorporating both the demands of the CGT (especially for no cut in pay as a direct result of worktime reductions) and the pleading of management for exemptions, delays, and flexibility in the use of overtime. In fact, it was merely an enabling act: hours reductions became legal only after decrees were promulgated for each industry in a complex and slow process.[45]

The law's authors hoped that this legislation would encourage the French to adopt English-style collective bargaining. Until early June, all went well as national eight-hour contracts were signed in the metal, railroad, textiles, printing, leather, shoe, and construction industries. Collective bargaining even yielded reduced hours for some retail clerks (typically, nine-hour days) and for restaurant workers (twelve to fourteen hours of "presence" at work). Largely because of the eight-hour law, 1919 was an unprecedented year for the collective contract. Some 557 were signed (as compared with the prewar high of 252 in 1910); 331 of these included worktime reductions.[46]

The Labor Ministry also slowly promulgated hours decrees after obtaining advice from unions and employer associations. These decrees often simply mirrored collective contracts. Where unions were weak, decrees were produced from "mixed committees" of employers and workers. All decrees allowed exemptions for specialists, modified the eight-hour rule to accommodate the *semaine anglaise,* and approved annual overtime quotas (usually between 60 and 150 hours).[47] To be sure, in the decade that followed labor inspectors were generally rather conservative in issuing citations and were unsympathetic with unions that refused to accept overtime provisions. Still they seemed to enforce the decrees, investigating complaints—even those published in the communist *l'Humanité*—and they often relied on unions to "signal" infractions of the law.[48]

The eight-hour law in France was as much a substitute for collective bargaining as a supplement to it. In Britain, the existence of powerful unions led to relatively successful national bargaining and government mediation to enforce a broad-based hours standard. In France, a similar end was reached when a threatened insurgency provoked parliamentary initiatives for a decree system.

The result in both countries was a dramatic reduction of worktime, a clear concession to labor. Not only did the "high politics" of peacemaking and loose coalitions of labor and well-placed reformers play roles, so also did militant collective bargaining and the threat of an insurgency unleashed by the example of the Russian Revolution. This fortuitous cluster of forces prevailed over the normal inertia. This opening for change followed some of the patterns of similar crises in 1847–1848, 1936–1938, and 1945–1947, which also produced reforms. The pressure for increased leisure, a quest that had been contained for a generation, became irresistible in the international conjuncture of 1919. Yet this configuration began to shift after June 1919 toward the employers' advantage when labor insurgency and unity abated and when the prospect for an international labor standard faded.

The Closure, July 1919–1920

In both Britain and France, attempts to consolidate the downward push of worktime in March and April 1919 did not end the rank-and-file movements for short hours. Militant opposition to the compromises made by union officials as the price for reduced hours continued to flare up. Yet by the end of the summer the hours movement had faded and employers were able to retake the offensive.

Engineering union leaders in Britain were embarrassed by the unwillingness of their members to abandon the forty-four-hour week in January 1919. Nevertheless, from April through July British engineering locals pressed for an eight-hour weekday with four hours of work on Saturday morning. Under the forty-seven-hour agreement, the weekday stint would actually be eight and a half hours (because of the Saturday half-holiday). Numerous districts refused overtime, a traditional tactic of forcing action in bargaining. Moreover, the forty-four-hour idea spread to numerous other trades; proponents included shipyard workers, tugboatmen, bricklayers, and cabinetmakers. In May, in Sheffield, it became a municipal movement and won the support of a majority of trades. More diverse were the protests against new work rules imposed to "compensate" for reduced worktime. Dockers in Liverpool refused to unload liquors after management eliminated their traditional drinking breaks. Factory workers protested the elimination of the breakfast break and the afternoon tea.[49]

By July and August, however, these expressions of worktime militancy had been eclipsed by national-level bargaining. In July, the cotton textile trades finally agreed to a forty-eight-hour settlement; and the engineering unions abandoned for a second time their goal of a forty-four-hour week after the engineering employers refused to negotiate other issues until the unions capitulated on hours.[50]

Why did the forty-four-hour movement fail? In many cases, local unions lacked the support of their national federations who held the real power. Employers had little reason to negotiate with the local union and owners often were forbidden to do so by their trade organizations. Moderate union officials distrusted shop steward radicals in much the same way as the French *majoritaires* feared the radical *minoritaires*. The forty-four-hour movement collapsed along with the shop steward cause. Moreover the overtime embargo had little effect because of the postwar slackening of demand. Finally, the trade union leadership was clearly skeptical that British industry could remain competitive against other nations whose workweeks extended to forty-eight hours or more.[51] After July few new reductions took place, leaving minor trades and farmworkers out of the new world of the short hours.[52]

In France, late spring brought a similar hope of a broader change but by summer the hours movement had also collapsed. May Day did not, as had been feared, unleash a general strike. Rather it was a broad and largely peaceful celebration. In all major cities and industrial regions, participation was widespread: rallies, sometimes punctuated with pro-Soviet speeches, were mixed in the holiday atmosphere of dancing and family picnics—surely a celebration of the new leisure.[53] Yet, in May and June the eight-hour law did not, as expected, quiet labor militancy. At the same time, the law revealed divisions that would stall the insurgency by July.

Militant Parisian clothing, shoe, and bank workers struck in May for the most advanced aim, the forty-four-hour week (an eight-hour day with the *semaine anglaise*). They were rapidly defeated. Yet construction workers in Paris demanded and won (temporarily) a uniform eight-hour day throughout the workyear, not the seasonally adjusted workday desired by employers. Strikes broke out in the departments both for an immediate eight-hour day and to force employers to raise pay to compensate for reduced worktime. Even without a national contract, some employers were obliged to reduce hours and, in August, even lowly road repair crews demanded less worktime. By June 2, Paris retailers also felt pressure from the leisure movement and organized (as they had in 1906) to prevent Sunday shop closings, which they believed (incorrectly) that unions would soon win.[54]

The Interfederal Cartel also continued its work. Miners struck on June 16 to defend an eight-hour bill opposed by the Senate. The threat of a sympathy strike from the maritime union led the Senate on June 24 to give in. Fears of similar interfederal action produced an eight-hour law for commercial sailors soon thereafter.[55]

Yet CGT leaders were unable either to control the insurgency or to maintain syndicalist unity. For example, in June, against the will of the Metalworkers' Federation, the Seine metalworkers union struck for a forty-four-hour week and a raise in piece rates. Quickly, however, the issue of hours was lost as politics dominated debates, and even the Parisian leadership could not hold the reins. By June 25, while workers drifted back to the factory, the Interfederal Cartel refused to support a sympathy strike. The Parisian movement disintegrated into recriminations between the leadership, compromised by its cooperation with the war effort, and the *minoritaire* opposition, with its pro-Soviet tendencies. On this reef, the Interfederal Cartel broke apart in July.[56]

On July 17, *minoritaires* pushed the CGT leadership into a one-day political strike for amnesty for political prisoners and for a more rapid demobilization of soldiers, thus sidetracking the still-unfinished business of implementing the eight-hour day. When it became obvious that the strike lacked support, the CGT canceled the job action. Reformist leader Francis Millon admitted that "fears of the new recruits" led to this failure. Perhaps too, as a Railway union official suggested, the reduced workday may have satisfied many workers.[57]

The CGT's ability to press for negotiated worktime reductions was exhausted by the end of July. Although the strikes of April and May 1920 were significant, they accomplished nothing positive; rather they confirmed the communist-reformist split. Winning the eight-hour law in 1919 was one of the few achievements of the union movement in the postwar period.[58]

When the insurgency that forced the eight-hour day on the employers had subsided, the internationalism that had supported the reduced workday itself was weakened. It was in this context that the long-awaited Washington Conference of the International Labor Organization was convened in November 1919. The meeting was compromised from the start with the refusal of the United States to participate. Barnes was shocked by the often hostile attitude of conservative American Senators who viewed delegates as "Bolshevik agents." And Jouhaux reported that "Americans only understand force and violence" in their rejection of the concept of international labor legislation.[59]

Although the conference was officially an outgrowth of the Versailles Treaty, the absence of the United States, the leading economic power, significantly reduced the chances of international labor legislation. Employer representatives declared that the eight-hour day was unworkable and insisted on a minimum of three hundred hours of annual overtime (in effect a nine-hour day). At the same time, labor delegates demanded an eight-hour day and claimed no need for overtime beyond a five-year period of seventy-five hours per year. Developing countries, where workweeks often reached seventy or more hours, argued that a forty-eight-hour standard was unrealistic. The result was a convention that was a study in moderation: it was to be applied only to transportation and industry, not commerce or agriculture. The convention tolerated flexible workweeks (although insisting on a nine-hour daily maximum). Developing industrial countries, including India and Japan as well as several new eastern European countries, were allowed longer workweeks, at least for a transition period. Still, even though national delegations voted eighty-three to two in favor of the convention, there was no certainty that governments would ratify it.[60]

Organized efforts to overturn the eight-hour victories of the spring of 1919 appeared soon after the signing of the Washington Hours Convention. Although the British delegation, headed by George Barnes and Tom Shaw, had been in large part responsible for the moderation of the convention, the British government delayed ratification. Only on July 26, 1921 (just before the eighteen-month grace period for ratification was to expire) did the British cabinet inform the ILO that the convention was too rigid to earn its approval. This refusal signaled other nations to reject the convention. By the end of 1921, only Rumania, Greece, and Czechoslovakia had ratified it.[61]

While union insurgency and hopes of an international hours standard waned, so did the promise of a universal eight-hour day in Britain and France. By the fall of 1919, reduced demand for industrial labor had limited the ability of British unions to enforce an overtime embargo as a means of work sharing. While the TUC formally advocated a forty-four-hour week to reduce unemployment, wage cuts forced jobholders to seek overtime to make ends meet. The immediate postwar ideal of reduced worktime began to lose appeal as depression placed many on a forty-hour week with corresponding pay cuts. Increasingly the TUC and Labour party stressed higher unemployment benefits and public works as the solution to rising jobless rates.[62]

The renewed power of British management became obvious. By June 1920 the National Wage Board acceded to the demands of employers by giving the railways a nine-hour shift (with one-hour overtime). In the building trades, an arbitration award of August 1923 largely conceded the employer position. In textiles, steel, and engineering, management continued to raise the hours question in bargaining.[63]

British employers were even more successful in blocking the spread of the eight-hour day. In the summer of 1919, British agriculture balked at applying the forty-eight-hour standard. In early 1920 maritime interests succeeded in opposing an eight-hour watch on British ships and blocked a Genoa Convention on seaman's hours. After repeated lobbying by business in 1920, the government abandoned its eight-hour bill. Only 75 percent of British workers had forty-eight hours by 1922.[64]

Nevertheless, there were few successful reversals of the gains of early 1919. The issue of hours may have been used merely as a bargaining chip by some employers for winning wage reductions. Indeed, wage decreases rather than worktime increases were common results of negotiations. The British system of unregulated overtime, limited only by the cost of the premium rate, usually provided a flexible schedule that accommodated commercial rush work. Of course, the protracted depression in major prewar industries (shipbuilding, engineering, mining, and textiles especially) muted the need of longer hours.

The central point remains that despite the advances toward a universal workweek in Britain in 1919, the reversals of the postwar depression confined the new standard to the more stable and unionized trades. The traditional arguments against a legal eight hours and in favor of an industry-determined variable workweek prevailed in commerce, agriculture, and maritime sectors.

Organized reaction to the short-hours movement of 1919 was even stronger in France. In the metal industry, employers frequently ignored the eight-hour contract that had been signed by their representatives in April. Conflicts over relay and split shifts, overtime, and pay delayed hours decrees in the metal industries until August 1920. This conflict was replayed in many major industries.[65]

The difficulties of retail clerks, especially in small towns, were even greater. A decree in early 1921 applied the eight-hour day only to shops in towns larger than one hundred thousand residents and excluded small stores. The regulation of the French petty bourgeoisie was as difficult in the 1920s as it had been before the war.[66]

The process of implementing the eight-hour day was extremely slow. By the end of 1920, only 27 percent of the eligible workers were covered by a decree, largely because of the snail's-pace progress in commerce, food processing, and transportation. And employers utilized legal exemptions in the decree laws.[67] The law that had in 1919 helped to consolidate a shorter workday was by 1920 used to frustrate and even reverse that process.

Discontinuity and Reform: A Comparison of France and Britain

A conjuncture of factors—both national and international, institutional and "discontinuous"—created this unique reallocation of personal time in industrial Europe after World War I. That opportunity was very brief, lasting scarcely more than six months. It was followed by a closure when that extraordinary configuration collapsed. The rapid disintegration of labor militancy in the summer of 1919 was the consequence of the inability of unions to maintain an organizational advantage in conditions of a weakening labor market. Despite the innovations of the Triple Alliance and Interfederal Cartel, that cohesion was quickly dashed over questions of strategy. In any case electoral defeats in both countries immediately after the war guaranteed that the balance of political power would ultimately shift toward deregulation. Dreams of national planning, workers' control, and nationalization collapsed at the same time as did hopes for more advanced reductions of working hours. With the decline of labor militancy, neither reformist union officials nor middle-class political allies at home or around the ILO were capable of sustaining the momentum.

Although incomplete and under repeated attack by the summer of

1919, the eight-hour day had still become an international standard. What made 1919 unique was that the pent-up demand for less work had exploded so widely across occupational boundaries and national frontiers. Yet the practical settlements took place within distinct national sociopolitical structures. The hours question was resolved in Britain through a cluster of nationwide collective bargaining agreements, whereas in France it was guided by legislation and decree law. In Britain, the eight-hour day had a less radical impact on the economy, and employers were better prepared to adapt to it than in France. Business resistance was therefore sporadic and largely isolated to problem industries like mining. Moreover, immediately after the war, the British labor movement enjoyed not only larger numbers than the French (8.5 million members compared with merely 2 million in France), but the British unions were often relatively well-oiled machines, at least the match of nationally organized employer groups in heavy industry.[68]

The radicalism of the British shop stewards was helpful in serving as a wedge to hasten negotiations, especially when they involved state-union participants. Cluster bargaining was facilitated by a government bureaucracy that was willing to present a shorter workweek to employers as a fait accompli before government-controlled industries were returned to private hands. Thus, the government was able to avoid the industrial disruptions that would have been likely if concessions had been delayed. Moreover, British labor largely rejected direct action, pinning its hopes on electoral victory of the Labour party. A formal national hours settlement was not required; it would have only confirmed, guaranteed, extended, and perhaps contained the terms of negotiated settlements. Ultimately the collective bargaining system was capable of restraining the advanced worktime goals of the labor insurgency (e.g., in textiles and especially engineering) without significant state intervention.

In France, the course of action went largely in the other direction—from the top down. This was not merely still another manifestation of the fabled *etatisme* of the French or the inability of contesting groups to negotiate directly in French society.[69] Rather it was a product of the relatively weak and divided character of French unions, the equally fragmented nature of national employer organizations, and surely the fact that an eight-hour day had a much greater immediate economic impact on the firm in France than it did in Britain. This only enhanced the distance between employer and worker, which impeded any solution other than on the national political level. Organized French labor—weak and divided on the shop floor—was obliged to lean on parliamentary mediators, to invoke the prospect of open-ended industrial action, and thus to provoke "emergency" legislation. The April 1919 law not only empowered the state to take direct action and to precipitate hours negotiations but, through its decree powers, to guarantee a new hours standard. Thus, the decree-deliberating process and the ongoing debate about the eight-hour law became in France the foci of the struggle over worktime. It was through the flexibility of the state's decree laws that employers sought to contain the hours movement and, by the end of 1919, to begin to reverse it.

The coming of the eight-hour day largely confirms conventional views of the contrast between British and French industrial relations—the emerging voluntarist bargaining system of the British as opposed to the discontinuous state-mediated pattern of reform of the French. Yet this contrast can easily be exaggerated. Both reforms required state intervention. In Britain, coal, railroad, and engineering hours agreements involved government mediation. And even if the Whitley Councils were to be "voluntary," the trade boards for smaller, less organized industries involved professional leadership from the Ministry of Labour. Yet both nations also required business-labor bargaining. The French eight-hour law only enabled ministerial decrees, which were often based on the written advice of trade organizations and even were patterned on contracts. If the British method produced a wider impact in the short run, the French government was surprisingly persistent in carrying out the law by gradually extending worktime decrees to provincial centers and commercial sectors. By the end of the 1920s the hours standards in both countries were comparable.

The eight-hour day was perhaps the key social reform won after World War I. It cannot be simply explained by an econometric model, or by long-term social trends. Rather its proximate cause was an international political crisis facilitated by a fragile coalition of labor and reformers in the face of business opposition. Ultimately it was the fruit of a long campaign for a new distribution of work and leisure. Although industrialization may have created the opportunity for liberating time from labor, its realization was essentially political. Indeed the eight-hour day played a key role in the ideological contest in the 1920s. It would help shape the twentieth-century debate about the relationship between reform and economic growth.

7

Worktime, Growth, and an International Labor Standard

The movement for an eight-hour day went far beyond the issue of how much time could be bought and sold. It challenged the traditional wisdom that social reforms must be subordinated to economic growth and that international competition must set the labor standard. Its promise was prosperity driven by a more efficient use of time and a rising labor standard based on international cooperation. These ideals met bitter resistance and suffered major disappointments in the 1920s.

From the vantage point of the late twentieth century, and particularly given the recent resurgence of economic liberalism, it is tempting to see these ideas as largely chimeras. Rather than a threat to the status quo, many might also argue that the eight-hour day was but a phase in economic modernization and corporatism. According to this view, workers abandoned control and participation in workplace decisions to a rising managerial technocracy in exchange for shorter working hours and increased consumption. Labor's role in this "reform coalition" could be seen as a junior partnership with progressive business in the creation of "corporate capitalism." A similar perspective is that the eight-hour day ushered in an era of more intense and less meaningful work, which was compensated by the "freedom" to participate in the manipulated world of mass consumption.

These common themes of modernization, corporatism, and consumerism are not, however, particularly helpful in understanding the goals, contests, achievements, and failures of the eight-hour reformers. Moreover, they do no justice to either the motives or experiences of workers in this first decade of the modern worktime standard.[1]

This chapter will attempt to clarify the fate of the "three-eights" in this critical period. More important, it will place this reform in the broader context of an emerging ideological contest within twentieth-century industrial democracies.

Ideology in Context, 1919

Those who advocated liberating time from work were obliged to speak the language of political economy. An apologetic that had emerged a generation earlier was refined in a bargaining, advocating process. The subsequent doctrine was broad enough to bridge class cleavages and capable of claiming the hegemonic position of representing the "national interest."

The overriding theme was that a firm commitment to technical efficiency and, even more, to intense work was a necessary concomitant to any reduction in the workday. In March 1919, Jouhaux went so far as to exclaim, "it is simply necessary to choose between an intense effort for eight hours or a limited effort for ten hours. . . . We must combat the spirit of routine among employers but also among workers." This view was confirmed at the bargaining table when French metalworkers agreed to cooperate in mechanization; they even accepted no increase in piece rates with shorter hours and expected workers to increase output proportionally to worktime reductions.[2]

British union leaders made similar claims. J. B. Brownlie of the engineers union, for example, assured employers that more "science" and "new methods" would overcome any loss of output due to worktime reductions. Others borrowed from work scientists their claim that an eight-hour day with the one-break system was the equivalent of a nine-hour day or longer. Leaders of all major British unions denounced ca'canny and insisted that the purpose of short hours was to improve social life, not to restrict output.[3]

Given the problem of economic reconstruction and relatively low productivity (especially in France), this position had obvious apologetic value. It also was a part of the broader and widely shared hope that the

technological upsurge—so strikingly developed for war—could be utilized to raise the labor standard in peace. This ideology might have been
the basis for a "modernization" of European industrial relations and for
labor-management corporatism. Instead, this era was generally characterized by conflict, not cooperation.

This vision of economic growth encountered many enemies. Not
only were French communists unwilling to abandon the alternative of
revolution, but, more important, the British rank and file often opposed technology that threatened the entrenched position of skilled
unions.[4] Yet even the engineering union leader Brownlie noted that
while he did not encourage "dawdling," getting workers to the job on
time and keeping them productive was "management's problem."[5] In
Britain, innovation seemed to be more in the employers' rather than the
national (or skilled workers') interest. In France, the need to recover
from the devastation of war and economic backwardness (as well as to
give organized labor a negotiating role in introducing change) produced
a more positive attitude toward innovation.[6] However, French labor
also evidenced an opposition to this technological strategy, especially
among the remnants of anarchosyndicalism.[7]

These negative views, however, were surely in decline. In fact, there
was surprisingly little overt opposition to the productivist line of the
CGT among the *minoritaires,* who by 1920 were dominated by the
communists. In fact, following Lenin's example, the French communists linked short hours and productivism in much the same way as did
the reformists.[8]

Probably more important to the failure of this economic model was
the resistance of most business. As discussed in chapter 4, the "progressive wing" of management was extremely small. Even commitment to
economic modernization was very ambiguous; most French employers
generally delayed costly and risky innovations as long as possible.[9] In
Britain, the "progressive businessman" was perhaps even rarer. Rejecting innovation in an unprofitable market, coal and other industries
sought to retrench with work-force reductions, wage cuts, and, in some
cases, longer working hours.[10]

The era of managerialism trumpeted by the American James Burham
and others had hardly made an appearance in Europe. When French labor reformers offered cooperation in the "National Economic Council," business organizations rejected them. The Industrial Conference of
1919 in Britain was dead by 1921 and the Whitley Councils had largely
faded before or during the General Strike of 1926.[11]

In a word, class collaboration was impossible because of the lack of a willing partner in business. This is not really surprising. The ideology of hours reformers violated the traditional notion that the market was to set the conditions and pay of labor. And many employers saw the shortening of the workday as essentially a wage issue, drastically modifying the ratio of output to wages. But the hours reformers went even further.

For organized labor the introduction of new technology was not only to be an integral part of the eight-hour day, it was to be a democratic process. As detailed in chapter 4, reformist French workers strove to participate in and enjoy a share of the benefits of labor-saving innovation in the form of reduced fatigue and shorter working hours as well as higher living standards.[12] Their British counterparts also participated in various ad hoc groupings like the Institute of Industrial Psychology and the Scientific Management Committee of the building industry.[13] These efforts were futile and probably naive; but they hardly are proof of business-labor corporatism. Rather they were attempts to redefine the nineteenth-century ideal of "workers' control" in the context of technological growth and the opportunities of access to the decision-making process. As Jonathan Zeitlin and others have noted, formal negotiating machinery enhanced labor control over the workplace rather than coopted it.[14] This new version of workers' control (albeit shared with management) was a clear threat to classical liberalism. Thus, the conflict over the eight-hour day in the 1920s encompassed these wider ideological issues.

A second major theme of the hour reformers was that the reduction of worktime could be secured only by international agreement. They believed that conventions set by the International Labor Organization could modify the game of global economic competition. The Washington Convention became a substitute for the workers' international and May Day agitation for the "three eights." Ratification of the convention would assure that an economic arms race would not destroy the labor standard so painfully won in countries where labor was well organized; it would thus prevent the downward pressure of competition from lowering that norm to the lowest prevailing level. Throughout the 1920s, ratification of the Washington Convention and the stabilization of an international hours standard were major issues in the labor movements of both countries (indeed throughout western Europe).

The ILO was not a bourgeois tool that forced labor into the mold of capitalist internationalism. The tripartite structure of the International

Labor Organization, with its national delegations of labor, management, and government members, hardly promoted class harmony. Instead this organization was a relatively open (if rather ineffective) forum in which European labor offered alternatives to the economic nationalism that prevailed in the ranks of most European business. The Washington Convention became not a vehicle for promoting labor peace, as perhaps some of its supporters in 1919 had wished it to be, but an emblem of a distinct international labor program, supported by a fragile transnational bureaucracy in the Geneva-based ILO.

Although governments wavered in the unstable political climate of the 1920s and 1930s, employers generally stood united against the convention. This passionate opposition reflected a commitment to market capitalism, the idea that commodity prices, costs of production, and marginal productivity should determine hours in any particular country—not labor diplomacy. If, in the 1920s, international constraints on arms and treaties governing territorial matters were grudgingly accepted, parallel limits on labor standards were anathema.

The doctrine of the market was, of course, paralleled by economic nationalism—the insistence that economic growth depended upon "beggaring thy neighbor" or evading the same fate from a competitor. Because hours were such a visible and obviously simple way of gaining an edge over the foreigner, European business insisted on leaving open the option to modify hours. The ILO then was hardly a polite conclave of irrelevant reformers; it was a playing field on which some of the most fundamental questions of twentieth-century capitalism were fought. The eight-hour day was the greatest issue of international labor diplomacy in the 1920s.

These arguments will be developed in an investigation of two broad issues, each with a special focus on one country: France and the political contest over the impact of the eight-hour day on economic growth; and Britain and the mixed success of labor diplomacy.

Time, Technology, and the Defense of Social Reform in France, 1921–1925

In the fall of 1921, most of industrial Europe pressed for a longer workday. The expectation of economic expansion following the postwar slump encouraged competing industries to work overtime and to raise the threshold before bonus rates applied. In this resurgence of economic nationalism, employers in each country argued that the nonratification of the Washington Convention forced them to increase hours to remain competitive. Dutch employers succeeded in raising weekly worktime from the forty-five-hour level won in 1919 to forty-eight hours, putting Holland in parity with neighboring competitors. Steel plants in Germany locked out workers who refused to accept the international standard of forty-eight hours instead of the forty-six gained after the war. By the end of 1922, under pressure to meet allied reparation demands, the German government overcame labor opposition and granted employers the right to use additional overtime with a limit of a 25 percent bonus. The most serious assault was a Swiss law in July that raised the workweek to fifty-three hours. The Swiss Parliament cited the failure of the Washington Convention and "economic difficulties" (primarily a labor shortage and a lack of raw materials) as reasons for breaking with the forty-eight-hour norm.[15]

This erosion of the international hours standard, accompanied by the postwar recession, encouraged French business to attack the eight-hour day. From November 1921 to November 1922, hardly a business association failed to condemn the eight-hour law as fatal to its industry and French economic power. The Union of Economic Interests led the campaign using its ties with the National Bloc and the Steel Committee. In December 1921, the General Confederation of French Production, which represented sectors of heavy industry, demanded the suspension of the law "until economic conditions are normal again." Small business and commerce also joined the crusade.[16]

Paralleling this business offensive came a flood of bills in the Chamber to revise or suspend the eight-hour law. They ranged from proposals simply to liberalize overtime rules to calls for the suspension of the law for five years and restoration then only "if the economic and financial situation of the country permits."[17] The conservative Social and Democratic Republican party announced its support for revision in December 1921 and members of the Union of Economic Interests met Premier Poincaré on March 15, 1922, demanding larger exemptions from the law.[18]

Despite talk of suspension, many business leaders agreed with business lobbyist Raphael Georges-Levy that it was "difficult . . . to demand today an abrogation of a law that appears so important in the eyes of the masses." Instead employer associations more often pressed for revisions of worktime decrees, often demanding, as did shoe manufacturers, an increase in annual overtime from sixty to three hundred hours (in effect a nine-hour day). In May, the Union of Metallurgical Industries renounced their 1919 agreement with the CGT, insisting on a flexible daily schedule of up to ten hours and trebling annual overtime to three hundred hours. This offensive led to inconclusive results against determined union opposition.[19]

Employers had more success winning liberal rulings from friendly bureaucrats like Divisional Inspector Berthiot of the Lyon region. In the spring of 1922, Berthiot made widely publicized concessions without the advice of unions, granting, for example, a fifty-four-hour week to the textile industries by legally dubious means. These Berthiot Settlements were applauded by national business associations as a model for increasing flexibility. Unions claimed that the fifty-four-hour norm, however, had removed the burden of proving the need for overtime and had resulted in the restoration of the ten-hour day in some cases.[20]

Even more rewarding were campaigns of the shipping and railroad industries to raise hours, again with the aid of a friendly bureaucracy. Because foreign shippers failed to reduce the hours of commercial sailors (despite ILO pressure), French employers claimed uncompetitively high labor costs. The Ministry of Merchant Marine drafted a new decree that essentially ratified the employer position. On September 5, it restored a 1907 regulation that set the sailors' watch at twelve hours. This became the new definition of the eight-hour day (as hours of "effective work") and allowed shipowners to eliminate a third shift. In railways an impasse in June over the "effective work" of employees whose tasks were intermittent (e.g., clerks and guards at small stations) allowed the Ministry of Public Works on September 15 to increase their workday. The government justified these changes by noting the recent upward revision of hours on British and Spanish railways.[21]

Along with this important political assault on the short workday, employers launched an ideological attack on the economic and social rationale for this reform. Perhaps the most thorough of these broadsides was written by André François-Poncet, the director of a news service owned by the Steel Committee and a member of a major heavy-industrial family. His book *La France et les huit heures* was a systematic refutation of the CGT's optimistic ideology of growth and social and cultural progress.[22]

François-Poncet refuted the tripartite and international politics implicit in the 1919 law, declaring that the eight-hour law was a mere political expedient made in the emergency of 1919—not a vehicle for so-cial peace. The government imposed it on business in an effort to reward the moderate Left for its cooperation in containing the Bolshe-vik flood. Now that this threat had subsided, revision was essential. Probably the greatest problem with the law was that it imposed collec-tive bargaining on employers. François-Poncet declared that labor and management could never agree and that this made "irresponsible func-tionaries" the mediators of inevitable disputes. Despite the flexibility of the law, it was still an unacceptable intervention into the labor market and was, for François-Poncet, the "advent of socialism." Moreover, the eight-hour law was passed with the expectation that the Washington Convention would be ratified. But, according to François-Poncet, that convention was now a "dead letter" insofar as no serious nation would give up its sovereignty to this vague and unworkable principle.[23]

The employers' campaign against the eight-hour day was part of the nostalgia for economic liberalism. With few exceptions, businessmen sought to minimize bargaining with labor. In an expanding economy, instead of making costly increases in the work force or in production capacity, they preferred the expedient of raising hours. Yet employer ideology went beyond traditional liberalism. Business seldom openly denied the right of the nation to intervene in the labor market. After all, employers encouraged government involvement in recruiting foreign labor in the 1920s. Even François-Poncet demanded not the revocation of the eight-hour law but its "liberalization." Employers shifted to a new ideological plane, arguing that sacrifice was necessary for national economic survival. Because the international economy was presumably immune to effective control, any attempt to regulate hours at the na-tional level was dangerous and must be minimized. This position, of course, remains at the heart of the contemporary opposition to government-sanctioned improvements in the labor standard.

The CGT responded by defending collective bargaining and declar-ing the economic feasibility and social necessity of an international hours standard. After the expulsion of communist-led unions in 1921, the CGT became thoroughly committed to a "politics of presence." Not only did its leadership defend the eight-hour law before the Chamber in March 1922, but it worked with sympathetic Radicals to mobilize sup-port. Mining, metal, rail, and maritime unions defended the integrity of the decrees of 1919–1920 as products of collective bargaining.[24] More-over, the CGT launched an unprecedented petition campaign in favor of the eight-hour day as an "acquired right" and a "fruit of twenty years of effort," which the "proletariat will not allow . . . to be mutilated much less suppressed."[25]

A key to winning public support was to prove that the new hours standard was international—despite employer claims. The CGT and allied press gave wide publicity to studies undertaken late in 1921 by German unions and an independent team of Dutch investigators that showed that the eight-hour day was in fact the norm in German industry. Members of the "Amsterdam" International Federation of Trade Unions claimed in a detailed report that the eight-hour day was observed throughout industrial Europe. Through their links with the ILO, unions were able to make the topic of hours the leading theme of the International Labour Conference in October 1922 in Geneva.[26] The French also supported a referendum led by the Swiss labor movement to regain the eight-hour day. The referendum won overwhelmingly on February 17, 1924—an event seen by both sides as a victory of the eight-hour day in Europe as well as in Switzerland.[27]

Only when these political tactics did not work did the CGT advocate strikes and, then, as symbolic actions. In response to the decree that raised hours for commercial sailors, the CGT organized on September 19, 1922, a twenty-three hour strike and held mass rallies in port towns and major industrial centers. Yet the CGT did not endorse wildcat strikes (often led by communists), which lasted until November 19. Instead, the CGT organized a coalition with officers and ship captains, lobbied Poincaré, and finally supported an unsuccessful parliamentary interpellation in November against the decree.[28] Yet so critical was the eight-hour day that the CGT joined Catholic and even communist unions in Lyon and in mining and railway industries in defense of this increase in leisure. The eight-hour day was not "a gift" from the government but a "conquest of workers" and evidence of organized labor's contribution to French society.[29]

The CGT defended the eight-hour day in terms very different from those used before or after the 1920s. Infrequently did it advocate reduced worktime to create jobs or raise wages. The labor movement had abandoned the "redistributionist position" common in the CGT before the war (see chapter 3) that claimed that reduced hours would lower productivity and thus "create new jobs, raise wages, and expropriate capital."[30] Instead, CGT leaders assumed that the eight-hour day would have no immediate impact on production and, in time, would increase output. The CGT thoroughly opposed economic Malthusianism—the restriction of production—as a threat to French growth. Anarchist ideals of a static economy had been largely purged from the CGT by 1919 and played little role in the Communist-led Confédération Générale du Travail Unitaire (CGTU), especially after the few remaining anarchosyndicalists were ousted by 1924.

The unions' solution to the challenge of the world economy was to improve productivity through mechanization and even scientific management. They argued that war-related dislocations (tariff policy, credit and exchange factors, and increased raw material prices) caused France's postwar recession—not shorter hours.[31] Against advocates of longer hours, Emile Basly of the miners' union argued that "it is those with the best and most powerful machinery; it is those with the spirit of initiative backed up with a capable financial organization" who will prevail in the market.[32] This put French labor in a rather ironic position of defending economic modernization. For both the CGTU and CGT, an idealized view of Taylorism became a stick used to beat the mule of French "routine," which had not only produced relatively low wages but threatened to restore long hours.[33]

By November 1922, opponents of the eight-hour day in France had retreated and the future of this norm was assured, at least in manufacturing. The offensive against the eight-hour day had succeeded primarily in those industries where it was the least defensible. Despite union arguments that all time at the employer's disposal was work, the railway and shipping industries easily prevailed with their distinction between "presence" at work and "effective" work. Not only was this principle well established in retail trades and food service, but the lack of an international eight-hour day in transportation made defeat almost inevitable.

Yet, given the conservative political climate, the nearly prostrate unions, and the failure of the Washington Convention, it is surprising that the eight-hour law itself remained unscathed. Of course, major industrial groups may have been content with new and more liberal regulations, which allowed seasonal adjustments in the workday. Still, despite strong lobbying, the 1919 eight-hour contracts held in mining, metal, and other industries. In fact "eight-hour decrees" continued apace in light industries and the service sector.[34]

The opposition was no more successful because business failed to rally support for its antiregulation ideology in Parliament. Both Radicals and the Catholic hierarchy supported the eight-hour day. Conservatives, like Poincaré, believed that restoration of the ten-hour day would unleash the social unrest that had been so recently silenced. Even the Social and Democratic Republican party abandoned its opposition to the law by November 1922.[35] It was politically foolhardy to oppose openly this very popular reform. E. Basly, a CGT official, claimed that office workers as well as industrial workers were "frightened by the campaign against the eight-hour day," an observation confirmed by conservatives like François-Poncet.[36]

Reduced worktime also had important support inside the government where hours reformers continued to exert some influence despite the post-1919 reaction. The Ministry of Labor supported the law, even against the Ministries of Commerce and Public Works, which were more responsive to business. In fact, Minister of Labor Albert Peyronnet, a member of a small centrist party, repeatedly supported the reformers' linkage of short hours and efficiency: before the Chamber in February 1922, he praised the procedure of labor-management negotiation for setting hours and implied that employers should cooperate with those workers who had accepted a "better technical organization of work in order to compensate for reduced output." His ministry, under the daily direction of reformer Arthur Fontaine, produced studies that supported the economic and social arguments for the eight-hour day. Drawing on these studies, Peyronnet declared that the eight-hour day was a vehicle of social progress, leading "to suburbanization, the increase of workers' gardens, greater attendance at professional courses and libraries, and the decline of alcoholism."[37]

Yet the official evidence hardly proved these claims. Not only had alcohol consumption been decreasing since 1911, long before the reduction of worktime, but the efforts of employers to build leisure facilities were exaggerated. Further, the government emphasized the positive economic impact of shorter hours by publishing only survey data that showed improved productivity with the eight-hour day while leaving contrary evidence in their files.[38] Government studies on the impact of the eight-hour day were at least as much propaganda in favor of reform as collections of fact.

The French Labor Ministry responded to employer opposition in the 1920s in the same way as did British labor inspectors to a similar reaction to the ten-hour day between 1847 and 1850: it defended the law for promoting labor peace, advocated innovation, and advertised the social and ultimately economic value of leisure time.[39] The elected government could not openly ally itself with a "politics of social regression," as Peyronnet admitted in 1922.[40]

The unions also played an active role. They were even able to regain lost ground in the years after 1922. Following the election of the Cartel des Gauches in 1924 and Justin Godart's appointment as minister of labor, the CGT leadership demanded the reversal of those rulings in 1922 that had undermined the eight-hour day. By December, Godart ended the "Berthiot Settlements" that had automatically granted employers additional hours. Inspectors became less willing to grant overtime and recuperation of hours "lost" to holidays. By February 1925, a new minister, Antoine Durafour, directed the inspectors to limit overtime to certain appropriate months and thus to safeguard the integrity of the eight-hour norm. Moreover, the government modified the 1922 extension of the workday of railroad workers and sailors.[41] The eight-hour day had, at least, a precarious foothold in manufacturing.

To be sure, the eight-hour day was continually attacked throughout the 1920s, especially during expansionary periods (1926 and 1928–1929). The defense of this reform preoccupied the CGT throughout the decade.[42] Still, hours decrees slowly advanced into agriculture-related industry and the tertiary sectors. Overtime allowances and violations in union-weak sectors meant that the promise of a reduction of the workweek by twelve to twenty-four hours was not always fulfilled. Yet the law in the 1920s was certainly not a dead letter awaiting the resurgence of labor during the Popular Front. Overtime allowances seldom were over one hundred fifty hours a year and overtime had similarly compromised the ten- and twelve-hour systems that had prevailed before the 1919 law. The Labor Ministry enforced the law in the 1920s (admittedly unevenly) as seen in the mountains of files in the National Archives. By 1931, every eligible sector had its decree.[43]

Even in the conservative 1920s the idea prevailed that social reform was not only consistent with but could also drive economic growth. Neither the ideology of the sovereignty of the market nor the paranoia of economic nationalism with its theme of pragmatic austerity could overcome this common faith: short time meant more efficient time or, at least, it was worth the economic risk.

Britain and the Fate of the International Hours Standard, 1921–1929

Whereas in France the debate over the eight-hour day was sited in the national economic arena, in Britain the issue was displaced largely to the international plane. Nothing like the furor of

1921–1922 in France or a similar uproar in Germany in 1923–1924 occurred in Britain. Yet, because of the pivotal role that the British economy played even in the 1920s and because of Britain's traditionally pacesetting role in the reduction of worktime in Europe, the United Kingdom was at the center of the battle over the international eight-hour standard. The attitude of the British government was a determining factor in the fate of the Washington Hours Convention and the repeated but futile efforts to guarantee that worktime would not be lengthened.

To say that the British government sabotaged the Washington Convention is to exaggerate only slightly. This may appear odd. After all, as numerous experts (including Tory ministers of labor) wrote, the general ratification of the Washington Hours Convention would have tended to raise the hours standards of Britain's competitors. This could only benefit Britain, which on average continued to have the shortest working week in Europe.[44] Yet only in brief spells when the Labour party was in power was the convention treated seriously. We could attribute this hostility to the technical difficulties of conforming the convention to the British railway agreement of 1919.[45] Perhaps it was also a problem of contrasting political styles—the legalistic approach of the British in comparison with the French support, "*en principe*," of the eight-hour standard while liberally interpreting the clauses of the convention. It may have simply been another form of British isolationism and general mistrust of continental partners in the ILO. Yet these interpretations obscure the deeper role that the Hours Convention played in the ideological contest of the decade after the eight-hour breakthrough.

In 1920 and 1921, the issue of ratification reached a climax. The ILO director, Albert Thomas, privately implored the British to accept their duty of promoting postwar stability by ratifying the convention. This would remove the pretense that allowed the Germans to return to their "imperialist ideas" by raising working hours and gaining an unfair economic advantage. Further, "the great effort demanded of Germany [for reparations] should be possible of accomplishment within the framework of universal conventions." Thomas claimed that "an organisation of labour might play a great part in the more solid establishment of peace" by reducing economic competition. Nonratification risked the danger of "throwing the organised workers into despair." Even British Ministry of Labour staff warned that by refusing to ratify "we are not only rejecting an international settlement but are also rejecting a national settlement which may have even more serious consequences."[46]

Ultimately, however, the opposition of organized business was decisive in turning Whitehall from these arguments. Having defeated national hours legislation, employers insisted that shorter hours not be imposed by international treaty.[47] The government stressed the technical problem with railways in its letter to Thomas rejecting ratification. Still, the broader pressure of business and an unwillingness to remain the leader in international labor reform were surely the main reasons for nonsupport. As the prime minister noted, the Germans, Russians, and particularly the Americans had not even participated in the Washington Conference and thus were "left untrammeled by hour restrictions."[48]

This action did not end the battle for ratification. Not only did Thomas conduct an untiring diplomacy throughout the 1920s to coax reluctant European governments into signing the convention, but even within the British government there were frequent demarches toward ratification or compromise. Thomas, for example, sponsored a massive study of world production in the hope of showing no harmful results from shorter hours; the 1924 International Labour Conference stressed the positive effects of the new leisure.[49]

The response of the British government, however, depended on both international conditions and domestic politics. As we have seen in 1922 and 1923, employer pressure in France (as well as in the Low Countries and Switzerland) for increased hours frustrated Thomas's efforts at diplomacy. In December 1923, following the collapse of passive resistance in the Ruhr, Germany began to threaten the norm with new regulations that raised the workday up to ten or even twelve hours in some sectors of the steel and mining industry. In early 1924, the Poles imitated this policy.[50] In this context, Whitehall simply asserted that British employers would accept no limits on overtime.[51]

In January 1924, the election of a minority government in London slowly modified the picture. Tom Shaw, principal British delegate at the Washington Conference in 1919, became the new minister of labor. For him, uniform labor standards were to be the foundation of "fair trade."[52] Tom Shaw and Albert Thomas arranged for a meeting of the ministers of labor of all the major European nations in Berne on September 8, 1924. The big powers felt the need to control the general deterioration of the hours situation, especially when the Germans, who claimed hardship due to the impending reparations settlement, threatened to extend their already lengthening workweek. After much special-interest pleading, the ministers finally issued a joint statement pledging action to ratify the convention. The Germans also promised to restore the eight-hour day in heavy industry. Still, there were no agreements on details of overtime allowances or other differences in national practices. The biggest setback, however, was the inability of Britain to pass an eight-hour law.[53]

Although the British cabinet approved of Tom Shaw's forty-eight-hour bill in 1924, opposition from the transport and munitions industries frustrated its passage. The defeat of the coalition government in the elections of December 1924 brought a conservative cabinet that formally rejected worktime legislation in May 1925.[54]

Yet again on the continent the political climate favoring ratification improved. Not only did the Germans begin to lower hours in steel and mining in 1925 but their labor minister, Dr. Braun, supported the convention. The French Cartel of the Left partially reversed the long-hours policy of the previous government. In July 1925, the Chamber endorsed the convention pending German ratification. Already in 1923 and 1924 the Italians and Austrians had conditionally adhered to the treaty.[55] As a result, the British were in no position to reject Thomas's proposal to convene a conference of European ministers of labor in London.[56]

Again, however, British business opposition to international labor agreements frustrated this initiative. Although engineering employers joined unions in supporting an international hours agreement in order to end the worktime advantage of continental competitors, the National Confederation of Employers' Organisations (NCEO) was uncooperative.[57]

In March 1926, the ministers of labor of Germany, Italy, France, Belgium, and Britain issued a series of "conclusions" which largely addressed British objections. Minister of Labour Arthur Steel-Maitland announced to the NCEO on April 20 that he had succeeded in winning all practical concessions from his continental colleagues. This agreement, he argued, would help to make Britain more competitive by raising the labor costs of continental economic rivals.[58]

The response of the NCEO was entirely negative: not only did they protest that the London Conference did not go far enough, but that any agreement would be enforced only in Britain with its strong unions, whereas on the continent the rules would be ignored. More to the point, they simply rejected the idea of restricting hours by any agreement. Lord Weir not only found "almost incredible" that this pro-business government would take up the "agenda of the government that it had so recently defeated." He claimed that an hours convention would "introduce the State as the controlling agent in this vital matter of hours and make it possible for the trade unions of this country and their political leaders to use it as a weapon for hampering production and to advance their policy of discouraging private enterprise." Ernest Moir asked, "Why should we, a country which can alter its laws from day to day, be bound by any international agreement to do something which it is certainly not evident . . . will improve the conditions of our labour and of our trade?" Not only did British industry require a flexible workday for seasonal industry, but given their unmatched wage bill (including social benefits) and the alleged failure of the British worker to increase productivity, "the worker may admit soon to the need not only to work harder but longer hours."[59]

In response, Steel-Maitland asked whether the "desire though unexpressed at the moment, is to try to increase the ordinary working week in this country." If so, he claimed, "the trade union movement would look upon the forty-eight-hour week as the Ark of the Covenant and their resistance to any attempt to extend beyond the forty-eight hours would be stronger than their resistance to any other proposal that was placed before them. . . . Isn't it wiser to try to get the same higher standard accepted by our principal competitors?"[60]

Organized business, however, preferred to leave its options open. Of course, having just returned to the gold standard, the British faced the prospect of competing with the burden of an overvalued pound. British industry also lacked confidence that it could lower costs and raise output through innovation. When the engineering union argued that if employers worked with labor in industrial modernization, the threat of the American car industry could be overcome, Allen Smith of the Engineering Employers Federation offered a most pessimistic response: the British simply "don't have the driving mental discipline" evident in newer industrial economies, that this has been true "for generations," and thus the cooperation of labor would not change a thing.[61]

This defeatist attitude in part explains the seemingly irrational opposition of British business to the convention. Britain's increasingly outdated physical plant was concentrated in industries that faced a global competition from regions where wages and benefits were lower and unions weaker. What is surprising is not that industrialists preferred the shortcut of raising hours to "modernization," but that they did not actually do it more often. From the employers' standpoint, the market, not an abstract social yardstick, must set the norm in wages and hours. This attitude would be vividly illustrated in the coal crisis that erupted in the spring of 1926.

In the British coal industry the line of conflict between ideologies of worktime was clearly drawn. Not only did coal suffer from a declining share of world market, but in 1919 the industry lost an hour of daily worktime. Moreover, the coal industry was a natural arena for the political contest over working hours to be played out in Britain: coal still dominated the British economy with over one million miners. And, since 1890, the hours debate in that industry had been an important political issue. Repeated parliamentary commissions, labor legislation, and wartime government control of the mines brought the state into the collective bargaining process.[62]

Although the government returned the mines to private control in 1921, union demands for a higher minimum wage in 1921 and 1924 led to raises, sweetened by wage subsidies provided by the state. Complaining of uncompetitive labor costs, in 1923 the Mining Association demanded a reversion back to the "eight-hour" system of 1908. Finally in 1925, when the government announced that wage subsidies would be discontinued, the prospect of a substantial wage cut and threat of increased hours created an industrial crisis.[63]

In hopes of avoiding a crushing national coal strike, the government appointed the Coal (Samuel) Commission. Employers testified that they needed to raise hours even more than a wage cut: they noted that, despite the official seven-hour day, miners worked at the coal face only five and one-half hours, output had dropped 11 percent from 1913 despite promises of increased effort, and shorter hours required additional "day men" (support workers on a time wage). As a result, Britain was placed in an unfair market position. American miners worked eight hours at the coal face; French mines obtained additional minutes of output because of less time lost by miners to get to the coal. According to the Mining Association, the solution was to increase the workday by an hour and to lower piece rates in order to induce greater output. This would insure more coal at a lower unit cost, allow British coal to meet and perhaps beat the world price, and enable the miners to minimize the inevitable wage reduction.[64]

In response, the miners (represented by Richard Tawney and others) claimed that their workday was really seven hours and thirty-nine minutes (as "winding time" getting to and from the pit was not included in the seven-hour day). This was but a slight deviation from the national standard and was justified by the horrific character of mine work. Moreover, as an alternative to longer hours and pay cuts, they stressed the need for nationalization, mechanization, marketing cooperatives, and development of alternative uses of coal. The real problem was a global overproduction of coal. Decline in output was a result not of the seven-hour day but of short time—the fact that many miners worked far less than a forty-two-hour week. A longer workday, they argued, would mean the loss of at least a hundred thousand jobs because it would exacerbate the problem of overproduction.[65]

The Samuel Commission's report, while agreeing with management's claim for the need for a wage cut, clearly rejected the lengthened workday. Its argument was simple: although an extra hour per day would allow an increase of thirty million tons of coal, this would only lead to lower prices. If output were maintained, 130,000 miners would be laid off. Whatever temporary advantage the British coal industry might gain would be eliminated when foreign industries raised their hours in retaliation. In 1919, the seven-hour day had created jobs during a world coal shortage; however, to raise hours in 1925 during a coal glut would only result in a "general lowering of the standard of leisure in all mining countries." Instead, the commission proposed only a more flexible workweek and wage cuts that, at least, could be easily adjusted upward as market conditions improved.[66]

The recommendations of the Samuel Commission, however, were swept away in the bitter events of 1926. The miners held firm with their famous slogan, "not a penny off the pay, not a minute on the day." In April, having already won a pledge from the TUC for a general strike, the miners refused any concessions; this led to a lockout on May 1. While the general strike from May 5 to 15, 1926, has attracted much attention, the subsequent nine-month coal lockout/strike was surely more important.[67]

Clearly the mine owners saw the increase of worktime as their primary objective. In April, the Mining Association offered the Miners Federation a choice of either a modest wage cut in exchange for an "eight-hour day" or a draconic decrease in pay. By May, they raised their ultimatum to an eight-hour day or a blanket refusal to negotiate a national wage package—in effect, a renunciation of collective bargaining. On May 14, just as the general strike collapsed, the government announced its support for legislation that acceded to the owner's wishes. The "eight-hour" miner's bill became law on July 1, considerably embittering the miners' strike, which continued for another six months. Winston Churchill believed that the owners had agreed to support a modest wage cut and a national wage in exchange for favorable legislation. However, having made no settlement with the miners, the coal owners found no reason to meet the miners when the unions finally agreed to resume bargaining in August. Despite angry words from Churchill for the Mining Association's refusal to bargain, and to carry out their "agreement," by November the owners essentially won a total victory when the miners were obliged to return to an "eight-hour" day and to wages set by the district colliery owners.[68]

Several authors have claimed that the cabinet and the prime minister, Stanley Baldwin, had underestimated the miners' feelings about working hours when they accepted a "compromise" on worktime as a basis of a settlement on wages.[69] Yet, given the bitter history of mining hours in Britain, in which Baldwin himself had played an active role when he opposed the 1908 hours law, no one in authority could have believed that increased worktime would have led to a negotiated end to the strike. In the words of Sidney Webb, cabinet members were playing the role of "parliamentary agents to the coal owners" by rejecting the findings of the Samuel Commission.[70] The immediate impact on the mining towns was unemployment and reduced wages by 20 percent.[71]

The coal crisis of 1926 may have been a no-win situation given the glut on the world market, the labor-intensive character of the industry, and the inability of producers to create a cartel. Yet it shows clearly the central role of worktime in this period. For the mine owners the solution was to lower production costs and increase output in the hope of winning a larger market share. The least costly means of doing this was to raise the hours of miners and reduce the work force. The coal crisis of 1926 also illustrates the profound reluctance of British industry to risk an international solution to the hours question: the coal owners and the government attempted to undercut the competition by a unilateral break from the de facto 1919 hours settlement.

The result, again, was a setback for the Washington Convention. Minister of Labour Steel-Maitland abandoned his own diplomatic success at the London Conference of March 1926. Moreover, in June, the Italians made legal a nine-hour day whenever it was "mutually agreed upon" between management and labor. The British Ministry of Labour was privately relieved by the Italian action because it displaced some of the British responsibility for scuttling the convention.[72]

Yet Steel-Maitland could hardly evade the issue indefinitely. The affair was a diplomatic embarrassment, especially after the French conditionally ratified the convention in February 1927 and the Germans promised to do so; also on the domestic political scene, Steel-Maitland warned the cabinet that the "opposition will make very great play" of government inaction and that the next Labour government might ratify the convention.[73] Further Labour Ministry staff wanted to prevent a general slide into international worktime competition. Nevertheless, when Steel-Maitland attempted to revive the London Conference settlement in early 1927, he was confronted by a mining hours law that appeared to violate the convention; a more formidable problem was organized business, which was probably even more intransigent than it had been in 1926.

The Tory government again offered a solution to the impasse: it proposed a bill that would "interfere as little as possible with existing conditions" and would become the basis of a revised convention. Yet even when offered an opportunity to consult privately on revisions, employers still were adamantly opposed to any action.[74]

Despite a more pliant TUC after the debacle of 1926, the NCEO and Mining Association rejected or evaded all concrete proposals. Without cabinet support, Steel-Maitland suffered the indignity of seeing employer groups repeatedly attack his concessions and evade his offers for further negotiations. This put the Ministry of Labour staff in a quandary. They could hardly propose revision of the convention to the ILO without a firm political support from British employers. Thus, using the nearly Byzantine procedures of the ILO, the British delayed action. Finally, in January 1929, Steel-Maitland called on other ministers of labor to propose still another revision of the convention. This effort dragged on throughout the spring accomplishing little but creating a deadlock at the ILO.[75]

In July 1929, with the election of a Labour government, British policy shifted back to support for the Washington Convention and hours legislation. Yet, Margaret Bondfield, the new minister of labor and former labor organizer, was beset with the same opposition as her predecessors. Although the cabinet agreed to introduce a bill in February, it had a low priority and was repeatedly delayed over details throughout 1930. In August 1930, this moderate leftist government managed to pass legislation that reduced a half-hour off the miners' workday. Yet, in November, Bondfield had to request an end to the delays instigated by Whitehall bureaucracies. No action was taken and the country slipped into the depression. The new National Government turned more conservative and labor agitation for a forty-hour week began to displace the Washington Hours Convention.[76]

After more than a decade of painstaking negotiation, the principle of an international labor standard had hardly dented the armor of economic nationalism. By 1930, the Washington Convention had been ratified unconditionally only by small European states. The refusal of Britain to endorse it made meaningless the conditional ratifications of France, Italy, and Spain. The major powers were also reluctant to support other labor conventions. Still the hours convention played a particularly central role in the attempt to reform competitive capitalism in the 1920s. Its failure paralleled the well-known inability of the Western capitalist democracies to forge a lasting peace out of the dreams of the fourteen points of Wilson.

Perhaps the whole system of international labor conventions was too cumbersome. Not only did it involve the usual conflicts inherent in the diplomacy of nation states but also the confrontations inevitable in tripartite corporatism. Tom Shaw declared in 1924 that the Washington Convention grew out of the fears of the peacemakers of world revolution in April 1919. Once that threat had passed, the prospects of labor diplomacy were few.[77] Surely also the refusal of the United States, the driving power in world capitalism, to participate in this reform crippled its chances. The dominance of free marketers in the United States contributed to the unwillingness and perhaps inability of Britain to maintain its traditional leadership in advancing the labor standard.

Yet the convention, even if not signed by the major powers, probably restrained potential "violators" of the informal eight-hour norm, much in the way that unratified arms accords were respected in the 1980s. It is not surprising that labor diplomacy failed—after all, so did arms control, trade and exchange stabilization, and territorial agreements. Non-ratification deprived industrial reformers of a guaranteed hours standard, forced them into an ongoing defense of the eight-hour day, and occasionally allowed employers in threatened industries like coal to reverse the gains of 1919. Nevertheless, the eight-hour day generally prevailed even if the ideology of an international labor standard did not.

For over a generation the eight-hour day represented to classical liberals a threat to the sovereignty of the marketplace. Yet, despite the efforts to reverse the concrete gains of 1919, there was no return to nineteenth-century liberalism. Rather, a broad consensus affirmed that the "three eights" was not a ticket to economic armageddon; instead, for some, it was a wedge for industrial modernization and, for others, a guarantee of social peace.

Less successful was the claim that an international hours standard should be the base of global trade and competition. Labor's relative access to power in the national arena was not achieved on the higher ground of interstate relations. It became increasingly apparent that labor's inability to create an international labor standard negated its influence over firms, industries, and nation states.

8

Meanings of Free Time:
Leisure and Class in the 1920s

The contest over time was waged largely in the arena of work. In an age that measured value primarily in economic terms, time was little more than an index of efficiency, a yardstick of production. Of course, a reallocation of time obviously meant at least the possibility of more leisure. Yet both managers and labor leaders seldom thought in terms of the value of personal time. Long gone were the defenders of religious festivals and the communal values of local fairs and games. Although privatized mass commercial leisure had emerged in the second half of the nineteenth century, it was largely ignored by almost everyone who addressed the question of free time. Recreation was defended as essential to the smooth functioning of the human motor, and the value of time for the cultivation of civic and familial virtues was praised. Still, free time, disconnected from economic and public functions, was problematic to both labor leader and employer in the early twentieth century. The debate over leisure did not even turn on the right to consume; few thought of leisure time in terms of broadening the mass market. Rather, it revolved around familiar nineteenth-century themes—the social utility of leisure and the best means to "organize" it.

Yet what meaning and use did time liberated from the long workday have for wage earners? Is there evidence that workers sought a reduction in the normal day for leisure rather than higher wages through overtime? Does the eight-hour day signify a changing leisure and work ethic? We have noted that underlying the politics of the short-hours movements of the late nineteenth century was a complex change in workers' attitudes toward time (chapter 3). Wage earners were increasingly intolerant of irregular work schedules and the "porous," yet interminable, workday under the control of an employer. The desire for personal time was one objective in shortening the "ends" of the workday and winning at least a weekly holiday. These practical demands for liberty were clear indicators of a growing individualism in the working classes. They were also pragmatic adaptations to an increasing concern of the twentieth-century worker—the coordination of worktime and family time. This new leisure ethic was not a revolt against the work ethic of the nineteenth century. Rather the desire for free time was accompanied by a general willingness to compress or even intensify worktime as the economic price of temporal freedom.

This chapter will investigate two related issues that emerged in the 1920s: the ideology and politics of leisure as part of the ongoing debate over the utility of noneconomic time; and signs of a new work and leisure ethic within the working classes during the postwar struggle for the eight-hour day. Included will be a brief perspective on the uses of leisure time in the interwar period.

Organizing Leisure after the Eight-Hour Day

Paralleling the economic debate over worktime was a struggle around the social and cultural utility of leisure. Like the economic dimensions of the question of worktime, the controversy over the efficacy of leisure was deeply rooted in the nineteenth century. By the 1880s in Britain, early Victorian anxiety over mass leisure had softened, and, despite continued frustration over the "wasted" free time of workers and the commercialization of leisure, even conservatives ceased struggling against popular leisure. Few British accepted either state or even private national leisure programs. Even Tom Shaw, when he was minister of labor in 1924, showed no interest when Albert Thomas sought to survey workers' leisure programs. For Shaw, leisure was a private affair. Of course, British trade unions, especially at the local level, took considerable interest in organizing leisure for their members.[1] In

France, however, the question of the purpose of leisure played a central role in the national conflict over worktime in the 1920s. The following discussion then will focus on France but introduce British evidence when appropriate.

French employers continued to argue that work alone brought salvation: leisure would dissipate the majority who lacked the training and intelligence to make proper use of unregulated time. François-Poncet declared that the only beneficiary of the eight-hour day was the cabaret; and the Deputy M. Josse claimed that the eight-hour law had created a "moral crisis" and was a "symbol of laziness."[2] Yet in a democratic age, such traditionalist views were seldom expressed in public.

More common were appeals for the "organization of leisure." Indeed François-Poncet found the eight-hour day premature because proper leisure institutions had yet to be founded. Recommendations for a national leisure policy followed well-worn paths: arguing that "the first educator of the worker is quite naturally the employer," Léon Pasquier, a prominent industrialist from Lyon, advocated that business should offer vocational education to help wage earners rise "up the social scale" and to "enlarge their intellectual horizon." Such education should also "teach the nonsense of high wages" isolated from economic realities. Support should be given to independent nonreligious social organizations to provide young working men with wholesome recreation and diversions. Others, especially mine operators in the north and east, favored Catholic organizations that proved to be helpful in "rooting" Polish workers recently recruited from the Ruhr or Galacia. These groups would provide activities to help eliminate the "social diseases that threaten the race: alcoholism, immorality, birth control, tuberculosis."[3]

According to employer opinion, organized leisure should encourage worker domesticity. Lodgings should be sufficient to accommodate large families; more housing should be built in suburban locations far from the factory so that children would cease being "vagabond[s] in the street while the father haunts the bar." The worker's garden was still the means to "develop in the worker a sense of property and of saving." It would also tie the male wage earner to the home and family, and provide him an activity corresponding to the wives' domestic duties. Early nineteenth-century paternalistic solutions to the social problem of leisure time—*embourgeoisement* through indoctrination, sublimating recreation, a "pro-family" housing policy, and the utopia of planting the "uprooted" urban worker in the soil of the *petit coin*—were very much alive nearly a century later.[4]

Middle-class British treatment of popular leisure stressed similar themes. Constance Harris in her study of working-class leisure in Bethnal Green (1927) followed the tradition of Booth and Rowntree in emphasizing the inadequacies of popular leisure despite the efforts of recreational planners. Monotonous jobs, she argued, made for "stupid, boring or perhaps vicious" leisure activities. She observed adults sitting in windows "watching the life of the streets" while the daily routine became "a kind of grey treadmill, without much hope or many desires." Because youths were "given freedom far too soon," they became "ardent individualists," with little desire to join clubs or attend vocational classes in the evening. On holidays, instead of exploring the countryside, the people of Bethnal Green, a working-class suburb, went to the nearby parks, crowded around pubs, played rounders, or danced. Rowntree's mid-1930s study of York revealed the same concern over gambling and drinking as did his study at the turn of the century— although he admitted that the latter had decreased since the war. Another survey published in 1933 expressed disappointment in the quality of woman's leisure—"unorganised social intercourse with neighbours at her shopping and housework."[5]

Few bourgeois writers considered seriously that leisure time might develop consumer industries or that appetites wetted by the dreams of the good life might bind workers more tightly to wage labor. Most European employers would have rejected the resolution presented to the International Chambers of Commerce in 1929 in defense of the new leisure: "Enlarged buying power supports the market for large-scale production and for a great variety of specialties and services, while reasonable leisure facilitates new use and enjoyment of more products and services." This view, held in the 1920s by a thin layer of "progressive" businessmen (influenced by groups like the American Twentieth Century Fund of Edward Filene), had hardly percolated down into the rank and file of European businessmen.[6]

The French ideal remained to control workers' leisure directly rather than to trust the temptations of the marketplace with its demoralizing entertainments and its lure of "wasteful" spending. The indirect stabilization of the mass market did not fit either economic reality or the ideology of the traditionalist French bourgeoisie. Yet even Henry Ford, the great proponent of mass-consumption leisure, shared many of these paternalistic notions.[7]

Nevertheless, French and, even more, British elites opposed the overtly politicized leisure practiced by Mussolini's *dopo lavoro,* the Nazi's

Kraft durch Freude, or the Soviet's trade unions. In Britain, the Workers' Education Association with its multiclass membership promoted local and voluntary leisure activities. Western Europeans disdained the manipulative character of state-organized leisure, which they believed only fostered loyalty to the totalitarian nation.[8] Yet the differences between totalitarian and democratic leisure can be exaggerated. Both were extensions of Victorian leisure ideology, sharing a common desire to thwart the "evils" of urban proletarian family life.[9]

Like employers, organized labor and reformist allies drew on nineteenth-century models to define their leisure goals. Justin Godart, the Radical deputy, still stressed that time freed from work would finally allow workers to "fulfill their duties and to exercise the rights of man and citizen." According to a British trade union official, shorter hours meant "that men and women might educate themselves to become better citizens." The shorter workday, according to a French communist in 1923, provided the proletarian with an "integral life" having "less the character of being merchandise." The nineteenth-century linkage of short hours and political activism was obviously still alive.[10]

Reformers also recognized that free time was a potential social problem. Labor officials and socialist leaders, often from the ranks of proud craft trades, were wary of the culture of less skilled manual workers. However, spare time was more an opportunity than a temptation. As Albert Thomas wrote: "Either the eight-hour day will be a deception and a disaster for the country, or else it will be the first step in the . . . decisive and peaceful revolution that the proletarians are seeking."[11]

Labor leaders addressed the wider question of the private meanings of leisure. Following an ideology already well developed in the 1890s, labor writers claimed that reduced time at work actually decreased alcoholism and cited statistics showing substantial decline in liquor consumption since 1914. Alcoholism, they argued, was a product of overwork where physical and mental exhaustion, along with a scarcity of time, combined to prevent the development of more healthful diversions. Reduction of the workday allowed wage earners to spend less time in the factory milieu where a drinking culture flourished. Especially if short worktime was accompanied by the replacement of the *casse croute* with the one-break system, workers would have less opportunity and need to blunt the rigors of a long day with a few *"petits verres"* during work breaks.[12] Moreover, a reduced workday would provide workers with the time necessary to abandon the overcrowded tenements located near the factory for the more spacious suburbs. French socialists praised the uplifting value of gardens as well as chicken and rabbit husbandry as positive alternatives to the lure of the cabaret or pub.[13]

Most important, the shorter workday would allow wage earners to "enjoy fully the life of the family." The father would benefit for he could develop a positive role in the family, contribute his skills and labor in the garden and in home improvements, and have sufficient time to "direct and supervise" the upbringing of his children. Women workers, of course, would have more time to make the home an attractive alternative to the bar for husbands.[14]

But, according to a CGT report on leisure in 1919, the man constantly at home "always is a slave." Male workers, at least, also needed more athletic fields, libraries, and diverse forms of enlightened recreation. In this report, Jouhaux advocated the founding of "maisons de vie social"—centers that would include a swimming pool, meeting halls, libraries, cinemas for "clean" films, restaurants, and a museum— all of which (typical to CGT folklore in this period) were thought to exist everywhere in the United States. The public recreational needs of women were largely ignored. Apparently trade unionists assumed that women's time released from wage work would be "domesticated" in the family.[15]

Throughout the 1920s, labor organizations continued to advocate popular education. For example, in 1922 the CGT established the Commission for Education and Leisure in Paris to coordinate sports and cultural programs. Most of these activities were local and generally short-lived. French communists established a federation of sports societies and even a newspaper, *Le Sport ouvrier*. And CGT supporters ran weekly excursions from Paris for municipal workers. There were similar efforts in Rouen, Toulouse, Lyon, and Nantes. Unlike their British counterparts, the CGT supported the initiatives of the ILO to coordinate popular leisure organizations; in 1929, French reformists organized a national leisure committee in order to broaden the appeal of workers' leisure beyond the confines of organized labor. This committee developed elaborate plans for educational tours, conferences, educational films, amateur theater, choral societies, and even dances, gardening, and sports.[16]

All of this effort reflected a rather conventional nineteenth-century socialist vision of leisure for self-improvement. Like their employers, unions had neither a commitment to mass consumption nor even much consciousness of the threat or promise of leisure organized by employers. In 1922, CGT writer Eugène Morel complained that, due to a lack of facilities, workers had little to do but to watch "cheap police films." Far from fearing employer manipulation of organized leisure, Morel denounced business for not being more active in sponsoring various forms of uplifting recreation. In France at least, the 1920s brought less a struggle over the uses of leisure than a conflict over its simple availability.[17]

Organized leisure, however, sponsored either by the Right or Left, was never the success in Britain or France that it would be in Italy, central Europe, or Russia. French employers made some headway in supporting workers' gardens, providing playing fields, sponsoring choral and theater groups, and even patronizing company libraries. Yet these efforts were largely concentrated in the mining and heavy-industrial regions of the north and east where the paternalism of large industrialists like the Wendels and Schneiders had long reigned. Although Renault and Thompson Houston initiated fairly ambitious sports clubs and other forms of welfare capitalism in the Paris region, reports from prefects in 1922 reveal practically no employer activity in the west or south. Employer-provided workers' gardens increased from 77,000 in 1919 to 160,000 in 1922; yet this was scarcely more than a gesture.[18]

In Britain, the number of "allotments" or workers' gardens also grew. In York, for example, they increased from 120 in 1899 to 1,544 in 1938, but Rowntree estimates that most of this rise took place during the war. Private gardening in Britain (as well as France) was already common, especially in rural areas. In the 1920s, the government doubled the value of education grants, which allowed the number of local adult education classes to increase from 219 in 1913 to 3,004 in 1938. Other local initiatives also bloomed in this period. The Men's Institute at Bethnal Green was founded in 1920 with 200 members; it enrolled 1,000 by 1925 in mostly home-improvement classes. And the Worker's Travel Association in the depth of the depression (1934) still organized trips for 27,361 tourists. The number of workingmen's clubs increased from 1,558 in 1913 to 2,488 by 1926. Yet, as all observers admitted, these examples of organized uplift paled in the light of increased commercial leisure and "wasted time."[19]

Gaston Rives's survey of French leisure in the mid-1920s found that, outside of the mining areas, workers mistrusted recreation facilities sponsored by employers or even those run by the Church. Workers resented these thinly veiled attempts to make them more loyal and productive employees; they identified leisure with "liberty" and thus resisted any collectivization of spare time.[20]

The Left was no more successful. Trade-union educational organizations were at best short-lived. The French popular university had never overcome the doctrinal splits that weakened this movement in 1907. Moreover, even relatively popular workers' sports groups had to compete with 20,000 nonaffiliated societies. Clearly, many a worker refused to be "parked in amusements especially created for his use." Even the miner "ardent for his union . . . goes fishing or hunting in preference to a dance or cinema because he wants to be alone." Moreover, despite the hopes of labor leaders, Rives was not optimistic that domesticity would provide a practical alternative to the bar: "Domestic activities do not exhaust the curiosity and intelligence of the male." "Women," he claimed, "are not interested in politics, the trade, or the union. . . . Woman is rarely a confidante of man." This skepticism toward the domestic leisure utopia was probably shared by many laboring men in the 1920s. Although workers may have increasingly valued sports, contact with nature, and even domestic togetherness, individualism and the lack of resources impeded their expression in organized leisure.[21]

On the surface this analysis of leisure ideology suggests a surprising degree of consensus. Both labor and management drew on a similar font of nineteenth-century myths—the value of domesticity and enlightened recreation. The enemy was the threat of the bar to the family and the continued allure of traditional unedifying amusements (like gambling and drinking) that challenged the wholesome virtues of organized athletics and cultural enrichment.

Labor seemed to be stealing the ideology and organizations of the conservatives. Socialists and trade unionists hoped that the eight-hour day would create a domestic utopia. The new leisure would replace the family (patriarchal) work unit lost with the physical separation of work and domestic life. An improved domestic bond would emerge in newly liberated hours at more relaxed meals during longer evenings and on freer Sundays. As an alternative to the mostly male and youthful solidarities of bar culture, the new leisure could restore the values of rural life, offer the moral uplift of organized sports and physical fitness, and provide a wider intellectual vision.

Yet this was hardly a clear case of *embourgeoisement*. The leisure ideology of the Left was essentially an apologetic. In the context of an organized attack on the shorter workweek, worktime reformers claimed that spare time was an investment in an improved "race" of workers. In this sense the *patron*'s attack on the eight-hour day was not an argument in the national economic interest but a selfish and short-sighted attack on "civilization." This ideology allowed labor to win Catholic allies in the 1920s by its defense of family values.[22]

However, these "conservative" goals went well beyond political expediency: as we have shown in chapter 4, they had played important roles in campaigns for the *semaine anglaise* and the Sunday closing law before the war. They reflected the beliefs of the organized and perhaps most articulate sections of the work force. These values were responses to the perceived loss of family ties in the working classes in the nineteenth century and the growing concern among mature workers that their children were becoming prey to moral and physical degradation. Ultimately, they reflect the long-term battle within the working classes over the "irrational" element in traditional leisures of all classes.[23]

A New Leisure and Work Ethic

Still we must ask: What did the eight-hour day mean to wage earners? If workers seldom embraced organized leisure, did they hold radically different views from their leaders? The chasm between elite and popular values has long been a presumption of much "new" social history. One way to develop a clearer understanding of the popular meaning of free time is to analyze the underlying values expressed by workers and unions in the struggles over hours in the decade after the war.[24] I find tensions but not clear opposition between the values of workers and the ideology of labor elites.

The eight-hour day was a quest for leisure—not the traditional play of community-centered festivals, lengthy rest breaks, and irregular voluntary absences from work but a desire for a new distribution of work and leisure time. This quest for a uniform and compressed workday with longer, more predictable and more continuous periods of personal time began in the 1890s at the start of the eight-hour movement (chapter 3); in the 1920s, the process was largely completed.

Despite utilitarian justifications for free time, workers and their leaders believed that leisure was an unqualified right. "A 44-hour week was sufficient for any man," said an engineer, for it assured a free Saturday afternoon so that workers could "have the real leisure that the weekend is intended to provide." Ernest Bevin of the dockers union claimed that modern steamships allowed the "work to fit the men." And what the men needed was "time other than for work or waiting for work."

Shorter hours meant the end to the "inhumane system of dragging people out of bed at 5:00 and 5:30" and the abolition of the "barbarous and unnatural practice of starting work at 6 o'clock in the morning." Workers had the right to a full evening of leisure and should not be obliged to retire early (or be deprived of rest) in order to rise too early in the morning. The traditional distaste for waking before dawn, to clock in at 6:00 A.M. in winter months, had now become "unnatural."[25]

The assumption of a right to leisure was perhaps the most common interpretation that Britons gave to Lloyd-George's call for a postwar Britain "fit for heroes" and the one new "freedom" that the French government promised its returning soldiers. In the post-armistice blossoming of democratic claims, the new workday was defended as a right of citizenship, a concrete expression of social equality beyond the common entitlements of political citizenship. If a 9:00 A.M. start, a forty-hour week, or a two-week vacation were appropriate for management, they were good enough for workers.[26]

The idea of a "normal working day for all industries throughout the country" was an attempt to eliminate the often extreme, and sometimes irrational, variations in worktime between different regions and industries. Despite the claim of British dock employers that different work sites required different hours, the dock union insisted on national uniformity. One British unionist argued that differences in intensity, productivity, skill, and danger of work should be reflected in wages, not hours. To deny the eight-hour day was to deprive workers of citizenship and even manhood. To the British dockers, the forty-four-hour week was "a demand for a real change in status calling for adequate human conditions for our members, who in the old days were looked upon as food for shipowners' profits, and who were picked out from day to day for a few hours' work like cattle from a pen."[27] A French paperworker expressed similar sentiments in 1922 in a complaint to the government over the nonapplication of the eight-hour law in his trade: "As a defender of the fatherland, I was told that all were one at the front, now we are to be all united at home and all equal before the law"—particularly the law of the eight-hour day.[28]

This quest for equality was restated in many forms. Retail clerks in Britain demanded an early closing of stores (with an often not too gentle chiding of the industrial worker for his insistence on buying tobacco after 9:00 P.M.). The hours movement in 1919 spread to seamen, farmworkers, and restaurant staff—all of whom had been left out of earlier hours agitation.[29] Even the elite had difficulty criticizing this quest for leisure. In early 1919, Professor John Hobhouse admitted that he had never worked more than an eight-hour day (and Charles Darwin had labored scarcely more than four). This consensus over the value of leisure made it a "natural" right.[30]

The equity of a "normal day" did not, however, override the traditional status-conscious labor hierarchy. Especially in Britain, many conflicts over the post-armistice hours settlement reflected the disappointment of skilled workers that the prewar gap between their working hours and those of their "inferiors" had not been maintained. Engineers felt that if the textile workers won a forty-eight-hour week, they should get forty-four hours; they were incensed by the fact that such workers—dockers, bargemen, even "down to dressmakers"—had won this advanced goal and they had not. Similarly, builders expected a forty-hour week and railroad signalmen demanded a six-hour day, in part because of their desire to maintain an hours hierarchy. In 1919, coal miners insisted on a six-hour day, because the danger and "unnaturalness" of underground work justified a "privileged" schedule. Free time was a measure of status as much as was the level of consumption. Yet organized labor insisted on a forty-eight-hour weekly maximum for all wage labor no matter what the mental or physical demands of the job— even though management rejected this right of citizenship on economic grounds.[31]

Why did this quest for leisure become such an obsession after the war? One might agree with G. D. H. Cole who, in 1920, declared that it was a pent-up demand, frustrated by a generation when the workweek scarcely changed despite increased work intensity and productivity. Historian M. A. Bienefeld claims that wage increases experienced during the war produced a desire to "buy" leisure time. Minister of Labour Robert Horne argued that the "irrational" aspects of the hours movement resulted from the "passionate desire for an easier time after five years of strain." In 1919, workers were repulsed by the prospect of increased work discipline—even in order to compensate for reduced hours. This may help explain their resistance to new work rules, their desire to eliminate piece rates, and their opposition to overtime. A revolt against the overwork of the war years surely was expressed in the ca'canny that British employers and government officials saw as more a threat to postwar recovery than hour reductions.[32] Yet the demand for leisure went beyond postwar social psychology.

Moreover, the goal was the permanent right to personal time—not merely income or jobs. Union leaders insisted that hours reductions were not to be bargained away for economic concessions. In the French building trades, compensatory time rather than income was sought when overtime was required. British steel smelters were even willing to sacrifice the wages of higher paid skilled workers in order to pay for a third shift and thus to reduce the day from twelve to eight hours. Robin Williams of the British dockers pointedly insisted that the goal of shorter time was not to increase employment but to create a steady pattern of work and leisure for dockers currently in the trade.[33]

Of course, leisure objectives were hardly new to the eight-hour era. They had been informally expressed in the traditional work habits of diverse trades: note the absenteeism among miners, tardiness among engineers and shipbuilders, late-morning starts of seamstresses, and the periods of "playing" in seasonal trades like dockwork. These customs had hardly died during World War I. In Britain, miners still took off on sunny summer days and often made Saturday shifts unprofitable because of their "sport-loving" ways. They also sometimes refused to work after a man was killed or seriously injured. In France, skilled workers (especially in construction) continued to insist on a Monday half-holiday as opposed to the "modern" Saturday afternoon. In addition, traditional wakes, patronal fetes, and other traditional holidays surely did not die out in either country.[34]

Yet after the war, there was a perceptible change in the allocation of time sought by most workers. Perhaps the most basic goal was a uniform workday throughout the year, particularly in seasonal trades like construction, dockwork, or even automobile manufacturing. In May 1919, French builders briefly won an unvarying eight-hour day, despite efforts of employers to modify it according to the season. French clothing unions resisted employers who attempted to perpetuate the traditional cyclic workyear by demanding ten hours of work during the busy season and only six in the dead season. Repeatedly in the early 1920s, French metal, textile, railroad, and other unions opposed managements' efforts to establish a workyear (e.g., of 2,496 hours) with no limits on the workday. Likewise dockers on both sides of the channel sought a uniform workday throughout the year.[35]

In Britain, the ideal of a daily norm of eight hours along with a Saturday half-holiday was behind the call for a forty-four-hour week. The alternative—a forty-eight-hour week with the Saturday half-holiday— of course meant an eight-and-a-half-hour weekday. A regular eight-hour norm deviated sharply from the seasonal schedule so common before the war. It was, in fact, seldom achieved in Britain: the movement for the forty-four-hour week was won only in a few trades. Workers in both countries failed to end the variable workday in construction, wood and flour mills, and agriculture; and, through the regular use of overtime, employers perpetuated it in textiles and many other industries. Still, the uniform eight-hour day remained a goal and a sensitive point in negotiations throughout the interwar period.[36]

In France, the eight-hour norm was tested in the practice of "recuperating" time "lost" to holidays and vacations. In the early 1920s, French employers sought and often won the right to extend the workday before and after major public holidays. After 1922, labor inspectors granted recuperation time at the normal pay rate without union approval. Workers were frequently more hostile to recuperation time than to ordinary overtime. As a Catholic metalworker declared, "a holiday is not really a holiday if the day's rest is conditional on the making up of time lost." This was a sharp change in attitude from the commonly accepted prewar pattern of furious overtime preceding holiday periods.[37]

Moreover, following the eight-hour settlements of early 1919, there were numerous conflicts over the definition of "worktime." French legislation proved to be ambiguous (e.g., in the meaning of the expression "effective work"); in Britain, the proviso in contracts that the same "conditions of employment" be maintained caused numerous conflicts. One common problem was determining when worktime began and ended: employers insisted on starting the clock when profitable production commenced (beginning with the start up of machinery). They complained bitterly when workers continued to arrive at the factory gate at 8:00 A.M. When operatives left their machine at 11:45 A.M. in order to be out of the factory by noon or when dockers stopped unloading the ship before the whistle blew to get at the head of the pay line, employers saw "cheating" on the eight-hour day. For the wage earner, "work" meant time at the "disposal of the employer" or on the employer's property: when employers insisted on running machines up to the whistle or required employees to service machines and clean up on their own time, workers protested. Although union officials were often willing to concede the employers' point in the name of increasing output, wage earners often resisted.[38]

Yet even the unions fought employers' efforts to limit paid worktime in mines to "productive time" or "effective work." Before the war, both French and British miners had waged a long battle over the issue of eight hours "from bank to bank." In France the 1919 miners' hours law conceded this principle when it included both "windings" in the eight-hour day (first miner in the pit until last out) as well as the lunch break; this, owners complained, produced only six and a half hours of "effective" work at the coal face. In 1922, French mine operators unsuccessfully attempted to eliminate the half-hour lunch break from the paid workday. For the mine owner, of course, worktime (even on piece rates like in mining) should count only from the moment the worker reached the coal face to do "effective work." For the miner, all time in the mine should be counted; for him worktime was that duration in which the worker was deprived of personal liberty because the miner, from the descent, was literally trapped in the mine and susceptible to its dangers. One French miner, perhaps only half-seriously, suggested that he really "worked" nine and a half hours counting the time when he left his home at 5:30 A.M. until his return at 3:00 P.M.[39]

A related problem in France was "intermittent work." Employers distinguished between "presence at work" and "effective labor."[40] Management argued that sailors, railway employees, and waiters should be obliged to put in ten or even twelve hours in order to complete eight hours of "effective" labor.[41] Yet French mechanics on dock equipment complained that ten hours of presence to service machines took away from the "complete joy of hours of liberty." A British locomotive repairman on a similar schedule declared: "make the 8 hours and off the job. I don't want to be at work or even on the railway 10 hours for 8, or else my benefit and pleasure is gone." The issue was not physical exertion or even uncompensated hours; it was preserving the ultimately scarce resource—personal time. As we have already seen, although French miners won the point, this was not true of their British counterparts in 1926; French sailors and some railway workers also lost this argument in 1922, at least temporarily.[42]

This conflict over the definition of labor time was closely related to labor's growing insistence that work schedules be modified to accommodate the family and personal clock. First, this meant that many workers endeavored to compress worktime in order to liberate as much of the twenty-four-hour day from work and its environment as possible. For this reason French trades (dockers, builders, metalworkers, etc.) agreed to the suppression of the morning and afternoon food breaks. In this instance the values of workers and labor elites probably coincided.[43]

There were numerous exceptions, however. Many French workers continued to take a two-hour lunch, even though it extended the time span engaged in wage work. Of course, "moderns" like Albert Thomas complained that this custom deprived workers of time for family evenings; and insofar as it led to excessive midday drinking and eating, it hampered productivity. Still, this tradition prevailed—perhaps because, for many, the long midday break was precisely the family meal.[44]

While some British workers embraced the one-break reform, others, especially in engineering, raised objections. Presumably the one-break system guaranteed that the wage earner had an adequate breakfast with the family because work would not begin until as late as 8:00 A.M. Yet male workers protested when employers insisted that work start no *earlier* than 7:45 A.M. This seems less strange when one realizes that wives and other relatives who worked at textile and clothing factories began their shifts at 6:00 A.M., and that the price of a late start was a 5:30 P.M. finish. The engineer preferred a shorter lunch to a "late" leaving time because he wanted as much of the evening free "to go to the pictures" and for "time in the evening with his wife and family." The presumed advantage of an early-morning breakfast with the family did not impress those small-town workers who were reluctant to abandon the 8:00 A.M. breakfast break that they traditionally had shared with the family.[45]

British reformers had long advocated the two- or (more rarely) three-shift system. This they saw as a practical alternative to overtime and high overhead costs that followed from short hours on a single shift. Yet there was considerable opposition to these schemes. Not only did feminist groups agitate against multiple shifts as destructive of family life, but working women themselves, especially where alternative employment was available, resisted the two-shift system. It meant not only a late return from work for the second shift (often about 10:00 P.M.) but an early start for the first shift (often at 6:00 A.M.). In both cases, work schedules interfered with sociable leisure and the midwork break violated "natural" eating habits—that is, meals with family and friends. As a final example, locomotive engineers in Britain opposed the regular eight-hour day, preferring to work ten or even twelve hours on a long haul to the prospect of having to board away from home after eight hours on the train.[46]

What all these variations had in common, of course, were workers' claims that family schedules should take precedence over the work clock. While this insistence that worktime accommodate family time was not unknown in prewar Europe, surely the trend was accelerated after the war.

Worktime, Employment, and Overtime

One might object that all this misses a central point—that workers used the eight-hour day not primarily for leisure but to reduce unemployment or gain higher wages through overtime pay. Although evidence of these motives exists, they neither are as basic as often assumed nor can these economic goals be understood outside the specific context of postwar labor conditions. In France, work sharing was central to some of the conflicts over the eight-hour day, especially immediately after the armistice in war-related industries. Fear of job loss was also a primary concern of French seamen and railway workers when, in 1922, employers sought to extend hours and eliminate a third shift.[47]

Yet this issue was seldom the central concern. After the war, France experienced not unemployment but a labor shortage, obliging employers to import some 1.5 million immigrants in the 1920s.[48] Even where job sharing was the goal, it had essentially a social purpose: for example, a construction union in Lille insisted on eight hours (a reduction from seasonal highs of twelve) in order to "distribute work to the largest possible number of family heads in the trade and thus to avoid the migration of these heads of families." The old workers' ethic—that all in a trade should have sufficient worktime to be able to maintain a family before any should work more hours—still lay behind much of the objection to overtime. It was also an expression of the "right of settlement"—that no family man be obliged to leave his village or neighborhood in order to work. It was a rejection of the old journeyman's "tour."[49]

In Britain, there is a stronger argument that the quest for shorter hours was primarily an effort to combat unemployment. This was clearly the objective in the strike for a forty-hour week in Glasgow in January 1919; and it lay beneath the agitation for the forty-four-hour week and the wildcat embargoes of overtime in engineering trades, where postwar economic conversion threatened shipbuilders and arms manufacturers.[50]

Yet again we must put this motive in a social context. Those who opposed overtime sought to reduce job competition between veterans and home-front workers. Some feared that without work sharing, soldiers would be kept in the army and the unemployed would be forced to relocate or even to join the reconstruction work in France.[51] Union leaders, like Robin Williams of the dockers, saw in the forty-four-hour week a dignified alternative to the Out-of-Work Donation. For the public, a shorter week was a less costly alternative to the dole and it placed the burden of economic downturn on employers. Most fundamentally, said Williams, the work-sharing demand could no longer be ignored for workers would no longer suffer silently during recessions; they expected either jobs or income, and preferably the former. The goal of reducing unemployment through work sharing reflected a more complex social psychology than expressed in the economics of unemployment.[52]

These arguments made sense in the optimism of 1919. But they gradually faded as economic pressures dissolved whatever labor solidarity existed. By summer, union leaders complained that workers would no longer sacrifice paid worktime for the justice or enlightened self-interest of aiding the unemployed. Moreover, work sharing never was embraced by many trades. For example, the British railroad union insisted on regular Sunday overtime instead of creating jobs through a forty-eight-hour limit.[53]

Opponents of reduced worktime frequently argued that the eight-hour day was merely a pretense for raising wages by applying overtime rates earlier. In March 1922, French labor inspectors reported that whereas unions opposed overtime, workers did not. In 1924, Paul Rives wrote that the eight-hour law was "only a minimum wage law." Workers expected that income beyond the subsistence level was to be earned on overtime and frequently through moonlighting. In 1919, the British minister of labor and employers agreed.[54] Trade union leaders often shared this view.[55]

Yet can we adequately explain this behavior in terms of economic self-interest and claim that the worker had become an "economic" man? In France, certainly, there is countervailing evidence. Many French unions consistently advocated strict limits on overtime, even when it was paid at a premium rate. In 1922, metalworkers repeatedly opposed employers' efforts to raise the annual overtime limit from 100 to 300 hours. That year textile unions protested a revised decree that allowed up to 250 hours of annual overtime. Again, in 1924 and 1925, as the political wind shifted in a more favorable direction, construction, metal, and leather workers demanded and partly won reduced overtime.[56]

An obvious response to this evidence is that the rank and file seldom shared with their leaders this opposition to overtime. Often this was true; but again we must explore the context. Part-time French farmers willingly worked ten or more hours per day at paid industrial jobs when there was little to do on their small farms. In the village of Montboison, for example, the employer of a small foundry in 1920 complained that his workers insisted on a ten-hour day in winter but only eight hours in the spring during planting.[57] This was, of course, an old adaptation of the rural farmer to part-time wage labor.

More common, however, French industrial workers accepted over-time in order to cope with the more modern pressure of wages that lagged behind prices. To be sure, the French eight-hour law formally conceded the principle of eight hours of work for ten hours of pay. Still in 1919 and 1920, decreases in real wages through inflation plus wage cuts during the 1921 recession made this victory meaningless. In the spring of 1920, Lyon textile and metal industries offered overtime to inflation-threatened workers rather than increased hourly wages. In Rennes, employers insisted that workers accept two hours of overtime at the discretion of management in exchange for any wage increase. Workers, especially in unorganized trades, sought and even petitioned inspectors for overtime to supplement wages below subsistence levels. When French unions in the building trades and heavy industry were weakened during the influx of immigrant workers in the early 1920s, workers accepted overtime in order to keep up with inflation.[58]

French unions responded to these threats in a variety of ways. Some sought prohibitively high overtime rates. In a few skilled trades, like printing, these rates (often at time-and-a-half) were sufficient to dis-suade employers from the "systematic" use of overtime. However, in other industries (like shoes) no overtime premium existed or it was only 10 to 25 percent over the hourly rate. Unions that lacked the organiza-tional power to bargain for a high overtime rate fought against decrees that granted employers overtime. As noted in chapter 7, these efforts were beginning to be successful from late 1924.[59]

At the same time, French business was ambiguous about the benefits of overtime. While clinging to the managerial right to determine when and how much overtime was necessary, employers seldom used all of their overtime allowances. For some, business activity seldom required overtime; for others, premium rates produced higher wage bills with little increase in weekly output. A few even preferred that workers use their "extra" time raising food in gardens, which would reduce wage pressures.[60]

Most important for our understanding of French labor attitudes, overtime did not always maximize income. Not only was an overtime rate not always paid in France, but workers accepted overtime primarily in the context of declining real incomes. For unions (who generally sought the long-term interest of their members), overtime was primarily a threat to a new hours standard, "a first step toward the abolition of the eight-hour law" and the beginning of the restoration of a ten-hour day as the norm for the basic wage. Its use also meant the perpetuation of the irregular workyear, caused by seasonal and trade-cycle factors. A CGT official at Belfort claimed, if the eight-hour day were "constant and uniform, all crises of work would go away." A textile employer from Tourcoing agreed that when the workers refused overtime, this tended to "regularize production." Overtime may have helped managers avoid costly labor-saving technology. French textile union officials accepted overtime if it was due to the "unforeseen pressure of work," but not if it was a result of a "poor organization of work."[61] Finally, some unions refused to negotiate on overtime until the wages at the eight-hour level were sufficient to support a family or assure the spouse's traditional share of family expenses.[62]

Rives may have captured a more basic motive: "so as to prove that they owe the employer only 8-hours, that they have freedom . . . [and] as a means of protest," workers refused to do overtime. This assertion of a right to personal liberty, although frequently stifled by the economic necessity of low wages, was likely to be closer to the feeling of many workers than the strictly pecuniary motives ascribed to labor by many employers and antilabor bureaucrats.[63]

In the 1920s, many workers would have still agreed with Ruskin that "there is no wealth without life." In an economy where the consumer-goods market was still relatively undeveloped, workers preferred time to income. French studies conducted in 1913 showed little impact of additional income on workers' living standards.[64] At least in France, an essentially subsistence mind-set survived even in Roger Francq, leading postwar economic writer for the CGT and leader of the technicians union. He declared that a "shortening of the workday is the only way for workers to gain from rising productivity," implying no possibility of an increase in real income.[65] Only when a consumer economy developed after World War II in Europe did workers adopt an offensive economic strategy—and, with it, sometimes a preference of overtime income instead of leisure.

Eight Hours, the Weekend, and the Annual Vacation

If, in the 1920s, a consumer workers' culture had not yet emerged, neither had other values associated with later twentieth-century leisure society—the ideal of the two-day weekend and the annual vacation. To be sure, in the heady days of January 1919, Scottish shop stewards and some miners advocated a thirty-hour week based on a six-hour day, five-day week. Others, who promoted the more modest forty-hour week, also supported a five-day week. Yet some advocates of the forty-hour week were still thinking of a five-and-a-half-day week with a seven-hour weekday, not the two-day weekend. With the demise of the radical hours movement in 1919, the only proponents of a five-day workweek in Britain were employers in the metal, engineering, and chemical industries for whom a half-Saturday was no longer cost-effective. The social advantage of two continuous days free from wage labor rarely even entered trade union discussion in the interwar years.[66]

In France, the ideal of the weekend was even more muted. The butchers resumed their prewar quest for a full day of rest (on Monday) to replace the compromise of two half-days won in 1907. Yet these struggles were surprisingly few—probably because of the lack of organization in the retail trades. Moreover, while labor leaders often had embraced the *semaine anglaise* as a solution to the moral problem of the family, not all trades stepped into line. It became widespread in textiles and clothing industries in which women predominated; but in occupations in which men were concentrated, support for the Saturday half-holiday was mixed. For example, about 70 percent of engineering firms had adopted it in 1919; but builders and furniture workers in many regions preferred an eight-hour day, six-day week, as an alternative to a longer weekday. All French unions were opposed to a five-day week based on a forty-eight-hour norm as a threat to the "spirit" of the eight-hour law.[67] Most French employers also had little sympathy for the five-day week. A prominent business journal had only scorn for Henry Ford when he introduced the five-day week in 1926, claiming that the reform was only a smokescreen for Ford's declining sales and the overwork of his employees.[68]

For organized labor, the duration of daily labor took precedence over increasing the length of weekly rest. Workers preferred longer evenings to Saturday mornings (or a carefree Friday night). This may reflect the lack of consumer consciousness or insufficient money for "weekends" away from home or even spent in doing home improvements.[69]

The annual holiday with pay was also only a minor movement in the decade following World War I. Organized workers were rather slow in developing an interest in the long stint away from work. As we shall see in chapter 10, this movement would explode only in the 1930s.[70]

In both the idea of the modern weekend and the paid vacation, income substantially beyond the subsistence level was required. Today's office workers might consider a schedule of four days of ten hours for the benefits of a three-day weekend, or prefer an additional week's holiday to a few minutes shaved off the workday. Yet both contemporary attitudes toward time presume a relatively manageable workweek of forty hours, not forty-eight or more; and both are based on a relatively secure annual income, which made meaningful longer durations of leisure time.

The 1920s were but a step in the broader movement toward a goal of long continuous blocks of spare time. The primary objective was to liberate time from the traditional 6:00 A.M. to 6:00 (or 5:00) P.M. workday and to create a regular work schedule that synchronized with the family and personal clock.

Some Leisure Patterns in the 1920s

If the ideology of "organized leisure" and "rational recreation" had proved disappointing, commercial and passive forms of leisure clearly benefited from the reduction of worktime in the 1920s. The cinema partially replaced the pub as the leisure center of interwar Europeans. By 1934, 18.5 million movie tickets were sold weekly in Britain, a phenomenon greatly enhanced by the legalization of the cinema on Sundays in 1932. In a 1931 survey in Liverpool, an average of 9 percent of leisure time was consumed in watching movies and 8.7 percent was spent in bars compared with only 0.3 percent of free time used in edu-

cation. Cycling blossomed as did country excursions. Association football, organized in 1913, expanded by 1922, to four leagues. Books and
magazines that specialized in home improvements proliferated during
the 1920s. While piano sheet music sales dropped by 50 percent between 1925 and 1933, music was increasingly heard on phonographs
and especially radio. By 1939, 73 percent of British families owned ra-
dios (while only 15 percent possessed telephones). George Orwell
claimed in 1937 that "cutprice chocolate, the movies, the radio, strong
tea and the football pools quite likely . . . between them averted revolution." Mass commercial leisure may well have made a more privatized
working class, a fact that distressed the organized Left throughout the
interwar period.[71]

Yet this growth of a leisure ethic hardly implied the emergence of a
consumer society. The quest for short hours surely did not simply reflect a timeless truth—that people want to work as little as possible.[72]
To be sure, union leaders believed that workers would have to be educated to make "good" use of their leisure and to abandon economic
Malthusianism or ca'canny. The rebellions in the spring of 1919 against
the intensification of the work pace and the imposition of new worktime rules—even those that had been accepted by union leaders—may
well be proof of this revulsion against work.

It has been fashionable in recent labor history to claim a sharp divide
between the "typical worker" and the labor leadership. For example,
one might argue that leaders, not the rank and file, favored technological modernization as a means of solving the economic dilemma of
increasing output in less time. After all, can we believe that workers
really abandoned their customary war against modern work discipline?
Did they look beyond the formula of "the highest wages with the least
effort and time" to the problem of the collective output?

Some evidence appears to suggest that they did. In contrast to the
"traditional" rejection of work discipline, twentieth-century European
workers not only accepted the regularity of the work clock, but even
sought a greater uniformity and predictability in economic time than
was actually demanded by industrialists. Far from simply seeking to
minimize effort, they adapted to the mechanical world in a pragmatic
attempt to synchronize social time and worktime. Many workers may
not have had much use for the moralizing rhetoric of their leaders (although older, more sedentary workers in many cases probably identified with this ideology). Nevertheless, wage earners generally recognized the linkages between effort and living standards. In the postwar

period, there is little evidence that workers objected to attempts to raise productivity—if it did not mean loss of jobs.[73] Like their leaders, most wage earners recognized the need for innovation in order to compensate for reduced hours. In the 1920s, French employers seldom complained of worker opposition to productivity measures, and, if British management often blamed go-slow attitudes for high costs, legitimate fears of layoffs prompted most of this behavior. The linkage between productivity and leisure was so obvious that organized British and French workers were slow to question the impact of economic rationalization upon work and economic stability in the 1920s. Demonstrating this will be part of my task in the following chapter.

9

Labor and Rationalization

The 1920s were an era of economic growth. Despite or because of the general reduction in worktime, European societies experienced a nearly unprecedented boom. By the mid-1920s, that growth and its future prospects were associated with *rationalization,* a term that had become a key code word throughout the industrial world. Like many such labels, the more common its use, the less clear was its meaning.

Rationalization was used as a synonym for Taylorism. Increasingly it also meant Fordism—a social as well as industrial system: it promised not only massive outputs of consumer durables but offered the high wages and short hours that guaranteed mass markets for these goods. Fordism was to be the key to a symmetrical economy, where wages and profits rose together and destructive fights over shares of the economic pie would become things of the past. Insofar as production became the principal yardstick of the successful society, Taylorism and Fordism could play leading roles. Rationalization was the goal not only of America's Herbert Hoover but of Europe's social democratic parties, Italy's fascism, and even Russia's socialism.[1]

The language of rationalization drew upon the nineteenth-century ideas of work science and even rational recreation. These themes were inextricably linked to the problem of the social allocation of time. Since

194

the 1880s, reformers claimed that time efficiency—the concentration of work into more intense and thus more productive duration—would liberate time from work and thereby both create mass markets and provide opportunities for social "betterment."

Between 1890 and 1920, labor support grew for the idea of a time-efficient mass-market economy and leisure society. Productivism—in France, labor's interpretation of Taylorism, and in Britain, the key to fatigue science—had played a central role in the apologetic for short hours for a generation. In the 1920s, the idea of the scientific organization of work was far from being merely a tool of the corporation during the second industrialization. It was a weapon of labor in its defense of a compressed workday.

Yet what impact did the eight-hour day have on economic development? Did it create jobs as promised by Guesde and Hyndman in the early 1890s or did it create unemployment as warned James Stephen Jeans and Yves Guyot before the war? Was the eight-hour day responsible for an increase or decrease in labor productivity? Did it promote a more efficient economy and encourage adoption of scientific management and mechanization as expected by Boilley and Mann in the late 1880s and Thomas and Leverhulme in 1918?

Moreover how did that world of more intense, more "managed" work look in reality? When, in the 1920s, the dreams of a labor-engineer alliance had faded along with workers' control of production and leisure, to what extent did British and French labor abandon the ideal of a time-efficient consumer society? Did they find an antiutopia in the Taylorized factory and the signs of a mass-consumption leisure? Or did they hold fast to the hope of a democratized world of leisure—and look for new meanings to work? We can begin to answer these questions in a further investigation of economic ideas and realities of the 1920s.

The Eight-Hour Economy in Britain and France

Despite expectations, worktime had an ambiguous or even irrelevant impact on the economic equation. The eight-hour day was not responsible for creating jobs, or eliminating them. It hardly led to economic decline; but neither was it the cause of a scientific revolution in industry. By briefly focusing on the economic fates of Britain and then of France in the 1920s, the linkages between work duration and economic rationalization can be explored.

In Britain, where fears of postwar unemployment fueled the short-hours movement, economic historian Peter Kane found a relationship between a decline in hours and additional employment: a 1 percent reduction in worktime yielded a 1.76 percent increase in jobs in 1919 and 1920.[2] But over a longer period, between 1920 and 1924, hours played an insignificant role. Kane attributes this to the widespread use of "systematic overtime," especially after 1922. This negated any job-creating role that a nominal forty-seven-hour week may have provided. However, mean weekly overtime hardly rose in the 1920s. Increased use of "systematic overtime" occurred only in the 1950s and especially the 1960s.[3] A better explanation is that firms after 1919 rapidly improved man-hour productivity, which obviated the need for additional manpower. Recent econometric analysis reveals that between 1924 and 1937 man-hour production in the British economy increased 1.5 percent per year, substantially higher than the rate of 0.9 percent during the prewar period (1873–1913) or 0.5 percent during a later period (1951–1973).[4] The postwar recessions of 1921 and 1926 also reduced demand for labor.[5] Moreover, rapid mechanization and innovation not only offset the job-creating effects of hour reductions, but contributed to at least temporary technological unemployment.[6]

One might argue, as do R. C. O. Matthews and his colleagues, that diminutions in worktime in 1919 were successful because they occurred at a cyclic peak when demand for labor was high. In consequence, production costs climbed; thus demand for labor decreased and the subsequent downward economic swing was exacerbated. Similarly, Matthews argues, recessions had followed other reductions in worktime (1870s and 1970s).[7]

Yet, it is difficult to assess the role, if any, of hours in the complexity of the business cycle. Probably more important to the slump in demand for British goods after 1920 was the wage bill (only partially related to worktime), which rose more sharply relative to marginal productivity after World War I than in any other modern period. Certainly British employers were much more concerned about wages, which, though declining after 1921, remained high throughout the interwar period relative to the prewar profit-wage ratio.[8] In any case, the British economic problem was not a labor shortage, created by a diminution of worktime, but rather unemployment—largely the fruit of technological innovation and, more important, of declining markets.

In France, the impact of shorter hours on employment should have been more direct. After all, the nominal reduction of worktime was substantially greater in France than in Britain (declining at least 18 percent in France from 1913 to 1929 in industry and commerce—double the rate in Britain).[9] The well-known facts of France's exceptionally low birth rate and war losses surely made the sharp drop in worktime even more likely to create labor shortages. These diminutions may well have created jobs, especially in continuous-process and growth industries (chemicals, steel, engineering, and railroads). It likely was a principal reason for the recruitment of over 1.5 million immigrant workers in the 1920s. These laborers filled places on the French occupational ladder in heavy construction, mining, metallurgy, and even seasonal agriculture when job opportunities in more stable and attractive industries opened up for French workers.[10]

Did the eight-hour day cause economic stagnation in France? E. H. Phelps-Brown estimated that between 1905 and 1930 the French distributed increased productivity on a ratio of six to four in favor of leisure over income (as compared with the ratio of four to six in Britain and two to eight in the United States). In the 1920s, the French worked an average of 1.6 hours less per week than did the Americans—despite a much less productive economy. The French economic historian, Jean Fourastié, has alleged a relationship between the forty-hour week and the economic (and military) failure of the Popular Front. From a desire to restrict output and share work, and even from an unwillingness to recognize the strict relationship between consumption and production, some critics argue, the French prematurely distributed leisure and thus allowed their economy to lag behind competitors.[11] By contrast, others have associated the economic "miracle" of the 1950s and 1960s with the stable and relatively long workweeks of French industry in that period.[12]

Nevertheless, is there sufficient evidence to conclude that worktime reductions impeded economic growth? There may be some validity to this claim for the forty-hour week. This, however, is surely an exceptional case because introduction of the forty-hour week took place in one of the least auspicious economic and political moments in the twentieth century. A better test case would be the impact of the eight-hour day (forty-eight-hour week) during the 1920s. Oddly, those who argue that worktime reductions impeded growth have not addressed this example even though it was an even sharper drop in hours than occurred in the late 1930s.[13]

Yet Jean-Jacques Carré and his associates have found that between 1921 and 1929 man-hour production rose 5.5 percent per year as compared with the 2 percent rate between 1896 and 1913. Increased man-hour production may be explained in part by the "efficiency offset." E. F. Denison estimates that 100 percent of the loss in man-week production down to forty-eight hours was recovered in improved hourly output. And other estimates are considerably more optimistic as to the point when the offset becomes only a proportion of the decrease in worktime.[14]

More important, between 1919 and 1929 the man-year growth in production was not much lower (5.1 percent) than the man-hour rate, despite the loss of perhaps six hundred hours per man-year (or 20 percent from the ten-hour day). Even though the British experienced a more modest loss of worktime (about 9 percent), increases in French man-year production were substantially superior to the British in the period from 1896 to 1929 (1.5 to 0.6 percent). The French index of industrial production rose by 1929 to 148 (1913 = 100) compared with an index of 125 for Britain.[15]

Even more significant, France's growth in the 1920s was comparable with that of the boom of the 1950s (a 5.1 percent annual growth in all productive sectors). This was true despite the fact that the industrial workday actually rose slightly in the latter period (1 percent from 1949 to 1963) while it fell dramatically in the 1920s. It is, of course, possible that with longer hours in the 1920s, the production index would have been even higher. Yet it is as likely that without the shock of having less labor time at their disposal, French employers would have not been obliged to have made the substantial investments that contributed to the boom of the 1920s.[16]

An Opportunity to Rationalize: Compressing Time and Intensifying Work

It is reasonably clear that output and even productivity were not affected by the reduction of worktime. In France at least, productivity rose while worktime fell. In Britain, productivity increases surely offset the work-sharing potential of reduced labor time. Does it follow from this that the eight-hour day actually facilitated the introduction of scientific management or work efficiency measures that account for these increases in productivity? As discussed in chapter 4, this had been the prediction of short-hours advocates.

In both countries, economic rationalization was the byword of economic reformers. In Britain, Taylorism began to receive increased attention in business and engineering journals after the war.[17] However, there is little evidence that Taylorism was widely introduced in the factory. Both inadequate capital from the City and managerial conservatism meant that the rationalization movement that swept the United States, Germany, and France had relatively little influence in Britain. In the United Kingdom, rationalization meant primarily merger and market sharing rather than managerial innovation to increase productivity.[18]

In any case Taylorism never had a good press in Britain. Work-efficiency specialists like P. Sargant Florence and Charles Meyer, who had greater influence than industrial engineers, continued to attack Taylorism for its neglect of the "human factor."[19] More important, employers lacked the managerial controls over the work process (e.g., relative to the United States) necessary to implement scientific management. Such typical Taylorite measures as time and motion study and functional foremen were nearly impossible in British engineering plants.[20]

British employers generally preferred indirect methods of increasing productivity like the premium-wage bonus systems. These schemes removed the economic risk of other incentive plans for they lowered the price paid per unit as output increased. As an alternative to scientific management in the early 1930s, a few British firms employed the Bedaux system. Unlike scientific management, Charles Bedaux's plan was simple, inexpensive, and claimed to accommodate the findings of fatigue science. Pay rates were to be based on the "scientific" determination of the time required both to undertake and to recover from a given task. Yet the managerial techniques of scientific management or even Bedaux or other bonus plans were relatively unimportant compared with mechanical improvements.[21]

To be sure, efforts of British work scientists continued throughout the interwar period. In 1918, the Industrial Fatigue Research Board (IFRB) encouraged management-labor cooperation in the steel industry.[22] In 1920, the Industrial Welfare Society, a group of moderate labor leaders and progressive businessmen, sought to foster new industrial welfare schemes in hopes of improving productivity.[23] The government likewise supported several commissions to study industrial efficiency.[24]

Still none of these efforts had much impact. The IFRB was repeatedly frustrated by employer indifference to its efforts. In 1920, *The Times Engineering Supplement* criticized the IFRB for ignoring engineering problems and the costs of increasing labor efficiency. In 1925, the IFRB's *Annual Report* admitted that, despite attempts to win employer cooperation in its research, few managers took much interest. By

1926, a major effort at promoting a shift system in textiles had converted only fifty firms. Given depressed markets, few employers had an incentive to add a second shift. Women workers frequently resisted the "Leverhulme" scheme as a threat to family and social life.[25]

British work science played an increasingly conservative role. In the 1920s, the discipline lost its propaganda function as specialists devoted themselves to narrow technical studies. With the failure of labor-management cooperation, work scientists were unable to play a mediating role. The IFRB redirected its efforts to finding solutions to the growing problem of boredom and nervous fatigue. Investigators favored regulated rest breaks, variations in job assignments, and vocational selection (e.g., to weed out extroverts); they even supported piped in music and group singing (to restore traditional work rhythms). At the same time, fatigue researchers began to define the eight-hour shift as the optimum work spell, below which absenteeism and other inefficiencies would rise. They legitimized the "naturalness" of the eight-hour day and abandoned the old dream of a progressive reduction of worktime.[26]

In France, the impact of the workday on industrial innovation was equally ambiguous. Certainly the eight-hour work regime helped to spark a widespread interest in the "scientific organization of work." French engineering groups, led by Charles de Freminville, Henri Le Châtelier, and Henri Fayol, popularized scientific management in French business circles. The Redressement Français, organized in 1925 by electrical goods manufacturer Ernest Mercier, proposed a French "Institute of Work." In the face of the less favorable exchange rate resulting from the stabilization of the franc in August 1926, the Redressement called for new measures to intensify production. Writing for the Redressement, Auguste Detoeuf noted:

We must develop . . . within management the belief that upon them alone depends the productivity of their enterprises, that the easy measures such as demanding fatiguing work or longer workdays from their employees or offering them less money for the same work . . . lead to a poor output, while difficult measures, those which demand the systematic study of the conditions of the functioning of the enterprise, have an enormous impact on production.[27]

Added to the now common generalities of "Taylorism" was a renewed fascination with the philosopher-industrialist, Henry Ford. Not only had Ford's assembly line Model-Ts, based on the principle of high output and the mass market, captured the European entrepreneurs' imagination, but Ford's five-dollar, eight-hour day had equally impressed reformers and labor with the dream of a consumers' "socialism." European authors praised Fordism for its promise of unlimited growth based on efficient time at work and mass consumption at leisure. This literature followed the well-worn path of nineteenth-century travel writings, claiming to show the European future in the innovations of the New World.[28]

By the mid-1920s, both French and international organizations, organized along tripartite lines, had adopted scientific management and Fordism as solutions to the economic and social problems of capitalist democracy. Albert Thomas helped to organize the French Association for Social Progress, which won the collaboration of E. Mercier and other leading business leaders. The International Scientific Management Committee, which since 1925 had included representatives of French business, in 1927 invited French labor delegates to participate.[29] Further, in 1924, the International Congress for the Scientific Organization of Work met in Prague with full French participation.[30] Finally, the French government commissioned a National Economic Council, which in March 1928 supported the study of the technical problems of scientific management.[31] At the center of this growing network was Albert Thomas and his vision of a time-efficient economy.

Yet employers were no more willing to sign onto this program than they had been earlier in the decade to embrace the CGT's power-sharing schemes.[32] The business press was also skeptical that scientific management—and especially Ford's assembly-line techniques—could be adapted to the quality-goods sector of French manufacturing.[33] In 1922, the Union of Metallurgical and Mining Industries questioned whether "any technical improvements [were] left to be made" and suggested that small manufacturers lacked the capital or markets necessary to adopt new equipment or to Taylorize. These firms, "closely linked to large-scale plants," could not be sacrificed.[34] Léon Pasquier, the president of the Lyon-based Metallurgical Association, neither was interested in nor indicated much understanding of Taylorism: scientific management works "only in new countries" and was a threat to apprenticeships and to technical education—hardly the response of a modernizing employer.[35]

There are few quantitative sources that inform us about the impact of scientific management on the eight-hour economy in France. Probably our best data are from a French government survey of seventy factories (conducted between 1921 and 1927) that was designed to illustrate the ways in which these firms adapted to the eight-hour day. This source clearly indicates the limited changes in the labor process stimulated by worktime reductions. This survey was by no means a sample of French industrial adaptation to the eight-hour day; but it can be used to indicate the experience of mostly *successful* firms responding to the challenge of intensifying worktime.[36]

Only one of the firms adopted time and motion studies, a key component of scientific management, while 51 percent introduced none or only one innovation that could be even loosely associated with Taylorism (Table 9-1); only 13 percent adopted as many as four to seven of these innovations. In a few mass-production factories, a simplified version of Taylorism was applied, at least in combining bonus-pay systems with improved internal transport. Yet in none was there any mention of the fine points of work science (such as vocational screening or predetermined rest breaks to eliminate fatigue). Half of the firms adopted piece work (but not necessarily the sophisticated bonus system advocated by Taylor); and 41 percent introduced new factory transportation (from push trucks to complex conveyor systems). Yet the less ambiguously Taylorite innovations (Table 9-1, innovations 3 through 7) were men-

Table 9-1 *Innovations Introduced after the Eight-Hour Day in Seventy French Factories (1921–1927)*

"TAYLORITE" INNOVATIONS	
1. Piece work and bonus pay systems	50%
2. Internal transport	41
3. Serial or line production	17
4. Additional machinery	16
5. Increased division of labor	10
6. Expanded plant	8
7. Improved training	4

"TRADITIONALIST" INNOVATIONS	
1. Improvements in old machinery	31%
2. Stricter control of worktime (suppression of breaks, etc.)	24
3. Increased surveillance	24
4. Additional drive power to machines	17
5. Increased machine speed	16
6. Increased work load	7

Source: "L'Adaptation des conditions de production et de travail à la loi du 23 avril 1919 sur la journée de huit heures," *Bulletin du Ministère du travail* (April–June, July–September, October–December 1924; January–March 1925; and July–September 1927).

Table 9-2 *Levels of "Taylorization" by Type and Size of Factory*

TYPE OF FACTORY	LOW[a] % (NO.)	MEDIUM[b] % (NO.)	HIGH[c] % (NO.)
Traditional (textile, leather)	65 (17)	27 (7)	8 (2)
Artisan/workshop	60 (9)	33 (5)	7 (1)
Mass production/heavy industry	34 (10)	48 (14)	17 (5)
Total	51 (36)	37 (26)	11 (8)

SIZE OF FACTORY			
Less than 25 workers	50 (5)	40 (4)	10 (1)
25–100 workers	58 (11)	26 (5)	16 (3)
101–999 workers	46 (11)	42 (10)	12 (3)
Total	51 (27)	36 (19)	13 (7)

[a]"Low Taylorization" is 0–1 innovations as listed in Table 9-1 under "Taylorite Innovations."
[b]"Medium Taylorization" is 2–3 innovations.
[c]"High Taylorization" is 4–7 innovations.
Source: See Table 9-1.

tioned much less often. With the possible exception of mechanical improvements, there were no significant differences between any of these innovations and the ability of the firms to recover output lost to shorter hours.

Apparently cheap traditionalist innovations like increasing work discipline and eliminating tardiness were just as likely to enhance productivity as were "scientific" innovations. For example, a small maker of eyeglasses had only to speed up the grindstones and insist that his workers arrive and leave on time to increase production by 27 percent over the ten-hour day. The workers themselves in a small engineering firm practiced "informal" Taylorism, increasing production as needed to compensate for a more compressed workday.[37]

There is some evidence, however, that smaller, less mechanized, and more specialized firms were less likely to adopt Taylorite innovations than were larger factories or plants that mass-produced goods (Table 9-2). Still, larger factories, relying on relatively complex technology, seemed to have combined new or improved machinery with "increased discipline" (rather than scientific management, properly called) to increase production. The old "driving" system of the nineteenth century had hardly died.[38] In two instances the owners actually suppressed a bonus-pay system (which the workers had opposed) and instead introduced mechanical changes. A bicycle factory introduced a machine in

1922 that increased the productivity of piece-rate workers by 50 percent over 1914, whereas productivity before this change was more than 10 percent below the 1914 level. At the same time, the work force was reduced by one-third. A similar pattern occurred in other assembly plants. Especially important was the introduction of conveyor belts, elevators, trollies, and other transportation devices.[39] Yet, as Patrick Fridenson and others have shown, in the 1920s even in the automobile industry the skilled worker survived the onslaught of Taylorism.[40]

These findings suggest several conclusions. First, in French industry there was sufficient slack both in the utilization of manual labor and in the use of existing machinery to allow many firms to avoid Taylorite innovations. We may assume that employers recovered lost output by the most economical means possible—in general, not much innovation in machinery or managerial method was required. Second, there was scarcely any difference in the response of large mass-production factories and small specialty workshops in their propensity to introduce Taylorism. Third, the ready availability of machine and process technology allowed employers to recover lost productivity easily, without Taylorism or work science. This was particularly true in larger and more fully mechanized plants.

In a word, the eight-hour day had a limited impact on the introduction of scientific management to France. The reduced workday, however, probably did encourage the more rapid introduction of machine technology than would have otherwise occurred; it likely created a more closely supervised work environment than was common during the more "porous" ten-hour or longer workday. This was probably also the British experience.[41]

The Dream and Nightmare of Rationalization

Despite its limited impact on the shop floor, the idea of rationalization, like that of industrial "science" in the previous generation, continued to dominate the ideological language on both sides of the bargaining table. The concept remained a vital one in part because it appeared to be Europe's future as revealed in America. Sufficient signs of that future had already appeared in the 1920s to allow observers to raise the question of the costs and benefits of a mass-production, consumer economy. Some within the circle of labor did not like what they saw. Yet these voices were surely only a minor dissonance in a chorus of praise for the future society combining mass production and leisure. A sharp bifurcation of time into the unfreedom of work and the liberty of leisure was increasingly accepted as the inevitable price of economic growth.

In Britain, during the postwar euphoria, productivism had been repeatedly challenged by those who saw any increase in hourly output as only a benefit of capitalist profit. In 1920, the British machinist William Watson argued that increased output would only allow an "inept, inefficient, unscrupulous class to regain its stability and strengthen its position." Taylorism meant "wasted wealth going to rate fixers and clerks of all sorts." In the late 1920s, R. M. Fox in the TUC's *Labour Magazine* condemned Ford's new auto plant in Ireland. That factory, he claimed, hired not skilled fathers but rather their unapprenticed sons who became "white mice that turn a revolving wheel. Ford would take them out of the cage sooner and give them more to eat" but the use of "short hours is not a remedy for uncongenial occupations. . . . The joy is taken out of leisure when the worker broods over the dull, tedious work to which he is chained." Yet these comments scarcely echoed widely in the British labor press.[42]

Far more substantial was the French critique of Fordism and rationalization. Elite journals presented nostalgia for the diversity of French civilization, making a vague appeal to the quality of French goods and a rejection of that mass culture of Fordism.[43] By contrast the press of labor and the Left attacked Fordism from a different perspective. André Philip, a young socialist law professor, rejected the typical uncritical praise of the American consumer economy in his reflections on a visit to the United States. He conceded that scientific management had contributed to the relatively high wages and short hours of American workers. Yet this was achieved at the price of "their liberty, personality and intelligence." Increased output resulted in the almost total cultural hegemony of financial and industrial interests. The captain of industry was seen by Americans as "able, by his will alone, to realize the universal well-being of all the working class." Philip concluded that rationalized capitalism tended to "diminish exploitation but to increase oppression." To combat this, socialists must not limit themselves to the struggle for material betterment. They should also be a *"force d'éducation"* to "create men who are masters of themselves and capable of realizing themselves."[44]

Philip's fear of the American Babbitt was echoed in Ilya Ehrenburg's

The Life of the Automobile. In this stinging mockery of Ford and his French imitator, André Citroen, Ehrenburg paints a dreary picture of the mass-production worker:

Pierre no longer believed in anything. When he was young, he had worked quietly and calmly. He had worked ten hours a day, but nobody pushed him. He had loved his tools and the iron. He relished the work. He mastered his trade. In those days, he read books and went to meetings. He believed in the victory of labor and in the brotherhood of man. But then it turned out that his mastery was useless. The milling machine worked with an accuracy of one-hundredth of a millimeter. Pierre no longer ran the machine, the machine ran him. Now he attached shackle-plates. He forgot about the brotherhood of man. He understood only one thing. Nothing could possibly change. The conveyor belt moved. Against that, all arguments were powerless.[45]

Within the ranks of labor activists, the most consistent critiques of rationalization came from the small and ephemeral Syndicalist League. Created by the former communists Pierre Monatte and Maurice Chambelland, the Syndicalist League hoped to organize independent but revolutionary trade unions. In contrast to the reformist's acceptance of Taylorism, which the league held to be only a speedup, the league advocated that workers "go slowly." Members also rejected the communist distinction between capitalist and socialist rationalization: "Let the workers in no case abandon absolute control over working conditions in either the bourgeois or workers' state," one member declared in 1927.[46]

For the Syndicalist League, workers' control meant basically regulating the speed of work. The productivity movement was management's "revenge" on labor for winning the eight-hour day, an attempt to force workers to do ten hours of labor in eight hours. If wage earners accepted this, they would have "gained nothing" from the shortened workday. The rank and file should impose a general slowdown, boycott Taylorized plants, and generally "fix the work rate for all."[47]

Work was not a necessary means toward prosperity or the price for "free" time; it was the embodiment of personal worth and an expression of individual autonomy, both of which were threatened by scientific management. However, in contrast to the anti-Taylorism of the prewar period, these independent radicals did not defend traditional skills. Their concern was merely with the quantity of work, an obvious reflection of the fact that industrial labor was finally becoming measurable as mere units of output.

As a viable strategy of French labor, syndicalism was dead by 1914.

By the time of the Renault strike of 1913, if not sooner, the goal of skilled workers' control had been abandoned. To the extent that the syndicalist tradition survived World War I, it surely had failed in May 1920. The ideal of artisan management of production persisted in the 1920s only in the episodic and pale afterglow of groups like the Syndicalist League.[48] In response to increased pace and discipline, workers generally embraced individual rather than collective solutions: absenteeism, turnover, or, where possible, informal restriction of output.[49]

Far more prominent than these critical voices was the affirmation of economic rationalization as the instrument of leisure and plenty. In postwar Britain, labor moderates like Brownlie, Hill, and Henderson had argued that industrial innovations would give workers a "right to a basic day as short as is commensurate with maximum efficiency." In light of the "enhanced capacity to produce" created during the war, a dividend of time as well as wealth was the workers' right. Tom Mann and others embraced the promise of Leverhulme's six-hour day and government-sponsored fatigue research. For these veterans of the short-hours struggle, worktime and industrial efficiency were inextricably linked.[50]

During their reassessment of policy following the disastrous coal miners' strike of 1926, the TUC embarked on a course largely favorable to the rationalization movement that was sweeping Europe and America. In 1928, the TUC joined various tripartite conferences that welcomed rationalization. At the TUC meeting in 1929, Ben Tillett argued that economic rationalization "cannot be resisted" and yet it "can be adapted to hasten the progressive development of the standard of living of the people."[51]

A "Memo on Technological Unemployment," issued in 1928 by the Industrial Committee of the TUC, refuted the growing fear among American trade unionists that technology was creating unemployment. Joblessness was caused by lack of innovation, which made British goods uncompetitive. A policy of "high wages," coupled with raising the age for leaving school and lowering retirement ages, would expand markets, create new jobs, and also improve productivity. The committee pointedly did not recommend further reduction of the workday, which, it feared, might cause "additional overhead charges" and "hinder the movement of labor from a stationary or declining industry to an expanding one."[52]

The former syndicalist engineer William Watson and Transport

Worker's Federation leader F. J. Maynard argued for a mass-production economy. William Watson, who in 1920 denied that workers should increase output for capitalists, wrote differently a decade later. Even in a mass-assembly factory, Watson argued, the machine operator could maintain autonomy as he could "properly work and think at the same time." Watson was convinced that the new factory would not displace the skilled machinist but only change his tasks. Maynard responded to R. M. Fox's critique of Fordism by arguing that a "scientifically organized mass production . . . is the only method by which we can raise production." Work can be "joyful" for only a "limited number of jobs. . . . I welcome the engineer who lightens the tasks and the organizer who shortens them. . . . No one wants to leave their well-lighted, warmed factory [and] eight hours with an electric sewing machine" to return to the nineteenth century's Satanic mills. Fordism, he asserted, is superior to other forms of the speedup for it is "accompanied with high wages and shorter hours." Maynard concluded that we must abandon the old traditions of the individualist skilled worker for "team work can be as enjoyable."[53]

These sentiments may simply reflect the crisis of British labor. Substantially weakened during the recession of 1921 and even more during the General Strike and coal miners' lockout of 1926, the TUC leadership may have been grasping at corporatist and technological straws. Yet this interpretation presupposes that a direct struggle for economic redistribution or control was the only appropriate behavior of organized labor. The goal of increasing productivity, however, was not merely in the employers' interest, nor did it necessarily mean ceding control of innovation to management. The views of the TUC's Industrial Committee reflected a position of workers within an economy that was becoming less competitive. Indeed, in the face of the threat of American economic domination, this view was thoroughly rational.

Yet this embrace of rationalization in the late 1920s suggests also a jelling of attitudes about mass-production society. Not only had labor leaders largely abandoned an ideology of workplace autonomy,[54] but they realized that the major issue was now coping with the monotony and "joylessness" of modern work. Thus, labor intellectuals waxed enthusiastic about the possibilities of "group" work or "thinking" while doing repetitive labor. They shared much with the British fatigue scientists who wrote of the comforting potential of rest pauses and "muzak." Few would have questioned the conclusion that life was becoming radically segmented into periods of economic instrumentalism and leisure autonomy. Indeed, despite real concern with preserving work rules, this bifurcation was becoming a virtue.

What is perhaps more surprising is just how little discussion of rationalization there was in Britain during this period. This, of course, may simply reflect the fabled nonideological character of the British labor movement. It just as likely indicates the relative lack of economic innovation in British industry in the 1920s.

By contrast, in France, the question of rationalization dominated the thinking of both wings of labor in the late 1920s. Despite its inability to control or even influence the rationalization process, the reformist CGT continued to support Taylorism (or Fordism) as the only way of guaranteeing the eight-hour day and of increasing the French standard of living.[55]

An instructive example of this seemingly unnatural embrace of American capitalism by French trade unionists is the career of Hyacinthe Dubreuil. A machinist for over twenty years, by 1920 Dubreuil had risen through the ranks of the Metalworkers' Federation to become secretary of the CGT in Paris. Known as an anticommunist, he drew the attention of Albert Thomas. In February 1927, through the good offices of Thomas and the American Industrial Relations Council (a Rockefeller Foundation affiliate), Dubreuil began a fifteen-month tour of "scientific factories" in the United States. As a former machinist, Dubreuil was a credible advocate of scientific management to a French working-class audience.[56] In a successful series of books Dubreuil praised the "scientifically run" American factory as an alternative to the old pattern of "discord and class war." He argued that both the "aristocratic pride" of the French factory owner and the "excessive individualism" of the French worker should be replaced by a "democratic" supervisor and a worker whose "remarkable trait" was a "natural placidity" in receiving orders and accepting change. Most important, Dubreuil saw the American factory as a solution to general scarcity through mass production. For Dubreuil this was a sign that the United States was moving "toward some form of socialism." Dubreuil presented an idealized image of how industrial society ought to be—a Saint-Simonian meritocracy and consumer democracy.[57]

This uncritical embrace of mass production characterized not only Dubreuil. An ILO study argued that without the tacit cooperation of labor organizations and a rested and well-paid worker, the dream of efficient production and a mass-market economy was illusory. In this way of thinking, the argument that labor had to be directly involved in implementing the new technology now seemed to be irrelevant. Likewise the social and moral problem of intense mass-production work was reduced to a psychological dimension:

The work—the sport almost—of rapidly assembling on the conveyors in the Ford factories would be impossible in conditions uncongenial to the workers. In this case, as in case of gang work, the spectacle of rhythmic movements of one's workmates may act as a stimulus that can be intensified by rhythmic sounds or singing.[58]

Like Maynard and Watson, Dubreuil and A. Thomas's ILO no longer expected that work be interesting or meaningful. As to the problem of monotony, according to the ILO report, its "most important cause" was the "incompatibility of some workmen's character to conveyor work." These were "ill-humored persons" for whom "the execution of movement is inhibited. . . . All activity becomes laborious to them."[59] Finally, these studies rejected the notion that technological unemployment was possible. This was an extreme position. Yet it was not far from the opinion of the influential Belgian socialist Henri de Man, who in his *Joy of Work* also stressed the need to develop a group spirit in mass-production work and to provide workers not with personally satisfying tasks but with job security and leisure time.[60]

These views, of course, did not go unchallenged in the CGT. Both the worship of American mass production and the possibility of collaboration with the "progressive" employer were questioned. The survival of these sentiments in the trade union press is summarized in this skeptical query of 1929: "Is it true civilization if morality flows only from material progress, if joy is contained totally within physical rest." Neither the inevitability of work without "joy" or leisure without self-development were conceded. Yet these doubts receded into the background of an articulate working-class culture.[61]

More important, those trade union writers with ties closer to the rank and file than the CGT executives (e.g., regional or trade delegates) were not nearly so enthusiastic for scientific management. They expressed serious doubts that innovating employers were easing work and raising wages or that jobs were being preserved. Voices defending crafts skills against mechanization and further divisions of labor still rose on the floors of infrequent union debates in spite of the increasingly centralized and even authoritarian character of French unions. Yet these doubters had little influence over policy.[62]

These facts make it all the more necessary to place this infatuation with rationalization into context. It emerged in these most extreme forms during a second major campaign against the eight-hour day between 1926 and 1928. Not only did the stabilization of the franc in August 1926 threaten French exports and thus oblige industry to retrench, but the attack on the eight-hour day in Italy and Britain in the summer of 1926 offered French employers an opportunity to raise still again the worktime issue. French labor responded as it had in the early 1920s. The CGT leadership declared in October 1926 that the necessary "increase of production ought to be sought within the framework of the eight-hour day." In a barrage of articles in *Le Peuple* between November 1926 and March 1927, the entire ideology of the time-efficient economy was rehearsed. The eight-hour day was "a revolution in daily life" that promised not only to "restore the family" and foster social betterment but to contribute to a rationalized economy. Innovations were the practical alternative to the shortcuts of longer hours and pay reductions.[63]

Likewise, the earlier dream of a democratic control over technology had not been abandoned. This was the point of CGT participation in the scientific management movement. The CGT had rather definite, if unrealistic, conditions for the introduction of economic innovation. According to the CGT's manifesto on productivity (October 1926), rationalization was unacceptable if it neglected the question of fatigue, led to the discharge of older workers, or made workers "interchangeable." It was tolerable if innovations led to lower-priced goods and provided wages commensurate with increased productivity, full employment, and, of course, guaranteed short hours. These concerns naturally reflected rank-and-file fears that paralleled later anxieties over automation.

French unions had not simply accepted a trade-off and rigid bifurcation of time between the "compulsion" of working hours and the freedom of leisure time. Continued desire to control or influence the workplace—even in this truncated form—reveals that the idea of autonomy had not been shifted entirely to leisure time.[64]

The problem, of course, was that the CGT leadership had no effective mechanisms for organizing industrial workers' control. And their increasing abandonment of the arduous effort of organizing mass-production workers only compounded the problem. In the end, in spite of themselves, they encouraged the split between work and leisure time.

Despite the deep ideological divisions within the French labor movement, the CGT's rivals in the communist party and the closely linked trade union federation, the CGTU, held views on rationalization that were similar. The CGTU criticized the CGT for accepting capitalism as long as it was productive and was willing to distribute time and income. In fashioning its own position on rationalization, the CGTU found itself in an anomalous situation: it shared with the CGT a belief in the progressive function of technological innovation (derived from Marxism).[65] The CGTU's position was also colored by Lenin's advocacy of Taylorism and by the Soviet Union's stress on time efficiency throughout the 1920s and during the early Five Year Plans.[66] However, to avoid class collaboration and, more important, to win new union members, the CGTU also vigorously attacked the "consequences" of capitalist innovation.[67]

The solution to this ideological dilemma was the distinction made between capitalist and socialist rationalization. This doctrine emerged in 1926 partially in response to the CGT's campaign for scientific management. In contrast to the capitalist distortion, socialist rationalization did not waste energy in class exploitation; rather it realized the dream of the eight-hour day. Indeed socialism could realize the seven-hour day, which had been introduced in some Soviet factories in the mid-1920s. While the CGT used an idealized image of Fordism to criticize the failure of French business to innovate, the CGTU posed an equally romantic picture of Soviet society for essentially the same purpose.[68]

Like the CGT, the communist unions demanded that the benefits of increased productivity be shared by those workers who were forced to submit to more intense production.[69] In contrast to the CGT, which increasingly abandoned the struggles on the shop floor for interest-group politics, the CGTU was committed to organizing new workers. They were interested especially in the larger and more concentrated industries. However, attempts of CGTU activists to penetrate new sectors, such as the automobile industry, obliged them to attack the new work methods.[70]

During the boom years of 1929 and 1930, communist labor organizers filed dozens of reports in *l'Humanité* condemning the new factories. The Michelin rubber workers were pictured as a "vast army of 18,000 people making the same mechanical movements under the watchful eyes of the company's band of young and loyal stooges." Moreover the CGTU also defended the skills of Breton fishermen, Parisian metalworkers, and carpenters whose immediate economic interests were threatened by innovation.[71]

By 1929, under pressure from the rank and file, the CGTU leadership went a step further by demanding workers' control over innovation on the shop floor. It advocated the suppression of time and motion studies and "dangerous machines" (as determined by the workers' delegates), rest breaks for conveyor workers, and even a reduction of the speed of the belts by "collective action" where needed. This policy was clearly a concession to organizers.[72]

The French communists in the 1920s faced a contradiction: they wished to affirm the rationalization of work and yet to avoid supporting modernizing capitalists. They rejoiced in the emergence of the mass-production worker, and yet they defended the immediate interests of the French laborer in the painful transition to a modern economy. Communists encouraged shop-floor agitation against the new work methods. Still, in the end, the main thrust of their policy was hardly distinguishable from the "reformist" CGT—higher wages and shorter hours in compensation for Taylorism and mechanization. Thus, they too legitimated the division between work as instrumental time and leisure as compensatory freedom.

Shortly before World War I, the mainstream of French labor moved away from a decentralized and craft-based syndicalism and toward an organized movement committed to mobilizing the industrial work force. Recognizing the need for a more productive economy, the French labor movement began to seek the means of making economic innovation serve the long-term interests of labor. Lacking an ability to organize the new unskilled industrial workers until 1936, and facing a *patronat* who failed to innovate, the French labor movement confronted an ironic situation: it proposed an ideology appropriate for a labor movement that it could not organize and for an economy that did not yet exist. Despite the obvious differences between Dubreuil and the communists, not only did both extremes favor a mass-production economy but they saw in it the future of French labor. The central problem—which the division of the Left and the poor organization of labor made impossible to solve—was how workers were to use innovation to improve both their material conditions and the quality of time at work and leisure.

This positive assessment of Europe's future as a mass-production society is certainly intelligible. In one sense, its context—the defense of the eight-hour day and, increasingly, the appeal of a productivity-based wage—explains the vitality of rationalization discourse. In another sense, it represents a compromise with a world out of labor's control—an effort to cope with the realities of an economy where work necessarily has lost its intrinsic meaning. Yet was this a sellout (perhaps premature) to consumer capitalism, an inability to see socialism as other than democratic leisure and commodity absorption? Certainly the old linkage between the progressive reduction of worktime and technological progress seemed to have been supplanted by a growing interest in a shareout of goods. The notion of leisure as an opportunity to create a working-class culture rather than as time for privatizing consumption seemed also to decline in the 1920s. As we shall see, the 1930s led to a revival of the short-hours movement. Yet its rationale was almost entirely economic rather than social.

Still, it would be unfair to interpret labor's response to rationalization as *embourgeoisement*. In a material world, where job insecurity and limited consumer choices still prevailed, to condemn organized labor's response as a sellout to mindless though well-paid work seems insensitive at the least. In any case, efforts (however inadequate) to find a new meaning to workers' control was a kind of halfway house between the personal freedom of leisure time and the compulsion of rationalized worktime. Moreover, collective action was still necessary to give expression to these private goals of free time.

10

The Right to Time in the Twentieth Century

This book has been about the origins of the social right to time. In the century after 1840, a *standard* of leisure was partially achieved. During this period, the intensification of work made the reduction of labor a biological necessity while the time freed for consumption facilitated economic growth. Yet it was against both the prejudices of elites and the pressures of the market that the eight-hour norm became a right of citizenship. This era marked the transition between time allocated according to the exigencies of nature, custom, and especially authority and the contemporary desire for highly individualized distributions of time. This middle period was characterized by the quest for an equality and simultaneity in social time—sited primarily within the family rather than the traditional community. The decades following World War II saw both a sharp decline in interest in reducing the hours standard and the advent of more individualistic quests for free time such as the vacation. These changes grew out of the events of the 1930s.

The very idea of a standard of labor time met vigorous resistance in the 1920s and continued to be opposed in the name of the free market and growth in the 1930s. Hopes that the forty-eight-hour ceiling would be lowered were frustrated in the 1930s by the impotence of labor, by nationalistic competition, and ultimately by the alternative of economic growth through mass consumption. Since the 1930s there has been relatively little decline in worktime, while the share of enhanced productivity distributed as income has been greatly increased.

At the same time, the demand for leisure was hardly finished with the Great Depression. If, in Europe, the forty-hour week was largely a failure in the 1930s, the annual paid vacation was a great success. Ironically, in spite of massive unemployment and deep ideological fissures within Europe, the vacation became a near universal ideal. It responded to deep needs that transcended ideology and economic system. In the generation after World War II, the vacation became the leisure concept of choice for most Europeans: the one- or two-week holiday expanded to four or more weeks in the prosperity of the 1950s and 1960s.

In this last chapter, I propose to sketch an explanation for this transition from the end of the progressive improvement in the hours standard to the beginnings of individualized leisure dominated by the annual vacation. Finally, I ask: What did these changes mean for the historic quest for free time and for contemporary attitudes toward work and leisure?

Depression and the Forty-Hour Week

The shrinkage of world markets in 1930–1931 brought a sudden end to British and French infatuation with Fordism and rationalization. Many faced joblessness and, more often, short-time work (with corresponding reductions in pay). Others experienced overtime and more intense labor when employers sought to reduce unit costs and to undercut competitors.[1] These trends tended to vindicate those critics of rationalization whom, in the 1920s, organized labor ignored. Whereas employers blamed the slump on the world market (especially their inability to compete because of high labor costs), organized labor attacked rationalization. A new consensus emerged on the Left that increased output per worker had not been balanced by either increased income or job security. The consequence was "underconsumption" and thus depression. The only solutions were salutary wage increases and job sharing by means of reduced hours.[2]

In Britain, this about-face was complete by September 1931. A TUC report called for a forty-hour week with no reduction in pay as "one of the ways in which the workers may share in increased productivity." In 1932, in the midst of deflation, the TUC's representative at the International Labor Organization, Arthur Hayday, bluntly demanded, "cut work time, not wages." Repeatedly over the next two years, trade unions presented evidence of the jobs lost in steel, textiles, shipbuilding, engineering, and mining due to recent mechanization. Contrary to their expectations in the late-1920s, employment was not shifting to new industries.[3] Even Harold Browden, an owner of the Raleigh Cycle Company, argued in October 1932 that employment was no longer a sufficient means of distributing purchasing power.[4] The only apparent solution to this dilemma was to find new mechanisms for allocating demand to balance supply. Although some trade unionists favored increasing the wages of those with jobs,[5] most preferred increasing aggregate purchasing power by reducing hours and thus obliging employers to increase jobs—without decreasing pay.

The British metalworkers union argued that the "problem of unemployment is in its essence a problem of undistributed leisure." While the goal of industrial society is to "free mankind from the burden of unnecessary toil . . . , instead of more leisure we have more unemployment."[6] Like the short-hours advocates of the 1880s, they asserted that it was morally superior to provide all wage earners with both compensated work and autonomous time instead of dividing the labor force between those suffering the poverty of idleness and those fatigued by overwork.

Yet the forty-hour movement did not turn on the distribution and meaning of time. The cultural value, for example, of the two-day weekend hardly entered the discussion in Britain.[7] Rather, labor leaders conceived the forty-hour week as an economic solution to essentially a "Keynesian" problem—"underconsumption." It was specifically offered as an alternative to the prognosis and therapy provided by employer groups and conservative governments.[8]

The National Confederation of Employers' Organisations (NCEO) summarized the dominant view of British business in December 1933: it was not mass purchasing power and productive capacity that were out of balance but wages and prices. Since the war, high wages, bolstered by social services and a labor standard set by government and "sheltered" industries, had priced British goods out of the world market. According to the NCEO, a forty-hour week would only oblige employers to expand facilities, increase supervisory staffs, and hire the "unemployables." It also would have a disproportionate impact upon labor-intensive sectors (already at a disadvantage with low-wage countries). Instead, the NCEO offered the solutions of lower taxes, reduced labor costs, and the abandonment of the gold standard, all of which would cheapen British goods on the world market.[9] In sum, the hours debate of the 1930s was subsumed under the old struggle between the advocates of the home market versus the world market.

Economists Colin Clark and P. Sargant Florence and the reformist International Association for Social Progress and the League of Nations Union supported the forty-hour week (with the maintenance of pay rates) as a way of expanding domestic consumption. This group also generally stressed the need to increase productivity and abandon the old prejudices against shift work in order to utilize existing capital fully. Yet, even if the threat to British competitiveness was real (e.g., vis-à-vis Japanese textiles), Clark argued that a shift to a home market and a larger public sector would eliminate most of this problem.[10]

A nearly identical debate took place in France. The CGT became rapidly disillusioned with Fordism in 1930; a forty-hour campaign followed in 1931, which was officially adopted in 1933. The new reduction of worktime was to solve the "disequilibrium of consumption and production" caused by "disorganized rationalization" and "overwork." The communists agreed, going still further in resurrecting the Soviet example of the seven-hour day.[11]

Jouhaux reasserted the linkage between technical innovation and the progressive reduction of worktime. In February 1933, he called the forty-hour week a "step" in the continuous reduction of worktime. The CGT observed that "we must recognize that the industrial system creates two products: goods and leisure." There should be a balance between the two so that leisure did not become unemployment.[12] Yet again, as in Britain, shorter hours were primarily intended to stimulate consumption; both job sharing and new time to consume were objectives. A two-day weekend would encourage suburbanization and with it domestic consumption.[13]

In turn, French employers countered with an analysis that was virtually identical to that of their British competitors.[14] Again, the remnants of the reform network, especially the Association for Social Progress, gave intellectual support to the concepts of technological unemployment, underconsumption, and the distributionist function of the forty-hour week.[15]

Moreover, these trends were part of an international movement. The forty-hour week dominated the Stockholm meeting of the International

Federation of Trade Unions in 1930. Sections of the American labor movement had advocated a forty-hour week in 1927 and, at the depth of the depression, the American Federation of Labor supported the introduction of the Black-Connery thirty-hour bill. Although Europeans generally ignored the thirty-hour concept, they repeatedly referred to the American example in the worktime provisions of the National Recovery Act of 1933.[16]

The principal forum was again the ILO. In October 1931, the tripartite Governing Body of the ILO barely supported the trade union proposal for an official commission to consider the relationship between unemployment and hours. Yet, in the following July, the Italian government requested a special conference to consider a uniform hours standard in order to reduce competition and to reabsorb the unemployed. The Governing Body responded by organizing a Tripartite Preparatory Conference in January 1933. Both the Italians and the ILO staff conceived of this meeting as an opportunity for shaping the agenda of the upcoming World Economic Conference. The ILO's report adopted the underconsumptionist interpretation of the depression. This concept was not merely a response to the economic emergency but an "essential element in long-range social planning." Albert Thomas's ideology of time efficiency still prevailed in the ILO, although his leadership was soon to pass to the British bureaucrat Harold Bulter, upon Thomas's unexpected death in 1933.[17]

These hopes were again dashed by the implacable opposition of business representatives supported by Germany, Japan, and, again, Britain. Only eighteen of thirty-five representatives endorsed a motion for a general forty-hour convention. The proposal of the trade unions for forty hours without pay reductions failed when Italy and other governments refused to join. At the end of this meeting the British employer representative, Forbes-Watson, took pleasure in reporting that short-hours advocates would have no influence on the World Economic Conference.[18]

Forbes-Watson was right. Instead of a general forty-hour convention, the ILO adopted a piecemeal program of special conventions for separate industries. Even then the June 1933 meeting of the International Labour Conference did little but distribute a questionnaire for future study. When the ILO staff introduced the idea of wage stabilization into an inquiry in 1934, Mussolini's delegates withdrew their support. The Fascist objective was to "share the misery," not to impose a burden on profit by raising the wage bill. In the following year,

Mussolini, like Hitler before him, abandoned the ILO and international solutions to the employment problem. Although the ILO plodded on, passing special forty-hour conventions for mining, textiles, and other industries in 1937 and 1938, these measures were delayed and few nations ratified them.[19]

In any case, by 1937 the opportunity for international solutions to the depression had long passed. Instead each nation adopted variations of a "beggar thy neighbor" approach to creating markets and jobs. Eventually the fascist solution of autarky and war economy dominated.[20]

What had failed at the international level was not abandoned in the national arena. The British TUC continued to press for forty-hour standards through the normal channels of collective bargaining. The Iron and Steel Trades Conference proposed four six-hour shifts and engineering unions pressed throughout 1934 and 1935 for an eight-hour, five-day week. Managers in some modern plants, where the Saturday half-holiday proved to be unprofitable, approved the latter plan. But the Engineering Employers' Federation held fast, as they had so often in the past, to the prevailing forty-seven-hour standard.[21] Attempts of the Labour party to introduce a forty-hour week in municipal governments also met with little success.[22]

One of the great anomalies of British labor in the 1930s was its nearly complete inability to affect national economic policy. This was obvious in the failure of the unions to win a forty-hour week in any important sector. Britain had clearly lost leadership in advancing the labor standard; the traditional tactic of collective bargaining was no longer effective.

On the continent, the pattern was quite different. In October 1934, Italy established a weak forty-hour statute (with corresponding reductions in pay); in June 1934, the Czechs adopted a forty- to forty-two-hour week with only a partial wage drop. Most important, by 1934 both wings of the French labor movement embraced the forty-hour week with no change in weekly wages. In 1935, with the formation of the *Rassemblement Populaire,* the forty-hour week became the cornerstone of an antideflationary economic program. Along with agricultural price supports and legal encouragement of collective bargaining, the forty-hour week was designed to increase purchasing power. Shortly after the election of the Popular Front government, a wave of strikes forced through a forty-hour law. This legislation was not only modeled after the eight-hour law of 1919, but both laws shared similar origins in social crises. What was different was that the 1936 law was passed in international isolation.[23]

There were, of course, renewed efforts by the British TUC in 1936 to revive a flagging forty-hour movement but with little impact. Ironically, by 1938, the United States—a nation that had abstained from the 1919 legislation—had adopted a forty-hour law. Yet the international coalescence of reform and insurgency, which had nourished the eight-hour movement of 1917–1920, was missing in 1936. The surprising support of the Italian Fascists in 1932 for an international reduction of worktime proved to be short-lived and was founded on wage-cutting principles opposed by the west European and American trade unions. When Hitler destroyed the German labor movement in May 1933, a strong supporter of international economic recovery through a work-time policy disappeared, severely weakening the prospects for the later success of the French Popular Front. Finally, the failures of labor diplomacy at the ILO guaranteed an international context unfavorable to the reformist experiments of the Popular Front. Shop-floor or ballot-box victory was as insufficient in the 1930s as a similar socialist experiment would prove to be in the early 1980s in France. Little could advance the labor standard in one country in the face of an unfavorable international market and hostile foreign policies.

Like the situation in 1919, the new French hours law was gradually implemented by bureaucratic decree. By the beginning of 1937, three and a half million industrial workers enjoyed the forty-hour week, and by September 1938, it was in theory nearly universal except in agriculture and the professions.[24] Yet capital flight, declining productivity, and inflation helped to produce trade imbalances in 1937 and 1938.[25] While labor inspectors tolerated overtime and recuperation hours, business opposition to the unilateral disarmament of the French economy became unrelenting. Even the CGT leader, René Belin, warned in early 1937 that the forty-hour week would survive only if production rose. The collapse of the Popular Front by May 1937 led to a series of decrees that suspended the law. Despite protest strikes in November 1938, the pressure to mobilize the economy in anticipation of war undermined political support for the forty-hour week.[26]

Although the law was officially restored in February 1946, it was again suspended during the reconstruction. Indeed, it remained under a cloud for a generation. Economists and politicians have identified it with the failure of the Popular Front government to revive the French economy on the eve of war and to prevent the German conquest in 1940.[27] Yet it is surely simplistic to blame these calamities on the forty-hour week. Rather it seems more reasonable to put the failure of this reform in context. In this century, any real improvement in a national labor standard has almost always paralleled a similar change on the international level. This, of course, was impossible in the 1930s.

The problem was also intellectual. Many associated the forty-hour week with economic Malthusianism. Of course, advocates claimed that the forty-hour week meant a demand-side economic recovery, an indirect means of deepening the home market. Supporters argued that productivity should and could increase with shorter worktime. Still, the concept implied a sharing of work when not much was being produced. It seemed to reject economic growth. The very notion of distributing leisure as well as goods increased this suspicion. In a context of massive unemployment and diminished consumption, this seemed to suggest the opposite of obvious economic priorities.[28]

Moreover, there was a clear (and for some economists) a superior alternative to the reduction of worktime: government spending could stimulate demand. This had the advantage over the job-sharing schemes of the short-hours movement of not imposing on capital the burden of redistributing demand. Neither option was acceptable to conservative British Treasury officials; nor were they able to withstand the conservative backlash to the Popular Front in France. Nevertheless the long-term solution would be predominately the Keynesian one. In the United States, the Roosevelt administration blocked the thirty-hour bill, opting instead for a number of fiscal measures. In France, the forty-hour week was quietly shelved after its brief postwar revival as incompatible with the "Battle of Production" and the Finance Ministry's plan for stimulating growth. In Britain, the immediate postwar demand for a forty-hour week was scrapped in 1946 for a more modest forty-four-hour week and unions increasingly abandoned their traditional rejection of multiple shifts.

Holidays and the Quest for Leisure in the 1930s

Whereas the forty-hour week failed in Europe, the annual paid vacation succeeded. The holiday could be understood as an alternative to the far more expensive concession of a shorter workweek. Yet the holiday movement was more than a consolation prize; it was the site of an expanded language of leisure.

Up until 1919, few wage earners demanded extended paid leave from work. To be sure, since 1911 the TUC had called for "total and sustained freedom from toil." Excepting printers, miners, and railwaymen, however, vacations had not been on the collective bargaining agenda in either country. Of course, a revised British Factory Act in 1901 guaranteed minors and women the right to six holidays per year (which were sometimes extended to men), and regional annual shutdowns of plants that coincided with traditional festivals (e.g., Lancashire wakes week and the Stockton race week) carried on from the nineteenth century. Yet these "vacations" had little in common with the twentieth-century movement for extended holidays. They were derived from traditional religious celebrations or communal fairs and sporting events, with the exception of the British August Bank Holiday. Seldom did they provide the opportunity for individual travel and escape from work and home environments. Moreover, they were generally uncompensated. Even though vacation savings schemes were common in Lancashire and Yorkshire textile towns, few British workers could afford to extend their holiday beyond a long weekend. For many, an annual shutdown—in order to refurbish machinery or because of slack sales—was merely a seasonal "lockout." Of course, both French and British civil servants and clerks enjoyed an annual holiday of several weeks. In fact, it was a mark of white-collar status. For employers to discriminate against the production worker was perhaps justified on grounds that the clerk earned no overtime and that paper work could be made up after the vacation. For the laborer, however, the lack of a paid vacation reflected his low social position and, as likely, the employers' view that the wage earner was incapable of benefiting from more than brief spells of rest away from work.[29]

Only in the postwar wave of collective bargaining were paid vacations granted in British railways, chemicals, printing, bootmaking, and mining and construction trades.[30] In France in 1919, isolated groups of printers and bakers won a one-week paid vacation (in the latter case to compensate them for night work). Holidays with pay were far more common in central and eastern Europe. Between 1919 and 1925, legislation provided paid vacations in six eastern and central European countries. However, demands of French miners and metalworkers in 1923 and 1924 for a one-week vacation fell on deaf ears. In 1923, only 4 of 144 collective contracts in France included holiday provisions. In 1925, vacation bills offered in French and British parliaments also failed.[31]

Nevertheless, during the Great Depression, the paid vacation had far broader support than the forty-hour week. In July 1931, the French

Chamber of Deputies passed a bill providing a one-week vacation for all except farmworkers. Again, as had so often occurred in the past, the rural-dominated Senate locked the bill in committee where it remained until the election of the Popular Front government in 1936. In Britain, legislators were also relatively receptive to holiday legislation. Bills were repeatedly introduced, obtaining second readings in Parliament in 1929 and 1936.[32]

Although wary of legislation, employers' reactions to the paid vacation were not nearly so hostile as they had been to a shorter workday.[33] Business found that the vacation was a perquisite that could enhance work discipline (by denying it to workers with less than one-year employment and to wage earners with bad records of absenteeism). Vacations also did not necessarily threaten annual production goals: they often coincided with seasonal slowdowns in demand or production. Moreover, they reduced man-year hours by only forty to eighty rather than by four hundred or more as required in the shift from a forty-eight- to forty-hour week. Especially when holidays were taken during a plant shutdown, employers would not have to invest in additional staff or equipment.[34]

Beyond these practical advantages of the vacation, the right to leisure was gaining legitimacy. By the early 1930s, the work science journals *Industrial Welfare* and *The Human Factor* were beginning to focus on the inadequacy of leisure opportunities. Articles noted the health and social potential of Fascist and Soviet leisure programs even when they attacked state-controlled culture.[35] By July 1933, the TUC's monthly, *Labour Magazine,* began to devote a regular column to the Workers' Sports Association by George Elvins.[36]

In France, the Ministry of Labor supported vacation legislation. Even conservatives like Deputy Duval-Arnould, an old opponent of the eight-hour law, favored the 1931 holiday bill, for "vacations are necessary in the modern world." Managers who did not provide them were creating an "unfair competition between employers."[37]

The ILO helped to organize international support for the workers' right to a vacation. In 1934, an associate of Albert Thomas, Louis Piérard, organized an International Committee on Workers' Spare Time.[38] By 1935, the International Labour Conference of the ILO discussed the vacation question. In the next year, it passed a modest draft convention for a six-day paid holiday by the impressive margin of ninety-nine to fifteen.[39]

These trends suggest a growing openness toward the idea of mass leisure.[40] Whereas in the 1920s social critics often feared that increased free time threatened cultural standards,[41] by the early 1930s authors increasingly accepted the legitimacy of mass leisure. John C. Hammond, C. Delisle Burns, and Bertrand Russell proposed a progressive democratization of leisure. The reduction of worktime for the masses had created a "widening of choice for the majority," "a democratic civilization," and a "freer and subtler community between all men," claimed Burns. Rather than condemn mass entertainment, Burns argued that "leisure is the time for going beyond what men know of life or can say of it." Russell claimed that instead of the traditional leisure class, which "produced a few Darwins and many fox hunters," "ordinary men and women, having the opportunity of a happy life, will become more kindly and less inclined to view others with suspicion."[42]

A recreation rhetoric emerged in the debates over holiday-with-pay legislation. The vacation was necessary for self-development and to discover new environments. The TUC report to the Commons in 1937 stressed that workers needed time, not only for recovery from fatigue but for creating "opportunities to engage in activities and pursuits more satisfying to their individual inclinations than the daily routine." The worker was "not merely a machine to be kept in reasonable working order, but a human being with a life of his own to be lived and enjoyed." For both clerk and blue-collar worker, "change of environment is absolutely necessary." A paid holiday alone could compensate for the increased pace of work since the last reduction of worktime in 1919. As if to underscore their belief in the necessity of leisure, the TUC was willing to allow employers to refuse holiday pay to those who took jobs during their vacations.[43]

The British government, however, remained a reluctant participant in this movement. In the fall of 1936, a vacation bill (for eight days of paid holiday for twelve months of employment) easily reached a second reading. The TUC lobbied the minister of labor. In February 1937, however, the government sidetracked immediate legislation by calling for an investigative committee led by Lord Amulree.[44] Witnesses from employer associations stressed technical difficulties but not the vacation in principle.[45]

The Amulree Committee's recommendations, which became law in July 1938, only authorized trade boards and other statutory bodies that mediated wage disputes in weakly organized industries to provide holidays with pay. In the meantime, bargaining rounds in heavily unionized sectors generally produced one week of paid holidays.[46] By the end of

1938, fifty holiday agreements had been signed, raising the number of *manual* laborers with a paid holiday to four million.[47] The British remained true to their collective bargaining tradition, although in the context of an international movement (and, indeed, they lagged behind vacation gains on the continent).

In France, the habitual logjam of senatorial reaction was broken by the labor insurgency of June 1936. Along with other reforms, a two-week paid holiday bill was passed on June 21 with no open opposition. Yet the *congé payé*, today identified with the Popular Front, was in fact not part of the electoral program of 1935. It was the product of a far broader consensus, supported by the Catholic Right with its promise of family leisure.[48]

Nevertheless, the idea of the workers' holiday quickly captured the imagination of both the French Popular Front and the British Left. In the summer of 1936, Léo Legrange became the Popular Front's undersecretary of state for sports and leisure. He not only sponsored a program of inexpensive family railroad excursions but administered the building of 253 sports arenas. The agricultural ministry even offered guided tours of Paris to young farmworkers. Still, the Popular Front opposed "directed leisure." Rather, as Legrange put it, "we must make available to the masses all kinds of leisure which they may choose for themselves."[49] Voluntarism reigned in France: Paris trade unions obtained chateaux in the countryside for vacation visits of their members. Teachers' unions organized the club, Vacations for All, which sponsored camps and youth hostels. In March 1937, the CGT opened its own tourist office.[50] To be sure, these efforts had limited success. As early as March 1937, the Popular Front's commitment to mass leisure was flagging when appropriations were substantially reduced. Yet the concept of "democratic leisure" became an integral part of the political and social goals of the Popular Front.[51]

British enthusiasm for leisure and tourism was even more concrete. By 1937, fifteen million of Britain's forty-six million people took one or more weeks of holiday away from home. There was a rapid growth of leisure voluntarism—for example, increased membership in camping clubs and the immense success of Billy Butlin's first holiday camp in 1937. By 1939, two hundred commercial camps had emerged. Moreover, there was a new interest in organized workers' leisure: the National Savings Committee, which had been founded in 1916 to encourage "thoughtful spending and purposive saving," attempted to enlist business support for holiday savings programs.[52] The Workers' Travel

Association provided an array of inexpensive excursions and holiday camps. A few Labour-controlled towns like Lambeth organized their own summer camps. By 1939, central government funding was available for such facilities. In July 1937, a writer in the *Labour Magazine* predicted the end of the "beanos, the fun fairs, and the noisy makeshift hilarity which has done duty for the holiday of the many." In its place would emerge a popular tourism, an opportunity for the exploration of nature, and the foundation of a new understanding between different trades and nationalities.[53]

In Britain, there was widespread interest in spreading over the holiday season to ease the August congestion in the seaside resorts. Still, the short school vacation in summer and the understandable British desire to flee the dirty industrial towns for a sunny beach in August made it unlikely that officials could woo workers into accepting a cooler and perhaps damper vacation in September or June.[54]

The general appeal of the vacation was part of a broad international movement for democratic leisure. In 1938, the International Committee of Workers' Spare Time gathered government and labor delegations from the Western democracies. It met to counter a similar meeting held by the Nazis two years earlier. Its chairman, Louis Piérard, expressed concern about "boredom during daily rest or holidays" and the consequent "burst of dreary incuriosity," which led to "unadorned idleness without recreation" and to vice. The solution was to train workers to use their leisure wisely and to provide them with a wide variety of recreational choices. Although delegates envied the government resources at the disposal of their fascist and Soviet counterparts, they were adamant that leisure, like freedom, was to proceed from the individual, not the collectivity.[55]

But what did this individual want? Doubtless, he wanted mostly personal experiences, rather than political education, cultural exchanges, or even encounters with nature. The British Federation of Miners published a pamphlet in 1938 informing members on their vacation rights. It featured a series of pictures of a young miner showering away the last of the coal dust for a week, collecting his vacation pay, packing his wife and two small children onto a train, and ending with a picture of the miner frolicking on the beach with his tots, over the title "Then a dip . . . Happy!" In a 1937 essay contest on the theme, "How I would like to spend my holiday," British workers offered images of sea breezes and water and of "children burying their sleeping parents in the sand." The vacation was to be a father's gift to his family and an opportunity to experience parenting outside the routine stress of the industrial world. The vacation was a chance for romance, chumming with child-hood mates, and simply just "letting the world go by" in a brief escape from the world of the clock. These strictly private images—varying with the infinite variety of age, family situation, and personal pro-clivity—probably reflected the aspirations of most workers.[56]

Labor leaders fully recognized that individuality could be expressed primarily in time away from work rather than in the work experience itself—even if leftist intellectuals sometimes did not. However, a per-haps unsolvable problem remained: How were the humane values of the labor movements to be inculcated into this leisure culture—and the ceding of this terrain to the merchandisers to be avoided? The advocates of a democratic leisure recognized this problem even if they lacked the organization, resources, or perhaps imagination to resolve it. Ulti-mately, the contest was not between totalitarian and liberal democratic leisure but between "organized" and commercial leisure. For many rea-sons, the latter has generally prevailed.

A Quest for Time and the Twentieth-Century Worker

It is easy to come to the pessimistic conclusion that the dreams of the nineteenth-century short-hours movements remain un-fulfilled. Some may blame workers for this failure. *Embourgeoisement*—privatization and consumerism—is commonly alleged to be the culprit.[57] Yet this approach often obscures the fact of the limited political, eco-nomic, and even cultural power of those advocating reduced hours or creative uses of free time. It also ignores the different problems that time reforms face in contemporary society.

By the 1960s, it appeared that the era of the progressive reduction of worktime had ended. Despite vast increases in productivity since the war, little of it had been distributed as free time. And despite the grow-ing inability of the world economy to allocate goods through employ-ment, the idea of work sharing as an alternative to the dole or other forms of social marginization had hardly reached the policy level.[58]

Moreover, the shorter-hours movement may have reached an ideo-logical impasse insofar as leisure has been defined as time to consume.

Rooted in the eight-hour movement, a general tendency to identify leisure with consumption guaranteed that wage earners would not seek further reductions of worktime at the cost of income. During the Great Depression, "Keynesian" liberals had identified shorter hours with stagnation—as attempts to spread unemployment rather than to restore economic growth. As an alternative, they advocated increased consumption and expanded markets through fiscal policy—and, in America especially, military spending and overseas expansion. When the forty-hour week became the standard in the prosperous 1960s in Europe, it provided an economic balance of income and consumption. If, in the 1920s, growth and short hours were linked, by the 1960s they were disassociated.[59]

Surely Albert Thomas would have been disappointed by the fact that time freed from work has often not produced cultural or political alternatives. The labor movement has failed to organize and uplift the working class; and the expansion of commercial leisure has undermined loyalties to class. Not only the longer evening but the vacation has been depoliticized and privatized. Even if the 1960s term, "affluent worker," seems inappropriate in the more sober decades that have followed, "class consciousness" has hardly been resurrected. George Orwell's claim that consumer culture had defanged the working class in the 1930s still rings true.[60]

Surely the replacement of the long laborious workday with the productive (but eased) eight-hour shift has had other than merely happy results. Unintentionally, the ardent campaigns for time efficiency in the 1920s may have contributed to the long-term process of deskilling labor. As the opponents of rationalization noted, work without initiative and interest has hardly provided a psychology conducive to the fulfillment of human diversity in leisure hours.

Yet the matter is more complex than working-class "capitulation" to consumerism and the deskilling of labor. We must also consider the broader world of industrial culture, the difficulties of policy formation, and political power—the very issues that had frustrated advocates of the eight-hour day before World War I.

Instead of progressively reducing worktime, contemporary industrial societies have created service and bureaucratic jobs, often without any clear norms of productivity or even utility, that replace manual labor made redundant by the machine. By the 1970s and 1980s, however, even these jobs appeared to be threatened by competition, computers, and a reduced commitment of elites to assure full employment. This has contributed to a rebirth of the short-hours movement throughout the industrial West. Yet few policy makers have heeded the call of trade unions and some economists to distribute income by sharing work. Perhaps industrial cultures are, as yet, unwilling to "delink" the distribution of goods from a "reasonable" time at labor. Even more likely, we are still afraid of additional leisure—at least for the other guy.[61]

Moreover, as has been shown by the efforts in the early 1980s in Germany, the Netherlands, and France to reach a thirty-five-hour week, appeals to collective interest may no longer inspire individual wage earners as they often did before World War II. More important, the goal of reducing the working day may have lost that appeal that attracted so many to the "three eights" at the beginning of the century. Time lost in commuting and the marginal usefulness of, for example, an additional half-hour per day, may make other allocations of free time much more attractive. Individualized packages of free time such as additional vacation, child-care leave, earlier retirement, and flextime have partially replaced the social ideal of a uniform reduced workweek. Yet the personalization of scheduling to accommodate the variety of family and life-course needs may appear to unions to undermine the established time standard and open the door to the individual labor contract.[62]

The nineteenth-century quest for social time has been frustrated by the advent of shift work. The efforts of unions and women's groups early in our century to preserve family time by opposing "unnatural" hours has succumbed to the logic of Lord Leverhulme, the work science experts, and the drive after 1945 to increase production. Although attempts of chain stores in Britain to extend hours to Sunday failed in 1986, the value of social time, so long defended by the Early Shop Closers, is increasingly attacked as contrary to American-style consumer convenience. Family time has been further undermined by the growth of the two-income household. The nineteenth-century domestic ideal has been frustrated by a "domestic speedup" as worktime has encroached on the hours available for child care, domestic chores, and familial interaction. Yet, again the problem is not clearly *embourgeoisement:* both economic pressures and women's desire for equal opportunity have created this new form of time scarcity. The labor movement, which formerly dominated the short-hours cause, surely cannot be expected to find solutions without the collaboration of women's and other groups.[63]

Perhaps the greatest problem today, however, is the inability of reformers to recreate the international coalition that supported the eight-hour day in 1919. In some ways the generation of World War I was a golden age of labor internationalism—when a rough economic equality between industrial states existed. Even then, however, uneven political development (e.g., the impotence of American labor reformers and British fears of decline) frustrated the internationalists at the ILO. Since the 1920s, the opportunities for the advance of an international labor standard have nearly disappeared. Economic nationalism in the 1930s and, recently, the advent of authoritarian Third World industrial powers have further undercut efforts to raise that standard in Europe. Increased competition between oppressed Third World and Western labor has frustrated even those workers who have had a foothold in the state, limiting their ability to break with the discipline of the international market and to liberate time. The problem of reducing work may prove in the long run to have as much to do with the difficulty of recreating an international movement for free time as it does with the cooptation of consumerism.

If any simple conclusion to this book is possible, it is that the goal of decreasing hours was (and remains) hard to obtain—often taking a generation or more of agitation, organizing, and coalition building. It has also required unique conjunctures—political, economic, and international.

However, our analysis may suggest more. Even though the time problem today is very different than it was in the early twentieth century, there remain some important parallels. The long-term trend of industrial economies toward growth without concomitant job creation is likely to produce new pressures for the reduction of work as it has so many times in the past. Perhaps the tendency of these economies to converge toward a similar labor standard may help revive an international desire for shorter worktime. Free-time movements have also been responses to cultural needs—quests for social and family time that have hardly been replaced today by the pure economic compulsion to consume. The two-income family with its burden of wage hours is a likely site for the building of a new quest for time. Of course, it may be expressed in terms radically different from the eight-hour or "weekend" struggles of the late nineteenth century. This new movement may include a coalition of women, labor, and other reform groups; it may well seek alternative allocations of life time in the pursuit of both work and personal and family goals.[64]

The quest for time may find still new expressions. Whether the era of shortening hours has ended and whether the uses of leisure will ultimately prove to be as disappointing as they have been to so many in the past remain open questions. There is an optimistic side to the historian's insistence that change is slow and complex.

Appendix

A Brief Comparison of British and French Working Hours in the Nineteenth Century

The difference in French and British working hours in the nineteenth century is a good measure of the contrasting levels of industrial development between the two countries. During the 1830s, French textile factory hours were commonly longer by two or more hours.[1] Whereas skilled trades in Britain seldom worked more than a ten-hour day, their counterparts in France usually labored twelve or even thirteen hours. French miners at midcentury endured ten- or eleven-hour days, again one or two hours longer than British hewers.[2] As Table Appendix-1 illustrates, these differences persisted into the 1890s. The imprecision and vastly different modes of data collection preclude an adequate and full comparison.[3] Still, in 1900 for most French the workday stretched from at least 6:00 A.M. to 6:00 P.M. for six days a week, requiring ten or more hours of effective labor; the British wage earner increasingly was at work only from 7:00 A.M. to 5:30 P.M. (for scarcely more than nine hours of labor) and had Saturday afternoon off.

The comparatively long hours of the French surely were indicators of that nation's relative economic backwardness and, more specifically, of a lack of time thrift. Both French and British observers attributed these differences in worktime to the inefficient technology and less disciplined work force of France. In turn, long hours led to reduced labor efficiency and made it possible for firms to avoid costly investments in plant or machinery.[4]

The workday and week were more "porous" in France. This was both a cause and an effect of the long workday. In 1899, when most British factory workers had one or two daily breaks in a ten-hour day, many French textile operatives were employed for twelve hours per day and thus frequently required three rest breaks. The result was a workday in France that extended from 5:00 A.M. until 7:00 P.M. Half-hour *casse-croûtes* at 8:00 A.M. and 4:00 P.M. as well as an hour (or longer) break at noon were essential to sustain a productive work force through such a long day. These breaks also contributed to lost output due to time wasted in the frequent shutdowns, the inefficiency of early morning work before breakfast, and the drinking in which workers engaged to compensate for the tedium of the long day.[5]

Because of extended hours and frequent employment of married women, French managers sometimes allowed women to nurse their babies at work; working children played in the shop courtyard and napped behind machines. Progressive textile manufacturers in Lille during the Second Empire were unable to save time by persuading their workers to eat in the factory even when cheap food was provided. Instead, these workers insisted on their ninety-minute lunch at home. Work discipline in France was particularly erratic in women's trades like garment making where mothers regularly arrived as late as 10:00 A.M. and left as early as 5:00 P.M. because of family demands. Still, French miners in the 1890s also worked hours that varied inversely with coal prices, no matter what the official hours policy was.[6]

In France, skilled and relatively well-paid artisans continued to take the traditional Monday holiday deep into the century. Community holidays and drinking clubs survived into the 1870s in regions less affected by industrialization. At the same time, these factors contributed to the low rate of productivity and the long official workday. The artisan culture, of course, was well known in Britain.[7] Although comparative research needs to be done in this area, Saint Monday and other forms of "porous" worktime surely survived longer and more widely in France where craft traditions persisted until the end of the century.

At the core of the problem of long hours in France was the prevalence of seasonal employment. Industries affected by agriculture, weather conditions, and annual variations in water power depended on long

Table Appendix-1 *Nominal Weekly Hours in British and French Industry:*
ca. *1890–1900*

	BRITAIN	FRANCE
Bakers	69.8	78–96
Brickmakers	54–69	96–108 [a]
Chemical workers	53–70	64.5–72
Construction	50–55	72–48
Foundry laborers	72–48	72–84
Metalworkers (engineers)	53.7	63–66
Miners (hewers)	42.5–55	51–60
Paper workers	66–78	63
Printers	53–54	60
Railway workers		
Ticket agents	56–62	90–96
Guards	64–70	96–108
Retail clerks	81.5	66–96
Restaurant waiters	96	101
Sailors	72	
Textile workers	56	66–72
Tailors	54–96	66–96

[a] For a six-month season

Source: For British hours, Royal Commission of Labour, 1892–1894, various volumes; Board of Trade, *Return Relating to the Hours of Employment in Various Trades* (London, 1890), pp. 9, 25, 32, 54–55. For French hours, Ministère du commerce, *Rapports sur l'application pendant l'année . . . des lois réglementant le travail* (1887), p. 14, (1888), pp. 39, 44, (1890), pp. 37, (1895), pp. 234; *Salaires et durée du travail dans l'industrie française* (Paris, 1898), 4: 95, 435, 469; *La Petite Industrie: Salaires et durée du travail* (Paris, 1893), 1: 58–62; Office du Travail, *Bordereaux de salaires pour diverses catégories d'ouvriers en 1900 et 1901* (Paris, 1902), p. 134; Conseil supérieur du travail, *Rapports et documents sur la réglementation du travail dans les bureaux et magasins et dans les petites industries de l'alimentation* (Paris, 1901), pp. 72, 79, 116; Maurice Bonneff, *La Classe ouvrière* (Paris, 1910), pp. 99–104, 112, 116, 156–67; Charles Rist, *Réglementation légale de la journée de travail de l'ouvrier adulte en France* (Paris, 1898), pp. 215–20, 242–54; Valentin Viard, *La Réduction de la durée du travail de l'employé* (Paris, 1910), pp. 13, 22–25.

workdays to compensate for lost time and to complete work on perishable goods. Seasonality also characterized industries where demand varied during the year. Custom-made products, especially fashionable clothing, typically required lengthy workweeks during the rush season, which were followed by unemployment or short hours in the "dead season." Employers sought to reduce inventory and investment by concentrating production into brief periods during the peak of demand. Days worked per year varied widely even within the same trade in

France. Louis Blanc claimed in 1848 that many trades provided work only three to six months. As late as 1906, carpenters in the department of Alpes-Basse worked only two hundred days per year, whereas others in Marseilles labored three hundred. Hours per day of carriage makers in the 1880s varied from fourteen hours during the busy season to only seven or eight in winter. Sometimes this seasonality was due to workers, like those employed in the mines of Carmaux in the 1870s, who quit the mines from July to September to work the farms.[8]

Again the difference with the British was relative: seasonal employment and, with it, long workdays were common on British docks, the garment districts of London's East End, and the gas works, for example.[9] Indeed, Table Appendix-1 reveals an extraordinary diversity of working hours in both countries. What clearly distinguishes twentieth-century workers from their predecessors is the absence of these great differences in worktime.

Yet again the French problem with seasonality was certainly greater than in Britain. An uneven workyear was more characteristic of the French economy where agriculture continued to prevail over industry. It was also a pattern associated with France's relatively large luxury craft sector. Thus, a combination of relatively late mechanization, the persistence of traditional work culture, and an industrial base that preserved a seasonal production pattern all contributed to the longer workday in France. These economic and cultural factors combined with a political regime that was slow to adopt shorter hours as a legislative goal. This, of course, reinforced the tendency of French industry to lag behind in the adoption of new technology.

Notes

Chapter 1: A Question of Time

1. Anthony Giddens, *Central Problems in Social Theory* (Berkeley, 1979), pp. 200–1; and Jacques Attali, *Histoire du temps* (Paris, 1982), pp. 112–23, 139–77. See also Jacques Le Goff, *Time, Work, and Culture in the Middle Ages* (Chicago, 1980), chap. 1; Mircea Eliade, *Cosmos and History: The Myth of the Eternal Return* (New York, 1953), chap. 1; and Nels Anderson, *Work and Leisure* (London, 1961), pp. 52, 71.

2. The problem of the scarcity of time and the necessity of synchronizing personal and social needs is stressed in Wilbert Moore, *Man, Time and Society* (New York, 1963), pp. 3–68.

3. Attali, *Histoire du temps,* pp. 11–12; Don Parkes and Nigel Thrift, *Making Sense of Time* (New York, 1978); Georges Gurvitch, *The Spectrum of Social Time* (Dordrecht, 1964), esp. pp. 12–94; Maurice Halbwachs, *La Mémoire collective* (Paris, 1950), chap. 3; M. P. Sorokin and R. K. Merton, "Social Time: A Methodical and Functional Analysis," *American Journal of Sociology* 42 (1937): 615–69; and Pitrim Sorokin, *Socio-Cultural Causality, Space, and Time* (Durham, 1943). For modern historians' interpretations, see David Landes, *Revolution in Time: Clocks and the Making of the Modern World* (Cambridge, Mass., 1983); and Stephen Kern, *The Culture of Time and Space, 1880–1918* (Cambridge, Mass., 1983).

4. Lewis Mumford, *Techniques and Civilization* (New York, 1934), p. 14; Attali, *Histoire du temps,* pp. 192–95; Carlo Cipolla, *Clocks and Culture: 1300–1700* (London, 1967); and Werner Sombart, *Der Moderne Kapitalismus,* 3rd ed. (Leipzig, 1919), pp. 809, 828–31.

5. Karl Marx, *Capital* (New York, 1967), 1: 235–56. Among the numer-

ous treatments of this theme, see Brighton Labour Process Group, "The Capitalist Labour Process," *Capital and Class* 1 (Spring 1977): 3–43; and Dan Clawson, *Bureaucracy and the Labor Process* (New York, 1980). Compare with Stephen Wood, ed., *The Degradation of Work? Skill, Deskilling and the Labour Process* (London, 1983).

6. John D. Owen, *The Price of Leisure* (Rotterdam, 1969), chaps. 2 and 3; and John D. Owen, *Working Hours: An Economic Analysis* (Lexington, 1979). For a balanced treatment of these theories, see M. A. Bienefeld, *Working Hours in British Industry: An Economic History* (London, 1972), pp. 143–48, 162–79.

7. Sidney Pollard, *The Genesis of Modern Management* (London, 1964), pp. 106–209; and Craig Littler, "Deskilling and the Changing Structure of Control," in Wood, *The Degradation of Work,* pp. 122–45.

8. The classics are, of course, E. P. Thompson, *The Making of the English Working Class* (New York, 1963); and Michelle Perrot, *Les Ouvriers en grève: France, 1871–1890* (Paris, 1974). For an important discussion of the dilemmas of nineteenth-century British social and labor history, see G. Stedman Jones, *Languages of Class* (London, 1983). Somewhat similar analysis appears in Steven Kaplan and Cynthia Koepp, eds., *Work in France* (Ithaca, N.Y., 1985).

9. Judith Stone, *The Search for Social Peace: Reform Legislation in France, 1890–1914* (Albany, 1985); and Sanford Elwitt, *The Third Republic Defended: Bourgeois Reform in France, 1880–1914* (Baton Rouge, 1986); A. Robson, *On Higher Than Commercial Grounds: The Factory Controversy, 1830–1853* (New York, 1983); and U. R. Q. Henriques, *Before the Welfare State* (London, 1979). Steward Weaver, *John Fielden and the Politics of Popular Radicalism, 1831–1847* (London, 1987); and Robert Sykes, "Some Aspects of Working Class Consciousness in Oldam, 1830–1842," *History Journal* 23 (1980): 167–85, and Sykes's forthcoming book on Lancashire working-class radicalism.

10. Eric Hobsbawm, *Laboring Men* (New York, 1964), pp. 371–86.

11. Edward P. Thompson, "Time, Work-Discipline and Industrial Capitalism," *Past and Present* 38 (1967): 56–97, esp. 86.

12. Thompson, "Time," pp. 57, 61, 94. See also Nicole Samuel, *Le Temps libre: un temps social* (Paris, 1984), pp. 9–10.

13. See, for example, John Rae, *Eight Hours for Work* (London, 1897), pp. 1–15; and Thorold Rodgers, *Six Centuries of Wages* (London, 1884), chap. 1; Alfred Franklin, *La Vie privée d'autrefois* (Paris, 1889), 5: 125–26, 138; and Henri Hauser, *Ouvriers du temps passé* (Paris, 1927), pp. 78–81. Alternative views are presented in Bienefeld, *Working Hours,* pp. 20–25; C. K. Dobson, *Masters and Journeymen: A Prehistory of the Industrial Revolution* (London, 1980), p. 94.

14. Gösta Langenfelt, *The Historic Origins of the Eight Hours Day* (Stockholm, 1954). Recent analyses included Michael Harrison, "The Ordering of the Urban Environment: Time, Work and the Occurrence of Crowds, 1790–1835," *Past and Present* 110 (1986): 134–58; Michael Sonenscher, "Work and Wages

in Paris in the Eighteenth Century," in *Manufacture in Town and Country before the Factory*, ed. Maxine Berg, Pat Hudson, and Michael Sonenscher (New York, 1983), pp. 162–67. See also Steven Kaplan, "Réflexions sur la police du mode du travail," *Revue historique* 529 (1979): 17–37.

15. Gaston Bouthoul, *La Durée du travail et l'utilisation des loisirs* (Paris, 1924), p. 80; Joffre Dumazedier, *Sociology of Leisure* (New York, 1974), p. 34; and Bienefeld, *Working Hours*, p. 17.

16. Sonenscher, "Work and Wages," pp. 150–51, 166; see also William Reddy, *The Rise of Market Culture: The Textile Trade and French Society, 1750–1900* (New York, 1984), chap. 1.

17. This thesis was first and most fully developed in E. A. Furniss, *The Position of Labor in a System of Nationalism* (New York, 1919), esp. pp. 118, 120–54, 233–335. For the preclassical economic theorists who insisted that workers preferred leisure to income and thus that subsistence wages alone would assure an adequate level of production, see Arthur Young, *Northern Tour* (London, 1770), pp. 289–91; Josiah Child, *New Discourse* (London, 1693), preface; William Petty, *Political Arithmetic* (London, 1755), p. 132; and N. E. Restif de la Bretonne, *Les Nuits de Paris* (Paris, 1963). See also Sonenscher, "Work and Wages," p. 150; Kaplan, "Réflexions," pp. 17–37; and Roger Picard, *Les Cahiers de 1789 et les classes ouvrières* (Paris, 1910), pp. 17–18.

18. Picard, *Les Cahiers*, pp. 108–11; and Attali, *Histoire du temps*, pp. 205–6.

19. Major contributions to this substantial literature have largely been British. These include R. W. Malcolmson, *Popular Recreations in English Society 1700–1850* (Cambridge, 1973); John Walton and James Walvin, *Leisure in Britain, 1780–1939* (Manchester, 1983); Peter Bailey, *Leisure and Class in Victorian England: Rational Recreation and the Contest for Control, 1830–1885* (London, 1978); Robert Storch, ed., *Popular Culture and Custom in Nineteenth-Century England* (London, 1982); E. Yeo and S. Yeo, eds., *Popular Culture and Class Conflict, 1590–1914* (Brighton, 1981); Hugh Cunningham, *Leisure and Industrial Revolution* (New York, 1979).

20. Thompson, "Time," pp. 81–83; Sidney Pollard, "Factory Discipline in the Industrial Revolution," *Economic History Review* 2nd ser., 16 (1963): 256–70; Neil McKendrick, "Josiah Wedgewood and Factory Discipline," *Historical Journal* 4 (1961): 30–55; and A. W. Coats, "Changing Attitudes to Labour in the Mid-Eighteenth Century," *Economic History Review* 2nd ser., 11 (1958–1959): 35–51. See also Marx, *Capital*, 1: 197–302.

21. Eileen Yeo and E. P. Thompson, *The Unknown Mayhew* (New York, 1971), pp. 77, 111–12, 123, 185–94, 387, 393, 422; Duncan Bythell, *The Sweated Trades: Outwork in Nineteenth Century Britain* (London, 1978); James Schmiechen, *Sweated Industries and Sweated Labor: The London Clothing Trades, 1860–1914* (Urbana, Ill., 1982); and Reddy, *Market Culture*, pp. 120–24.

22. D. A. Reid, "The Decline of St. Monday, 1776–1876," *Past and Pres-*

ent 38 (1967): 56–97; and Jeffrey Kaplow, "La Fin de la Saint-Lundi: Etude sur le Paris ouvrier au XIXe siècle," *Le Temps libre* 2 (1981): 107–18.

23. Eric Hopkins, "Working Hours and Conditions during the Industrial Revolution: A Re-appraisal," *Economic History Review* 25 (February 1982): 52–67; G. C. Allen, *The Industrial Development of Birmingham and the Black Country, 1860–1927,* 2nd ed. (London, 1966), pp. 166–69, 314–43; Patrick Joyce, *Work, Society, and Politics: The Culture of the Factory in Later Victorian England* (Brighton, 1980), chaps. 3–5; Raphael Samuel, "The Workshop of the World: Steam Power and Hand Technology in Mid-Victorian Britain," *History Workshop* 3 (1977): 49–60; and Clive Behagg, "Controlling the Product: Work, Time and the Early Industrial Workforce in Britain, 1800–1850," in *Worktime and Industrialization: An International History,* ed. Gary Cross (Philadelphia, 1988), pp. 41–58.

24. Benjamin Franklin, *Autobiography* (New York, 1932), esp. pp. vii, 93–95; A. Daumard, *Oisiveté et loisirs dans les sociétés occidentales au XIXe siècle* (Amiens, 1983), pp. 9–21; and Phillip Scranton, *Proprietary Capitalism* (New York, 1982).

25. Thomas Wright, *Some Habits and Customs of the Working Classes* (1867; reprint: New York, 1967), pp. 111–19.

26. Moore, *Man, Time, and Society,* pp. 45–66; Samuel, *Le Temps,* pp. 9–15; John Lowerson and John Meyerscough, *Time to Spare in Victorian England* (Brighton, 1977), p. 22; and Alasdair Clayer, *Work and Play: Ideas and Experiences of Work and Leisure* (London, 1974), pp. 2, 62, 93–94.

27. Patrick Joyce, ed., *Historical Meanings of Work* (London, 1987). Especially germane here are Richard Whipp, "'A Time to Every Purpose': An Essay on Time and Work," pp. 210–36; Keith McClelland, "Time to Work, Time to Live: Some Aspects of Work and the Reformation of Class in Britain, 1850–1880," pp. 180–209; and Robert Gray, "The Languages of Factory Reform in Britain," pp. 143–79.

28. For a basic bibliography, see n. 19. See also James Walvin, *Besides the Seaside* (London, 1978); John A. R. Pimlott, *The Englishman's Holiday* (London, 1947); Robert Gray, *The Labour Aristocracy in Victorian Edinburgh* (New York, 1976); Helen Moller, *Leisure in the Changing City, 1870–1914* (London, 1976); and especially Brian Harrison, *Drink and the Victorians* (Pittsburgh, 1971). French studies are sparse. Note Patrice Boussel, *Histoire des vacances* (Paris, 1961); and R. Guerrand, *La Conquête des vacances* (Paris, 1963).

29. See, for example, Neil Smelser, *Social Change in the Industrial Revolution* (Chicago, 1959). A full discussion and bibliography appear in chapter 2.

30. Bienefeld, *Waking Hours,* p. 17.

31. James R. Marchant, *The Shop Hours Act, 1892* (London, 1892); and John Hallsworth and R. H. Davies, *The Working Life of Shop Assistants* (London, 1892). See also chapter 4.

32. The classic expression of this idea is in Paul Lafargue, *The Right to Be Lazy* (1880; reprint: New York, 1910). For sociological treatments of the rela-

tionship between leisure and individualism, see Dumazedier, *Sociology of Leisure,* pp. 36, 39–40; Anderson, *Work and Leisure,* p. 62; and George Soule, *Time for Living* (New York, 1955), p. 94. For American sources, see David Roediger and Philip Foner, *Our Own Time: American Labor and Working Hours* (Westport, Conn., 1988); and Roy Rosenzweig, *Eight Hours for What We Will* (New York, 1983).

33. L. Hantrais, P. A. Clark, and N. Samuel, "Time-Space Dimensions of Work, Family and Leisure in France and Great Britain," *Leisure Studies* 3 (1984): 301–17; Dumazedier, *Sociology of Leisure,* p. 36; Samuel, *Le Temps,* pp. 7–14; Michael Young and Peter Willmott, *The Symmetrical Family: A Study of Work and Leisure in the London Region* (London, 1973); and Rhona Rapoport and Robert Rapoport, *Leisure and the Family Life Cycle* (London, 1975). See also John Hammond, *The Growth of the Common Enjoyment* (London, 1933).

34. Lujo Brentano, *Hours and Wages in Relation to Production* (London, 1898), popularized this idea. He also believed that because of the new industrial work discipline, workers would be able to produce as much in eight hours as in ten or more.

35. Clark Kerr, John Dunlop, et al., *Industrialism and Industrial Man* (Cambridge, Mass., 1964), p. 219; Alain Touraine, *The Post-Industrial Society* (New York, 1971), p. 54; and John H. Goldthorpe, *The Affluent Worker: Industrial Attitudes and Behaviour* (London, 1968). For Marxist views, see James O'Connor, *The Fiscal Crisis of the State* (New York, 1973), pp. 23–26; and especially David Gordon, Richard Edwards, and Michael Reich, *Segmented Work, Divided Workers* (New York, 1982), pp. 14–15.

36. Reinhard Bendix, *Work and Authority in Industry* (New York, 1956), chaps. 5 and 7; and James Burnham, *The Managerial Revolution* (New York, 1941). See also Keith Middlemas, *Politics in Industrial Society* (London, 1979); Martin Fine, "Toward Corporatism: The Movement for Capital-Labor Collaboration in France, 1914–1936" (Ph.D. dissertation, University of Wisconsin, 1971), esp. pp. 4–129; and John Godfrey, "Bureaucracy, Industry, and Politics in France During the First World War" (Ph.D. dissertation, Oxford University, 1974). For a view of corporatist leisure, see Robert Goldman and John Wilson, "The Rationalization of Leisure," *Politics and Society* 7 (1977): 157–87.

37. Stuart Ewig, *Captains of Consciousness* (New York, 1976), pp. 24, 30.

38. Sebastian De Grazia, *Of Time, Work, and Leisure* (New York, 1967), pp. 195–223; Jürgen Habermas, *Legitimation Crisis* (Boston, 1975), pp. 37, 75; and Georges Friedmann, *The Anatomy of Work* (Glencoe, Ill., 1961), pp. 103–14.

39. For the best analysis of this, see Bienefeld, *Working Hours,* pp. 145–48, 162–78, 193, 197.

40. Ibid., pp. 143, 194, 197; and Jean Bouvier, "Le Mouvement ouvrier et les conjonctures économiques," *Mouvement social* 48 (1964): 3–28.

41. Brian McCormick, "Hours of Work in British Industry," *Industrial and*

Labor Relations Review 12 (April 1959): 423–33; and Jean-luc Bodigeul, *La Réduction du temps de travail* (Paris, 1969), pp. 23–64.

42. David Brody, "Time and Work during Early American Industrialism," unpublished essay, 1987; and Thomas Smith, "Peasant Time and Factory Time in Japan," *Past and Present* 111 (May 1986): 165–97.

43. Charles Rist, *Réglementation légale de la journée de travail de l'ouvrier adulte en France* (Paris, 1898), p. 228.

44. For estimates of the impact of industrialization on annual work hours, see Fred Best, ed., *The Future of Work* (New York, 1973), p. 88; Samuel, *Le Temps,* p. 53; Jean Fourastié, *Des Loisirs pour quoi faire* (Paris, 1970), p. 35; and H. A. Phelps Brown, *A Century of Pay* (London, 1968), p. 211.

45. Ivan Illich, *Shadow Work* (Boston, 1982); De Grazia, *Of Time,* chap. 1 and pp. 233–40; and S. B. Linder, *The Harried Leisure Class* (New York, 1970).

46. Interesting treatments of the democratization of leisure appeared in Britain and the United States in the 1930s. See particularly Bertrand Russell, *In Praise of Idleness and Other Essays* (London, 1935); John C. Hammond, *The Growth of the Common Enjoyment* (London, 1933); and C. Delisle Burns, *Leisure in the Modern World* (London, 1932). On this theme, see also Barry Jones, *Sleepers Wake! Technology and the Future of Work* (London, 1982).

Chapter 2. Policing Time: The Nineteenth-Century State and Working Hours

1. Contemporary accounts include Philip Grant, *The History of Factory Legislation: The Ten Hours Bill* (Manchester, 1866); Alfred [Samuel Kydd], *The History of the Factory Movement,* 2 vols. (London, 1857); and Karl Marx, *Capital* (New York, 1967), 1: 270–98. Among the twentieth-century surveys are R. G. Cowherd, *The Humanitarians and the Ten-hours Movement in England* (Boston, 1956); E. L. Hutchins and A. Harrison, *A History of Factory Legislation* (London, 1926); U. R. Q. Henriques, *Before the Welfare State* (London, 1979), chaps. 4 and 5; John S. Hodgson, "The Movement for Shorter Hours, 1840–75" (D. Phil. dissertation, Oxford University, 1940); A. Llewellyn, *The Decade of Reform* (New York, 1971); A. Robson, *On Higher Than Commercial Grounds: The Factory Controversy, 1830–1853* (New York, 1985); and John Ward, *The Factory Movement, 1830–1855* (London, 1962).

2. Ward, *Factory Movement,* and his "The Factory Movement" in *Popular Movements, 1830–1850,* ed. John Ward (London, 1970); Patrick Joyce, *Work, Society and Politics* (New Brunswick, N.J., 1980), pp. 323–27; and R. L. Hill, *Toryism and the People 1832–46* (London, 1929). For a contrary view, see David Roberts, *Paternalism in Early Victorian England* (London, 1979).

3. A. J. Taylor, *Laissez-faire and State Intervention in Nineteenth-Century Britain* (London, 1972); O. MacDonagh, "The Nineteenth Century Revolution in Government: A Reappraisal," *Historical Journal* 1 (1958): 52–67; O. MacDonagh, *Early Victorian Government 1830–1876* (London, 1977); and W. H. Greenleaf, *The Rise of Collectivism* (London, 1983).

4. John Foster, *Class Struggle and the Industrial Revolution* (London, 1974), pp. 207–10; David Thompson, *The Chartists: Popular Politics in the Industrial Revolution* (New York, 1984), p. 333; and D. C. Moore, "The Other Face of Reform," *Victorian Studies* 4 (June 1961): 7–34. For a valuable critique of this thesis, see Stewart Weaver, "The Political Ideology of Short Time: England, 1820–1850," in *Worktime: An International History*, ed. Gary Cross (Philadelphia, 1989), pp. 77–102.

5. Neil Smelser, *Social Change in the Industrial Revolution* (Chicago, 1959).

6. For Britain, note especially Weaver, "The Political Ideology"; and Stewart Weaver, *John Fielden and the Politics of Popular Radicalism, 1831–1847* (Oxford, 1987). Robert Gray, "The Languages of Factory Reform in Britain, c. 1830–1960," in *Meanings of Work*, ed. Patrick Joyce (New York, 1987), pp. 143–79; Robert Sykes, "Some Aspects of Working Class Consciousness in Oldam, 1830–1842," *Historical Journal* 23 (1980): 167–85; and Robert Sykes's forthcoming book on Lancashire working-class radicalism. For France, see Lee Shai Weisbach, *Child Labor Reform in Nineteenth Century France* (Baton Rouge, 1989).

7. Adam Smith, *Wealth of Nations* (New York, 1937), pp. 78–83; Cris Nyland, "Capitalism and the History of Worktime Thought," *British Journal of Sociology* 4 (December 1986): 513–34; K. O. Walker, "The Classical Economists and the Factory Acts," *Journal of Economic History* 1 (1941): 168–77.

8. Nyland, "Capitalism," pp. 520–34; and Howard Marvel, "Factory Regulation: A Reinterpretation of the Early English Experience," *Journal of Law and Economy* 20 (1977): 379–402.

9. Marx, *Capital*, 1: 542. See also Douglas Booth, "Karl Marx on the State of the Regulation of the Labor Process," *Review of Social Economy* 36 (1978): 137–58; and Harry Cleaver, *Reading Capital Politically* (London, 1979), p. 78.

10. For example, Lord Ashley in 1844 and William Greg in 1832 argued that shorter hours would improve labor efficiency and thus compensate for reduced hours of production. "The Ten Hours Bill, The Speech of Lord Ashley, M.P. (May 10, 1844)," in *Prelude to Victory*, ed. K. Carpenter (New York, 1972), p. 15; and William Greg, "An Enquiry into the State of the Manufacturing Population, and the Causes and Cures of the Evils Therein," *The Ten Hours Movement in 1831 and 1832*, ed. Kenneth Carpenter (New York, 1972), pp. 4–5.

11. Ward, *Factory Movement*, p. 18; Alfred [Kydd], *Factory Movement*, 1: 18–38; Hutchins and Harrison, *Factory Legislation*, pp. 5–7.

12. Alfred [Kydd], *Factory Movement*, 1: 40–85; Hutchins and Harrison, *Factory Legislation*, pp. 19–38; "The Factory Question" (1837), in *The Battle for the Ten-Hour Day Continues, 1837–1843*, ed. Kenneth Carpenter (New

York, 1972), p. 406; John T. Ward and W. Hamish Fraser, eds., *Workers and Employers* (London, 1980), pp. 46–47; John Fielden, *The Curse of the Factory System* (London, 1834), pp. 7–12; and Kenneth Carpenter, ed., *The Factory Act of 1819* (New York, 1972).

13. Alfred [Kydd], *Factory Movement,* 1: chap. 7, esp. p. 100. See also the following collections of documents edited by Kenneth Carpenter: *Richard Oastler: King of the Factory Children; The Ten Hours Movement in 1831 and 1832;* and *The Factory Act of 1833* (New York, 1972); Ernest L. Woodward, *Age of Reform* (London, 1962), pp. 120–42; C. Driver, *Tory Radical: The Life of Richard Oastler* (New York, 1946); and J. C. Gill, *The Ten Hours Parson: The Life and Work of George Stringer Bull* (London, 1959).

14. Karl Marx, *On Britain* (New York, 1975), pp. 99–100.

15. Weaver, "Political Ideology," pp. 77–89; Weaver, *John Fielden,* chap. 8; and T. R. Tholfsen, *Working Class Radicalism in Mid-Victorian England* (New York, 1977).

16. See Gray, "Languages of Factory Reform," for a brilliant analysis of the texture of short-time discourse.

17. E. P. Thompson, *The Making of the English Working Class* (London, 1963), p. 340. See also Sykes, "Some Aspects of Working Class Consciousness"; and Weaver, *John Fielden.*

18. Smelser, *Social Change,* pp. 180–85, 188–92, 196–212, 235, 240, 257–58, 265–66, 280–86; and Maxine Berg, *The Machinery Question and the Making of Political Economy, 1815–1848* (New York, 1980), pp. 23–27. For a critique of Smelser, see Craig Calhoun, *The Question of Class Struggle: Social Foundations of Popular Radicalism during the Industrial Revolution* (Chicago, 1982), esp. pp. 191–96.

19. Hutchins and Harrison, *Factory Legislation,* pp. 412–13; Ward, *Factory Movement,* p. 125; Richard Oastler, "Eight Letters to the Duke of Wellington," (1835) in Carpenter, *Richard Oastler,* pp. 44–45, 162–63, 168; and Friedrich Engels, *Condition of the English Working Class* (Stanford, 1968), pp. 162–65. See also R. G. Wilson, *Gentlemen Merchants* (Manchester, 1971); and Gray, "Languages of Factory Reform," pp. 7–8.

20. Smelser, *Social Change,* pp. 297–98; Alfred [Kidd], *Factory Movement,* pp. 48–49, 64, 68–69, 85–93; Hutchins and Harrison, *Factory Legislation,* pp. 76–77; and Weaver, *John Fielden,* chap. 5.

21. Smelser, *Social Change,* esp. pp. 286, 266.

22. "The 'Ten Hours Question': A Report Addressed to the Short Time Committee of West Riding of Yorkshire" (1842), in *Battle for the Ten Hour Day Continues,* ed. K. Carpenter (New York, 1972), pp. 19, 23–32.

23. Neil W. Thompson, *The People's Science: The Popular Political Economy of Exploitation and Crisis, 1816–1834* (New York, 1984).

24. William Kenworth, "Inventions and Hours of Labour" (1842), in Carpenter, *The Battle for the Ten Hour Day Continues,* p. 9.

25. John Fielden, letter to *Pioneer* (December 21, 1833); and Fielden, *The Curse*, pp. 34–35.

26. John Doherty, *Poor Man's Advocate* (March 17, 1832), cited in Gray, "Languages of Factory Reform," p. 150.

27. "The Ten Hours Question," in Carpenter, *The Battle for the Ten Hour Day Continues*, pp. 4–5; Lord Ashley, "The Ten Hours Bill," in Carpenter, *Prelude to Victory*, p. 24; and Greg, "An Enquiry," in Carpenter, *The Ten Hours*, pp. 18–28, 30–31.

28. *Pioneer* (December 21, 1833).

29. Ivy Pinchbeck and Margaret Hewitt, *Children in English Society* (London, 1973), 2: 406.

30. Alfred [Kydd], *Factory Movement*, 1: chap. 13; P. Gaskell, *Artisans and Machinery* (London, 1936), p. 89; Charles T. Thachrah, *The Effects of the Principal Arts, Trades and Professions* (London, 1832); and John Brown, *A Memoire of Robert Blincoe An Orphan Boy* (Manchester, 1832).

31. For example, George Bull calculated that working-class parents spent only four and a quarter hours per week with their children. They had no time for "parental influence and filial affection" (cited in Smelser, *Social Change*, p. 281).

32. Pinchbeck and Hewitt, *Children*, 2: 387–405; and M. Hewitt, *Wives and Mothers in Victorian Industry 1750–1850* (London, 1975), p. 12.

33. Greg, "An Enquiry," in Carpenter, *The Ten Hours*, pp. 2–31; Ashley, "The Ten Hours Bill," in Carpenter, *Prelude to Victory*, pp. 6–8; Oastler, "Eight Letters," in Carpenter, *Richard Oastler*, pp. 78–81, 146–47; Alfred [Kydd], *Factory Movement*, 1: 197–99.

34. For example, Lord Ashley observed the stretch out on the spinning mules, which meant that the spinner who walked eight miles on the mule in 1815 was walking twenty by 1832. Ashley, "The Ten Hours Bill," in Carpenter, *Prelude to Victory*, pp. 12–14.

35. M. J. Cullen, *The Statistical Movement in Early Victorian Britain* (Brighton, 1975).

36. Ashley, "The Ten Hours Bill," in Carpenter, *Prelude to Victory*, p. 17; and Nassau Senior, *Industrial Efficiency and Social Economy* (1847; New York, 1928), 2: 307–8.

37. An exception is Oastler's innovative argument that drunkenness (as well as the profanation of the Sabbath) was not the product of excess leisure but of overwork; see Oastler, "Eight Letters," in Carpenter, *Richard Oastler*, pp. 146–47.

38. E. P. Thompson and Eileen Yeo, *The Unknown Mayhew* (New York, 1971), p. 53; and *Journal of the Statistical Society of London* 1 (1839): 55. See also Gray, "Languages of Factory Reform," pp. 174–75.

39. A. Ure, *Philosophy of Manufacturers* (London, 1835), p. 301; and Senior, *Letters* (London, 1837), p. 23.

40. "A Letter to Sir John Hobhouse, M.P. on 'the Factory Bill' by a Manufacturer," in *The Ten Hour Movement (1832)*, ed. Ken Carpenter (New York, 1972), p. 20.

41. Robert Greg, "Factory Question and the Ten Hours Bill, 1837," in Carpenter, *The Battle for the Ten Hour Day Continues*, pp. 74–104; Robert Torrens, "A Letter to Lord Ashley on the Principles Which Regulate Wages," (1844), in Carpenter, *Prelude to Victory*, pp. 1–80; and Senior, *Letters*, pp. 12–13.

42. "The Justice of Exposing Tyrannical Employers," prospectus for *The Poor Man's Advocate* (1932–1933), cited in Gray, "Languages of Factory Reform," p. 150.

43. *Cobbett's Weekly Political Register* (December 14, 1833), cited in Weaver, "Political Ideology," p. 93.

44. Weaver, "Political Ideology," pp. 78, 91; Richard Price, *Masters, Unions and Men* (New York, 1980), p. 53; and G. S. Bull, "To the Friends of the National Regeneration Society," *Crisis and National Co-operative Trades' Union Gazette* (April 26, 1834), cited in Weaver, "Political Ideology," p. 91.

45. John Fielden, "To the Electors of Oldham" (1832), Fielden Manuscripts, University of Manchester, cited in Weaver, "Political Ideology," p. 94.

46. Bull, *Crisis* (April 26, 1834).

47. *Bulletin de la Société industrielle de Mulhouse* 1 (1828): 325; Louis René Villermé, *Tableau de l'état physique et moral des ouvriers employés dans les manufactures de coton, de laine, et de soie* (Paris, 1840), 2: 97–98; Victor Mataja, "Les Origines de la protection ouvrière en France," *Revue d'économie politique* (1895): 529–36, 739–57; and William Reddy, *The Rise of Market Culture: The Textile Trade and French Society, 1750–1900* (New York, 1984), pp. 169–71.

48. Eugène Buret, *De la misère des classes laborieuses en Angleterre et en France* (Paris, 1840), 2: 159–70; Pierre Bigot de Morogue, *De la misère des ouvriers et de la marche à suivre pour y remédier* (Paris, 1932), p. 23; Adolphe Blanqui, *Les Classes ouvrières en France pendant l'année 1848* (Paris, 1849), p. 77; Villermé, *Tableau*, 2: 89, 97; Louis René Villermé, "Sur la durée trop longue du travail des enfants dans beaucoup de manufactures," *Annales d'hygiène publique et de médecine légale* 18 (1837): 164–76; J. C. L. Sismondi, *Nouveaux principes d'économie politique* (Paris, 1927); and Alban de Villeneuve-Bargemont, *Economie politique chrétienne ou recherches sur la nature et les causes du pauperisme en France et en Europe* (Paris, 1837). See also Katherine Lynch, "The Problem of Child Labor Reform and the Working Class Family in France during the July Monarchy," *Proceedings of the Annual Meeting of the Western Society for French History* 5 (1977): 228–36; and Hilde Regaudias, *Les Enquêtes ouvrières en France entre 1830 et 1848* (Paris, 1936).

49. Charles Dupin, *Moniteur* (March 1, 1840): 350; Mataja, "Les Origines," pp. 530–38; and Blanqui, *Les Classes*, p. 31.

50. Louis Blanc, *Histoire de 10 ans* (1844), 4: 106; *Moniteur* (September 9, 1848): 2363; *Le National* (September 4, 1840); Charles Rist, "La Durée du travail dans l'industrie française de 1820 à 1870," *Revue d'économie politique* (1897): 371–73; and Emile Levasseur, *Histoire des classes ouvrières et de l'industrie en France de 1789 à 1870* (Paris, 1904), 2: 165, 241, 243.

51. Louis Reybaud, *Le Coton, son régime, ses problèmes, son influence en Europe* (Paris, 1863), pp. 227–44; H. A. Frégier, *Des Classes dangereuses de la société dans les grandes villes et des moyens de les rendre meilleures* (Paris, 1840), 1: 76–80, 111–32, 340–46, 376–77, and 2: 186–202, 340–46; Villermé, *Tableau,* 2: 37, 66–68; and Blanqui, *Les Classes,* pp. 60, 66, 192, 202, 207–15, 227, 231.

52. Speech of Guy Lussac, *Moniteur* (February 1, 1840): 459; and debate in Chamber, December 12–29 1840, *Moniteur* (December 22, 1840): esp. 2488. See also Levasseur, *Histoire,* 2: 127–29; and Majata, "Les Origines," p. 541.

53. Blanqui, *Les Classes,* 225–28; *Bulletin de la Société industrielle de Mulhouse* 1 (1828): 325–35; and E. Béres, *Les Classes ouvrières* (Paris, 1836), p. 154.

54. *Moniteur* (December 22, 1840): 2485.

55. *Moniteur* (December 29, 1840): 2541–42.

56. *Moniteur* (December 22, 1840): 2488–89; and (December 29, 1840): 2542.

57. Levasseur, *Histoire,* 2: 131–32; Mataja, "Les Origines," pp. 545–47, 739, 750–51; and Reddy, *Market Culture,* p. 239.

58. *Moniteur* (February 14, 1847): 337; (June 29–30, 1847): 1830, 1844; (February 15, 1848): 390–94; and (February 18–23, 1848): 426–94. See also Pierre Pierrard, *La Vie ouvrière à Lille sous le Second Empire* (Paris, 1965), pp. 163–64.

59. Note especially J. Epstein and D. Thompson, eds., *The Chartist Experience* (London, 1982); D. Thompson, *The Chartists;* Maurice Augulhon, *Une Ville ouvrière au temps du socialisme utopique: Toulon de 1815 à 1851* (Paris, 1971); and John Merriman, *The Red City* (Oxford, 1986).

60. *Manchester and Salford Advertiser* (January 15, 1842), cited in Alfred, *Factory Movement,* chaps. 12–15; Hutchins and Harrison, *Factory Legislation,* pp. 64–66; Woodward, *Reform,* pp. 148–49; and Weaver, *John Fielden,* chap. 8.

61. Karl Marx, *Selected Works,* ed. Victor Adorasky (London, 1842), 2: 439.

62. BPP, "Report of Inspectors of Factories," 25 (1847–1848): 245; Marx, *Capital,* 1: 290–98; and Hutchins and Harrison, *Factory Legislation,* p. 102.

63. Robert Gray also stresses that hours laws were "seen as the moral voice of the community," and he develops the notion of the role of the 1847 law as a part of a "symbolic social settlement" between alternative discourses; see "Languages of Factory Reform," pp. 5, 20, 25–54. See also William G. Carson, "Symbolic and Instrumental Dimensions of Early Factory Legislation," in

Crime, Criminology and Public Policy, ed. Robert Hood (London, 1974), esp. pp. 129–34.

64. *Moniteur* (February 18, 1848): 511; (March 2, 1848): 521, 529; and (March 4, 1848): 537. Louis Blanc later claimed that the March 2 decree "was given in fear of the pressure of events. . . . It was less the work of government than of the workers themselves." Louis Blanc, *Histoire de la Révolution de 48* (Paris, 1880), 1: 167–71.

65. Blanc, *Histoire de la Révolution,* pp. 58–60; *Moniteur* (August 30, September 5, 9, 1848): 2235, 2296, 2236–64. See also Agricol Perdiguier, *Discours sur la fixation des heures de travail* (Paris, 1849).

66. Blanc, *Histoire de la Révolution,* p. 87; and Reddy, *Market Culture,* pp. 210, 220.

67. Charles Rist notes that the average workday in Lyon, St. Etienne, and Marseille was twelve in 1848. This was possibly a drop from the 1830s but it was above the eleven and ten hours demanded by the decree. See Rist, "La Durée," pp. 383–85; *Moniteur* (March 10, 1848): 581, and (April 5, 1948): 765; and Reddy, *Market Culture,* pp. 205–6. Note also Michel Chevalier, "Question des travailleurs," *Revue des deux mondes* 21 (March 1848): 1056–86.

68. *Moniteur* (August 30, 1848): 2236–37; (September 5, 1848): 2295; and (September 9, 1848): 2362–63, 2369–70. See also Charles Rist, *Réglementation légale de la journée du travail de l'ouvrier adulte en France* (Paris, 1898), pp. 38–49.

69. *Moniteur* (September 5, 1848): 2295; (September 9, 1848): 2362–63; (September 10, 1848): 2378, 2381; Blanc, *Histoire de la Révolution,* pp. 25, 51.

70. For details see Rist, *Réglementation,* chap. 5.

71. Joyce, *Work, Society and Politics,* pp. 58, 64; and Berg, *The Machinery Question,* p. 29.

72. Hours legislation was extended to branches of the textile trades (e.g., bleaching and dye works in 1860 and hosiery in 1864) and to "dangerous trades" (like match and percussion cap manufacturing) in 1864. In that same law of 1864, children under thirteen were allowed only to work half-shifts, a provision that reinforced the trend (caused by higher wages) to remove children from the industrial work force. In 1867, the ten-hour day was applied to all manufacturing, including workshops employing fewer than fifty workers (although rules were less stringent for the smaller shops). By 1871, a centralized inspection system was established. By 1874, the protected classes in textiles were granted a ten-hour weekday and a half-Saturday. In 1878, an act consolidating the piecemeal legislation was passed. Although it was strict for textile employers (including two-hour meal breaks within a workday, which could not extend beyond a twelve hour period), it provided a sixty-hour week for nontextile factory workers and additional loopholes for domestic trades. Hutchins and Harrison, *Factory Legislation,* chaps. 7–8; Woodward, *Reform,* pp. 589–90;

Monica Hodgson, "The Working Day and the Working Week in Victorian England" (M.Phil. thesis, University of London, 1974), pp. 15–29; Gertrude Tuckwell and Constance Smith, *The Workers' Handbook* (London, 1908); and A. E. Peacock, "The Successful Prosecution of the Factory Acts, 1833–55," *Economic History Review* 38 (May 1984): 197–210.

73. BPP, "Annual Report of the Chief of Factory Inspectors," 25 (1912–1913): 14–15, 29, 103, 145.

74. Reddy (*Market Culture,* pp. 235–44) found that there was only one inspector for the entire northern textile region in the 1850s, until he was fired in 1867 at request of Chambers of Commerce.

75. Rist, *Réglementation,* pp. 50–60, 90–105.

76. Ibid., pp. 52–60.

77. Tallon was so suspicious of the threat of dissipating luxury that he was convinced that American experiments with the eight-hour day had led not only to the closure of a "great number of factories" but that the new leisure had created "new germs of demoralization." See Eugène Tallon, *Législation sur le travail des enfants dans les manufactures* (Paris, 1875), pp. 247–56, 389–92. Note also Tallon, *La Vie morale et intellectuelle des ouvriers* (Paris, 1877).

78. According to Simon, the working-class couple "when love has left, are no more than two associates, who pool their salaries. The men, who are more free and who, sometimes do more fatiguing work, and finding discomfort at home in cold and dirty rooms, with no one attending them, go to the bar." See Jules Simon, *L'Ouvrière* (Paris, 1861), pp. 59–63; and idem, *L'Ouvrier de huit ans* (Paris, 1867), pp. 73–129. See for similar ideology, Denis Poulot, *Question sociale: Le Sublime ou le travailleur comme il est en 1870 et ce qu'il peut être* (Paris, 1872), pp. 192–202; Paul Leroy Beaulieu, *Le Travail des femmes au XIXe siècle* (Paris, 1873); and Frédéric Le Play, *Les Ouvriers européens: Etudes sur les travaux, la vie domestique et la condition morale des populations ouvrières de l'Europe* (Paris, 1877–1879), esp. 4: 109–10.

79. Tallon, *Législation,* pp. 136–37, 141, 148–50; and Simon, *L'Ouvrier de huit ans,* pp. 138, 210–22. See also Michelle Perrot, "De la nourrice à l'employée: travaux de femmes dans la France du XIXe siècle," *Mouvement social* 105 (October–December 1978): 3–11; and Joan Scott, "L'Ouvrière. Mot impie, sordide: The Working Woman in the Discourse of French Political Economy," in *Meanings of Work,* ed. Patrick Joyce (New York, 1987).

80. This movement culminated at St. Quentin in 1879 where four thousand textile workers struck for a ten-hour day. See Michelle Perrot, *Les Ouvriers en grève* (Paris, 1973), 1: 288; and Rist, *Réglementation,* pp. 120–32, 150–57.

81. Rist, *Réglementation,* pp. 130, 150–57; and Levasseur, *Questions ouvrières* (Paris, 1907), p. 437. See also Martin Nadaud, *Leonard* (1895; reprint: Paris, 1976).

82. France ChDoc (March 22, 1881), pp. 584–85.

83. Another opponent added that piece rates naturally regulated worktime. Thus, no further legal reductions were justified. France ChDoc (March 22 and 29, 1881), pp. 592–600, 663.

84. See the speeches of Auguste Ballue, France ChDeb (March 29, 1881), p. 670, and of Nadaud, ChDeb (March 22, 1881), pp. 601–2.

85. France ChDeb (March 29, 1881), p. 673. Note Waddington's stress on the physical deterioration caused by the new factories, in ChDeb (March 29, 1881), p. 663.

86. Examples are in Waddington's speech, France ChDeb (March 29, 1881), p. 663, and that of Nadaud, ChDeb (March 22, 1881), p. 601. Still the deputy from Lyon, Auguste Ballue, went further. He argued that there could be no improvement in the lives of children without time for adults to uplift the "generation." Implicitly, he rejected the efficacy of the substitutionary role of the state. See ChDeb (March 29, 1881), p. 670.

87. Senator Alexandre Oudet noted that the Orleanist upper house in 1847 had voted for a law regulating women's hours—a measure lost in the turmoil of revolution; he claimed that women were physically incapable of more than eleven hours of work. Yet Senator Ernest Feray held the majority view when he rejected an "exceptional law" for one sex. This argument could not be easily repulsed. See France SDeb (February 24 and 25, 1881), pp. 107, 111–12, 123–24. For the debate between de Mun and Yves Guyot, see France ChDeb (June 11, 1888), pp. 1726–32.

88. France SDeb (February 24 and 25, 1882), pp. 101–3, 118–23. See also Rist, *Réglementation*, pp. 156–65; Raoul Jay, *La Limitation de la journée de travail en France* (Paris, 1904), pp. 10–12; and Nadaud, *Leonard*, pp. 475–76.

89. Maurice Ansiaux, *Heures de travail et salaries* (Brussels, 1896), p. 125; and Rist, *Réglementation*, pp. 167–68.

90. For discussion, see Jay, *La Limitation*, pp. 16–17; Levasseur, *Questions*, pp. 439–41; Edouard Payen, *La Réglementation du travail réalisée ou projetée: Ses illusions et ses dangers* (Paris, 1913), p. 10; Paul Balsenq, *La Limitation légale de la journée de travail dans l'industrie française, loi du 30 mars 1900* (Paris, 1910), pp. 2–5; and Jean-luc Bodigeul, *La Réduction du temps de travail* (Paris, 1960), pp. 64–65.

91. Conseil supérieure du travail, *Rapport* (Paris, 1895), pp. 106–7; (1896), pp. 83, 119; (1899), pp. xviii, xxx, 189, 510; *Bulletin de l'inspection du travail* (1894), p. 852; Office du Travail, *Salaires et durée du travail: La Petite industrie* (Paris, 1893), 1: 273.

92. For discussion, see Rist, *Réglementation*, pp. 166–71; Jay, *La Limitation*, pp. 20–25; Levasseur, *Questions*, p. 442; and Balsenq, *La Limitation*, p. 9.

93. *Bulletin de l'Office du Travail* (March 1904), pp. 200–4; (March 1905), pp. 198–205; and (May 1905), pp. 420–39; and Conseil supérieur du travail, *Rapport* (Paris, 1902), p. xxxv.

94. Conseil supérieur du travail, *Rapport* (Paris, 1904), p. xxx; (1905),

p. liv; (1911), p. xxvii; Balsenq, *La Limitation*, pp. 72–73; Jay, *La Limitation*, pp. 37–40; and *Bulletin de l'inspection du travail* (1902), p. 21. See also F^{22} 333, Justin Godart, *Rapport sur l'application des lois réglementant le travail* (Paris, 1906), p. 8.

95. Conseil supérieur du travail, *Rapport* (France, 1899), p. 66; (1902), pp. xxxv, xlvii; (1903), p. xxx; (1904), pp. xxvii–xxviii, xxxiii–xxxviii, 34; (1905), pp. xliv, 7–10, 105; and (1906), p. xxxiv.

96. *Bulletin de l'Office du travail* (September 1907), pp. 903–6; (January 1911), p. 27; and (September 1911), p. 870; Conseil supérieur du travail, *Rapport* (Paris, 1902), pp. xxxiv, xxxvi, xxxix; (1904), pp. xlii–xliv, 27; (1905), pp. xxxi–xxxii, 1, 7, 103, 141, 221, 275; and (1911), p. xxxix.

97. France SDeb (March 18, 1904); Conseil supérieur du travail, *Rapport* (Paris, 1902), pp. xlix, lii–lvi; and (1905), p. xli; and *Bulletin de l'Office du travail* (August 1912), pp. 852–54. Additional details are in Balsenq, *La Limitation*, pp. 155–60; Justin Godart, "Rapport relatif à la réglementation du travail," France ChDoc Annex (March 21, 1907), no 876; François Fagnot and Alexandre Millerand, *La Durée légale du travail: Des Modifications à apporter à la loi de 1900* (Paris, 1905); and Ministère du Travail, *Lois, décrets et arrêtés concernant la réglementation du travail* (Paris, 1913). See also Ministère du travail, *Le Problème de la réduction de la durée du travail devant le parlement français* (Paris, 1918).

Chapter 3. Challenging the Liberal Economy of Time, 1886–1912

1. Jules Guesde, "La journée de huit heures," *L'Ere nouvelle* (1894): 231.

2. Richard Price, *Masters, Unions, and Men: Work Control in Building and the Rise of Labour* (Cambridge, 1980), pp. 38–39; D. A. Reid, "The Decline of St. Monday," *Past and Present* 71 (May 1976): 56–97; D. A. Reid, "Labour, Leisure and Politics in Birmingham c. 1800–1875" (Ph.D. dissertation, University of Birmingham, 1985); Clive Behagg, "Controlling the Product: Work, Time and the Early Industrial Workforce in Britain, 1800–1850," in *Worktime and Industrialization: An International History*, ed. Gary Cross (Philadelphia, 1989), pp. 41–58; and William Reddy, *The Rise of Market Culture: The Textile Trade and French Society, 1750–1900* (Cambridge, 1984), pp. 136–37.

3. Reddy, *Market Culture*, pp. 120–24, 186–87, 20–21, 67, 328; Price, *Masters, Unions, and Men*, pp. 39–42, 158, and chap. 3; and Eric Hobsbawm, *Labouring Men* (London, 1964), pp. 371–86.

4. For example, Gareth Stedman Jones in *The Language of Class* (London, 1983), pp. 235–38, sees the era of the New Unionism as a part of a "defensive

culture" of British labor that emerged in the last third of the nineteenth century. See also E. P. Thompson, "Homage to Tom Maguire" in *Essays in Labour History in Memory of G. D. H. Cole*, ed. Asa Briggs (London, 1971), pp. 286–87.

5. Price, *Masters, Unions, and Men*, pp. 39–42, 158, and chap. 3; Hobsbawm, *Labouring Men*, pp. 371–86; and Jones, *Language of Class*, pp. 235–38. For a different assessment that stresses the controls that workers gained in formal bargaining structures, see Jonathan Zeitlin, "From Labour History to Industrial Relations," *Economic History Review* 40 (1987): 159–84.

6. James E. Cronin, *Labour and Society in Britain, 1918–1979* (London, 1984), chap. 1.

7. For example, Reddy (*Market Culture*, p. 301) noted that the demand for a ten-hour day in an 1880 strike of French textile workers was dropped for a modest claim for an eleven-hour day and the original demand was replaced by "more urgent issues" (like improving work materials). At the same time, the new program of the textile workers abandoned the ten-hour day "until such time as the workday was reduced by legislation."

8. See, for example, M. A. Bienefeld, *Working Hours in British Industry: An Economic History* (London, 1972), pp. 122–26; George D. H. Cole, *A Short History of the British Working Class Movement* (London, 1948), p. 249; and Hugh Clegg, *A History of British Unions Since 1889* (London, 1964), pp. 53–54.

9. On the nine-hour movement, see George Howell, "Great Strikes: Their Origin, Cost, and Results," *The Cooperative Wholesale Society Annual* 7 (1889): 266–311; and The Nine Hours' League, *The North East Engineers Strikes of 1871* (Newcastle, 1891). In the LSE Pamphlet Collection, see "Balance Sheet of the Late Strike and Lockout in the London Building Trades, July 24, 1859–May 1, 1860" (London, 1860), and "The Balance Sheet of the Carpenters and Joiners Short Time Movement of 1872" (London, 1872). Note also John Burnett, *History of the Nine Hours Movement at Newcastle and Gateshead* (London, 1872); Philip Bagwell, *The Railwaymen* (London, 1963), pp. 37, 50–54; Monica Hodgson, "The Working Day and the Working Week in Victorian Britain, 1840–1900" (M. Phil. thesis, University of London, 1974), pp. 39–53, 155; Raymond Postgate, *The Builders' History* (London, 1923), pp. 169–75, 209–11; and Price, *Markets, Unions, and Men*, pp. 45–52.

10. Cole, *Short History*, p. 211; Sidney Webb, *The History of Trade Unionism* (London, 1950), p. 298. Note also the numerous histories of the Factory Acts cited in chapter 2, n. 1.

11. Trade Union Congress, *Report of the Proceedings . . .* (1887), p. 36; Brian McCormick and J. E. Williams, "The Miners and the Eight Hours Day 1863–1910," *Economic History Review* 35 (1959): 238–50; Henry Pelling, *A History of British Trade Unionism* (New York, 1966), pp. 89–90; Robert Currie, *Industrial Politics* (Oxford, 1979), pp. 89–96; E. A. P. Duffy, "New Unionism in Britain, 1889–1890: A Reappraisal," *Economic History Review* 14 (1961): 312–13; and idem, "The Eight Hour Day Movement in Britain, 1836–1893,"

Manchester School of Economics and Social Studies 36 (1968): 208, 217–18; Eric Hobsbawm, *The Turning Point of Labour, 1880–1900,* 2nd ed. (London, 1977), pp. 55, 109; and Tom Mann, *Memoirs* (London, 1923), pp. 58–60.

12. Earl (Thomas) Brassey, *Lectures on the Labour Question* (London, 1878), chap. 2. See also the work by the American Carroll Wright: *Comparative Wages, Prices, and Cost of Living: Massachusetts and Great Britain 1860–1883* (Boston, 1889).

13. See F. Domela Niewenhuis's article in *The Eight Hours Working Day* (January 25, 1890), pp. 11–12. The problem of systematic overtime is treated well by Hodgson, "The Working Day," pp. 68–84.

14. Each of these trades experienced long workdays; in some, hours were concentrated in seasonal and unpredictable stints (e.g., in dock and gas work); in others, worktime was spread over periods of sixteen hours or more (rails and trams); in still more, workers were obliged to work night shifts (bakers and smelters). Bagwell, *Railwaymen,* pp. 131–40; Bienefeld, *Working Hours,* pp. 118–119, 183–84; Clegg, *British Unions,* p. 234; Cole, *Short History,* pp. 207, 256, 300; E. H. Phelps-Brown, *The Growth of British Industrial Relations* (London, 1955), pp. 126–32, 135; Hobsbawm, *Labouring Men,* pp. 161–62, 170; Webb, *Trade Unions,* pp. 344, 379–80, 391–93; Keith Burgess, *The Origins of British Industrial Relations: The Nineteenth Century Experience* (London, 1975), p. 204; Helen Lynd, *England in the Eighteen Eighties* (New York, 1945), esp. chap. 1 and pp. 195–231; Hubert L. Smith and Vaughan Nash, *The Gas Workers' Strike* (London, 1889). Testimonies of unions are in *Royal Commission on Labour Minutes of Evidence* (RCL), report 5, part 2, pp. 106–8, 157, 210–12, 229; report 3, group B, pp. 114–21, 126–28, 318–19, 351–52, 360–61, 469–71; report 5, group B, p. 153; report 2, group C, pp. 18–19; report 3, group C, pp. 332–43, 611.

15. Ministère du Commerce, *Enquête sur les modifications à apporter aux lois du 9 octobre 1848 et du 19 mai 1874 sur le travail dans l'industrie* (Paris, 1885), p. 129; and Michelle Perrot, *Les Ouvriers en grève: France, 1871–1890* (Paris, 1974), 1: 83, 93, 95–96, 287–88, 320. See also Michael Hanagan, *The Logic of Solidarity: Artisans and Industrial Workers in Three French Towns 1871–1914* (Urbana, Ill., 1980), pp. 66–67.

16. M. Spuller, "Commission d'enquête parlementaire sur la situation des ouvriers de l'industrie et de l'agriculture en France," France ChDoc (Paris, 1884), pp. 141–43, 148; Maurice Dommanget, *Histoire du premier mai* (Paris, 1953), chap. 3; and Jean Bodiguel, *La Réduction du temps de travail* (Paris, 1969), pp. 34–69.

17. Sidney Webb, "The Limitation of the Hours of Labour," *Contemporary Review* 56 (December 1889): 859. The literature advocating a legal eight-hour day in Britain during this period is vast and includes: Henry Hyde Champion, *The Parliamentary Eight Hours Day* (London, 1890); A. K. Donald, *The Eight Hours Work Day* (London, 1890); George W. Foote and George B. Shaw, *The*

Legal Eight Hours Question: A Public Debate (Glasgow, 1891); H. M. Hyndman, "Eight-Hours, The Maximum Working Day," *New Review* 1 (August 1889): 166–87; H. M. Hyndman, *Mr. Gladstone and the Eight Hours Law* (London, 1892); and H. M. Hyndman with Charles Bradlaugh, *Eight Hours' Movement: Verbatim Report of a Debate* (London, 1890); Tom Mann, *What a Compulsory Eight Hours Working Day Means to Workers* (London, 1886); Tom Mann, *The Eight Hours Day: How to Get It by Trade and Local Option* (London, 1891); L. Ramsay, "The Eight Hours Movement," *Westminster Review* (December 1890): 642–57; John Rae, *Eight Hours Work* (London, 1894); John Rae "The Eight Hours Day and Foreign Competition," *Contemporary Review* 65 (February 1894): 189–206; and especially Sidney Webb and Harold Cox, *The Eight Hours Day* (London, 1891).

18. TUC, *Proceedings* (1887), pp. 35–37.

19. Fernand Pelloutier, *La Vie ouvrière en France* (Paris, 1900; reprint: Paris, 1975), pp. 52–53. See also Jacques Julliard, *Fernand Pelloutier et les origines du syndicalisme d'action directe* (Paris, 1971); and Bernard Moss, *The Origins of the French Labor Movement, 1830–1914* (Berkeley, 1976).

20. *Eight Hours Working Day* (December 7, 1889), p. 7; and TUC, *Proceedings* (1887), p. 37; (1888), p. 15; and (1891), pp. 48, 52–55.

21. Examples of fears of international competition are noted in TUC, *Proceedings* (1889), pp. 37, 52–54, and (1890), p. 50; RCL, report 5, part 2, p. 306. Concerns over the impact of eight hours on wages were stated in TUC, *Proceedings* (1887), p. 37; and RCL, report 5, part 2, p. 211. Opposition to a legal eight-hour day by task-oriented workers was clear in RCL, report 5, part 2, pp. 106–7, 305; report 2, group A, p. 335; and report 3, group A, pp. 45–49, 211–12; and report 2, group C, p. 199.

22. *La Révolte* (February 1, 1886).

23. William Shaxby, *The Case against Trade Union and Legislative Interference* (London, 1898), pp. 11–12, 22–23; Yves Guyot, *La Tyrannie socialiste* (Paris, 1893), pp. 5, 114–15, 121–22; Jean Desmets, "Les Conséquences de la journée de huit heures," *Réforme économique* (July 12 and 26, 1907): 843, 875–76; and Henri de Moly, "La Réglementation du travail en France et les catholiques," *Réforme sociale* 4 (1891): 592–94. A list of hostile reports from French Chambers of Commerce on the reduction of worktime are in F[22] 334. Robert Giffen's views are stated in RCL, report 4, pp. 486–88. See also T. G. Spyers, *The Labour Question: An Epitome of Evidence and the Report of the Royal Commission of Labour* (London, 1894), p. 69; and Charles Bradlaugh, "Regulation by Statute of the Hours of Labour," *Fortnightly Review* new ser. 47 (March 1890): 440–60, esp. 454.

24. John A. Hobson, "The Cost of a Shorter Day," *National Review* (April 1890): 121, 194–99; and Léon Donnat, *La Réglementation du travail: Discours prononcé au Conseil Municipal de Paris, le 29 juillet 1886* (Paris, 1886), p. 24. Alfred Marshall took a similar view in the RCL, report 4, part 2, pp. 288, 504.

Opponents' concerns over international competition are evident in Charles Bradlaugh, *The Eight Hours Movement* (London, 1889), pp. 130–31; John Robertson, *The Eight Hours Questions* (London, 1893), chap. 9; and J. S. Jeans, *The Eight Hours' Day in British Engineering Industries: An Examination and Criticism of Recent Experiments* (London, 1894), p. 16.

25. For Britain, see Robertson, *Eight Hours,* chap. 12; Shaxby, *Interference,* p. 5; and Jeans, *Eight Hours' Day,* pp. 33–36. For France, note Ministère du Commerce, *Rapport concernant l'application en 1900 des lois réglementant le travail* (Paris, 1900), p. 5, where a prominent factory inspector declares, "The mechanical tools, today generally used to the maximum effectiveness, cannot easily be improved for the reduction of labor time." See also Paul Balsenq, *La Limitation légale de la journée de travail dans l'industrie française, loi du 30 mars 1900* (Paris, 1910), for a discussion of French business pessimism regarding the possibility of work intensification. A negative assessment of workers' leisure appears in H. Wallon, "Rapport sur la réduction des heures de travail dans les usines et manufactures," *Bulletin de la Société industrielle de Rouen* (1885): 289–91.

26. Cited in Bradlaugh, "Regulation by Statute of the Hours of Labour," p. 443. See also Albert de Mun, *La Question sociale* (Paris, 1878); and Benjamin F. Martin, *Count Albert de Mun* (Chapel Hill, N.C., 1978).

27. Paul Lafargue, *The Right to Be Lazy* (1880; reprint: Chicago, 1907).

28. Webb and Cox, *The Eight Hours Day,* pp. 145–51. Webb explained the omission of "moral" arguments for the eight-hour day when he wrote, "popular opinion is . . . now running so strongly in favour of a general shortening of the hours of labour that complicated social or physiological reasoning on the point is unnecessary." See Sidney Webb, "The Limitation of the Hours of Labour," *Contemporary Review* 56 (December 1889): 866.

29. *Labour Tribune* (June 21, 1890); Rae, *Eight Hours Work,* p. 252; Champion, *Eight Hours Day,* p. 520; RCL, report 3, group B, p. 265; report 2, group B, p. 194; Duffy, "New Unionism," p. 312; and McCormick and Williams, "Miners," p. 241.

30. Mann, "Compulsory Eight Hours," p. 12, and also pp. 13–18, 30. See also, for example, RCL, report 2, group B, pp. 346–47, 362–63; report 2, group C, pp. 41, 387–92; and report 3, group B, pp. 157, 162.

31. Hyndman, "Eight Hours, The Maximum," pp. 267–71; Sidney Webb, *Problems of Industrial Democracy* (London, 1898), pp. 106–35; Webb and Cox, *The Eight Hours Day,* pp. 118–19; Mann, "Compulsory Eight Hours," pp. 1–17; and Rae, *Eight Hours Work,* pp. 318–22.

32. Richard Wilson of the Bradford Power Loom Overlookers Society in RCL, report 2, group C, pp. 12–13.

33. Webb and Cox, *The Eight Hours Day,* pp. 110–13, 118–20; Webb, *Problems,* pp. 128–133; Foote and Shaw, *Hours Question,* pp. 9, 11, 14–17, 22–24; Ramsay, "Eight-Hours," pp. 647–53; and Hubert Thompson, *The*

Theory of Wages and Its Application to the Eight Hours Question (London, 1892), p. viii and chap. 1 on the socialist use of Mill and George. See also John Garraty, *History of Unemployment* (New York, 1978), pp. 70–71, 102, for an interesting discussion of wage fund theory and the theory of employment.

34. Guesde, *Le Problème et la solution: Les huits heures à la chambre* (Paris, 1894); Lafargue, *Right to Be Lazy*, chap. 2; and Victor Delahaye, "Les 8 heures du travail," *Revue socialiste* 10 (1885): 315–28.

35. *Voix du Peuple* (March 26, 1905); CGT, *La Journée de huit heures* (Paris, 1906); and CGT, *La Journée de huit heures dans le bâtiment* (Paris, 1904). See also Louis Neil, *La Journée de 8 heures* (Paris, 1905), pp. 15, 20, 28; and CGT, *Congrès confédéral* (Paris, 1904), p. 214.

36. See, for example, *Voix du Peuple* (November 19, 1904; August 15, 1904; February 19 and April 23, 1905). See also CGT, *Journée*, pp. 5, 6, 14; and Emile Pouget, "La Conquête de la journée de huit heures," *Le Mouvement socialiste* 151 (April 15, 1905): 361.

37. Donnat, *La Réglementation*, pp. 6–7; Paul Boilley, *La Journée de huit heures* (Paris, 1886), pp. 11, 50–53.

38. Boilley, *La Journée*, pp. 53. Indeed this conflict appeared between "re-distributionists" like the anarchist Louis Niel and the "productionists" like Paul Delesalle who, between 1904 and 1906 argued over the impact of shorter hours on employment. See also *Voix du Peuple* (March 26, 1905); and Emile Gautier, *Les Endormeurs: Heures de travail (Propos anarchistes)* (Paris, n.d.), pp. 12, 18.

39. Paul Brissac, "La Réduction de la journée de travail," *Revue socialiste* 15 (1887): 298–305; and Boilley, *La Journée*, pp. 6–7. See also Paul Boilley, "Les 3 huits et la théorie du travail intensif," *Revue socialiste* 2 (1886): 702–15. For French views of American technology, see chapter 5, n. 7.

40. Mann, "Compulsory Eight Hours," pp. 6, 11–12; Ramsay, "Eight Hours Movement," p. 650; Karl Marx, *Capital* (New York, 1967), 1: 407–17.

41. Champion, *Eight Hours Day*, pp. 114–17; Webb and Cox, *The Eight Hours Day*, pp. 150–51; Man, "Compulsory Eight Hours," pp. 6–7; and RCL, report 5, part II, p. 345.

42. CGT, *Journée de huit heures*, p. 1; and *Voix du Peuple* (December 11–18, 1904).

43. George Gunton, *Wealth and Progress* (New York, 1887), pp. 4–5, 11, 21–32, 84, 88, 212, 232–48, 260–66; and Lujo Brentano, *Hours and Wages in Relation to Production* (London, 1894), esp. chap. 1. For further analysis, see Daniel Horowitz, *The Morality of Spending Attitudes toward Consumer Society in America, 1875–1940* (Baltimore, 1985), chap. 3.

44. Guesde, "Journée de huit," p. 25; G. Stedman Jones, *Outcast London* (London, 1971), chaps. 3 and 4; Ministère du Commerce, *Salaire et durée du travail: La Petite industrie* (Paris, 1893); Sidney Webb, ed., *Seasonal Trades*

(London, 1912); and Norman Dearle, *Problems of Unemployment in the London Building Trade* (London, 1908).

45. RCL, report 2, group C, pp. 412–15, 146–47, 356–57; and report 2, group B, pp. 90–91, 136–38.

46. Léon Bonnef and Maurice Bonnef, *La Classe ouvrière* (Paris, 1911), p. 23.

47. Because miners worked on a piece rate, short hours would not only prevent the greedy from producing more than a fair share but also even out the workyear. See *Labour Tribune* (November 28, 1891); and RCL, report 2, group A, p. 88.

48. Amalgamated Society of Engineers (ASE), *Notes on the Lockout* (London, 1898), p. 34. "Final Report of the Amalgamated Committee of the Bookbinding Trade of the Metropolis on the Eight Hours' Movement" (London, 1892), LSE Pamphlet Collection. The issue of overtime continually occupied the negotiations between the engineers and their employers after 1900. See MRC, EFF, H series.

49. Brissac, "La Réduction," p. 298.

50. *Mines (Eight Hours) Bill: Deputation from the Representatives of Miners of the U.K. to Henry Mathews et al.* (London, 1890), pp. 4–5, 9–11, 15; and RCL, report 5, part 2, p. 104.

51. RCL, report 5, part 2, p. 205; report 3, group B, pp. 45, 472–73. The "watch" system is described in *Le Petit parisien* (August 1, 1906) and in correspondence in F^{22} 341.

52. Hodgson, "The Working Day," pp. 31–33, 120–37; and William Whatley, *The Workers' Daily Round* (London, 1913), pp. 101–2.

53. ASE, *Notes on the Lockout*, p. 42; and W. Walker Stephens, *Higher Life for Working People: Its Hindrances Discussed* (London, 1899), pp. 80–81.

54. Niel, *La Journée*, p. 11; *L'Ouvrier métallurgiste* (May 1, 1906); *Voix du Peuple* (December 11, 1904); Perrot, *Les Ouvriers,* 1: 291–92; and Charles Rist, *Réglementation légale de la journée de travail de l'ouvrier adulte en France* (Paris, 1898), p. 139.

55. *Labour Tribune* (February 21, and June 13, 1891).

56. RCL, report 1, group C, pp. 338–39.

57. RCL, report 3, group C, p. 13; Webb and Cox, *The Eight Hours Day,* pp. 152–57; and Charles Coriolon, *Le 1ᵉʳ mai et la journée de 8 heures* (Paris, 1891), preface; *Voix du Peuple* (February 26, 1905). See also Niel, *La Journée,* p. 5, who claimed that differential life expectancies for the poor and the rich were the result of long working hours. Note the impact of technology on worktime demands of French artisans in Hanagan, *Solidarity Artisans,* 66–67.

58. MRC Engineering Employers Federation (EEF), H 4/8–11, EEF Memo, February 1902; in the same file see, H 4/9–11, and H 4/10–11 for additional EFF and ASE conflict over the one-break system, 1902–1907. See

also Horace Allen, "Better Hours for Workmen," *Cassiers' Magazine* (December 1901): 167–68.

59. *Preliminary Report of the Amalgamated Committee of the Bookbinding Trade on the 8 Hours Movement (From December 1890 to June 1891)* (London, 1891), pp. 1–2; and RCL, report 2, group B, pp. 427–28.

60. ASE, *Notes,* p. 34.

61. Jones, *Language of Class,* pp. 205–8, 218–19. See also Standish Meacham, *A Life Apart* (Cambridge, Mass., 1977), chaps. 4 and 5; and Stephens, *Higher Life,* pp. 80–84, 88.

62. RCL, report 5, part 2, p. 104; RCL, report 2, group C, pp. 67–68; and Mann, "Compulsory Eight Hours," p. 13.

63. *Voix du Peuple* (May 1, 1906, and December 10, 1904); Niel, *La Journée,* pp. 5–11; and CGT, *Journée de huit heures,* p. 1.

64. RCL, report 3, group C, p. 17.

65. See chapter 1, n. 19.

66. Benjamin Hunnicutt, "The End to Shorter Hours," *Labor History* 12 (December 1984): 373–404.

67. The results of a membership poll on the issue in 1888 were ambiguous, thanks, according to advocates, to the obstruction of eight-hour opponents in the leadership. TUC, *Report of Proceedings* (1887), pp. 36–38; (1889), pp. 47–48, 54, 56–58; (1890), pp. 48–53; and Duffy, "New Unionism," pp. 307, 313–16.

68. *Congrès national du Parti ouvrier* (Roubaix, 1884), pp. 20–21; Rist, *Réglementation,* pp. 123–27; and Dommanget, *Premier mai,* pp. 51–61.

69. The First International declared that the eight-hour day was the "preliminary condition, without which all further attempts at the improvement and emancipation must prove abortive." It would secure "the possibility of intellectual development, social intercourse, and social and political action." "Resolutions of the First and Third Congress of the International Working Men's Association" (London, 1866 and 1868), LSE, Webb Collection, E.B. 7.

70. In 1886, British delegates to the congress, who were dominated by the conservative Parliamentary Committee of the TUC, balked at this proposal, claiming the lack of a mandate to vote on labor legislation. This attitude, according to Cesar Paepe, "fell like a douche of cold water on the Congress." At the 1888 meeting, the British delegation was divided over the question. Although a majority of the congress supported a resolution favoring legislation (proposed by Tom Mann), British and anarchosyndicalist opposition from Italy remained a serious problem. See *Report of the International Trades Union Congress (Paris, August, 1886)* (London, 1887), pp. 20–21; and *Report of the International Trades Union Congress* (London, 1888), pp. 1–24. Both were found in the LSE, Webb Collection, E.B. XXIV, 51–52.

71. Dommanget, *Premier mai,* pp. 54–56, 62, and 117; Duffy, "Eight

Hour," p. 211; William E. Murphy, *History of the Eight Hours Movement* (Melbourne, 1896 and 1906), 2: 75–81.

72. Of course, delegates sought a number of other protective labor reforms at the same time. Dommanget, *Premier mai,* p. 117; and *Eight Hours Working Day* (December 17, 1889).

73. Dommanget, *Premier mai,* pp. 121–31; and Murphy, *Eight Hours Movement,* 2: 86.

74. *Le Temps* (March 16, 1890); *Le Combat* (May 4, 21, and 26, 1890); *Le Matin* (March 21, 1890); *L'Egalité* (March 17 and 22, May 3, 1890); *Le Figaro* (March 7 and May 2, 1890); and *Le Petit parisien* (May 3, 1890). See file of Mayday petitions in Archives de la Préfecture de Police (PP), B³ 41. Note also Michelle Perrot, "The First of May 1890 in France: The Birth of a Working-Class Ritual," in *The Power of the Past: Essays for Eric Hobsbawm,* ed. Pat Thane, Geoffrey Crossick, and Roderick Floud (Cambridge, 1984), pp. 143–72.

75. *Labour Tribune* (May 10, 1890); *Workman's Times* (May 1, 1891); "The Legal Eight Hours Demonstration in London, a Brief History of the Movement" (London, 1891), LSE Pamphlet Collection; *Star* (May 5, 1890), cited in Hobsbawm, *Turning Point,* p. 111; *Arbeiterzeitung* (May 23, 1890), cited in Lynd, *Eighteen Eighties,* p. 238. See also Alexander Trachtenberg, *The History of May Day,* 7th ed. (New York, 1935); and Frederick Giovanoli, *Die Maifeierbewegung* (Karlsruhe, 1923).

76. See France, ChDoc (January 18, 1890), no. 257, p. 99. Dommanget gives a full account of the decline of the eight-hour agitation in France; see *Premier mai,* pp. 180–200; TUC, *Proceedings* (1891), p. 29, and (1892), p. 22; See also Duffy, "Eight Hours," pp. 346–51; Phelps-Brown, *Growth of Industrial Relations,* chap. 4, esp. pp. 181–90; and *The Times* (August 17, 1892).

77. Hyndman, *Mr. Gladstone and the Eight Hours Law;* Duffy, "Eight Hours," pp. 350–51; and Shaxby, *Interference,* p. 15.

78. In Britain, while major opponents of the legal workday left the Parliamentary Committee in 1891, the trade unionists and members of Parliament Charles Fenwich and John Wilson opposed the miners' eight-hour bill as did Durham and Northumberland miners. Although cotton weavers were won over to the legal approach in 1892 during a major recession, as trade increased in 1894, these workers lost interest. Railway workers were divided over strategy, as were dockers. In an attempt to address this problem, Tom Mann and the Fabians drafted bills that would have allowed workers in any industry to vote inclusion (or alternatively exclusion) from the eight-hour day. This only added to the confusion when the TUC in 1893 voted both for a universal eight-hour law and a resolution allowing voluntary exclusion. Clegg, *British Unions,* pp. 95, 241–43; TUC, *Proceedings* (1893), pp. 5, 25; Rae, *Eight Hours Work,* pp. 322–32; Mann, *The Eight Hour Day;* and Webb, *Problems,* pp. 123–24.

79. *Labour Gazette* (June 1894): 208; (November 1894): 340; and (July

1905): 196; Duffy, "Eight Hours," pp. 346–55; Office du Travail, *Notes sur la journée de huit heures dans les établissements industriels de l'état* (Paris, 1906); Chemins de fer de l'état, *Réglementation du travail des chemins de fer* (Paris, 1901); and J. Couppel du Lude, *La Réglementation et le contrôle de la durée du travail dans les chemins de fer* (Paris, 1905).

80. *Interim Report in Connection with the Eight Hours Movement of the Bookbinding Trade of the Metropolis of London* (London, 1892); and London United Trade Committee of Carpenters and Joiners, "The Eight Hours Movement, 1891" (London, 1892), both at LSE, Webb Collection, E.B. LXXIII. Also RCL, report 2, group C, pp. 263–65; Clegg, *British Unions*, pp. 127, 243–44; and Hodgson, "The Working Day," p. 106. For pessimistic French views regarding the eight-hour day, see Rist, *Réglementation*, pp. 129–30.

81. Hodgson, "The Working Day," pp. 106–8; and Currie, *Industrial Politics*, chap. 2.

82. Peter Stearns, *Lives of Labor* (New York, 1976), pp. 377–78.

83. Among the numerous investigations of the engineers strike are R. O. Clarke, "The Dispute in the British Engineering Industry, 1897–98: An Evaluation," *Economica* 37 (1957): 128–37; Nigel Todd, "Trade Unions and the Engineering Industry Dispute at Barrow-in-Furness, 1897–98," *International Review of Social History* 20 (1975): 33–47; E. Wigham, *The Power to Manage: A History of the Engineering Employers' Federation* (London, 1973), pp. 38–43; Jonathan Zeitlin, "The Labour Strategies of British Engineering Employers, 1890–1922," in *Managerial Strategies and Industrial Relations: An Historical and Comparative Study*, ed. Howard Gospel and Craig Littler (London, 1983); Jeffrey Haydu, "Factory Politics in Britain and the US: Engineers and Machinists, 1914–1919," *Comparative Studies in Society and History* 27 (January 1985): 33–56.

84. ASE, *Notes on the Lockout*, pp. 18, 36–39, 41, 90–91, 100–66. See also n. 83.

85. ASE (George Barnes), "Reply to Col. Dyer," pp. 9, 77, and "Election of the General Secretary," pp. 15–17, both in *Notes on the Lockout;* Federated Engineering and Ship Building Employers, "Freedom to Management: Employers and the 48 Hour Demand," (Glasgow, 1897); and Federated Engineering Employers and Affiliated Trade Unions Joint Committee, "Joint Conference Held in London, 1897," (Glasgow, 1897). These and similar sources are in LSE, Webb Collection, E.B. XLIX.

86. *Eight Hours Movement as Affecting the Iron and Steel Industries* (reprint from the *Iron and Coal Trades Review*) (London, 1898), pp. 3–4, 26, 47–48, 52–53; Engineering Employers' Federation, "48 Hours' Dispute, July 1898 to January 1898," (Glasgow, 1898); and J. Stephen Jeans, "Labour Problems of Today with Special Reference to the Eight Hours Question in the Engineering Industry," (London, 1898). All of the above are pamphlets available at LSE.

87. *Daily Express* (April 1 and 26, 1901); *Evening Standard* (October 29,

1901, and September 5, 1904); and *Bulletin de l'Office de Travail* (January 1902), pp. 19–20, and (November 1903), p. 892. See also Edgard Milhaud, "La Journée de huit heures: Expériences pratiques," *La Revue socialiste* 43 (April 1906): 385–400; and F^{22} 13267 for file on government experiments with eight-hour days.

88. Pouget, "La Conquête," pp. 354–85; CGT, *Congrès national corporatif* (Bourges, 1904), pp. 205–20; *Voix du Peuple* (January 5 and 29, February 5 and 12, April 6, May 14, September 17, and December 12, 1905); and Dommanget, *Premier mai,* pp. 205–20.

89. Section française de l'Internationale ouvrière, *Premier Congrès national: Compte rendu analytique* (Paris, 1905), p. 42; Jean Jaurès, *L'Humanité* (April 16, 1905); Gaston Beaubois, "Le Mouvement des huit heures," *Mouvement socialiste* 173 (April 15, 1906): 428–41; and *Voix du Peuple* (October 10, 1904). See also Peter Stearns, *Revolutionary Syndicalism and French Labor* (New Brunswick, N.J., 1971), pp. 43–45.

90. *Voix du Peuple* (April 1, 2, 28, and 30, May 1 and 3, 1906); F^{22} 13267, Interior Ministry reports, March 29 to June 17, 1906; *Echo de Paris* (March 25, April 2, 7, and 11, 1906); and *L'Intransigeant* (April 16 and 19, 1906). See also A et Z, "Pour la réduction des heures de travail," *La Revue socialiste* (1906): 307–23, 433–51, 718–33; and Maxime Leroy, "La Journée de huit heures," *Revue de Paris* 14 (October 15, 1907): 243–52.

91. *Labour Gazette* (July 1895): 210, 223; (November 1895): 338; and (January 1896): 76; TUC, *Proceedings* (1910), pp. 190–91; Bagwell, *Railwaymen,* pp. 263–65; *Manchester Guardian* (November 4, 1905); *Ironmonger* (January 21, 1905); *Daily Chronicle* (September 29, 1904); *The Times* (September 2, 1904); *Reynold's Weekly Newspaper* (April 19, 1908); and John Hodge, "Conditions in British Iron and Steel Works" (London, 1912), LSE Pamphlet Collection. For details of hours agitation in engineering, see MRC, EEF Papers, 1 H 2/10–20, conferences between the EEF and ASE, 1912–1914; and John T. Brownlie, "The Engineers' Case for an Eight Hours Day" (London, 1914), LSE Pamphlet Collection.

92. "Working Hours in the Printing Trade, Report of the Conference of the Federation of Master Printers and the National Printing and Kindred Trades Federation" (Manchester, 1911), LSE Pamphlet Collection. Concern about speedup and the need for a compensatory reduction of hours to reduce fatigue and to save jobs was expressed at the TUC, *Proceedings* (1911), p. 231, (1912), pp. 50–51, and (1913), pp. 296, 318–19. See also TUC, *Premium Bonus System* (Manchester, 1910); and TUC, "Overtime: To the Officers of the Trade Unions" (London, 1907), both in LSE Pamphlet Collection. See also Bagwell, *Railwaymen,* p. 344; Phelps-Brown, *Industrial Relations,* chap. 6; and George R. Askwith, *Industrial Problems and Disputes* (London, 1920), pp. 353–54.

93. In the final form legislators dropped the earlier proposal for eight hours "bank to bank," producing instead an average of eight and a half hours in the

pits. In addition to McCormick and Williams, "Miners," see Clegg, *British Unions,* pp. 104–5, 242–43, 399, 464–65; Edward Welbourne, *The Miners' Unions of Northumberland and Durham* (Cambridge, 1923), pp. 243–52; Pelling, *Trade Unionism,* pp. 102–3; and J. W. F. Rowe, *Wages and the Coal Industry* (London, 1923), pp. 114–17, 155–69. Some primary sources are *Mines (Eight Hours) Bill, Deputation from Representatives of the Miners of the United Kingdom to Henry Matthews et al.* (London, 1890); RCL, report 5, part 2, p. 53–55; RCL, report 1, group A, pp. 130–33; report 2, group A, pp. 41–52, 70–71, 157–58, 180–83; United Kingdom, Home Department, Miners' Eight Hour Day Committee, *Reports on the Departmental Committee Appointed to Inquire into the Probable Economic Effects of a Limit of Eight Hours to the Working Day of Coal Miners* (London, 1907), 7 vols.; and especially the Webb Trade Union Collection, "Miners' Eight Hour Day," which contains thirteen volumes of newsclippings and published parliamentary hearings on the miners' eight-hour bill, 1901–1908.

Chapter 4. Family Time and Consumption Time: Shop Hours and the Origins of the Weekend

1. See, for example, the amusing popular sociology of the British Sunday, Mass Observation, *Meet Yourself on Sunday* (London, 1947).

2. A 1839 law that closed bars until 1:00 P.M. on Sunday was amended in 1854, extending the time to 3:00 P.M. Peter Richards, *Parliament and Conscience* (London, 1970), pp. 159–78; Monica Hodgson, "The Working Day and Working Week in Victorian England" (M. Phil. thesis, University of London, 1974), pp. 188–90; and Ken Carpenter, ed., *British Labour Struggles, Sunday Work, Seven Pamphlets, 1794–1856* (New York, 1972).

3. Brian Harrison, "The Sunday Trading Riots of 1855," *Historical Journal* 8 (1965): 219–45; and Brian Harrison, *Drink and the Victorians, 1815–1872* (Pittsburgh, 1971). See also Karl Marx and Frederick Engels, *Marx and Engels on Britain* (Moscow, 1953), pp. 415–17.

4. John Wigley, *The Rise and Fall of the Victorian Sunday* (Manchester, 1980).

5. Metropolitan Sunday Rest Association, "An Address to the Inhabitants of the Metropolis" (London, 1859), pp. 2–8; T. C. Horfall, "The Right Use of Sunday" (Ripon Diocesan Conference, 1896); George Holyoake, "The Rich Man's Six, and the Poor Man's One Day: A Letter to Lord Palmerston" (London, 1856)—all three are in Goldsmith Library; C. Hill, "The Day of Rest" (London, 1884), LSE Pamphlet Collection; and Robert Cox, *The Literature of*

the Sabbath Question (Edinburgh, 1865). See also John A. R. Pimlott, *The Englishman's Holiday* (London, 1948), pp. 160–72. Other sources on the British Sabbath include R. L. Greaves, "The Origins of English Sabbatarian Thought," *Sixteenth Century Journal* 21 (1981): 19–37; and Peter Richards, *Parliament and Conscience* (London, 1970).

6. London Society for Promoting the Due Observance of the Lord's Day, "Summary of Statutes for the Observation of the Lord's Day in Force in 1910" (London, 1910), and Society for Promoting Christian Knowledge, "Report of the Sunday Advisory Committee, Oct. 1905" (London, 1906), both in LSE Pamphlet Collection. See also Hodgson, "Working Day," pp. 190–210; and H. L. Stephens, "Sunday Closing in Operation," *Fortnightly Review* (August 1896): 285–90.

7. For background, see Léon Bonneff and Maurice Bonneff, *La Classe ouvrière* (Paris, 1910); Ministère du commerce, *La Petite industrie* I (1896); Conseil supérieur du travail, *Rapports et documents sur la réglementation du travail dans les bureaux et magasins et dans les petites industries de l'alimentation* (Paris, 1901); Ministère du Travail, *Salaires et durée du Travail dans l'industrie française,* 4 vols. (Paris, 1907); and F^{22} 340, Reports on the *repos hebdomodaire* (1889–1902) for the Labor Ministry.

8. A. Artaud, *La Question de l'employée* (Paris, 1909), p. 6; Valentin Viard, *La Réduction de la durée du travail de l'employé* (Paris, 1910), pp. 3–236; *Congrès international du repos du Dimanche 1900, Rapport no. II and III* (Paris, 1900).

9. For background see Georges Dupeux, *La Société française* (Paris, 1970); James McMillan, *Housewife or Harlot: The Place of Women in French Society, 1870–1940* (Brighton, 1981); Maurice Crubellier, *L'Enfance et la jeunesse dans la société française, 1800–1950* (Paris, 1979); and especially Louis Tilly and Joan Scott, *Women, Work, and Family* (New York, 1978), chap. 4.

10. Clive Behagg, "Controlling the Product: Work, Time and the Early Industrial Workforce in Britain, 1800–1850," in *Worktime and Industrialization: An International History,* ed. Gary Cross (Philadelphia, 1989), pp. 41–58; D. A. Reid "The Decline of St. Monday, 1776–1876," *Past and Present* 71 (1976): 77–101; Sidney Pollard, *A History of Labour in Sheffield* (Liverpool, 1959), p. 211; and Hodgson, "Working Day," pp. 176–80.

11. Hodgson, "Working Day," pp. 149–53, 166–71. A good summary of middle-class pressure groups appears in Albert Larking, *History of the Early Closing Association to 1864* (London, 1914), pp. 1–16; John Litwall, *The Half-Holiday Question* (London, 1856), pp. 1–24; and John R. Taylor, *Government, Legal and General Saturday Half Holiday* (London, 1857).

12. See Reid, "St. Monday," and Behagg, "Controlling the Product," for example, for this viewpoint.

13. Only 451 French businesses in 1903 reported granting a shorter workday on Saturday afternoon. These exceptions were concentrated in industries

where workers habitually commuted weekly from rural village homes. Others included a few banking and wholesale houses where management sought for themselves increased personal leisure, especially in the summer, and a few isolated textile firms in Roanne. F[22] 398, Reports of the Inspecteurs divisionnaire to the Minister of Labor 1912–1913; *Bulletin de l'Office du Travail* (March 1903), p. 203; Léon Armbruster, *Le Repos hebdomadaire* (Paris, 1905), chap. 1; Charles Berthomieu, *Du Repos hebdomadaire* (Paris, 1914), pp. 14–15; and R. Chassain de la Plasse, *L'Industrie roannaise et le chômage du Samedi soir* (Roanne, 1879). See also Michelle Perrot, *Les ouvriers en grève: en France* (Paris, 1971), 1: 292.

14. Jeffrey Kaplow, "La Fin de la Saint-Lundi: Etude sur le Paris ouvrier au XIXe siècle," *Le Temps libre* 2 (1980): 107–18.

15. John Dennis, *The Pioneer of Progress or the Early Closing Movement in Relation to the Saturday Half-Holiday and the Early Payment of Wages* (London, 1860), p. 47.

16. James Miller, *Labour Lightened, Not Lost* (London, 1855?), pp. 1–5, 10, 31; and Dennis, *Pioneer*, pp. 4, 10, 30–40.

17. Dennis, *Pioneer*, pp. 51–52, 75–78; Litwall, *Half-Holiday Question*, pp. 1–12; and Colin MacInnes, *Sweet Saturday Night* (London, 1856), pp. 106–23.

18. *Annual Report of the Early Closing Association* (hereafter cited as ECA) (London, 1855), pp. 1–6, in the LSE Library; and R. B. Grindrod, "The Wrongs of Our Youth Or the Evils of the Late Hours System" (London, 1843), Goldsmith Library.

19. Thomas Sutherst, *Death and Disease behind the Counter* (London, 1892).

20. ECA (1855), pp. 9, 15–16, 25–39; (1857), pp. 8–17; (1858), pp. 5–110; and (1860), pp. 22–24. See ECA (1903), p. 9, for a summary of a half-century of achievements.

21. In 1882, North London shops closed at 5:00 P.M. on Thursdays and South London shops did the same on Wednesdays. By 1891, the hour of closure had dropped to 2:00 P.M. or even noon in London, a practice followed by 1893 in eight hundred towns. See ECA (1903), esp. p. 9.

22. Managers required that shop assistants continually stand because otherwise retail employees might "give the customers the impression that there is little business done." This, of course, produced "leg fatigue." Thomas Davis, "Prize Essay on the Evils of Late Hours of Business . . ." (London, 1843), pp. 7–8, 9–10, 18–23, 30–36.

23. Thomas Honibone, "A Work for Early Closing" (London, 1843), pp. 9, 12, 15–16, Goldsmith Library.

24. ECA (1857), pp. 13–15.

25. ECA (1886), pp. 35–38, 43–48; and (1887), pp. 1–3, 7–9, 25–30.

26. While an ECA survey of shopkeepers in October 1886 found that an 8:00 P.M. closing law was supported by a majority of 966 to 832, this was

hardly a ringing endorsement. Tradesmen in working-class districts complained that most of their business took place after 8:00 P.M. Butchers and fruit dealers, dependent upon selling their stock each day, were reluctant to close at a fixed hour. Lubbock responded to this ambiguity with a proposal for an 8:00 P.M. closing on weekdays (10 P.M. on Saturday) and an option for districts and trades to "opt out" of the law upon the vote of two-thirds of affected shop-keepers. This proposal never got out of the select committee in 1886; instead Parliament remained within the bounds of protective legislation—restricting the hours only of the "dependent" work force to a maximum of seventy-four hours. ECA (1887), pp. 43–48; *Report from the Select Committee on the Shop Hours Bill* (June 16, 1892) in Trades Union Congress Archives, HC 1506; and James Marchant, *The Shop Hours Act, 1892* (London, 1892), pp. 1–40.

27. Michael Winstanley, *The Shopkeepers' World, 1830–1914* (Manchester, 1983), pp. 95–100; and William Stephens, *Higher Life for Working People* (London, 1899), p. 95. For additional background, see Philip C. Hoffman, *They Also Serve: The Story of the Shop Workers* (London, 1949); and Simon Rottenberg, "Legislated Early Shop Closing in Britain," *Journal of Law and Economy* 4 (October 1961): 118–30.

28. ECA (1901), pp. 17–19; Hoffman, *They Also Serve*, p. 12; ECA (1904), pp. 10–11, (1905), pp. 5–6, (1913), pp. 3–4; Winstanley, *Shopkeepers' World*, pp. 95–98; *Report from the Select Committee of the House of Lords on the Early Closing of Shops* (London, 1901); and R. A. Leach, *The Shops Act, 1912* (London, 1912).

29. RCL, report 3, group C pp. 418–19, 648; and report 5, part 2, p. 304. Note also ECA (1901), pp. iii–vii, 55, 60–62, 70–93; and ECA, *Report . . . on the Early Closing of Shops* (1901).

30. RCL, report 3, group C, p. 422; ECA (1901), pp. 26–28, 70–71; and Amalgamated Union of Shop Assistants, "Early Closing of Shops: The Attitude of the National Amalgamated Union of Shop Assistants" (London, 1903), LSE Pamphlet Collection.

31. Winstanley, *Shopkeepers' World*, pp. 95–101.

32. RCL report 3, group C, p. 648; and ECA (1901), p. 4.

33. Winstanley, *Shopkeepers' World*, p. 94; Hoffman, *They Also Serve*, p. 9; and Sutherst, *Death and Disease*, pp. 44–45, 50–60, 63–64.

34. Hoffman, *They Also Serve*, pp. 1–4; and Amy Bulley and Margaret Whitley, *Women's Work* (London, 1894), pp. 49–50. Williams Johnson of the Shop Assistants, in 1894, argued that the ECA was merely an educational organization for shopkeepers and did little for the assistants. RCL, report 3, group C, pp. 415–18, 424. For the frustration of the Early Closing Association at enlisting shop assistants into their group, see ECA (1893), p. 11.

35. Because of long hours and the tradition of apprenticeship, many store workers, especially in small specialty shops, lived on the premises. Assistants increasingly saw this as a violation of privacy; in effect, living-in was an exten-

sion of the truck system long in disrepute in production work. Shop assistants complained of having to leave their rooms on Sundays and, when in them, to follow codes of rules that they considered inappropriate for adults. Successful campaigns against the living-in system from 1901 to 1914 gained the support of H. G. Wells, Margaret Bondfield of the Women's Industrial Council, and the *Daily Chronicle*. See Hoffman, *They Also Serve*, pp. 18–48; William Paine, *Shop Slavery and Emancipation* (London, 1912), preface by H. G. Wells; Margaret Bondfield, "Conditions under Which Shop Assistants Work," *Economic Journal* 2 (March 1899): 277–86; and Joseph Hallsworth and R. J. Davies, *The Working Life of Shop Assistants* (London, 1910).

36. Bulley and Whitley, *Women's Work*, pp. 61–62; Hoffman, *They Also Serve*, pp. 1–4. See also *Shop Assistant* (1896–1913), especially in 1912 when clerks picketed shops that violated the 1912 Shops Act. Note also the testimony in RCL, report 3, group C, pp. 417–25. For material dealing with American store clerks, see Gary Cross and Peter Shergold, "We Think We are of the Oppressed: White Collar Work, Gender, and the Grievances of Late Nineteenth Century Women," *Labor History* 28 (Winter 1987): 23–53.

37. ECA (1915), pp. 2–4, 9–10; (1916), pp. 3, 5–6; (1917) pp. 3–5; and "Compulsory Closing, A Clarion Call to the Nation of Shopkeepers" (London, 1917), LSE Pamphlet Collection.

38. ECA (1918), pp. 2–5; (1920), pp. 3–9; and (1921), p. 4.

39. ECA (1926), pp. 2–3, 14–15; and ECA, *Report on the Inquiry into the Working of the Shops (Early Closing) Acts of 1920 and 1921* (London, 1927), pp. 9–12.

40. ECA, *Report . . . Shops* (1927), pp. 33–35, 48; ECA (1929), pp. 10–23; Hoffman, *They Also Serve*, p. 13; and Trades Union Congress Archive, HD 5106, trade union reports on shop assistant hours, 1919–1939. See also *Labour Magazine* (May 1828): 44; TUC, *Proceedings* (1927), pp. 443–45; and National Amalgamated Union of Shop Assistants, Warehousemen, and Clerks, "A 48 Hour Week. Evidence Submitted to the Select Committee of the House of Commons" (London, 1930), pp. 1–10, LSE Pamphlet Collection.

41. ECA (1922), p. 1; (1924), p. 11; and (1925), p. 8.

42. For material on the Sunday rest movement, see the pamphlets of the Congrès international du Repos du Dimanche in F[22] 349. See also Henri de Moly, "La Réglementation du travail en France et les catholiques," *Réforme sociale* 4 (1890): 585–606. Some sources of the Sunday closing movements in other countries are: Dennis Pellibone, "Caesar's Sabbath: The Sunday Law Controversy in the United States, 1879–1892" (Ph.D. dissertation, University of California at Riverside, 1981); and August Bebel, *Die Sonntags-arbeit* (Stuttgart, 1888). For British material, see n. 2.

43. F[22] 340, "Congrès international du repos hebdomadaire au point de vue hygiénique et social" (Paris, 1890), pp. 30–39.

44. F^{22} 340, "Congrès international du repos hebdomadaire au point de vue hygiénique et social" (Paris, 1890), pp. 75, 83–89; and "Repos du Dimanche en France depuis 1889, Rapport I" (Paris, 1890). On social Catholicism, see Antoine Murat, *Le Catholicisme social en France* (Bordeaux, 1980).

45. F^{22} 340, "Congrès international du repos hebdomadaire," pp. 40–43, 126–27. See also M. Blondeln, *Le Repos hebdomadaire* (Paris, 1904), pp. 45–46, 57.

46. René Martinat, *Repos du samedi après-midi dans l'industrie* (Paris, 1911), pp. 6–9, 10–12, 38, 138–39, 169; and F^{22} 340, "Le Repos partiel du samedi considéré comme un acheminement vers le repos absolu du dimanche" (1889). See also Raoul Jay, "Le Repos du dimanche et la nouvelle loi française," *Action Populaire Tract No. 122* (Paris, 1907).

47. Jacques Donzelot, *The Policing of Families* (New York, 1979), pp. 3–96.

48. F^{22} 341, Chamber of Commerce of Cambrai resolution of December 17, 1904, and letter of J. B. Weibel, paper manufacturer of Besançon to the Prefect of Doubs, April 5, 1906.

49. F^{22} 341, resolutions from chambers of commerce, 1904–1905. See also Fédération des industries et commercants français (Jean Cruveilhier), *Rapport sur la proposition de loi relative au repos hebdomadaire* (Paris, 1904).

50. See n. 51. For a careful study of the Parisian shopkeeper, see Phillip Nord, *Paris Shopkeepers and the Politics of Resentment* (Princeton, 1986).

51. For details, see F^{22} 341 for petitions and reports on demonstrations of workers' groups for the *repos hebdomadaire* between 1902 and 1906. See also Viard, *La Réduction,* pp. 48–61, 140–48.

52. F^{22} 341, report of a meeting of Union des commis et comptables de la Gironde, November 28, 1904; and Fédération des employés de France, *Congrès national corporatif* (Lyon, 1907), p. 22; *L'Action* (August 4, 1906).

53. A related campaign was the attempt to end the "watch," waiting required of young seamstresses until 9:00 or even 11:00 P.M. in order to serve customers in the fashionable garment districts of Paris after the theater. *Le Petit Parisien* (August 1, 1906); *Le Ralliement des employés* (April 1905); *Bulletin officiel, Bourse du Travail de Paris* (July 1, 1905); and F^{22} 341, petition of the Employés des Magasins du Havre, April 26, 1905.

54. *La Petite République* (August 25, 1906).

55. *Journal officiel de la République de la France* (April 10, 1907), p. 1230 (circular concerning implementation of *repos hebdomadaire* law of July 13, 1906). See also the press accounts in *Journal* (September 2, 1906); *Le Temps* (July 29, 1906); and *L'Action* (July 31, 1906).

56. France ChDoc (November 20, 1906) no. 440 in F^{22} 340.

57. A detailed file on the actions of the Paris employees is in Archives du Prefect de Police, B^{a} 1542.

58. *Journal des Halles* (September 8, 1906); F^{22} 344, police report on em-

ployees union, December 24, 1906; and Commissionaire de Police report, Nîmes, March 18, 1910.

59. Departmental council petitions are in F²² 340. Space does not allow an analysis of the success of the weekly rest law. These conclusions, however, reflect the contents of F²² 352, 354, and 394, as well as Bª 1543. See also Paul Aubriot, *Les Dérogations au repos collectif du dimanche* (Paris, 1914), pp. 6–7, who calculates that only 30 percent of retailers in 1912 granted the *repos hebdomadaire* to their employees thanks to exclusions in the law; in contrast, 93 percent of the industrial workers benefited from the weekly rest.

60. To facilitate the cleaning and repairing of machines, some employers favored a sixty-hour week with a short day on Saturday. This of course meant an eleven-hour weekday.

61. Raoul Jay, *La Semaine anglaise dans l'industrie du vêtement, la loi du 11 juin 1917* (Paris, 1918), pp. 5–7; Ivan Strohl, *La Réglementation hebdomadaire: Le repos du samedi* (Paris, 1903), pp. 10–14; Ministère du Travail, *Enquête sur la réduction de la durée du travail le samedi (Semaine anglaise)* (hereafter cited as *Semaine anglaise*) (Paris, 1913), pp. vii–ii, ix; F²² 398, labor inspector (Rouen) report, June 12, 1913; and Martinat, *Repos du Samedi*, pp. 137, 140, 177–78.

62. *Semaine anglaise*, pp. ix, iv–iii. See also Pierre Dumas, "La Semaine anglaise," *La Vie ouvrière* (December 20, 1911): 113–14; and Victor Vandeputte, *La Semaine anglaise ou le repos du samedi après-midi dans l'industrie textile* (Lille, 1912).

63. For example, see *Semaine anglaise*, pp. 225, 238–39, 240–45, 250, 252–53.

64. I develop this theme in my "Redefining Workers' Control: Rationalization, Labor Time and Union Politics in France, 1900–1925," in *Work, Community and Power: The Experience of Labor in Europe and America, 1900–1925*, ed. James Cronin and Carmen Sirianni (Philadelphia, 1983), pp. 143–72.

65. *Semaine anglaise*, pp. 240–41.

66. CGT, "Diminuons nos heures de travail, revendiquons la semaine anglaise" (Paris, 1911?); Vandeputte, "La Semaine anglaise"; Alphonse Loyau, "La Semaine anglaise en France dans l'industrie mécanique de la Seine," *La Vie ouvrière* 4 (1912): 369–85; and Edouard Vaillant, *Pour le jour de huit heures et la semaine anglaise* (Paris, 1913). See also Michelle Perrot, "Eloge de la ménagère dans le discours des ouvriers français au XIXᵉ siècle," *Romantisme* 13 (1976): 105–21; and CGT, *Affiches et luttes syndicales de la CGT* (Paris, 1978), for posters and cartoons dealing with this topic.

67. On these themes, see particularly the recent work of Lenard Berlanstein, *The Working People of Paris, 1871–1914* (Baltimore, 1984), chap. 4. For a view somewhat different from mine, see Michael Seidman, "The Birth of the Weekend and the Revolt Against Work," *French Historical Studies* 12 (Fall 1982): 249–76.

Chapter 5. Efficiency and Reform: Work Science, the State, and Time, 1890–1918

1. See, for example, Bernard Moss, *The Origins of the French Labor Movement, 1880–1914: The Socialism of Skilled Workers* (Berkeley, 1976); Jacques Julliard, *Fernand Pelloutier et les origines du syndicalisme d'action directe* (Paris, 1971); and Kathleen Amdur, *Syndicalist Legacy* (Urbana, Ill., 1986). See also Edward Bristow, "The Liberty and Property Defence League and Individualism," *History Journal* 18 (1975): 751–89.

2. Michelle Perrot, "The Three Ages of Industrial Discipline in Nineteenth-Century France," in *Consciousness and Class Experience in Nineteenth-Century Europe,* ed. John Merriman (New York, 1979), pp. 149–68, esp. p. 159.

3. For a most helpful view, see Anson Rabinbach, "The European Science of Work: The Economy of the Body and the End of the Nineteenth Century," in *Work in France,* ed. Steven Kaplan and Cynthia Koepp (Ithaca, N.Y., 1986), pp. 475–513.

4. Perrot, "Three Ages," pp. 149–51.

5. A concise analysis of European Taylorism is Charles S. Maier, "Between Taylorism and Technocracy," *Journal of Contemporary History* 5 (1970): 27–62. Note also Paul Gagnon, "La Vie Future: Some French Responses to the Technological Society," *Journal of European Studies* 6 (1976): 172–89; Yves-Claude Lequin, "Le Taylorisme avant 1914: Réponse technique et idéologique et exigences du monopolisme," *Cahiers d'histoire de l'Institut Maurice Thorez* 16 (1977): 14–36; Aimée Moutet, "Les Origines du système de Taylor en France, le point de vue patronal (1907–1914)," *Le Mouvement social* 93 (October 1975): 15–49; and George Humphreys, *Taylorism in France, 1904–1920: The Impact of Scientific Management on Factory Relations and Society* (New York, 1986).

6. Martin Fine, "Toward Corporatism: The Movement for Capital-Labor Collaboration in France, 1914–1936" (Ph.D. dissertation, University of Wisconsin, 1971), esp. pp. 4–129. See also Michael De Lucia, "The Remaking of French Syndicalism, 1911–1918" (Ph.D. dissertation, Brown University, 1972); and John Godfrey, *Capitalism at War: Industrial Policy and Bureaucracy in France, 1914–1918* (London, 1987).

7. Among the French authors who praise American productivity, see Maurice Waxweiler, "Les Hauts salaires aux Etats-Unis," *Revue sociale et politique* (1894): 237–45; Georges Alfassa, "La Commission industrielle Mosely aux Etats-Unis," *Revue populaire d'économie sociale* (August 1, 1903), pp. 11–45; "L'Enquête industrielle de la Commission Mosely aux Etats-Unis," *Bulletin de l'Office du Travail* (July 1903), pp. 576–80; Georges Blondel, *La France et les marchés du monde* (Paris, 1901); Emile Lavasseur, *L'Ouvrier américain* (Paris,

1898); Paul de Rousiers, *La Vie américaine* (Paris, 1892); and Fimin Roz, *L'Energie américaine* (Paris, 1908). An important essay on the technocratic impulse in French labor before the war is Michelle Perrot, "Le Regard de l'autre: Les Patrons français vus par les ouvriers (1880–1914)," in *Le Patronat de la seconde industrialisation,* ed. Maurice Lévy-Leboyer (Paris, 1979), pp. 293– 306. Influential American sources on the superiority of the American standard include Edward Young, *Labor in Europe and America* (Washington, D.C., 1875); and George Gunton, *Wealth and Progress* (New York, 1887). For a critical assessment of the superiority of the American labor standard, see Peter Shergold, *Working Class Life: The 'American Standard' in Comparative Perspective 1899– 1913* (Pittsburgh, 1982).

8. Among the many studies of scientific management are Samuel Haber, *Efficiency and Uplift: Scientific Management in the Progressive Era, 1890–1920* (Chicago, 1964); Sudhir Kakar, *Frederick Taylor: A Study in Personality and Innovation* (Cambridge, Mass., 1970); and Daniel Nelson, *Frederick W. Taylor and the Rise of Scientific Management* (Madison, Wis., 1980).

9. See Bernard Mottez, *Systèmes de salaire et politiques patronales* (Paris, 1966), for an account of experiments in bonus and piece-rate systems in late nineteenth-century France. See also Moutet, "Les Origines," pp. 16–17; Humphreys, *Taylorism,* pp. 48–58; and James Laux, "Travail et travailleurs dans l'industrie automobile jusqu'en 1914," *Mouvement social* 81 (October 1972): 14–23.

10. Georges de Ram, "Quelques notes sur un essai d'application du système Taylor dans un grand atelier de mécanique française," *Revue de métallurgie* (September 1909): 929–33. See also Patrick Fridenson, *Histoire des usines Renault* (Paris, 1972), pp. 71–72; E. Richié, *La Situation des ouvriers dans l'industrie automobile* (Paris, 1909), pp. 84–91; and J. P. Bardou, J. J. Chanaron, P. Fridenson, and J. Laux, *La Révolution automobile* (Paris, 1977). Sources on the 1913 strike are found in Michelle Collinet, *Esprit du syndicalisme* (Paris, 1950), pp. 41–47; Fridenson, *Histoire des usines,* pp. 73–78; Laux, "Travail," pp. 25–26; Moutet, "Les Origines," pp. 41–43.

11. Emile Pouget, *L'Organisation du surmenage* (Paris, 1914), pp. 53–54; and A. Merrheim, "Le Système Taylor," *La Vie ouvrière* (March 5, 1913): 309, and (February 20, 1913): 214 and 224. Pierre Coupat of the Fédération des mécaniciens de la Seine in 1906 also denounced the increasing specialization of work and the decline of long apprenticeships. See P. Coupat, "L'Enseignement professionel," *Revue syndicaliste* (December 1906): 84.

12. See n. 10 above. See also Jacques Rancière, "The Myth of the Artisan: Critical Reflection on a Category of Social History," in Kaplan and Koepp, *Work in France,* pp. 317–34.

13. Adophe Loyau, "Les Conditions de travail dans la mécanique," *Revue syndicaliste* (August 1907): 84; Victor Griffuelhes, "L'Infériorité du capitalisme français," *Mouvement socialiste* 28 (December 1910): 329–33; and Léon

Jouhaux, *La Bataille syndicaliste* (July 3, 1911). See also Bernard Georges and Denis Tintant, *Léon Jouhaux* (Paris, 1962), 1: 72–77.

14. Frederick W. Taylor, *The Principles of Scientific Management* (New York, 1967), pp. 19–24; and Frederick Taylor, "Testimony before the Special House Committee," in *Scientific Management* (New York, 1947), pp. 24–30.

15. Ervin Szabo, "Principes d'organisation scientifique des usines," *Le Mouvement socialiste* (January–February 1913): 128–32; and Griffuelhes, "L'Infériorité," pp. 329–33.

16. A. Merrheim, "Le Système Taylor," p. 304.

17. Collinet, *Syndicalisme,* pp. 44–45 and Christian Gras, "Fédération des Métaux en 1913–1914 et l'évolution du syndicalisme révolutionnaire français," *Le Mouvement social* 77 (October–December 1971): 98–101.

18. J. M. Lahy, "Le Système Taylor et l'organisation des usines," *Revue socialiste* (August 1913): 126–38; and J. M. Lahy, "L'Etude scientifique des mouvements et le chronométrage," *Revue socialiste* (December 1913): 501–20. See also J. M. Lahy, *Le Système Taylor* (Paris, 1916).

19. Bernard Thumen, "Organisons la production," *Cahiers du Redressement français* 2 (1927): 32–37. See also Bertrand Thompson, *Le Système Taylor* (Paris, 1916); and Bertrand Thompson, *L'Organisation des usines* (Paris, 1926), especially the preface. The engineering journal *Le Génie civil* became a vehicle of Taylorism in France during the war. Note, for example, *Le Génie civil* (November 4, 1916): 315; and (November 10, 1917): 307. Especially useful here is Humphreys, *Taylorism,* pp. 145–84.

20. Roger Picard, *Le Mouvement syndical durant la guerre* (Paris, 1928), pp. 58–72; "Rapport sur l'action générale de la CGT depuis août 1914," *Voix du Peuple* (December 1916): 7; Léon Jouhaux, *Les Travailleurs devant la paix* (Paris, 1918); and Georges and Tinant, *Jouhaux,* pp. 153–85.

21. William Oualid, *Salaires et tarifs* (Paris, 1929), pp. 90, 97; and D. Yovanovitch, *Le Rendement optimum du travail ouvrier* (Paris, 1923), pp. 238–40. For two studies on Thomas's role in the war industries, see Alain Hennebicque, "Albert Thomas et le régime des usines de guerre, 1915–1917," and Gerd Hardach, "La mobilisation industrielle en 1914–1918: Production, planification, et idéologie," in *1914–1918: L'Autre front,* ed. Patrick Fridenson (Paris, 1977), pp. 111–44 and 81–109. For other background on Thomas, see Martin Fine, "Albert Thomas: A Reformer's Vision of Modernization," *Journal of Contemporary History* 12 (July 1977): 545–64; Patrick Fridenson and M. Reberioux, "Albert Thomas, pivot du réformisme," *Le Mouvement social* 87 (April–June 1974): 85–98; and Thomas Schaper, *Albert Thomas, trente ans de réformisme social* (Assen, 1959).

22. *Bulletin des usines de guerre* (April 4, 1917): 273. See also François Bayle, *Les Salaires ouvriers et la richesse nationale, La Méthode de Taylor et le salaire moderne: Application à la fabrication du matériel de guerre* (Paris, 1919), pp. 41, 44–45.

23. *Le Génie civil* (February 8, 1919): 177–81; (February 15, 1919): 137; and (October 18, 1919): 179–80; Fridenson, *Histoire des usines,* p. 57; and André Citroën, "L'Avenir de la construction automobile," *Revue politique et parlementaire* (May 10, 1929): 241. Henri Le Châtelier, for example, claimed in 1919 that "there is no industrialist in France . . . rigorously applying the Taylor system." See *Information sociale et ouvrière* (September 14, 1919). See also Aimée Moutet, "Patrons de progrès ou patrons de combat? La Politique de rationalisation de l'industrie française au lendemain de la Première guerre mondiale," in *Recherches (Soldat du travail),* ed. Léon Marard and Patrick Zylberman (Paris, 1978), pp. 454–55, 476–86.

24. CGT, "Le Programme minimum de la CGT" (December 15, 1918), in *La Confédération générale du travail et le mouvement syndical* (Paris, 1925), pp. 165–71.

25. CGT, *Congrès national corporatif, compte rendu* (Paris, 1918), pp. 234, 184–92. See *Information ouvrière et sociale* (January 11, 1920) for a description of the National Labor council. A good recent analysis appears in Richard Kuisel, *Capitalism and the State in Modern France* (New York, 1981), pp. 59–69.

26. Rabinbach, "European Science of Work," pp. 472–94; R. Ribeill, "Les Débuts de l'ergonomie en France à la veille de la première guerre mondiale," *Le Mouvement social* 113 (February–April 1980): 3–26. For differences between work science and Taylorism, see Jules Amar and Armand Imbert, "A Propos du système Taylor," *La Technique moderne* (November 1, 1913), pp. 1–12.

27. Axel Honneth, "Work and Instrumental Action," *New German Critique* 26 (Spring 1982): 38–39; and Angelo Mosso, *Fatigue* (London, 1904), pp. 152–54, 172. Other major sources are Yovanovitch, *Le Rendement;* and Jules Amar, *Le Rendement de la machine humaine* (Paris, 1910).

28. Rabinbach, "European Science of Work," p. 498; and Jules Amar, *Le Moteur humain et les bases scientifiques du travail professionnel* (Paris, 1914), pp. 675–76. See also Maurice Anxiaux, *Heures de travail et salaires* (Paris, 1896); and J. C. Fromont, *Une Expérience industrielle de réduction de la journée de travail* (Brussels, 1906). For business proponents of shortening hours to increase output, see William Mather, "The Eight Hour Day: Report on a Year's Experiment and Its Results at the Salford Iron Works" (Manchester, 1894), LSE Pamphlet Collection; and Robert Hadfield and Henry Gibbons, *A Shorter Working Day* (London, 1892), pp. 135–54.

29. Important works by Jean Lahy include, "Recherches sur les conditions du travail des ouvriers typographes composant à la machine dite linotype," *Bulletin de l'inspection du travail* (1910), p. 98; and *Le Système Taylor et la physiologie du travail professionnel* (Paris, 1916). Armand Imbert's ideas are in "Congrès ouvriers et Congrès scientifiques," *Revue scientifique* (May 13, 1905): 234; "Statistique d'accident du travail," *Revue scientifique* (October 21, 1905): 526; and "Le Surmenage par suite du travail professionnel au XIVᵉ Congrès inter-

national d'hygiène et de démographie (Berlin, 1907)," *Année psychologique* 14 (1907): 232–48. See also Ribeill, "Les Débuts," pp. 32–33; and Rabinbach, "European Science of Work," pp. 498, 507.

30. Ilia Sachnine, *L'Influence de la durée du travail quotidien sur la santé générale de l'adulte* (Lyon, 1900); and Marc Pierrot, *Travail et surmenage* (Paris, 1911). See also E. Vaillant's bill, France, ChDoc (June 27, 1898), no. 115, pp. 1297–1302, which fully documents the efficiencies in British engineering firms that had adopted the one-break system. In his subsequent bill ChDoc (November 5, 1906), no. 374, pp. 58–60, he stressed the language of fatigue science in justification of an eight-hour law.

31. See, for example, Arthur Shadwell, *Industrial Efficiency: A Comparative Study of Industrial Life in England, Germany, and America* (London, 1909); Aimee Smyth Watt, *Physical Deterioration* (London, 1904); Charles Myers, *Industrial Psychology in Great Britain* (London, 1926); Charles Myers, *Mind and Work* (London, 1920); P. Sargant Florence, *Economics of Fatigue and Unrest: The Efficiency of Labor in England and American Industry* (London, 1924); and Joseph Ioteyko, *The Science of Labour and Its Organisation* (London, 1919).

32. Amar, *Le Moteur humain,* pp. 609–15, 675–76; A. Imbert, *Le Système Taylor* (Paris, 1920); and Lahy, *Le Système Taylor.*

33. Mosso, *Fatigue,* pp. 272, 299; Ribeill, "Les Débuts," pp. 25–33; and Josephine Goldmark, *Fatigue and Efficiency* (New York, 1912). Note also Florence Kelley, *Women in Industry: The Eight Hour Day and Rest at Night Upheld by the U.S. Supreme Court* (New York, 1916); and Felix Frankfurter, *The Case for the Shorter Workday* (New York, 1916).

34. Richard Soloway, "Counting the Degenerates: The Statistics of Race Deterioration in Edwardian England," *Journal of Contemporary History* 17 (January 1982): 136–64. See also in the same issue Robert Nye, "Degeneration, Neurasthenia and the Culture of Sport in Bell Epoque France," pp. 51–68. Contemporary sources include C. Morgan Webb (Standing Joint Committee of the Independent Labour Party), "The Eight Hours Day" (London, 1912), LSE Pamphlet Collection; and E. F. Stanley Kent, "An Investigation of Industrial Fatigue by Physiological Means: Interim Report," BPP (1911), XXIV, Cd. 8056.

35. Sachnine, *L'Influence,* pp. 1–20, 131, 141, 148–67, 191–202, 248–62; Pierrot, *Travail,* pp. 9–12. See also Goldmark, *Fatigue,* chaps. 2–3; Ligue française d'éducation morale (Jules Hayaux), *L'Education antialcoolique dans les milieux ouvriers* (Paris, 1913), p. 16; and Sidney Webb and Harold Cox, *Eight Hours Working Day* (London, 1891), pp. 143–44.

36. Amar, *Le Moteur humain,* pp. 295–301; Pierrot, *Travail,* pp. 17–19.

37. Goldmark, *Fatigue,* chaps. 1–3; Pierrot, *Travail,* p. 37.

38. PRO, LAB 2 427/1, "The Effect on Output of a Short Working Week in Trades Employing Women and Girls," by C. E. Collet for the Ministry of Labour (August 1914), pp. 1–9, 17–19, 23–25, 32–39, 55–56. Some of the

responses (which were not systematically gathered) denied that reduced hours could be generalized (because firms offering short hours retained the best workers) and doubted whether piece workers would accept hour maximums (e.g., see pp. 37, 40–41, 53).

39. PRO LAB 2 427/1, "The Effect on Output," pp. 23–25, 32–36.

40. "Annual Report of the Chief Inspector of Factories," BPP (1914–1916), vol. 21, p. 38.

41. PRO MUN 144/1, "Report of the Work of the Munitions Act" (September 11, 1915), and "Notes Affecting the Supply of Munitions" (July 3, 1916); Ministry of Munitions, "Report on Bad Time Keeping," BPP (1914–1916), vol. 40, pp. 1–4; PRO MUN 5/91 345/3, Correspondence from employers, 1915–1916; PRO MISC 144, v. 1, "Second Report of the Armament Output Committee" (May 13, 1915); and PRO HO 45/10734, Home Office memo (September 3, 1914).

42. Department of Education, "Munitions Holidays in Relays, Minutes of Evidence" (August 1, 1916), pp. 4–9, and (August 3, 1916), pp. 3–5, 42 (available at LSE); PRO MISC 1/1 "Glasgow and West of Scotland Armament Committee" (May 15, 1915); and PRO MUN 5/91 345/112, Ministry of Munitions memo (January 22, 1918). For similar material see Richard Croucher, *Engineers at War, 1939–1945* (London, 1982).

43. Health of Munitions Workers Committee (HMWC) "Report," BPP (1918), vol. 12, pp. 7–44, esp. p. 18.

44. HMWC, "Report," BPP (1918), vol. 12, pp. 23–28; and PRO LAB 2 254/8 "Commission of Enquiry into Industrial Unrest" (1917), pp. 4–5, 9.

45. PRO MUN 5/91 345/1, "Lost Time in Controlled Establishments" (May 27, 1916), and MUN 5/91 345/3, "Report on Bad Timekeeping" (October 1917), pp. 2–4. See also Health of Munitions Workers' Committee, "Report and Statistics of Bad Time Kept in Shipbuilding, Munitions, and Transportation Areas," BPP (1914–1916), vol. 40, p. 947.

46. PRO MISC 144, vol. 3, "Report of the Work of the Munitions Act" (September 11, 1915).

47. Ethel Osborne, Industrial Health (Fatigue) Research Board (IFRB), "Output of Women Workers in Relation to Hours of Work in Shell-making," *Report No. 1* (London, 1919), esp. pp. 6–9. H. M. Vernon, IFRB, "The Influence of Hours of Work and of Ventilation on Output in Tinplate Manufacture," *Report No. 1* (London, 1919), p. 29; HMWC, "Report," BPP (1918), vol. 12, pp. 45–48; HMWC, "Memorandum No. 5," BPP (1916), vol. 23, p. 449; and "Memorandum No. 12," BPP (1916), vol. 23, p. 501. Summaries of these memoranda are in "Annual Report of the Chief Inspector of Factories," BPP (1917–1918), vol. 20, p. 5.

48. HMWC, "Memorandum No. 5," p. 449; *Labour Gazette* (December 1917): 438; and MUN 343/100, "Health of Labour Committee Report" (August 24, 1917).

49. HMWC, "Final Report," BPP (1918), vol. 12, pp. 40–42; and "Annual Report of the Chief Factory Inspector," BPP (1917–1918), vol. 14, p. 161.

50. HMWC, "Final Report," pp. 42–43; and Board of Education, "Munitions Holidays" (August 3, 1916), pp. 75–93, and (August 6, 1916), pp. 6–9.

51. PRO MUN 5/90 342/100, Hours of Labour Committee Reports (May 11, November 22, December 6, 1916; January 23, March 20, May 19, June 11, 1917).

52. PRO MUN 5/90 343/100, Hours of Labour Committee reports (November 11, 1916; September 28, November 2 and 22, 1917; and February 23, 1918). MRC Engineering Employers' Federation (EEF), H 3/1, correspondence with Churchill (November–December 1917); and MCR EEF H 3/2, memo on the "Subcommittee for Postwar Problems" (November 11, 1917). See correspondence in MRC EEF H 3/9 for follow-up.

53. "Annual Report of the Chief Inspector of Factories," BPP (1919), vol. 22, pp. 2–3, 22–24; and "Report . . . on the Employment . . . on the Two Shift System," BPP (1920), vol. 19, pp. 12, 22. PRO LAB 2 821/9, Labour Ministry memo concerning the two-break system (July 1917); and PRO MUN 90/5 343/100, Hours of Labour Committee memo (September 24, 1917).

54. PRO MUN 144/3; in an undated memo, the Ministry of Munitions Welfare Department encouraged Welfare Supervisors to read HMWC memos as well as classic works in fatigue science by J. Goldmark and Arthur Shadwell, B. A. Whitlegge, and N. A. Brisco.

55. Lord Leverhulme, *The Six Hour Day* (London, 1918), pp. 5–8, 12, 28–29. See also Charles Myers, *Mind and Work,* pp. 162–74; and B. Seebohm Rowntree, *The Human Factor in Business,* 3rd ed. (London, 1937), pp. 16, 91.

56. Carter Goodrich, *The Frontier of Control* (London, 1920), pp. 173–74, 180–200, 204–9.

57. Judith Stone, *The Search for Social Peace: Reform Legislation in France, 1890–1914* (Albany, 1985), chap. 1; Sanford Elwitt, "Politics and Ideology in the French Labor Movement," *Journal of Modern History* 49 (1977): 468–70; and *The Third Republic Defended: Bourgeois Reform in France, 1880–1914* (Baton Rouge, 1986), esp. pp. 170–216. Anson Rabinbach, "Knowledge, Fatigue and the Politics of Industrial Accidents," paper presented to the Social Science History Association, Chicago, November 1985. Note also James Kloppenberg, *Uncertain Victory: Social Democracy and Progressivism in European and American Thought, 1870–1920* (Oxford, 1986).

58. Another important journal was *Questions pratiques de législation ouvrière et d'économie sociale* (from 1899). Other reformers were frequent contributors to mainline journals like *Revue politique et parlementaire.* For a useful discussion, see Stone, *Social Peace,* pp. 50–53, 201–5. Another example of this tradition is René Lavollée, *Les Classes ouvrières en Europe,* 3 vols., 2nd ed. (Paris, 1884–1896).

59. Other reformist institutions, including the Conseil supérieur du Travail (from 1900), a consultative committee representing business, labor, and politicians, and the Musée social (1895), included advocates of legislative reform. Elwitt, "Politics and Ideology," pp. 148–58; Stone, *Social Peace,* pp. 50–53. Parker James Moon, *The Labor Problem and the Social Catholic Movement in France* (New York, 1921), pp. 94–108, 170–83; Raoul Jay, *La Limitation légale de la journée de travail en France* (Paris, 1904), p. 215; Paul Ourmet, *Le Contrôle de la durée du travail* (Paris, 1910), pp. 26–27. Ministère du Travail, *Notes sur la journée de huit heures dans les établissements industriels de l'Etat* (Paris, 1907), pp. 8–41; "Etude sur l'influence de la réduction de la journée de travail sur le rendement industriel," *Bulletin de l'Inspection du Travail* 9 (1902): 397. Sources on the Office (Ministry) of Labor include Jean Tournierie, *Le Ministère du Travail, origines et premiers développements* (Paris, 1971); and Albert Peyronnet, *Le Ministère du Travail, 1906–1923* (Paris, 1923).

60. Raoul Jay, *La Protection légale des travailleurs* (Paris, 1910), pp. 46, 144–45; and Stone, *Social Peace,* pp. 15, 23. See also Arthur Fontaine, *Les Grèves et la conciliation* (Paris, 1897); and Paul Boncour, *Le Fédéralisme économique* (Paris, 1901).

61. Jay, *La Protection,* pp. 144–45, 156.

62. A. Maurice, *La Réglementation de la durée du travail des employés de chemins de fer* (Paris, 1960), chap. 1; and Charles Rist, *Réglementation légale de la journée de travail de l'ouvrier adulte en France* (Paris, 1898), chap. 1, on the invalidity of adult/minor distinction.

63. Some useful sources in this immense literature are John Rae, *Eight Hours for Work* (London, 1897); Victorine Jeans, *Factory Act Legislation* (London, 1892); Frederic Merttens, "The Hours and the Cost of Labour in the Cotton Industry," *Transactions of the Manchester Statistical Society* (1893–1894): 125–90; G. H. Wood, "Factory Legislation Considered with Reference to the Wages . . . of the Operatives Protected Thereby," *Journal of the Royal Statistical Society* 65 (June 1902): 284–320; Joseph Munro, "The Probable Effects of an Eight-Hours Day on the Production of Coal and the Wages of Miners," *Economic Journal* 1 (June 1891): 241–61; and William Stanley Jevons, *The State in Relation to Labour* (London, 1882), chap. 3. See also A. Fox, *History and Heritage: The Social Origins of the British Industrial Relations System* (London, 1985), pp. 246–308; and Pat Thane, *Foundations of the Welfare State* (London, 1981).

64. H. E. Phelps Brown, *The Growth of British Industrial Relations* (London, 1955), chap. 5; and Frank Wilkinson, "The Development of Collective Bargaining in Britain to the Early 1920s," King's College Research Center, Shop Floor Bargaining Seminar, March 2, 1981. See also Rodney Lowe, *Adjusting to Democracy: The Role of the Ministry of Labour in British Politics, 1916–1939* (Oxford, 1986).

65. Between 1907 and 1914, five bills for the legal eight-hour day were in-

troduced into Parliament: BPP (1907), vol. 2; (1908), vol. 2; (1912–1913), vol. 1; (1913), vol. 2; (1914), vol. 2.

66. Thomas Brassey in his two works, *Foreign Work and English Wages* (London, 1879), pp. 189–92, 303, and *On Work and Wages* (London, 1873), pp. 152–53, finds the superior productivity of British labor sufficient to withstand the competition despite a nine-hour day. Compare this with the pessimistic conclusions of J. S. Jeans, *The Eight Hours Day in British Engineering Industries: An Examination and Criticism of Recent Experiments* (London, 1894). Of course there were liberal and business supporters of the eight-hour day in Britain in the 1890s: William Mather, "Labour and the Hours of Labour," *Contemporary Review* 72 (1894): 609–31; William Mather, *The 48 Hours Week: A Year's Experiment and Its Results at the Salford Iron Works* (Manchester, 1894); and Sidney Chapman, *Work and Wages: Social Betterment* (London, 1914). Yet these progressives had little influence with the new associations like the Engineering Employers' Federation.

67. Joseph Schumpeter, *History of Economic Analysis* (New York, 1954), pp. 811–12; George Barnes, *History of the International Labour Office* (London, 1926), pp. 28–29; Benoît Malon, *Le Socialisme intégral* (Paris, 1894) 2: 80; and Moon, *Labor Problem*, pp. 123–39.

68. Malon, *Le Socialisme intégral*, 2: 82–85.

69. *Conférence internationale concernant le règlement du travail aux établissements industriels et dans les mines* (Leipzig, 1890), pp. 13–14; Justin Godart, *Les Clauses du travail dans le Traité de Versailles* (Paris, 1920) pp. 24–32; Malon, *Le Socialisme intégral*, pp. 90–91; H. Van Zanten, *L'Influence de la Partie XIII du Traité de Versailles sur le développement du droit international public et sur le droit interne des états* (Leiden, 1927), pp. 2–3; and Armand Julin, "Des Limitations naturelles aux lois internationales ouvrières," *Réforme sociale* 10 (1890): 193–200. See also Wilhelm II, *Ansprachen und Erlasse S.M. des Kaisers Wilhelm II* (Leipzig, 1891), pp. 72–76.

70. Stone, *Social Peace*, pp. 53–55, 206; Zanten, *L'Influence*, pp. 4–8; Georges Alfassa, "La Durée du travail et l'association nationale française pour la protection légale des travailleurs," *Revue Politique d'économie sociale* (1905): 11–45; International Association for Labour Legislation, British Section, "The International Association for Labour Legislation" (London, 1914), p. 1; and Association internationale pour la protection légale des travailleurs, *Deux mémoires présentés aux gouvernements des états industriels en vue de la convocation d'un conférence internationale de protection ouvrière* (Paris, 1905), p. 49, both in the LSE Pamphlet Collection. See also Paul Balsenq, *La Limitation légale de la journée de travail dans l'industrie française, Loi du 30 mars 1900* (Paris, 1910), p. 25; and the official journal of the Basel office, *Bulletin of the International Labour Office* (1906–1919).

71. Barnes, *History*, pp. 31–35; Godart, *Les Clauses*, p. 37; and especially Etienne Bauer, *Rapport présenté au Congrès mondial de l'Association internationale*

pour la protection légale des travailleurs: Origines, organisations, oeuvre realisée, documents (Brussels, 1910).

72. Paul Boulin (Association internationale pour la protection légale des travailleurs), *L'Organisation du travail dans les usines à feu continu* (Paris, 1912), pp. 1–14; and Arthur Crosfield, *A Plea for the Eight-Hours Day in Continuous Processes* (London, 1912). See also Paul Fromont, *Une Expérience,* esp. chap. 1. For a detailed account of the history of working hours in iron and steel, see Marsha Shields, "Collective Choice in Labor Markets. Hours Reduction in British and US Iron and Steel Industries, 1890–1923" (unpublished paper).

73. Lujo Brentano, "La Réglementation internationale de l'industrie," *Revue d'économie politique* 4 (1892): 105–26, esp. 122–24. See also Julin, "Des Limitations," pp. 202–14. Vaillant's eight-hour bills are in France ChDoc (June 27, 1898), no. 115; (November 17, 1910), no. 469.

74. PRO LAB 2 682/5, Report of the Silk Joint Industrial Council (December 19, 1918); PRO CAB 24 71, Bessborough letter to the Prime Minister (December 9, 1918); PRO MUN 5/90/343/110, Report of Hours of Labour Committee (November 20, 1916); and PRO CAB 24/73, Horne's report on the "Labour Situation" (January 1, 1919).

75. Reports in F²² 401 from the inspecteurs du travail (January 1919).

Chapter 6. Labor Insurgency, International Reform, and the Origins of the Eight-Hour Day, 1917–1924

1. Charles Tilly and Edward Shorter, *Strikes in France* (New York, 1974), pp. 66–68, 190; Peter Stearns, *Lives of Labor* (New York, 1976), pp. 252–57; Michelle Perrot, *Les Ouvriers en grève: France, 1871–1890* (Paris, 1974), 1: 260–63, 284; and E. H. Phelps-Brown, *A Century of Pay* (London, 1968), p. 208.

2. James Cronin, "Labor Insurgency and Class Formation: Comparative Perspectives on the Crisis of 1917–1920 in Europe," in *Work, Community and Power, the Experience of Labor in Europe and America, 1900–1925,* ed. James Cronin and Carmen Sirianni (Philadelphia, 1983), pp. 20–41; and Charles Bertrand, ed., *Revolutionary Situations in Europe, 1917–1922* (Montreal, 1977).

3. For example, see James Hinton, *The First Shop Steward Movement* (London, 1973). For France, see Anne Kriegel, *Aux origines du communisme français: 1914–1920* (Paris, 1964), 1: 193–351; Adrien Jones, "The French Railway Strikes of January–May 1920: New Syndicalist Ideas and Emergent Communism," *French Historical Studies* 12 (Spring 1982): 508–40.

4. Charles Maier, *Recasting Bourgeois Europe* (Princeton, 1975); and Dan Silverman, *Reconstructing Europe after the Great War* (Cambridge, Mass., 1982).

For an important analysis of the origins of the full reformist program, see John Horne, *Labour Reformism in France and Britain during the First World War* (forthcoming).

5. *Journal officiel de la République de la France, Lois et décrets* (April 25, 1919), p. 4266. For details, see Jean Beaudemoulin, *Enquête sur les loisirs des ouvriers français* (Paris, 1924), pp. 28–95; and Direction du Travail, *Travaux préparatoires de la loi du 23 avril 1919 sur la journée de huit heures* (Paris, 1919).

6. Justin Godart, *Les Clauses du travail dans le Traité de Versailles* (Paris, 1920), chap. 2. See also Horne, *Labour Reformism,* chaps. 4 and 5, who notes that the universal eight-hour day became the postwar demand of the CGT in December 1916 and was adopted by international trade union conclaves in 1917.

7. N. McKillop, *The Lighted Flame* (London, 1950), p. 113; Philip Bagwell, *The Railwaymen* (London, 1963), p. 365; *Daily Herald* (May 4, June 22, and October 19, 1918); PRO, CAB 24/67 "Labour Situation" (October 16, 1918); CAB 24/68, "Lab. Sit." (October 23, 1918); and CAB 24/74, "Lab. Sit." (February 5, 1919).

8. P. Dumas, "La Semaine anglaise en France," *Information sociale et ouvrière* (February 16, March 2 and 20, 1919); and James McMillan, *Housewives or Harlots* (London, 1981), pp. 153–56.

9. France, ChDoc, no. 5600 (January 28, 1919), p. 146.

10. See, for example, France, ChDoc, no. 5600 (January 28, 1919), p. 146; and Federation of Engineering and Shipbuilding Trades of the UK and ASE, *Application for the 44-Hour Week* (London, 1919), p. 7.

11. "Le programme minimum de la CGT," in CGT, *La Confédération générale du travail et le mouvement syndical* (Paris, 1925), pp. 165–66.

12. See chapter 5, nn. 20–22. See also G. D. H. Cole's rather hostile views of the "cult" of scientific management in *Labour Yearbook* (London, 1919), pp. 257–59.

13. See, for example, Board of Education, "Munitions Holidays in Relays, Minutes of Evidence" (August 3, 1916), pp. 75–87; typed copy at the LSE.

14. See chapter 5, nn. 54–56. MRC EEF H3/1 Memo by EFF chairman, Allen Smith (November 10, 1917); and MRC EEF H3/9 on EEF preparations for the reduction of worktime in 1918.

15. Ministry of Labour, *Industrial Report, no. 1, The Whitley Report* (London, 1917). See also PRO LAB 2 289/11/14 and LAB 2 299/7.

16. See chapter 5, n. 22; and CGT, "Le Programme minimum de la CGT," p. 165. For an analysis that finds that Thomas and the CGT developed independent and somewhat different commitments to the linkage of technology and social reform, see John Horne, "Le Comité d'Action (CGT-PS) et l'origine du réformisme syndical du temps de guerre (1914–1916)," *Le Mouvement social* (January–March 1983): 33–61.

17. See William Oualid, *Salaires et tarifs* (Paris, 1929), pp. 90–97, for an account by an assistant of Thomas. An important comparison of the impact of

the war on French and British industrial relations is in Duncan Gallie, *Social Inequality and Class Radicalism in France and Britain* (Cambridge, 1983). See also Horne, *Labour Reformism,* chap. 7; and Adrian Rossiter, "Experiments with Corporatist Politics in Republican France, 1916–1939" (Ph.D. dissertation, University of Oxford, 1986).

18. A. Merrheim, *Information ouvrière et sociale* (May 4, 1919). See also Kriegel, *Aux origines du communisme,* 1: 193–351; Robert Wohl, *French Communism in the Making* (Stanford, 1966); Max Gallo, "Quelques aspects de la mentalité et du comportement ouvriers dans les usines de guerre, 1914–1919," *Le Mouvement social* 56 (July–September 1966): 3–33; and Horne, "Le Comité d'Action," pp. 33–60.

19. F²² 318, "Recueil des Actes de la Conférénce de la Paix: Commission de législation internationale du travail" (1922), pp. 27–71; F²² 401, Report of the "Commission de législation internationale du travail" (no date); F²² 402, Ministry of Labor report (November 19, 1921); and 41 AS 12, Circulars of the Union des industries métallurgiques et minières, no. 1112–13 and 1136, for 1919.

20. George Barnes, *History of the International Labour Office* (London, 1926), pp. xi–xii, 39, 59; and PRO CAB 24/78, "Lab. Sit." (April 23, 1919, and May 7, 1919).

21. Godart, *Les Clauses,* pp. 5–6, 10–13.

22. Barnes, *History,* pp. 36–37; Godart, *Clauses,* pp. 32, 65. See also Louis Pasquet, *La Loi sur la journée de huit heures* (Lyon, 1921), pp. 20–21; and Georges Alfassa, "La Durée du travail et l'Association nationale française pour la protection légale des travailleurs," *Revue politique d'économie sociale* (1905): 11–45. Consider also the *Bulletin de l'Office international du travail* (1901–1914), and *Documents du travail* (1917–1922).

23. France ChDoc, no. 5050 (October 8, 1918), and no. 5305 (November 26, 1918); and Godart, *Clauses,* pp. 66–71.

24. F²² 319, "Note sur les conditions internationales de travail" (January 24, 1919); F²² 318, "Commission de législation internationale du travail" (February 2, 1919–March 14, 1919); and International Labor Office, "Report Presented to the Peace Conference by the Commission on International Labor Legislation" (Geneva, 1920); Bureau International du Travail, *Clauses des traités de paix relatives au travail* (Geneva, 1920), pp. 1–2; and *Voix du peuple* (April 1919): 233.

25. PRO CAB 24/71–72, "Lab. Sit." (November 27, December 2 and 18, 1918); and *Daily Herald* (December 11, 1918).

26. While various government agencies advocated the palliative of increasing the quantity and strength of beer, the Controller General of Civil Demobilization encouraged hours reductions. PRO CAB 24/71, Memo from Food Controller (December 6, 1918), and Memo from Home Office (December 2, 1918); CAB 24/73, "Lab. Sit." (January 1 and February 19, 1919), for Horne's

views. Lloyd George's quotation from CAB 23/8, meeting of cabinet (December 6, 1919), cited in Keith Middlemas, *Politics in Industrial Society* (London, 1979), pp. 142–43.

27. *Railway Review* (December 13, 1918); MRC, EEF H3/17, reports from shipbuilders (September 27, 1918); and an engineering and shipbuilding agreement (November 31, 1918). See also PRO LAB 2 1035/2, memos on engineering negotiations (December 1918).

28. Some of the wildcat strikes were precipitated by the employers' refusal to raise piece rates in order to compensate for worktime reductions, their insistence on a one-break system, and their attempts to increase discipline against tardiness. George Askwith, *Industrial Problems and Disputes* (London, 1920), p. 465; PRO CAB 24/73, "Lab. Sit." (January 1 and February 26, 1919); CAB 24/77, "Lab. Sit." (January 15, 1919); MRC EEF H3/20, report to EEF (December 7, 1919); EEF H3/18, conference at Coventry (January 28, 1919); EEF H3/17, negotiations with unions (January 9, February 26, March 3, and April 1, 1919); PRO LAB 2, 1035/2, Ministry of Labour report (February 10, 1919); *ASE Monthly Journal* (February 1919): 21–23, 28, 35–36; and *Labour Gazette* (February 1919): 20, 59, and (March 1919): 102.

29. For the Glasgow general strike, see Iain McLean, *The Legend of Red Clydeside* (Edinburgh, 1983); Harry McShane, *Glasgow 1919: The Story of the 40 Hours Strike* (London, n.d.); Scottish Trade Union Congress, *Annual Report* (April 1918), p. 37; *Daily Herald* (January 25, 1919); *Labour Leader* (October 17, 1918, and January 23, 1919); PRO CAB 24/74, "Lab. Sit." (January 29, 1919); and Ministry of Labour memo (January 24, 1919).

30. An independent strike among Belfast engineers and municipal workers suffered a similar fate after railworkers refused to join and construction unions negotiated separate worktime settlements. See *Daily Herald* (February 8 and 15, 1919); PRO CAB 23/9, report of union deputation from Glasgow (February 3, 1919); CAB 23/9, Ministry of Labour memo (February 4 and 6, 1919); PRO CAB 24/74, Ministry of Labour memo (January 24, 1919); "Lab. Sit." (January 29, February 5 and 19, 1919); *The Call* (January 9, 1919); *Railway Review* (February 7, 1919); *Labour Leader* (February 13, 19, and 20, 1919); and *The Times* (February 8, 13, and 19, 1919).

31. Railworkers obtained a guaranteed eight-hour workday over a six-day week, a limit of twelve hours "spread-over time," and periodic Sunday work at time-and-a-half pay. These had been critical issues for railway workers since the creation of the union. Added to the forty-four-hour week of dockers were two daily fifteen-minute "musterings" for work assignments. PRO CAB 24/75 to 24/80, "Lab. Sit." (February 5, 19; March 12, 19; April 2, 9; and May 21, 1919); LAB 2 1052/15 file on Triple Alliance (1919); PRO CAB 24/74, memo on railroad hours (January 24, 1919); CAB 24/77 report on Triple Alliance (March 22, 1919); *Railway Review* (April 4, 1919); *The Call* (March 13, 1919); *The Times* (March 7, 1919); *Daily Herald* (March 1, 1919); CAB 23/9, report

on meeting with coal miners (February 3, 1919) and discussion of Sankey Report (March 21, 1919); and CAB 24/77, deputation from miners to cabinet (March 22, 1919).

32. PRO CAB 24/73–77, "Lab. Sit." (January 15; February 2, 19; and March 2, 19, 1919); Raymond W. Postgate, *The Builders' History* (London, 1923), p. 440; CAB 24/89, Ministry of Labour memo on the builders (October 6, 1919); *ASE Monthly Journal* (February 1919): 34, and (March 1919): 35; *The Call* (January 9, February 27, June 26, 1919); *Daily Herald* (March 1, 1919); and CAB 24/77, Ministry of Labour memo on bakers (March 28, 1919).

33. PRO CAB 24/76 "Lab. Sit." (February 26, 1919); CAB 24/95 "Lab. Sit." (December 17, 1919); *Shop Assistant* (March 1, 22; April 5; July 14; and August 30, 1919); *The Democrat* (April 10, 1919); *Daily Herald* (March 19, 1919); CAB 24/74, Ministry of Labour memo on farmworkers (January 24, 1919); PRO LAB 2 740/15, file on farmworker hours (Spring 1919); LAB 2 466/9 notes on hours (March 1919); and Askwith, *Industrial Problems,* pp. 468–70. For details on iron and steel hours settlements, see MRC ISTC, MSS 36, E6; and Labour Research Department, *Steel* (London, 1925), pp. 70–77.

34. PRO CAB 23/10, report on meeting on Industrial Conference (April 3, 1919).

35. BPP, 1919, vol. 24, "Provisional Joint Committee of the Industrial Conference Report" (April 4, 1919), p. 501; PRO CAB 24/82, "Lab. Sit." (June 18, 1919); CAB 24/83, Ministry of Labour memo on "Hours of Employment Bill" (July 2, 1919); and CAB 23/10, cabinet meeting over farmworkers' hours (May 29, 1919).

36. Note the minor role of hours in the TUC, *Annual Proceedings* (September 1919), p. 375. See also Rodney Lowe, "Hours of Labour: Negotiating Industrial Legislation in Britain, 1919–1939," *Economic History Review* 35 (May 1982): 254–68; and Rodney Lowe, "The National Industrial Conference, 1919–1921," *Historical Journal* 2 (1978): 649–75.

37. F^7 13576, Ministry of Interior report (April 10, 1919); and Archives de la Préfecture de Police, B^a 1614, Commissaire divisionnaire reports (March 1919).

38. F^7 13576, "CGT note" (March 19, 1919); *La Bataille* (January 13, 1919); and *L'Humanité* (January 22, 1919).

39. The CGT leadership had little confidence that they could match the British unions. Not only did the metalworkers' A. Merrheim believe that "it will be totally impossible to apply the eight-hour day for two or three years in the provinces," but unions (especially those in textiles) in war-damaged regions favored exemptions from the eight-hour standard in order to prevent unfair competition. Jouhaux also feared that workers could be easily lured with the bauble of a wage increase and abandon worktime reductions altogether. He insisted that May Day agitation concentrate on hours to avoid distractions and to deny the radical *minoritaires* a forum. F^7 13576, reports on CGT Commission Ad-

ministrative (March 18, April 4 and 16, 1919); F⁷ 13273, report on CGT Comité confédéral (March 23, and April 7, 1919); *Le Peuple* (January 13, 1919); and *Le Journal* (January 17, 1919). Minutes of the "Loucheur Commission" are in F²² 401.

40. F⁷ 13576, CGT Commission Administratif meeting (March 19, 1919), and Comité confédéral meeting (March 25 and 28, 1919); *Information ouvrière et sociale* (March 23, 1919); *France libre* (February 28, 1919); F⁷ 13273, Interior Ministry report (April 18, 1919); F²² 420, Ministry of Labor report (April 29, 1919); and 41 AS 11, Union des industries métallurgiques, Circular 1134 (April 1919). See also Fédération des ouvriers des métaux et similaires de France, *Pour la défense de la journée de huit heures* (Paris, 1922), pp. 17–19.

41. *Bulletin du Ministère du Travail* (June–August 1919), pp. 288–89; and *Information ouvrière et sociale* (January 26, 1919). See also Jacques Julliard, *Clemenceau, briseur de grèves* (Paris, 1965).

42. *Information ouvrière et sociale* (March 6 and April 14, 1919); and F²² 401, "Loucheur Commission" (March 15, 21, and 27, 1919). For the "Minority Report," see France ChDoc, no. 5980 (April 19, 1919), p. 1185.

43. Gaston Tessier, *Les Conséquences économiques et sociales du régime des huit heures* (Prague, 1924), pp. 1–2; and F²² 401, "Loucheur Commission" (March 21, 27, and April 4, 1919).

44. France ChDoc, no. 5980 (April 10, 1919), pp. 1183–89; France ChDeb (April 16–17, 1919), pp. 1801–42; and France SDoc, no. 210 (April 22, 1919).

45. F²² 420, "Avant-projet relatif à la journée de huit heures" (April 1919); and *Information ouvrière et sociale* (April 13 and 23, 1919). For the law, see *Journal officiel* (April 25, 1919), p. 4266. Its essential provisions included: 1) an eight-hour day or forty-eight-hour week of "effective work" for commercial and industrial workers with "derogations"; 2) decrees required to implement the law for each industry and region based on the consultation of labor and management organizations; 3) temporary overtime for seasonal work, emergencies, and holiday recuperation (requiring prior government approval) and permanent overtime for specialists essential for normal operations; and 4) no pay cuts resulting directly from the law. No overtime premium was set, although they were common in contracts. The clause "effective work" allowed in the decrees a day of nine to twelve hours for those employed in "intermittent" work.

46. A Labor Ministry circular of May 27, 1919, stressed the desirability of a collective, not individual, contract to set hours. See F²² 427. For hour contracts, see F²² 427, 428, and 411, as well as F⁷ 12596. The *Bulletin du Ministère du Travail* (1919 and 1920) published quarterly reports on collective contracts. Also see Pierre Laroque, *Les Conventions collectives de travail* (Paris, 1934).

47. International Labor Office, *Hours of Labour, France* (Geneva, 1922), pp. 15–23. For an example of the mixed commission for gas works in 1923, see F²² 425.

48. These observations are based on F²² 409–28, which contain the Ministry of Labor files dealing with the implementation of the eight-hour law in various industries between 1919 and 1930. Especially useful are F²² 411, 414, 415, and 420.

49. PRO CAB 24/77–85, "Lab. Sit." (April 2, 9, 23; May 7, 14, 21, 29; June 4, 11, 18; July 2, 21, 30; and August 13, 1919); MCR, EEF, H13/1 EEF circular (June 6, 1919); *ASE Monthly Journal* (June 1919): 30–33; CAB 24/76, Home Office memo (April 10, 1919); CAB 24/84, report on "Committee on Night Baking" (July 16, 1919); Labour Research Department, *Monthly Circular* (January 1919), p. 2; *Labour Gazette* (June 1919): 245, and (November 1919): 485; and *Daily Herald* (May 12, 1919).

50. PRO CAB 24/78–86, "Lab. Sit." (April 23; May 7; June 4, 25; July 2, 30; August 13, 20; and September 3, 1919); *ASE Monthly Journal* (June 1919): 44, (August 1919): 15–20, and (September 1919): 16–17; and Federation of Engineering and Shipbuilding Trades of the U.K. and the ASE, *Application for the 44 Hour Week* (London, 1922).

51. MRC, EEF, H3/12 report from EEF affiliates on the overtime embargo (July 1919); *Application for the 44-Hour Week,* pp. 1–7; and PRO CAB 24/82 "Lab. Sit." (June 25, 1919).

52. By August, strikes of cabinetmakers for forty-four hours had failed. Attempts of bakers to achieve the prized goal of the abolition of night work had been deposited in the trashcan of a parliamentary committee and the hated old practice gradually returned. PRO CAB 24/81–88 "Lab. Sit." (June 11, 25; August 27; and September 3, 1919); and *Labour Gazette* (September 1919): 389.

53. See F⁷ 13273 for Interior Ministry reports on May Day 1919 in the provinces, and Bª 1614 for reports on Paris.

54. F²² 174, reports of clothing strike meetings (May 5, 6, 7, 10, and 14, 1919); CGT, *Congrès corporatif* (Paris, 1919), pp. 93, 108–9. Reports on similar strikes in the Seine shoe and construction industries are in F²² 174 (June 4 and 6; October 13; and December 31, 1919) and in *La Bataille* (May 21 and 27, 1919). For the banking strike, see *L'Humanité* (May 18, 1919); and F²² 411, letter from Fédération des commerçants détaillants en France (June 2, 1919). Provincial strike reports are in F²² 173.

55. In 1919, French miners wanted the eight hours to be calculated from the entry of the first and exit of the last miner, which employers claimed shortened the "effective" workday to six and a half hours. For the June 1919 miners' strike, see F⁷ 13576, Interior Ministry reports on the CGT (June 11, 12, 14, 18, 20, 1919); and F²² 173, strike questionnaire (July 16, 1919). See also Marcel Lombois, *La Loi du 24 juin 1919 sur la durée du travail dans les mines* (Lille, 1926).

56. Archives de la Préfecture de Police, Bª 1386, prefect of police reports (May 31–July 2, 1919), and an undated 120-page report on the strike. F⁷

13576, report on the CGT (June 5, 6, and 25, 1919); F²² 174 Labor Ministry reports on CGT (June 2–30, 1919); Fédération des ouvriers des métaux, *Congrès fédéral* (Paris, 1919), pp. 20–41; and CGT, *Congrès corporatif* (1919), pp. 93–108. Note also Christian Gras, "La Fédération des métaux en 1913–1914 et l'évolution du syndicalisme révolutionnaire français," *Le Mouvement social* 77 (October–December 1971): 87–88; and Bernard Abherve, "Les Origines de la grève des métallurgistes parisiens," *Le Mouvement social* 93 (October–December 1973): 75–81.

57. F⁷ 13576, reports on the CGT (June 11, July 9 and 21, 1919); *L'Humanité* (July 20, 1919); *Le Matin* (July 22, 1919); and *La Bataille* (July 22, 1919).

58. The *minoritaires* at the September Congress of the CGT opposed collective bargaining and continued to insist on a strike to win the forty-four-hour week. In November, they also condemned Jouhaux's participation in the Washington Conference as "*Millerandisme*" and succumbing to the "*duperie*" of the League of Nations. CGT, *Congrès corporatif* (Paris, 1919), pp. 208–10; and *Journal du Peuple* (October 16, 1919).

59. F²² 404, Bureau international du travail, "Rapport sur les huit heures" (June 1923). F⁷ 13577, report on the CGT (January 7, 1920); PRO CAB 24/95, report on the Washington Conference by G. Barnes (December 30, 1919); and PRO LAB 2 698/1, undated report on the Washington Conference (1921?).

60. Comité d'organisation de la Conférénce internationale de travail, *Rapport sur la journée de huit heures* (Geneva 1919), pp. 117ff.; and *International Labour Conference: First Annual Meeting* (Washington, D.C., 1920), pp. 222–27. See also James Shotwell, *The Origins of the International Labor Organization*, 2 vols. (New York, 1934); and H. Solano, ed., *Labour as an International Problem* (London, 1920).

61. Roger Picard, "La Journée de huit heures à l'étranger," *Les Documents du Travail* (March 1922): 1–14.

62. PRO CAB 24/97 "Lab. Sit." (January 28, 1920); CAB 24/125, Ministry of Labour memo (May 14, 1921); CAB 24/128, "Lab. Sit." (October 1, 1921); *British Trade Union Review* (November 1919): 3, (January 1922): 9–11, and (February 1922): 3–5; Amalgamated Engineers Union, "Some Comments on the Pamphlet entitled 'The Present Economic Position in the Engineering and Allied Industries'" (London, 1921), LSE Pamphlet Collection; and *FBI Bulletin* (March 31, 1919): 14.

63. In construction, the winter workweek (in December and January) was lengthened from forty-one and a half to forty-four hours; and for the rest of the year, it was increased from forty-four to forty-six and a half. *Labour Gazette* (January 1922): 6; (February 1922): 55; (September 1922): 366; (April 1923): 101; (August 1923): 280; (September 1923): 324; (January 1923): 4–5; (September 1923): 319; (January 1924): 4–5; and (July 1924): 237–38. See also

PRO LAB 2 435/4, file on railroad hours (1921); LAB 2 821/4, file on hours in iron and steel (1921–1923); LAB 2 1163/IR 1256/1925, file on iron and steel negotiations (1925); LAB 2 903/IR 633/22, deputation from General Federation of Trade Unions (July 17, 1922); and MRC ISTC MSS 36 I30a/8, joint conference of iron and steel industry (March 19–July 3, 1924).

64. In December 1919, chambers of commerce began sending delegations to the Ministry of Labor opposing the inflexibility of an eight-hour law. After the bill was modified to meet the provisions of the Washington Hours Convention, the resistance stiffened further. Shipowners' Parliamentary Committee, "The Hours of Employment Bill" (London, 1920); PRO LAB 2 740/4, file on sailors' hours (1920); *British Trade Union Review* (May 1920): 1–3; PRO CAB 23/11, cabinet discussion of Hours of Employment Bill and agriculture (July 4, 1919); LAB 2 1009/3 file on farmworkers' hours (1919); LAB 2 740/13, file on farm hours (1919); LAB 2 435/5, report on hours bill (November 29, 1919); and CAB 24/88–95 "Lab. Sit." (September 17, and December 17, 1919). For a more thorough analysis, see Lowe, "Hours of Labour." For the definitive treatment of the British Ministry of Labour, see also Rodney Lowe, *Adjusting to Democracy: The Role of the Ministry of Labour in British Politics, 1916–1939* (Oxford, 1986).

65. F^{22} 420, correspondence from: Prefect of Yonne (May 21, 1919); Tour metalworkers (July 23, 1919); Savoie metalworkers (July 21, 1919); Inspector divisionnaire of Lyon (September 26, 1919, and January 21, 1920); Rhône metalworkers (July 4, 1919); CGT metalworkers (December 27, 1919); and Ministry of Labor to Cabinet (October 10, 1920). For the decree process in the dock industry, for example, see F^{22} 417.

66. Clerks in large cities like Rouen, Lyon, and Paris had won the fifty-four-hour week in May and June 1919; but retail employees in smaller towns like Dieppe and Avignon continued to labor under a seventy-two-hour weekly schedule. F^{22} 412, reports on hour contracts: Nîmes (March 1, 1920); Nice (January 23 and September 12, 1920); Bordeaux (October 1, 1920); and Marseilles (August 24, 1919). See also F^{22} 408 for decree problems in food processing.

67. F^{22} 411 Labor Ministry circular (January 4, 1920), and *Bulletin du Ministère du travail* (January–March 1921): 39–40, and (October–December 1921): 432–35.

68. The role of corporatism is stressed by R. Keith Middlemas, *Politics of Industrial Society* (North Pomfret, Vermont, 1980). A contrary view is taken by Lowe, "The Industrial Conference." For recent analysis, see Steven Tolliday and Jonathan Zeitlin, eds., *Shop Floor Bargaining and the State: Historical and Comparative Perspectives* (Cambridge, 1985).

69. The classic on this theme is Stanley Hoffmann et al., *In Search of France* (Cambridge, 1963), esp. chaps. 1 and 5. See also Horne, *Labour Reformism,* chap. 7.

Chapter 7. Worktime, Growth, and an International Labor Standard

1. See chapter 1, nn. 35–38.

2. *Information ouvrière et sociale* (May 4, 1919).

3. PRO LAB 2 1052/15, report on conference of labor and management in dock industry (January 31, 1919). See also MRC EEF H3/18, "General Report of the Shipbuilders' Federation" (September 26, and October 17, 1918); MRC ISTC MSS 36 E6, minutes of iron and steel industry negotiations (December 10, 1918); PRO CAB 24/88 "Lab. Sit." (September 17, 1919); *The Democrat* (May 29, 1919); and Federation of Engineering and Shipbuilding Trades and the Amalgamated Society of Engineers, *Application for the Forty-Four Hour Week* (London, 1922), pp. 28–29.

4. "When workers recognize the essential conflict between capital and labor," said William Watson in *Workers' Dreadnought* (January 18, 1919), they "will strive to restrict output." *The Daily Herald* (November 2, 1918) warned that employers will concede a shorter day as a part of a plot to introduce "high speed machinery, standardisation, payment by results, and no trade union rules or regulations." See also William Watson, "Should the Workers Increase Output" (London, 1920), LSE Pamphlet Collection.

5. Trade union adviser G. D. H. Cole attacked scientific management as "essentially undemocratic." See G. D. H. Cole, "Gospel of Output," *Labour Yearbook* (London, 1919): 257–59; and idem, *Payment of Wages* (London, 1918), pp. 23–24, 68–76, 110–11. See also MRC EEF H3/17, report of Shipbuilding Federation (September 26, 1918); *ASE Monthly Journal* (February 1919): 87; and *The Call* (January 23, 1919).

6. Still, the moderate General Federation of Trade Unions called for increased output in coal and other basic-export goods in order to improve the slipping British position on the world market. It opposed the militant tactics of the "Triple Alliance" and advocated class cooperation. See *The Democrat* (May 29, June 5, August 15, and October 9, 1919).

7. *Information ouvrière et sociale* (November 7, 1918). Lingering examples of the anarchosyndicalist view are found in *La Révolution prolétarienne* (September 1926), p. 22, and (March 15, 1929), pp. 84–85.

8. See chapter 9, nn. 65–72.

9. Richard F. Kuisel, *Capitalism and the State in Modern France* (New York, 1981), pp. 59–69; and Aimée Moutet, "Patrons de progrès ou patrons de combat? La Politique de rationalisation de l'industrie française au lendemain de la Première Guerre mondiale," in *Soldat du travail,* special issue of *Recherches,* ed. Léon Marard and Patrick Zylberman (Paris, 1978), pp. 454–55.

10. See, for example, *System, The Magazine of Business* (August 1918, and

January 1920), for an advocacy of applying fatigue and efficiency research to labor-management cooperation. Also P. Sargant Florence, *Economics of Fatigue and Unrest and the Efficiency of Labour in English and American Industry* (London, 1924); and International Association for Social Progress (British Section), *Report on Hours of Work and Their Relationship to Output* (London, 1927).

11. PRO CAB 24/87 "Lab. Sit." (August 20, 1919).

12. CGT, *Congrès national corporatif, compte rendu* (Paris, July 1918), pp. 234, 184–92. See also *Information ouvrière et sociale* (January 11, 1920) for an account of the National Labor Council, an ill-fated scheme to create a policy-making body to link technologists with labor.

13. Industrial Fatigue Research Board, *Annual Report* (London, 1920); and George Askwith, *Industrial Problems* (London, 1920), pp. 353–54.

14. Jonathan Zeitlin, "From Labour History to Industrial Relations," *Economic History Review* 40 (1987): 159–84.

15. Detailed reports from the Ministry of Foreign Affairs (commercial attachés) on the status of the eight-hour day in Europe in 1922 are in F^{22} 401–3. See especially, F^{22} 401, Commerce Ministry to the Ministry of Labor (March 27, 1920) and F^{22} 403, the Ambassador at Berne to the Ministry of Labor (July 8, 1922). Note also *Journée industrielle* (May 8, 1922). For an accessible survey, see Roger Picard, "La Journée de huit heures à l'étranger," *Les Documents du travail* (March 1922): 1–14.

16. Union des industries métallurgiques et minières, *Les huit heures en Allemagne* (Paris, 1921); *Journée industrielle,* (December 12, 1921; February 24, and May 24, 1922); *Bâtiment et Travaux publics* (February 5, 1922); *L'Information financière* (June 29, 1922); and *Le Temps* (November 17, 1921). See also Gabriel Guyot, *La Loi de huit heures et ses conséquences économiques* (Paris, 1922), p. 85.

17. *Journée industrielle* (January 25; February 24; April 12, 20, and 23; June 2 and 29; and September 6, 1922). Other attempts to revise the eight-hour law include: France ChDoc, no. 882 (May 18, 1920), pp. 1471–73, and no. 1076 (June 15, 1920), pp. 1733–40. The latter bill gained the sponsorship of 113 deputies and a long list of business associations; it demanded general exemptions from the law for national economic salvation.

18. *Le Petit parisien* (February 9, and May 23, 1922); *Journée industrielle* (February 10, 23, 24, 26; and March 1, 8, 5, 1922); and *Le Temps* (February 1, 1922).

19. *Le Temps* (February 1, 1922); Fédération des ouvriers des métaux, *Congrès fédéral* (1923), pp. 21–24; *Industrial and Labour Information* (April 7, 1922), pp. 32–35, and (June 23, 1922), pp. 40–41; *L'Information française* (March 1, 1922); *Journée industrielle* (March 11, and August 22, 1922); *Bulletin de la Chambre syndicale de l'Ameublement* (September 1922), pp. 13–14; *Information sociale* (June 16, and August 17, 1922); and *Le Peuple* (July 6, and August 21, 1922).

20. Berthiot added overtime allowances, anticipated time lost to emergencies, and "recuperated" hours from holidays to the normal week. See F^{22} 420. Note also *La Voix sociale* (October 10, 1922); *Le Peuple* (August 9, 1922); *L'Usine* (May 20, 1922); and *Journée industrielle* (April 23, 1922). In F^{22} 415, 418, 411, and 404, labor inspectors' reports reveal that in 1922 Berthiot's policy was also applied in the furniture, textile, pubic service, and construction sectors.

21. *Journée industrielle* (August 2, and September 22, 1922); *Le Temps* (September 22, and October 2 and 8, 1922); *Le Peuple* (March 15; May 16; June 9, 17; July 20; August 3, 5; September 11, 27; October 1–29; and November 3 and 27, 1922). Summaries of the contest in the merchant marine and railroads appear in *Industrial and Labour Information* (September 26, 1922), pp. 30–33, and (October 24, 1922), pp. 13–16. For later modifications in the working hours in rails and shipping, see *Journée industrielle* (February 13, and March 11, 1925).

22. André François-Poncet, *La France et les huit heures* (Paris, 1922), pp. 10–14, 44, 70–77, 162, 166–70, 252–53. François-Poncet's views were shared by the Wholesale Food Producers who claimed that, with a more flexible law, "workers will no longer be able to continually demand a visit of the labor inspector who comes to discuss overtime." F^{22} 405, extract from the Syndicat des produits alimentaires en gros, *Bulletin mensuel* (February 1922). Other works opposing the eight-hour law include G. Guyot, *La Loi de huit heures et ses conséquences économiques* (Paris, 1922); Raphael Georges-Levy, "La Loi des huit heures, jugée par les faits," *La Revue des deux mondes* (February 1, 1922): 605–30; Paul Pic, "La Journée de huit heures," *Revue politique et parlementaire* (April 1922): 167–79; and Robert Veyssié, "Nos Chemins de Fer: Les Voyageurs victimes des huit heures," *Renaissance politique* (July 23, 1921).

23. François-Poncet, *La France*, pp. 14, 35–37, 162.

24. F^{22} 405 contains a large file of press clippings on the CGT's defense of the eight-hour day in 1922. See especially *Le Peuple* (May 13, June 26, and August 11, 1922); and *Réveil du Nord* (February 17, and May 17, 1922).

25. The petition appealed to women workers as well as blue-collar males by stressing that a reduced workday allowed more time for family. By July 5, the CGT claimed "about one million" signatures after a vigorous campaign. Between May 1 and July 7, 1922, the CGT daily, *Le Peuple*, published nineteen major front-page articles on the eight-hour day. See especially *Le Peuple* (May 13, June 3, and July 7, 1922); in September, the CGT Bureau confédéral called for a renewed drive for a second million signatures on the petition. See *Le Peuple* (September 9, 1922).

26. In June 1921, even the "apolitical" Christian trade unions demanded the ratification of the Washington Convention as the only way of saving this reform. *Information sociale* (March 3 and 17, 1922); *Journée industrielle* (July 2 and 3, 1922); International Federation of Trade Unions, *Enquiry on the Eight-*

Hours Day (Amsterdam, 1922); and F²² 402, report on Confédération internationale des Syndicats chrétiens (June 20–23, 1922). See also Bureau international du travail, *Conférénce internationale du Travail* (Geneva, October 1922).

27. Swiss unions launched this referendum to restore the old law with a petition drive that gained 203,000 signatures within fifteen days. Léon Jouhaux and Albert Thomas joined the campaign one week before balloting by participating in a widely publicized conference on the value of leisure. For a lengthy file on the restoration of the eight-hour day in Switzerland, see F²² 403. See E. P. Graber, *Nous défendrons les 48 heures: Comment augmenter la production* (Berne, 1924), for a Swiss socialist defense of the eight-hour day.

28. F²² 182, for the wildcat strikes against the lengthened workday in shipping. See also *l'Humanité* (September 27, 1922).

29. *Le Peuple* (June 26, 1922); *Réveil du Nord* (February 17, 1922); and Léon Jouhaux, preface to Raymond Manevy, *La Défense des huit heures* (Paris, 1922).

30. For example, see Emile Pouget, "La Conquête de la journée de huit heures," *Mouvement socialiste* (April 15, 1905): 361; and the *Voix du Peuple* (November 1904 to May 1906), which is saturated with articles in preparation for the 1906 general strike for the eight-hour day.

31. *Le Peuple* (February 1, May 20, June 1, and November 12, 1922); Manevy, *La Défense des huit heures,* pp. 40–49.

32. *Réveil du Nord* (March 11, 1922); and *Le Peuple* (January 30, 1922).

33. To be sure (as will be discussed in chapter 9) only a faction of the CGT leadership went so far as to glorify Taylorism and later Fordism. On French labor interest in Fordism, see Martin Fine, "Hyacinthe Dubreuil: Le Témoignage d'un ouvrier sur le syndicalisme," *Le Mouvement social* 106 (1979): 45–53. Note also H. Dubreuil, *Standards* (translated as *Robots or Men*) (New York, 1927); and Eugene Morel, *La Production et les huit heures* (Paris, 1927).

34. See n. 43, this chapter.

35. One CGT writer referred to M. Josse and other vocal deputies against the eight-hour day as a "lamentable clique of nobodies" in *Le Peuple* (July 1, 1922). The Radicals, Catholic unions, and Association nationale pour la protection légale des travailleurs defended the law as early as March 1922. See International Labor Office, *Hours of Labour in Industry, France* (Geneva, 1922), p. 44; and Tessier, *Un Progrès social,* p. 74. Catholic deputy R. Lafargue supported the law as a fruit of the postwar social reconciliation, and the Union sociale d'Ingénieurs catholiques feared the consequences for "social peace" if a "too brutal and hasty decision were taken" against the eight-hour day and a loss of prestige if France "appears to oppose the principle of the international regulation of work so indispensable for social progress." The Bishop G. G. Julien at the Semaine sociale de Caen spoke in more idealistic terms—that the eight-hour day "allowed the worker not to be treated as a machine. . . . Let the worker have the time to be a man and a Christian." ChDeb (July 7, 1922),

p. 800; *Journée industrielle* (April 7, 1922); *Semaine sociale de Caen* (1920), p. 141; *Le Peuple* (November 6, 1922); and *Le Journal* (August 21, 1923).

36. *L'Intransigeant* (November 6, 1922) and François-Poncet, *La France et les huit heures,* p. 14. There is also evidence that opponents may have been satisfied with their gains of 1922. *Journée industrielle* (April 23, 1922) opined that "perhaps we can be content" with the fifty-four-hour week in Lyon and with the hours increase in merchant marine and railroads.

37. *Journée industrielle* (February 26, 1922); and *Le Peuple* (October 30, 1922). Government studies favorable to the eight-hour day were published in the *Bulletin du Ministère du Travail.* They include: "L'exode en banlieue des employés et ouvriers parisiens et la journée de huit heures" (April–June 1923), pp. 153–56; "Enquête sur l'utilisation des loisirs crées par la journée de huit heures" (August–October 1920), pp. 402–9; "L'alcoolisme est-il en décroissance dans la population ouvrière?" (January–March 1923), pp. 39–54; and "L'adaptation des conditions de production et de travail à la loi du 23 avril 1919 sur la journée de huit heures," which appeared in the issues from April 1924 to March 1925 and again from July to September 1927. An analysis of these data is presented in chapter 9.

38. "Enquête sur l'utilisation des loisirs crées par la journée de huit heures," *Bulletin du Ministère du Travail* (October–December 1922): 408. See *Capital et travail* (September 6, 1923) for a critique of the Ministry of Labor's interpretation of alcohol consumption statistics.

39. For an interesting analysis of the British labor inspectorate, see Karl Marx, *Capital* (New York, 1965), 1: 407–17; and Douglas Booth, "Karl Marx on the State of Regulation of the Labor Process," *Review of Social Economy* 36 (1978): 138–58.

40. *Le Peuple* (October 30, 1922).

41. For details of the reversal of the "Berthiot Settlement," see F^{22} 418; and for the response of the metallurgical industry of Rhone, see M. R. Touchard, *La Journée de huit heures dans les industries de la métallurgie et du travail des métaux* (St.-Etienne, 1925).

42. In the fall of 1925 the ILO and CGT again campaigned to win ratification of the Washington Convention. This effort met a setback when, in the spring of 1926, Fascist Italy reinstated a nine-hour day, prompting international business demands for raised hours. Between November 1926 and March 1927, the CGT defended the economic and social benefits of the eight-hour day in twenty-six lengthy reports in *Le Peuple.* They are reprinted in Eugène Morel, *La Production et les huit heures* (Paris 1927). See also Albert Thomas, "The Eight-Hour Day," *International Labour Review* 6 (August 15, 1926): 154. In 1928, the CGT and the communist-led CGTU also defended the eight-hour norm against pressures for overtime as the economy heated up. For example, see *Le Peuple* (May 4, 1928); and *Voix du peuple* (March 1928): 145.

43. Decrees were enforced in banking (July 1923), food processing (1925–1927), wood (June 1925), laundry (August 1929), hotels (July 1930), and bakeries (1931–1933). These decrees were regularly published in the *Bulletin du Ministère du Travail.* See also F²² 406, list of decrees (November 22, 1932).

44. In a memo to the Cabinet on the eve of the parliamentary debate on the Washington Convention, Minister of Labour T. J. MacNamara claimed that to reject the convention "would allow a dangerous license to our trade competitors when it is our interest to bring them up to the existing British practice as to the regulation of overtime." PRO CAB 24/125 (June 23, 1921). Similar points were made during each of the subsequent debates on the convention without gaining Cabinet sympathy.

45. The railroad hours settlement of 1919 in Britain entailed regular Sunday overtime and was flexible regarding daily hours because of the difficulties of fitting long-haul transport into rigid schedules. Leaders of the National Union of Railwaymen, for example, opposed the daily hour limit in the convention and embarrassed the TUC by its opposition to the forty-eight-hour bill modeled after the ILO's formulas. Yet throughout 1920 Ministry of Labour officials were convinced that these difficulties could be overcome. PRO CAB 24/123, Ministry of Labour memo (May 25, 1921); CAB 24/123, Ministry of Labour memo (June 23, 1921).

46. PRO CAB 24/145, A. Thomas letter to Cabinet (July 1, 1921); LAB 2 821 IL 615/2, Allen Smith letter to Prime Minister (June 23, 1921); and "Minute Sheet" by Ministry of Labour staffer, Humbert Wolfe (June 25, 1921).

47. PRO LAB 2 821 IL/615/2, Arthur Henderson to Thomas Munro (June 17, 1921). See also LAB 2 435/4; LAB 2 903 IR 1633/22; and LAB 2 994 IL 125/34/24 for Ministry of Labour reports on Washington Convention (1920–1922).

48. PRO CAB 23/26, Cabinet meeting (June 30, 1921). See also *Hansard,* House of Commons Debate (May 27, 1921), cols. 486 and 545, for the discussion of the convention in Parliament. One of the key objections of the government was the presumed limits on overtime. This point was central to the formal rejection of ratification. CAB 24/160 Cabinet letter to Albert Thomas (July 23, 1921).

49. Albert Thomas, *The International Labor Organisation and the First Year of Its Work* (Geneva, 1921), introduction.

50. *Labour Gazette* (December 1923): 438; (March 1924): 83; (May 1925): 349. See also the ILO monthly, *Industrial and Labour Information* (1922–1923).

51. The British and French objected to the limit of nine hours per day while other states complained of the need to raise hours in order to lower production costs in the increasingly competitive European economy. PRO LAB 2 994 IL/125/34/24, "The Washington Hours Convention, A History" (February 1925); LAB 2 2018 IL 166/1935, report on ILO (June 1923); CAB 24/160, Ministry of Labour memo (May 17, 1923); LAB 2 2018 IL 166/1935, A.

Thomas to Ministry of Labour (May 7, 1923), and report on the ILO meeting (June 2, 1923); and CAB 24/161, Ministry of Labour memo (June 23, 1923).

52. PRO CAB 23/48, Cabinet meeting (June 18, 1924); CAB 24/166–7, Ministry of Labour memo (June 3, 1924); Ministry of Transportation memo (March 31, and May 14, 1924) and Admiralty memo (May 30, 1924); LAB 2 821 IR 345/100/1924, Chambers of Commerce letter to Ministry of Labour (May 28, 1924) and Chambers of Commerce deputation to Ministry of Labour (July 19, 1924); *Labour Gazette* (August 1924): 278; and *The Times* (September 9, 1924).

53. More than half of German industrial workers in Saxony and Westphalia put in over forty-eight hours per week. Reports on this conference held in Berne are in PRO LAB 2 994 IL 125/29/1924 (September 1924; May 5, 1925); and *The Times* (September 11, 1924).

54. PRO LAB 2 1168 IR 1256/2/25, Ministry of Labour memo (November 9, 1925).

55. *Labour Gazette* (February 1925): 41–42, and (May 1925): 159; *Industrial and Labour Information* (August 1924–May 1925); Albert Thomas, "The Eight-Hour Day, Taking a Reckoning," *International Labour Review* 14 (August 1926): 5–9; *Manchester Guardian* (February 6, 1925); and *The Times* (February 20, 1925). Discussions of these events appear also in PRO LAB 2 994 IL 125/34/24 and CAB 24/173, Ministry of Labour memo (April 23, 1925).

56. PRO CAB 24/178, Ministry of Labour letter to Ministers of Labor of France, Germany, Italy and Belgium (June 20, 1925); CAB 24/178, Ministry of Labour memo (January 22, 1926); PRO LAB 2 1004 IL 118/21/26 "Minute Sheet" (March 20, 1926); LAB 2 1003 IL 1181/13/26, deputation from General Federation of Trade Unions (March 15, 1926); CAB 24/179 report on the London Conference (March 19, 1926); and *Labour Gazette* (April 1926): 120.

57. PRO LAB 2 1168 IR 1256/2/25, notes on a conference between Minister of Labour Arthur Steel-Maitland, Engineering Employers' Federation, and the Amalgamated Engineers' Union (November 10, 1925). This meeting produced a unique joint statement favoring support for an hours limitation accord with the continent. See also *Labour Magazine* (December 1925): 380.

58. The London Conference limited the French practice of "recuperating" time lost to holidays, restricted the meaning of worktime to "time at the disposal of the employer," limited the tactic of extending hours of workers engaged in "intermittent work," and prohibited the suspension of the eight-hour day because of self-declared "commercial crises." After having abolished common loopholes utilized by continental competitors, the conference accepted the British custom that there be no maximum overtime but rather that an overtime rate of 125 percent be levied in order to discourage its systematic use. PRO CAB 24/179, memo on the London Conference (March 19, 1926); *Labour Magazine* (April 1926): 568; and *Labour Gazette* (April 1926): 120.

59. PRO CAB 24/179, Deputation of the National Confederation of Employers' Organisations to Ministry of Labour (April 20, 1926).

60. Ibid.

61. Ibid.

62. PRO LAB 27/1, "Diary of the Coal Dispute, 1918–1926"; Mining Association, *The Case for the Mine Owners* (London, 1925); Labour Research Department, *The Coal Crisis: Facts from the Samuel Commission, 1925–1926* (London, 1926); and Sankey Commission, *Coal Industrial Commission Report and Minutes of Evidence* (London, 1919). See also R. A. S. Redmayne, *Labour in the Coal-Mining Industry (1914–1921)* (Oxford, 1923); and J. W. F. Rowe, *Wages in the Coal Industry* (London, 1923).

63. PRO LAB 27/1 "Diary," pp. 20–32, and Mining Association, *Case,* pp. 25–27.

64. Mining Association, *Case,* pp. 9–11, 14–18.

65. Miners' Federation of Great Britain, *The Coal Crisis and the TUC* (London, 1925); Labour Research Department, *Coal Crisis,* pp. 10–77; House of Commons, *Report of the Royal Commission on the Coal Industry (1925)* (London, 1926); and House of Commons, *Royal Commission on the Coal Industry. Evidence* (London, 1925), vol. 2B, pp. 933–34, and vol. 2A, pp. 125–27.

66. House of Commons, *Royal Commission on the Coal Industry. Evidence,* 1: 165–79.

67. These facts are well documented in Geoffrey Skelley, ed., *General Strike 1926* (London, 1976); Page R. Arnot, *The General Strike of May 1926: Its Origins and History* (London, 1926); Gerard Noel, *The Great Lock-Out of 1926* (London, 1976); Chrisopher Forman, *The General Strike, May 1926* (London, 1972); Michael Morris, *The General Strike* (London, 1976); G. A. Phillips, *The General Strike: The Politics of Industrial Conflict* (London, 1976); and R. A. Florey, *The General Strike of 1926* (London, 1980).

68. PRO LAB 27/4, Ministry of Labour memos (April 14, 15, 29, 1926); *The Times* (April 24, 30; May 22, 1926); *Manchester Guardian* (April 5, 1926); LAB 27/1, "Diary," pp. 52–57; Miners' Federation, *Annual Proceedings* (London, 1926), pp. 753–54, 775–77; CAB 24/180, memos on revision of coal mining hours law (May 21, 22, 26; and June 17, 1926); LAB 2 647/11, coal miners' hours bill memos (April–July 1926); Miners' Federation, "Minutes of Proceeding of a Meeting between the Miners' Federation and Mining Association, August 19, 1926" (London, 1926); Miners' Federation, "The Coal Situation: Note of a Meeting between His Majesty's Ministers and the Mining Association, September 6, 1926" (London, 1926), pp. 12–15, in the archives of the TUC; *Labour Gazette* (August 1926): 280–83; *The Times* (September 6 and November 27, 1926); and LAB 2 657/11, undated memo on coal strike.

69. Noel, *Lock-Out,* p. 160, claims that Baldwin did "not realize the depth of bitterness against an eight-hour act." Morris, *General Strike,* pp. 301–2, also suggests that the eight-hour act of July 1926 was intended to "divide" miners.

70. Cited in Forman, *General Strike,* pp. 249–50. For hostility of miners to the eight-hour act, see LSE, Webb Misc. Coll., 31, 140, XII, "Miners' Leaflet No. 1," and June 12, 1926, dispatch of the Miners' Federation to union secretaries.

71. A. J. Cook, secretary of the Miners' Federation, claimed in 1928 that while costs per ton of coal had been reduced, pithead earnings actually decreased because of a drop in price. The Samuel Commission's estimate of lost jobs was on the mark at a 136,202 decline from March 1926 to December 1927. This was paralleled by a drop in weekly wage of almost 20 percent when overproduction led to short time. Although this drastic decline can hardly be attributable entirely to increasing hours (for 1927 was a year of global recession), that extra hour did not contribute to economic stability in the mining towns. Although massive retaliation from foreign competitors did not take place, the position of British mining was hardly improved as a result. Noel, *Lock-Out,* p. 137; Morris, *General Strike,* p. 276; Miners' Federation, *Annual Proceedings* (London, 1927), pp. 115, 302, 309, and (1928), pp. 910–14; and A. J. Cook, "The Effect of a Longer Working Day in British Coal Mines" (London, 1928), LSE Pamphlet Collection.

72. PRO LAB 2 1004 IL 188/21, Ministry of Labour notes (August 27, 1926).

73. PRO CAB 24/184, Ministry of Labour memo (February 14, 1927); and CAB 27/341, Ministry of Labour note to Washington Hours Committee (February 24 and March 7, 1927).

74. By July 1927 the draft bill exempted all commercial and agriculture-related firms, and allowed hour averaging and other provisions favorable to business. PRO LAB 2 992/11, "Coal Mining Industry and the Washington Hours Convention, A History" (1927?); and Ministry of Labour staff memos (April 4 and May 10, 1927); PRO POWER 20/24, Ministry of Labour memo (March 18, 1927); PRO CAB 24/184, Ministry of Labour memo (November 19, 1927); CAB 24/188, Ministry of Labour memo (July 18, 1927); and LAB 2 992/11, Ministry of Labour staff note (July 29, 1927).

75. PRO CAB 24/188–89, Ministry of Labour memos (July 18, and November 19, 1927); PRO LAB 2 992/11, report on meeting between minister of labor and National Confederation of Employers' Organisations delegates (July 29, 1927); LAB 2 992/12, "Minute Sheet" (July 1, October 31, November 13, 1927); LAB 2 992/13, "Minute Sheet" (December 14–15, 1927; and January 16, June 20, July 6 and 31, 1928); LAB 2 992/12, Minutes of conference between minister of labor and National Confederation of Employers' Organisations (Oct. 19, 1927); and CAB 23/55, Cabinet meeting (November 23, 1927). For the public position of the employers, see National Confederation of Employers' Organisations, *The Washington Hours Convention: A Statement of Facts* (London, 1927).

76. PRO CAB 23/61, Cabinet meeting (July 24, 1929); CAB 24/205,

Ministry of Labour memo (July 21, 1929); PRO LAB 2 2138 IR 420/13, deputation of Confederation of Employers' Federations (July 30, 1929); LAB 2 992/11, deputation of Mining Association (February 26, 1929); CAB 23/63, Cabinet meeting (January 15, 1930); CAB 24/206, Ministry of Labour memo (October 13, 1929); CAB 24/209, Attorney General memo (January 30, 1930); CAB 26/13, Ministry of Labour memo (April 9, 1930); *Labour Gazette* (May 1930): 163, 165, (August 1930): 281, and (November 1930): 404; and CAB 24/216, Ministry of Labour memo (November 3, 1930).

77. TUC, *Annual Proceedings* (1924), p. 188. See also Thomas, *The International Labor Organisation,* pp. 13–14, for a similar but more diplomatic assessment.

Chapter 8. Meanings of Free Time: Leisure and Class in the 1920s

1. PRO CAB 24 166, Ministry of Labour memo (March 24, 1924). The ILO questionnaire sent to Shaw asked for information on the problem of moonlighting; improvements in transportation and housing to facilitate workers' leisure; the possibility of one-break work shifts; and the question of the role of government, business, and labor in the organization of workers' leisure. None of these issues seemed to the British to be an appropriate government concern. For details of the ILO survey, see especially ILO, *Rapport supplementaire sur l'utilisation des loisirs des ouvriers* (Geneva, 1924). For a full discussion of British trade union leisure programs, see Stephen Jones, *Workers at Play: A Social and Economic History of Leisure, 1919–1939* (London, 1986), pp. 133–63. For the Victorian leisure debate, note especially John Lowerson and John Meyerscough, *Time to Spare* (Brighton, 1978), pp. 1–22; and J. M. Golby and A. W. Purdue, *Civilisation of the Crowd* (London, 1984), chaps. 1, 2, 4, and 5.

2. André François-Poncet, *La France et les huit heures* (Paris, 1922), pp. 10–14; and France ChDeb (July 7, 1922), p. 810.

3. François-Poncet, *La France,* pp. 70–77; Léon Pasquier, *La Loi sur la journée de huit heures: Quelques conséquences économiques et sociales* (Lyons, 1921), pp. 103–18; Czeslaw Kaczmarek, *L'Emigration polonaise en France après la guerre* (Paris, 1928), pp. 280–94; and Jean Beaudemoulin, *Enquête sur les loisirs de l'ouvrier français* (Paris, 1924), part 2.

4. Pasquier, *La Loi,* pp. 108–11; Yves Bacquet, *L'Organisation des loisirs des travailleurs* (Paris, 1919), pp. 218–19; and Robert Pinot, *Les Oeuvres sociales des industries métallurgiques* (Paris, 1924), chaps. 1–3. Other examples of this paternalism are Edouard Labbe, *Les Loisirs ouvriers* (Lille, 1929); Société d'Education Familiale de l'Aube, *Organisations des loisirs à la campagne* (Paris, 1932);

and Gaston Etienne, *L'Utilisation des loisirs des travailleurs* (St. Cloud, 1935). On workers' gardens, see Henri Robin, *Les Jardins ouvriers* (Paris, 1905); Louis Rivière, *La Terre et l'atelier: Jardins ouvriers* (Paris, 1904); Paul Bacquet, *Les Jardins ouvriers en France et le terréanisme* (Paris, 1906); and Ligue française du coin de terre et du foyer, *Congrès international des jardins ouvriers* (Paris, 1903).

5. Constance Harris, *The Use of Leisure* (London, 1927), pp. 1–2, 33–38, 60–62, 64, 66–67; B. S. Rowntree, *Poverty and Progress* (London, 1941), pp. 333, 354–62, 369–71; and International Association for Social Progress, *Inquiry into the Hours Problem* (London, 1933), pp. 7, 14, 29–33. See also L. Hubert Smith, *The New Survey of London Life and Labour* (London, 1934), 4: 315.

6. *International Chambers of Commerce, Congress* (July 8–13, 1929). For background on this "consumer strategy," see Stuart Ewig, *Captains of Consciousness* (New York, 1976), pp. 23–103.

7. David Roediger, "The Limits of Corporate Reform: Fordism, Taylorism, and the Working Week in the U.S., 1914–1929," in *Worktime and Industrialization: An International History,* ed. Gary Cross (Philadelphia, 1989), pp. 134–54. For comparative view on organized leisure, see Victoria De Grazia, "La Politique sociale de loisir: 1900–1940," *Les Cahiers de la recherche architecturale* 15–17 (1985): 24–35.

8. T. W. Price, *The Story of the Workers' Educational Association, 1903–1924* (London, 1924).

9. For example, members of the reformist Association for Labor Legislation claimed that the workers' garden was an "excellent component of social defense," arguing that it domesticated men. A change in housing design—eliminating the common room for a specialized living space—would create a place for reading and familial interaction and reduce the tendency of men to flee the home for the bar. See Georges Borderel and M. R. Picot, *L'Utilisation des loisirs des travailleurs* (Paris, 1924), pp. 10–11, 21. For the definitive study of *dopo lavoro,* see Victoria De Grazia, *The Culture of Consent* (New York, 1982).

10. F^{22} 404, undated speech by Godart; *Railway Review* (February 13, 1918); CGTU, *Congrès du bâtiment: Compte rendu* (1923), p. 210; and *Labour Leader* (January 23, 1919).

11. *Information ouvrière et sociale* (March 20, 1919); *Voix du peuple* (December 1919): 724. See also *Le Réveil du Nord* (May 18, 1924); and *Le Peuple* (July 19, 1922).

12. *Le Peuple* (June 22, 1923); *Ouvrier textile* (June 1923); *Le Réveil du Nord* (May 17, 1922); and even the communist *Humanité* (August 8, 1923).

13. For example, see E. Plevant's article in *Le Réveil du Nord* (May 17, 1922), or E. Antonelli in *Le Peuple* (June 28, 1923).

14. A petition in 1922 in defense of the eight-hour day declared that if the shorter day were lost, the wage earner would not "be able to educate himself or his family and women would have to return to the slavery of housework after a

longer workday." See *Le Peuple* (June 3, 1922). CGT propaganda also linked the shortening of the workday to the need for public housing. These together, said Dumoulin, would improve family life and make France "no longer a land of tuberculosis and alcoholism." See *Voix du Peuple* (June 1919): 359. See also Godart's undated speech in F²² 404, and especially "L'Exode en banlieue des employés et ouvriers parisiens et la journée de huit heures," *Bulletin du Ministère du travail* (April–June 1923): 153–56. For similar views of Catholic labor, see Gaston Tessier, *Un Progrès social: La Journée de huit heures* (Paris, 1923), pp. 121–22.

15. *Le Peuple* (November 23, 1921, and July 20, 1922); and *Information ouvrière et sociale* (May 18 and June 1, 1919).

16. Paul Crouzet, "L'Education populaire et les 8 heures," *La Grande revue* (October 1921): 23–54; *Le Peuple* (July 30, 1922); Becquet, *L'Organisation,* pp. 195–225; Gaston Rives, *La Corvée de joie* (Paris, 1924), pp. 60–97; and Congrès de la ligue de l'enseignement à Lille, *Loisirs ouvriers* (Lille, 1928).

17. *Le Peuple* (December 7 and 9, 1922); cf. De Grazia, *Culture of Consent.* A general consensus as to the ideal uses of leisure seems to have prevailed in France. See, for example, Jean Vignaud, "Les 8 heures de loisir," *Je sais tout* (September 25, 1919): 341–48, which surveys a wide range of French opinion.

18. F²² 404, Labor Ministry inspectors' reports on organized leisure (March 1922); "L'Enquête sur l'utilisation des loisirs crées par la journée de huit heures," *Bulletin du Ministère du travail* (August–October 1922): 408; Becquet, *L'Organisation,* pp. 223–29.

19. Rowntree, *Poverty and Progress,* pp. 333, 387; Becquet, *L'Organisation,* pp. 131; Harris, *Leisure,* p. 46; Working Men's Clubs and Institute Union, *Annual Report* (1913), p. 71, and (1926), p. 46; "Recreation in the Country: An English Experiment in Organisation," *International Labour Review,* 9 (June 1924): 829–30. Three fine surveys with sources are Jones, *Workers at Play;* John Lowerson and Alun Howkins, *Trends in Leisure, 1919–1939* (London, 1979), esp. pp. 7–54; and John Meyerscough, "The Recent History of the Use of Leisure Time," in *Leisure Research and Policy,* ed. I. Appleton (Edinburgh, 1974). See also Steven Jones, "The Leisure Industry in Britain, 1918–1939," *Service Industries Journal* 5 (1985): 90–105; and idem, "State Intervention in Sport and Leisure in Britain between the Wars," *Journal of Contemporary History* 22 (January 1987): 163–82.

20. Rives, *La Corvée,* pp. 175–78, 189–90, 207.

21. Adolphe Hodée, "L'Organisation des loisirs et de l'éducation populaire est un problème capital pour la démocratie, *Lumière* (August 11, 18, and 25, 1928); F²² 404, Labor inspector (Rouen) report (March 11, 1922); *Bataille* (September 24, 1919); Becquet, *L'Organisation,* pp. 22–26; and Rives, *La Corvée,* pp. 80, 29–30, 50, 185–86.

22. Fédération des ouvriers des métaux, *Pour la défense de la journée de huit*

heures (Paris, 1922), p. 4; and *Voix du Peuple* (December 1919): 724. Other examples of this theme are *Le Peuple* (June 22, 1923); *Le Réveil du Nord* (May 17, 1922); and *L'Ouvrier textile* (June 1923).

23. An example of this familial ideology appears in the CGT pamphlet, complete with cartoons illustrating the happy middle-class home life awaiting the worker after the reduction in hours, "Diminuons les heures du travail" (Paris, 1908?). See also Conseil supérieur du travail, *La Réduction de la durée du travail le samedi* (Paris, 1913).

24. Other ways of exploring this problem, of course, include detailed studies of working-class leisure activities. Beyond references to ongoing research in this area, this level of analysis unfortunately lies outside the limits of this study. My goal is not to analyze the specific content of workers' leisure but rather its availability and broader social significance.

25. *ASE Monthly Journal* (March 1919): 34; *Dockers' Record* (January 1919), p. 2; PRO LAB 2 1052/15, Conference of National Transportation Workers (January 31, 1919); and *Daily Herald* (December 21, 1918).

26. Federation of Engineering and Shipbuilding Trades of the United Kingdom and the Amalgamated Society of Engineers, *Application for the 44 Hour Week* (London, 1922), p. 8; *Daily Herald* (December 21, 1918): 8; and *Labour Leader* (January 23, 1919).

27. *Daily Herald* (December 21, 1918); and PRO LAB 2 1052/15, Dock employers' letter (February 24, 1919) and dockers' resolution (January 31, 1919).

28. F[22] 404, letter from paper worker from the Dordogne (March 9, 1922).

29. *Democrat* (July 18, 1919); and PRO CAB 24/77, report from the minister of labor (February 27, 1919).

30. Cited in *Railway Review* (February 27, 1919): 2.

31. Federation of Engineering and Shipbuilding Trades, pp. 11–13; PRO CAB 24/74, report from Ministry of Labour (January 24, 1919); *Railway Review* (January 24, 1919); *Daily Herald* (February 22, 1919); and PRO LAB 2 1035/2, Ministry of Munitions memo (January 23, 1919).

32. M. A. Bienefeld, *Working Hours in British History: An Economic History* (London, 1972), pp. 145–48; PRO CAB 24/73, "Lab. Sit." (January 1, 1919, and February 19, 1919); and Whitely Williams, *Full Up and Fed Up* (New York, 1921), pp. 21, 28, 47, 55, 58.

33. PRO LAB 2 1052/15, Federation of Transport Workers' Conference (January 31, 1919); MRC, ISTC, MSS 36, E6, bargaining conference (December 10, 1918, and January 20, 1919); and PRO CAB 24/73, "Lab. Sit." (January 15, 1919). For French construction workers, see *Voix du Peuple* (June 1919): 358, and *L'Ouvrier du bâtiment* (October–December 1924).

34. For example, see Ken Howarth, *Dark Days, Memories and Reminiscences of the Lancashire and Cheshire Coalmining Industry up to Nationalisation* (Manchester, 1978), pp. 1–3; PRO LAB 27/4, report from a government agent

(September 26, 1926); and House of Commons, *Report of the Royal Commission on the Coal Industry* (London, 1926), pp. 180–83.

35. F²² 174, Strike report of housepainters (December 31, 1919); *Bataille* (May 21, 1919); F⁷ 13576, report on the CGT construction workers (May 26, 1919); F²² 404, report on textiles workers of Lyon, (May 1923); F²² 174, report on clothing union (May 8, 1919); F²² 417, dossier on docks (April 1921); and F²² 410, inspector report on the glass industry (November 25, 1925). Other evidence of resistance to seasonal workdays are in F²² 415 and F²² 404.

36. For the forty-four-hour drive in clothing, for example, in France, see F²² 174, Paris strike reports (May–June 1919).

37. F²² 404, inspector's report (Lille, March 9, 1922); F²² 408, inspector's report (Rouen, May 3, 1922); F²² 411, Ministry of Labor circular (January 4, 1920); F²² 415, furniture workers' letter (December 14, 1924), and inspectors' report (September 21, 1925); and F²² 418, Ministry of Labor circular (November 19, 1925), as well as a file dealing with holiday time in the Rhone (May–November 1924). The minister of labor finally ended all recuperation time on July 27, 1933; see F²² 416. This conflict runs throughout F²² 411, 415, and 417. See also *Peuple* (February 27, and March 1, 1922). The quotation is from *Industrial and Labour Information* (August 4, 1922).

38. French examples in metalworking and docks are found in F²² 408, inspector report (February 1, 1920); F⁷ 13775, report from Montbrison bicycle plant (February 27, 1920); report from iron works at Bar le Duc (February 26, 1920); F²² 417, letter from CGT dockworkers (May 10, 1920); F²² 173, Haute Rhine strike report (June 1919); and Archives de la Prefect de Police, Bᵃ 1614, strike report on Panhard (May 26, 1919). For similar conflicts in Britain, see Federation of Engineering and Shipbuilding, *Application* p. 21; PRO LAB 2 1035/2, joint resolution on working hours in engineering (December 21, 1918); *Daily Herald* (January 11, 1919): 4; *Railway Review* (February 14, 1919); PRO LAB 2 1052/15, conference with Federation of Transport Workers (February 5, 1919); and LAB 2 688/5, dockers' contract (May 5, 1920).

39. F²² 282, dossier on mines conflict (Summer 1914); *Bataille syndicaliste* (July 6, 1914); *L'Echo du Nord* (July 7, 1914); *Le Matin* (June 13, 1919); and *Industrial and Labour Information* (May 26, 1922), p. 37. Note also International Labor Office, *Hours of Labor, France* (Geneva, 1924), p. 53; and *Le Peuple* (October 28, 1922).

40. *L'Ouvrier textile* (July–September 1919). "Intermittent work" meant that workers were "away from home, under the employer's control . . . for 14 hours per day for an equivalence of eight hours of production." See CGT, *Congrès confédéral* (1925), p. 134.

41. Note especially *Industrial and Labour Information* (September 29, 1922), pp. 30–33, and (October 24, 1922), pp. 12–16; ILO, *Hours of Labor, France*, pp. 9, 35; *Le Peuple* (July 20, and August 29, 1922); and *Journée industrielle* (November 23, 1922). On British railway hours, a summary appears in ILO, *Hours of Labor, Britain* (Geneva, 1924), pp. 27–28; for a similar complaint by

British miners, note Charles Forman, *Industrial Town: Self-Portrait of St. Helens in the 1920s* (London, 1978), p. 57.

42. *Railway Review* (February 7, 1919): 2. For revisions of railroad and sailor hours more favorable to labor, see *Industrial and Labour Information* (May 18, 1925), pp. 27–28.

43. According to *Information sociale* (March 13 and 20, and May 18, 1922), railroad and dockworkers signed away rest breaks in 1919, and the Ministry of Labor report, "L'Alcoolisme," pp. 39–54, notes widespread decline of the *casse-croûte,* a change that reduced on-the-job drinking. See also Jacques Valdour, *Ouvriers parisiens d'après-guerre* (Paris, 1921), pp. 84–86. Other French examples are found in *Information ouvrière et sociale* (March 16, 31, and May 18, 1919); F²² 417, inspector report on Rouen dockers (May 10, 1920), and F²² 174, strike report on Paris restaurant workers (June 8, 1920). Similar pressure for a compressed day among plate layers on British rails is reported in *Railway Review* (February 14, 1919): 2; of course, the one-break system (already discussed) was based on the same principle.

44. Paul Crouzet, "L'Education populaire et les 8 heures," *Grande revue* (October 1921): 37. A Parisian employer told an inspector that he was convinced that the French two-hour lunch (as compared with the American half-hour meal) was responsible for all of France's defeats since 1870. Yet the short break was rejected by dockworkers at Cette and Havre in F²² 417 (April 1 and 25, 1920) and by female metalworkers at Maubeuge (who got one and a half hours to prepare lunch) in F²² 404 (October 2, 1920).

45. *Daily Herald* (January 11, 1919): 10; MRC EEF, H3/18, conference at Bradford (January 10, 1919); MRC EEF, H3/3, EEF correspondence (January 14, 1919); *Industrial Peace* (April 1918), pp. 14–17; Federation of Engineering and Shipbuilding, p. 12; and "Annual Report of the Chief Factory Inspector," BPP (1919), vol. 22, p. 8.

46. "Report by the Departmental Committee on the Employment of Women and Young Persons on the Two-Shift System," BPP (1920), vol. 19, pp. 4, 16, 31, 36, 68–69, 95; and PRO CAB 23/9 (523), (6), Cabinet meeting (January 31, 1919).

47. French rail unions claimed that thirty-five thousand would lose their jobs as a result of longer hours while the figure for the sailor's union was three thousand. *Le Peuple* (November 27, and September 27, 1922); and *L'Humanité* (October 6 and 7, 1922).

48. See Gary Cross, *Immigrant Workers in Industrial France* (Philadelphia, 1983).

49. F²² 404, inspector report (March 20, 1922).

50. *Labour Leader* (January 23, 1919); *Workers' Dreadnought* (December 21, 1918, and February 8, 1919); *Daily Herald* (February 1, 1919): 8; *The Call* (January 23, 1919); *Railway Review* (November 1, 1918); and PRO CAB 24/73–74, "Lab. Sit." (January 15 and 23, 1919).

51. PRO CAB 24/71 and 24/21, "Lab. Sit." (January 1, 1919, and De-

cember 4, 1918); *Daily Herald* (February 1, 1919); and *The Call* (January 23, 1919).

52. PRO LAB 2 1052/15, Federation of Transport Workers conference (January 13, 1919). See also LAB 2 688/5 "Report by a Court of Inquiry Concerning Transport Workers" (1920), which stresses the benefit of regular work for dockers as a means of eliminating that "liberty to do nothing which they have come to prize" (p. 7).

53. Although the trade unionist might understand the worker with the "large family and the small wage" becoming an "overtime hog," working more than normal hours "blinds him to the real economic cheapness at which he is selling his labour power." See *Railway Review* (November 1, 1918).

54. F^{22} 404, inspectors' reports, March 1922; Jacques Valdour, *Ateliers et taudis de la banlieu de Paris* (Paris, 1923), pp. 176–77; and Rives, *La Corvée,* pp. 49–50.

55. In March 1919, Jouhaux warned against coupling worktime reductions with wage increases in negotiations "because the majority of workers, who having obtained satisfaction on the rise of wages, might desert the struggle for the reduction of working hours." The reform wing of the French miners' union advocated fining not only employers but workers who did overtime; and in 1923 the communist construction union expressed frustration when building workers regularly accepted a ten-hour day. French textile union officials claimed that workers cooperated with employers and inspectors in raising the overtime hours. *Voix du Peuple* (March 1919): 64; Fédération nationale des travailleurs du sous-sol et similaires (CGT), *Congrès fédéral* (1925), p. 30; Fédération national des travailleurs du bâtiment et des travaux publics (CGTU), *Congrès fédéral* (1923), pp. 215–16; and *L'Ouvrier textile* (May 1924).

56. For the struggle to prevent a raise in overtime, see Fédération des ouvriers des métaux, *Pour la défense,* pp. 8, 13–14; and Fédération des ouvriers des métaux, *Congrès fédéral* (1923), pp. 11–18, 21–24. Similar battles in construction are in *Voix du peuple* (June 1919): 358; and *L'Ouvrier du bâtiment* (October–December 1924). See F^{22} 418 for reports about overtime in the textile industry in the Rhône.

57. F^7 13775, police report (Montboison, February 16, 1920); F^{22} 404, inspector reports (Nantes, March 10, 1922; and Nancy, March 7, 1922).

58. *Bataille* (March 11, 1920); F^7 13775, reports on strikes in February 1920; F^{22} 420, inspector report (Rennes, April 22, 1920); F^{22} 404, inspector reports (Bordeaux, March 8, 1922; Nancy, March 9, 1922; Lille, March 9, 1922; and Dijon, March 1, 1922).

59. Opposition to all overtime was expressed, for example, by construction workers in *L'Ouvrier du bâtiment* (October–December 1924). Textile unions of Tourcoing in F^{22} 418 (June 28, 1922) rejected all overtime as did food workers in F^{22} 408 (May 19, 1925). The files F^{22} 404–31, largely devoted to the written comments of employers and workers regarding projected hours decrees in

specific industries, are filled with these intransigent opinions. However, overtime rates of 30 percent were acceptable to metalworkers near Belfort although they preferred a 50 percent raise in family allocations. F⁷ 13775, Belfort police reports (February 25, and March 10, 1920). Textile workers from Angers accepted rates of 25 to 50 percent. F²² 404, inspector report (Nantes, March 10, 1922). High overtime rates prevented the use of government-approved overtime in print trades according to F²² 404, inspector report (Rouen, March 11, 1922).

60. F²² 404, inspector reports (Nancy, March 9, 1922; and Dijon, March 11, 1922).

61. F²² 404, inspector report (Dijon, March 11, 1922); and F²² 408, inspector report (Tourcoing, September 26, 1922). Vandeputte made the same point when he argued that overtime be allowed only because of "unforeseen orders, not because of a poor organization of work"; see *L'Ouvrier textile* (July–September 1920), p. 5.

62. For example, Belfort metalworkers insisted that the first eight hours of pay be sufficient to meet family needs. F⁷ 13775, police report (March 10, 1920).

63. Rives, *La Corvée*, p. 166.

64. See Maurice Halbwachs, *La Classe ouvrière et les niveaux de vie* (Paris, 1913); and Peter Stearns, *Lives of Labor* (New York, 1976), p. 283.

65. *Information ouvrière et sociale* (October 9, 1919).

66. Scottish Trade Union Congress, *Annual Report* (1918), p. 53; PRO CAB 24/73, "Lab. Sit." (January 1, 1919); "Annual Report of the Chief Factory Inspector," BPP (1919), vol. 22, p. 12; CAB 24/87, "Lab. Sit." (August 20, 1919); and MRC EEF, H14/1, EEF letter to Coventry branch (June 17, 1919).

67. *Le Peuple* (February 12, 1923). For a file on the Saturday half-holiday with a fifty-four-hour week, see F²² 401. See also F²² 420, letter from Syndicat des mécaniciens . . . de France (September 26, 1919); F²² 404, inspector reports (Nantes, March 9–10, 1922; and Dijon, March 11, 1922); *Information ouvrière et sociale* (February 16, 1919); *Voix du Peuple* (June 1919): 380; *Industrial and Labour Information* (June 9, 1922), p. 23; *L'Ouvrier textile* (July–September 1919); *Journée industrielle* (August 26, 1923); and F²² 415 inspector report (Paris, May 27, 1922).

68. *Le Peuple* (October 6, 1926); and *Bulletin quotidien* (November 26, 1926) in F²² 402.

69. Wage-earning daughters may have preferred working for pay on Saturday morning to doing uncompensated housework under the demanding eye of mother, as claimed by John Benn, *Industrial Welfare* (August 1939), pp. 295–99.

70. See, for example, *Bulletin du Ministère du travail* (January–March 1922): 60, and (October–December 1922): 424. Note also chapter 10, nn. 31–43.

71. Richard Stone and D. A. Rowe, *The Measurement of Consumer Expen-*

diture and Behaviour in the United Kingdom, 1920–1938 (London, 1966), 3: 133, 159; Cecil Chisholm, *Marketing Survey of the United Kingdom,* 3rd ed. (London, 1938), pp. 51–56; John Walton and James Walvin, *Leisure in Britain, 1780–1939* (Manchester, 1983), esp. pp. 32–42; Lowerson and Howkins, *Trends in Leisure,* pp. 17, 36–39, 50–54; Jones, *Workers at Play,* pp. 34–62; and George Orwell, *Road to Wigan Pier* (London, 1962), p. 80. Other sources are Walter Greenwood, *Love on the Dole* (London, 1933); Rachel Low, *The History of British Film, 1918–1929* (London, 1971), pp. 39–43; James Walvin, *The Peoples' Game* (London, 1975); Sidney Dark, *After Working Hours* (London, 1929); Asa Briggs, *The History of Broadcasting in the United Kingdom* (London, 1979); and Mass Observation, *The Pub and the People* (London, 1943).

72. For a somewhat different view, see Michael Siedman, "The Birth of the Weekend and the Revolts against Work: The Workers of the Paris Region during the Popular Front (1936–38)," *French Historical Studies* 12 (Fall 1982): 249–76.

73. Few French labor inspectors' reports on the impact of the eight-hour day on industry (May 1920, March and May 1922) noted any complaints from employers that workers refused to accept innovation. Inspectors attributed the difficulties in improving productivity to shortages of capital rather than worker resistance to change; see F^{22} 404 and 408.

Chapter 9. Labor and Rationalization

1. See, for example, Angelo Pichierri, "Diffusion and Crisis in Scientific Management in European Industry," in *Contemporary Europe,* ed. S. Giner and M. S. Archer (London, 1978), pp. 55–73; Craig Littler, *Control and Conflict: The Development of Modern Work Systems in Britain, Japan, and the USA* (London, 1981); Judith Merkle, *Management and Ideology: The Legacy of the International Scientific Management Movement* (Berkeley, 1980); and Charles Maier, "Between Taylorism and Technocracy," *Journal of Contemporary History* 5 (1970): 27–62.

2. Peter Kane, "The Impact on Employment, of Worksharing and the Shorter Working Week in 20th Century Britain" (Ph.D. dissertation, University of London School of Economics and Political Science, 1982), pp. 77–79.

3. Estimates of mean weekly overtime in British industry remained unchanged between 1873 and 1913 at 2 hours. The figure for 1924 was 1.2 while the estimated overtime per week in 1968 was 4.3 hours. See R. C. O. Matthews, C. H. Feinstein, J. C. Olding-Snee, *British Economic Growth, 1856–1973* (Stanford, 1982), p. 70.

4. Industrial production fell from 99 in 1920 to 79.7 during the 1921 depression (1913 = 100). Recovery was slow with production reaching the 125 level only in 1929. See Sidney Pollard, *The Development of the British Economy, 1914–1980,* 3rd ed. (London, 1983), p. 52. More revealing, insured worker unemployment reached 22.2 percent in May 1921 and declined to single-digit figures only in 1924 and seldom dipped below 10 percent. Forrest Capie, *The Inter-war British Economy: A Statistical Abstract* (Manchester, 1983), pp. 20, 26, 63.

5. The causes of this prolonged stagnation are well known. Despite significant growth in new industries (automobile, electrical goods, chemicals, etc.) and a shift of employment from north to south, new sector growth was insufficient to counteract the decline in traditional industries (e.g., textiles, iron and steel, shipbuilding, and coal). Although demand grew by the mid-1920s, foreign competition had seriously cut British market share, and overcapacity plus managerial inertia had led to deep depressions in these industries. Useful sources include Charles Mowat, *Britain between the Wars, 1918–1940* (London, 1955); Roderick Floud and Donald McCloskey, *The Economic History of Britain since 1700* (New York, 1981); and Capie, *Interwar British Economy.*

6. While automobile production increased 201 percent between 1923 and 1933, the work force rose only 23 percent. Coal mining jobs decreased by 316,000 between 1913 and 1933. This can be partially explained by an increase from 8.5 to 42 percent in the share of coal cut by machines. Whereas 480 men were employed at sixteen drop hammers at a tool-making plant in 1918, by 1927 only 280 remained to operate twenty-two hammers. See Hubert Williams, *Man and the Machine* (London, 1935), pp. 75, 136–42, 65–68; and J. T. Walton Newbold, *Steel* (London, 1926), pp. 33–34.

7. Matthews et al., *Economic Growth,* p. 514.

8. Ibid., p. 314.

9. L. A. Vincent, "Population active, production, et productivité dans 21 branches de l'économie française (1896–1962)," *Etudes et conjonctures* (February 1965): 78–93.

10. Gary Cross, *Immigrant Workers in Industrial France* (Philadelphia, 1983), chaps. 2, 3, and 6.

11. E. H. Phelps-Brown, *A Century of Pay* (London, 1968), p. 210; Jean Fourastié, *Les 40,000 Heures* (Paris, 1965), pp. 76–80; and Jean Fourastié, *The Causes of Wealth* (Glencoe, Ill., 1960), pp. 168–71; and Alfred Sauvy, *L'Histoire économique de la France entre les deux guerres,* vol. 1 (Paris, 1965), chaps. 3 and 4; vol. 2 (Paris, 1984), pp. 221–22, 366–67; and vol. 3 (Paris, 1984), p. 95. See also Paul Combé, *Niveau de vie et progrès technique en France (1860–1939)* (Paris, 1965), pp. 162–63, 169.

12. Jean-Jacques Carré, P. Dubois, and John Malinvaud, *French Economic Growth* (Stanford, 1975), p. 220.

13. Vincent, as modified by Carré, estimates a 14 percent drop in mean an-

nual man-hours between 1913 and 1929 as compared to an 11 percent decline between 1929 and 1939. These are only crude guesses owing to the lack of full data on either nominal or real working hours. For example, Vincent's figures (especially before 1931) are calculated from comparisons of hourly pay with weekly wages based on data tabulated each October. It is likely that this procedure would have overestimated hours worked above forty-eight by the fact that overtime pay rates were evidently not taken into account. Carré et al., *Economic Growth* pp. 90–99. See also Jean Fourastié, *Des Loisirs pour quoi faire?* (Paris, 1979), p. 37.

14. Carré et al., *Economic Growth,* pp. 90–99; and Edward F. Denison, *Why Growth Rates Differ* (Washington, D.C., 1967), pp. 59–62.

15. Carré et al., *Economic Growth,* pp. 81–98.

16. Jean Bouvier et al., *Histoire économique et sociale de la France* (Paris, 1980), 4: 646–52; and Maurice Lévy-Leboyer, "Innovation and Business Strategies," in *Enterprise and Entrepreneurs in Nineteenth- and Twentieth-Century France,* ed. Edward Carter (Baltimore, 1976), pp. 116–29.

17. A. Vines, "Engineers' Views on Scientific Management," *Engineering and Industrial Management* (January 1, 1920): 12–14. Note the general efficiency theme in *Industrial Welfare and Personnel Management,* first published in 1920 by the Industrial Welfare Society. The same was true of *System* (1919–1925), a journal that stressed office as well as factory efficiency.

18. There is a consensus on these points. Note Littler, *Conflict,* pp. 99–145; G. Brown, *Sabotage* (Nottingham, 1977), pp. 148–59; Steven Wood, ed., *The Degradation of Work? Skill, Deskilling and the Labour Process* (London, 1982), esp. pp. 19–42; Howard Gospel, "The Development of Management Organisation in Industrial Relations," in *Management Strategies and Industrial Relations,* ed. Keith Thruley and Steven Wood (London, 1982); E. H. Lorenz, "The Labour Process and Industrial Relations in the British and French Shipbuilding Industries, 1880–1970" (Ph.D. dissertation, Cambridge University, 1983); and Charles Sabel, *Work and Politics: the Division of Labor in Industry* (Cambridge, 1982). Particularly helpful were two as yet unpublished papers by Wayne Lewchuk, "The Effort Bargain and Technological Change," and "The Effort Crisis and British Managerial Strategies."

19. Criticism of Taylor's neglect of the "human factor" can be found in Charles Myers, "Industrial Efficiency from the Psychological Standpoint," *Cassiers Magazine* (April 24, 1919): 332; and P. Sargant Florence, *Economics of Fatigue and Unrest* (London, 1924), pp. 76–77, 93–101, 118–23.

20. This lack of managerial controls is well documented by Lewchuk (see n. 18). See also Jonathan Zeitlin, "Craft Regulation and the Division of Labour: Engineers and Compositors in Britain, 1890–1914" (Ph.D. dissertation, University of Warwick, 1981); and Edward Wigham, *The Power to Manage: A History of the Engineering Employers' Federation* (London, 1973).

21. Littler, *Conflict,* pp. 101–42; William F. Watson, *Bedaux and Other Bonus Systems Explained* (London, 1932); Mark Jenkins, *Time and Motion Strikes, Manchester, 1934–37* (London, 1974); and General Federation of Trade Unions, "Report on the Bedaux and Kindred Systems" (London, 1932), LSE Pamphlet Collection.

22. Industrial Fatigue Research Board, *Annual Report No. 1* (London, 1920), pp. 1–17; and H. M. Vernon, "Fatigue and Efficiency in the Iron and Steel Industry," *Industrial Fatigue Research Board, Report No. 5* (London, 1920).

23. Included were trade unionists J. R. Clynes and Arthur Henderson, as well as the chemicals executive Henry Melchett and the chocolate manufacturer and social scientist B. S. Rowntree.

24. PRO LAB 2 817/14, reports on the Committee of Enquiry into the Production of Industry (March 2, 1920). A summary of the Balfour Commission appears in *Labour Gazette* (April 1928): 123. For the full report, see Committee on Industry and Trade, *Factors in Industrial and Commercial Efficiency* (London, 1927). See also Lyndall Urwick (Director of the International Management Institute in Geneva), *The Meaning of Rationalisation* (London, 1929).

25. *The Times Engineering Supplement* (August 1920, February 1921, June 1921), cited in Florence, *Fatigue and Unrest,* pp. 118–20; *Labour Gazette* (October 1927): 372; and "Annual Report of the Chief Inspector of Factories," BPP (1922), vol. 7, p. 86, and (1923), vol. 11, pp. 49–51.

26. T. Bedford, S. Wyatt, and H. M. Vernon, "Two Studies on Rest Pauses in Industries," *IFRB, Report No. 25* (London, 1924); S. Wyatt, "Studies in Repetitive Work, with Special References to Rest-Pauses," *IFRB, Report 32* (London, 1925); S. Wyatt and J. N. Langdon, *Fatigue and Boredom in Repetitive Work* (London, 1937); H. M. Vernon and T. Bedford, "Two Studies of Absenteeism in Coal Mines," *IFRB, Report No. 62* (London, 1931); and Florence, *Fatigue and Unrest,* pp. 349–50.

27. Auguste Detœuf, "La Réorganisation industrielle," *Les Cahiers du Redressement français* 7 (1927): 39. See also Richard Kuisel, "Auguste Detœuf, Conscience of French Industry: 1926–47," *International Review of Social History* 20 (1975): 149–74; and Richard Kuisel, *Ernest Mercier: French Technocrat* (Berkeley, 1967).

28. André Siegfried, *Les États-Unis aujourd'hui* (Paris, 1926); H. Dubreuil, *Standards* (Paris, 1927); Paul Devinat, *Scientific Management in Europe* (Geneva, 1927); and Bertram Austin and W. F. Lloyd, *The Secret of High Wages* (London, 1926). On Fordism, see Steven Meyer, *The Five Dollar Day* (Albany, N.Y., 1982); Henry Ford, *My Life and Work* (Garden City, N.Y., 1923); and especially Henry Ford, *My Philosophy of Industry* (New York, 1929).

29. ILO, *Director's Report, International Labour Conference* (Geneva, 1927), 32; *Industrial and Labour Information* (April 1, 1929), p. 27; Paul Devinat, "Le Mouvement européen en faveur de l'organisation scientifique du travail," *Les*

Cahiers du Redressement français 8 (1927): 16–18; *International Labour Conference* (Geneva, 1928), p. 563; and *Le Peuple* (May 4, 1928).

30. Not only did the French Ministry of Labor become involved, but in 1927 the ILO became a sponsor and helped to organize the International Scientific Management Institute. This institute gave uncritical support to Fordism. See Devinat, *Scientific Management in Europe;* and ILO, *The Social Aspects of Rationalisation* (Geneva, 1931).

31. *Le Peuple* (March 11, 1928, and January 17, 1929); and *La Voix du peuple* (April 1928): 273.

32. This was especially evident in 1926–1927 when a cyclic downturn combined with moves by Italy and Britain (in coal) to raise working hours as a means of gaining competitive advantage. For a summary, see Albert Thomas, "The Eight-Hour Day," *International Labour Review* 6 (August 15, 1926): 154–55. See chapter 7, n. 72.

33. *Information sociale* (June 20, 1929); and Albert de Tarlé, "L'Organisation rationnelle du travail industriel et les syndicats ouvriers," *L'Economie nouvelle* (March 1927): 78–81.

34. *Industrial and Labour Information* (April 7, 1922), pp. 32–35; and Léon Pasquier, *La Loi sur la journée de huit heures* (Paris, 1922), pp. 78–103.

35. Pasquier, *La Loi,* p. 83. Postwar interest in Taylorism is evident in the engineering journals; see, for example, *Le Génie civil* (February 8, 1919): 137, (February 15, 1919): 177–81; and (October 18, 1919): 379–80.

36. Indeed, the published data show a rate of success that contrasts to similar information collected in 1919–1920. The French government preferred to leave these earlier data in their archives rather than allow opponents to use their results in the campaign against the eight-hour day. These differences were in part the result of longer periods of adaptation of shorter hours in the published data and the fact that the unpublished results were gathered in 1919 and 1920, years of extraordinary labor unrest and readjustments made necessary by the shift from a war to a civilian economy. Whereas the published survey found an increase of 24.4 percent in daily output per worker over a mean of 3.7 years of experience with the eight-hour day, the rate for a study of fifty-four shoe factories with an average of 4.8 months under the eight-hour day revealed a 17.7 percent decrease in daily output per worker. In a study of fifty-six textile firms, operating eight-hour shifts for only 3.7 months, the decrease was 22 percent. The fact that at least one employer group demanded that its membership not cooperate with the later survey suggests that firms hostile to the reform and possibly those less likely to have adapted to the change were not included in the published data. These unpublished data appear in F^{22} 402. Information about the gathering of the published material is in "L'Adaptation des conditions de production et de travail à la loi du 23 avril 1919 sur la journée de huit heures," *Bulletin du Ministère du travail* (April–June 1924): 100.

37. F²² 404, inspector report (Nancy, March 9, 1922).

38. Michelle Perrot, "The Three Ages of Industrial Discipline in Nineteenth Century France," in *Consciousness and Class Experience in Nineteenth Century Europe,* ed. John Merriman (New York, 1979), pp. 160–66.

39. "L'Adaptation des conditions," *Bulletin du Ministère du travail* (April–June 1924): 110; and André Citroën, "L'Avenir de la construction automobile," *Revue politique et parlementaire* (May 10, 1929): 232–40.

40. Patrick Fridenson, "Automobile Workers in France and their Work, 1914–1983," in *Work in France,* ed. Steven Kaplan and Cynthia Koepp (Ithaca, N.Y., 1986), pp. 515–23; and Sylvie Schweitzer, *Des Engrenages à la chaîne: Les Usines Citroën, 1915–1935* (Lyon, 1982), pp. 60–62, 80–90; and Alain Pinol, "Travaux ouvriers et témoignages oraux: L'Exemple des usines Berliet pendant l'entre-deux-guerres," in *Mémoire vivante: Dires et savoirs populaires,* ed. Jean-Baptiste Martin (Lyon, 1982), pp. 152–57.

41. H. M. Vernon found that production levels were restored in tinplate and some steel plants within two to twelve months after the introduction of the eight-hour day. But he admitted that the largest gains in productivity were due not to reduced fatigue but to technological innovations. See his "Speed of Adaptation of Output to Altered Hours of Work," *IFRB Report No. 6* (London, 1920); and E. Farmer, "Comparisons of Different Shift Systems in the Glass Trade," *IFRB Report No. 24* (London, 1924).

42. R. M. Fox, "Fordism and the Future," *Labour Magazine* (January 1927): 405–6; and William F. Watson, "Should the Workers Increase Output?" (East London Workers' Committee, 1920), LSE Pamphlet Collection.

43. See, for example, Léon Rougier, "L'Avenir," *Revue des deux mondes* (June 13, 1930): 914–20, who complained that the new mechanization would lead to a decline of the privileged elites.

44. André Philip, *Le Problème ouvrier aux Etats-Unis* (Paris, 1927), pp. 147, 216, 225.

45. Ilya Ehrenburg, *The Life of the Automobile* (1929; reprint: New York, 1972), pp. 23–24.

46. *La Révolution prolétarienne* (July 1, 1928): 199–200, (February 15, 1926): 22, (March 15, 1927): 84–85, and (May 1927): 147–51.

47. *La Révolution prolétarienne* (November 1928): 275–81.

48. John Gerber, "Dissident Communist Groups and Publications in France during the Interwar Period," *Third Republic/Troisième République* (Spring 1980): 1–62. For a more optimistic view of syndicalism, see Katherine Amdur, *Syndicalist Legacy* (Urbana, Ill., 1986).

49. Fridenson, "Automobile Workers," pp. 521–25; Schweitzer, *Des Engrenages,* pp. 71, 80–82; Pinol, "Travail," pp. 140–46; Annie Foucaut, *Femmes à l'usine: Ouvrières et surintendantes dans les entreprises françaises de l'entre-deux-guerres* (Paris, 1982), pp. 96–101; and Jean-Paul Depretto and Sylvie

Schweitzer, *Le Communisme à l'usine: Vie ouvrière et mouvement chez Renault, 1920–1939* (Roubaix, 1984), pp. 54–63, 78–80.

50. Arthur Gleason, *What the Workers Want?* (London, 1920), interviews with Robin Williams, pp. 40–59 and Tom Mann, pp. 104–11. *British Trade Union Review* (January 1921): 9, (December 1920): 7, for favorable reports on electrification and scientific management. See Lewchuk, "The Effort Crisis."

51. George Skelly, ed., *The General Strike* (London, 1976) p. 412; and TUC, *Report of Proceedings* (1929), pp. 66–68, and (1931), pp. 220–22.

52. TUC, *Report of the Proceedings* (1929), pp. 198–99. See also TUC, "Memorandum on Technological Unemployment" (London, 1928), LSE Pamphlet Collection. This was a clear reflection of the views of the International Association for Social Progress with its mixed-class membership and linkages to the old reform coalition. On the committee were such leading reformers as Bertram Austin, C. H. Northcott, P. Sargant Florence, and G. D. H. Cole. See the International Association for Social Progress, British Section, *Report on the Hours of Work and Their Relationship to Output* (London, 1927), and *Report on the Policy of High Wages* (London, 1931).

53. William Watson, *Men and Machines* (London, 1935), pp. 150–57, 214–15, 219, 223; and F. J. Maynard, "Fordism vs. Individuality," *Labour Magazine* (February 1927): 474–75.

54. I do want to qualify this. Watson in the 1930s and Brownlie in the postwar period were conditional in their support of new methods. Watson continued to oppose the Bedaux system and Brownlie likewise was hostile to incentive systems that were imposed on workers. See Watson, *Men and Machines,* pp. 167–68, 219. Also by 1929 union voices hostile to the impact of rationalization on employment were heard. See, for example, TUC, *Report on the Proceedings* (1929), pp. 427–29, and (1931), p. 128–30, 219–20. The result was by 1933 the advocacy of a forty-hour week as a response to technological unemployment.

55. Note the enthusiastic reviews of Bertram Austin and Willis F. Lloyd, *The Secret of High Wages* (London, 1926), in *Le Peuple* (March 30, 1926), and *Information ouvrière et sociale* (April 15, 1926). See also A. Merrheim, *Information ouvrière et sociale* (May 4, 1919); and Léon Jouhaux, *La Bataille syndicaliste* (July 23, 1919).

56. Martin Fine, "Toward Corporatism" (Ph.D. dissertation, University of Wisconsin, 1971), pp. 279–83; H. Dubreuil, *La République industrielle* (Paris, 1924); and *Information sociale* (September 4, and October 2, 1924; January 3, and May 28, 1925; and July 29, 1926).

57. H. Dubreuil, *Standards* (translated as *Robots or Men*) (New York, 1927), pp. 36, 78, 172, 192; *Nouveaux Standards* (Paris, 1931), pp. 48, 110, 200, 213, 223–24.

58. ILO, *Social Aspects,* p. 280. See also Jules Moch, *Socialisme et rationalisation* (Paris, 1927), esp. pp. 37, 98; Devinat, *Scientific Management,* p. 30; and a series of articles by Charles Spinasse in *Le Peuple* describing model U.S. facto-

ries (e.g., the December 12, 1927, issue). Even Léon Blum shared a similar perspective; see *Le Populaire* (May 4 and 5, 1927).

59. ILO, *Social Aspects*, p. 279.

60. Henri De Man, *Joy in Work* (New York, 1929), esp. p. 67.

61. *Le Peuple* (January 29, 1929), as well as (January 11, 1927; May 12, and November 20, 1928; January 3 and 14, March 13, August 23, 1929; and March 5 and 13, 1930), for example.

62. See rank-and-file opposition to this policy on rationalization in CGT, *Congrès national corporatif: Compte rendu des débats* (Paris, 1929), p. 262; and *Voix du Peuple* (September 1929); 676, 679.

63. *Le Peuple* (October 30, 1926) for the CGT's "Manifesto on Productivity." Also important is *Le Peuple* (November 15, 1927), "Le Programme de la CGT." See Raymond Manevy *La Défense des 8 heures* (Paris, 1922), for a summary of CGT articles.

64. *Le Peuple* (October 15, 1926). See also Luchien Karsten and Ger Harmsen, "Le Premier mai: Jour de manifestation dans le mouvement ouvrier neerlandais, 1890–1940," a forthcoming chapter in anthology published by the International Institute of Social History.

65. François Fontenay, "A propos du Fordisme," *Les Cahiers du Bolchevisme* (October 9, 1926): 18–32. See also F. Fontenay, "C'est à qui la rationalisation?" *Les Cahiers du Bolchevisme* (January 15, 1927): 49–53.

66. V. I. Lenin, "The Immediate Tasks of the Soviet Government" (first published in *Pravda* [April 28, 1918]), in *Selected Works* (Moscow, 1967), 2: 663–64. See also James Bunyan, *The Origins of Forced Labor in the Soviet State, 1917–1921* (Baltimore, 1967); Jean Querzola, "Le Chef d'orchestre à la main de fer: Léninisme et taylorisme," in *Soldat du travail*, ed. Leon Marard and Patrick Zylberman (Special issue of *Recherches*), (Paris, 1978), pp. 59–94; Kendall Bailes, *Technology and Society under Lenin and Stalin* (Princeton, 1978). For a recent analysis and bibliography, see Lewis Siegelbaum and William Chase, "Worktime and Industrialization in the Soviet Union, 1917–1941," in *Worktime and Industrialization: An International History*, ed. Gary Cross (Philadelphia, 1988), pp. 183–210.

67. A. Losovsky, "La Trustation, la rationalisation et nos tâches," *L'Internationale syndicale rouge* (November 1926): 947–54; and M. Rubenstein, "Les Contradictions de la rationalisation capitaliste," *L'Internationale syndicale rouge* (January 1927): 3–11. See Jane Degras, ed., *The Communist International 1919–1943, Documents* (London, 1960), 2: 44, for the position of the Comintern on "capitalist rationalization" in a session held November 22 to December 6, 1926.

68. *La Vie ouvrière* (July 19 and September 1929). See also Siegelbaum and Chase ("Worktime") for a discussion of the seven-hour day in the Soviet Union. For other views on communist approaches to rationalization, see Pierre Saint-Germain, "La Chaîne et le parapluie: Face à la rationalisation (1919–1935),"

Révoltes logiques 1 (Spring–Summer 1976): 87–124; Depretto and Schweitzer, *Communisme,* pp. 20–28; and Patrick Fridenson, "The Coming of the Assembly Line to Europe," *Sociology of the Sciences* 2 (1978): 168–72.

69. CGTU, *Congrès national ordinaire, compte rendu des débats* (September 1927), p. 508, and (September 1929), pp. 527–29.

70. Degras, *Documents,* 2: 433; and *La Vie ouvrière* (June 28, 1929): 3.

71. *L'Humanité* (December 5, 1928 and March 15, 1929) for reports on automobile plants. *L'Humanité* (January 4; July 4, 8, 11, 28; and August 7, 1928) for evidence of CGTU defense of craft skills.

72. See, for example, *L'Humanité* (April 15, 1929) and *La Vie ouvrière* (May 1, 1929) for evidence of a greater shop-floor militancy within the struggling CGTU Metalworkers' Federation. Note also CGTU, *Congrès* (1929), p. 529.

Chapter 10. The Right to Time in the Twentieth Century

1. Allen Hutt, *The Condition of the Working Class in Britain* (London, 1933), pp. 22–23, 30, 61–65, 169–70; Walter Southgate, *That Was the Way It Was, 1890–1950* (London, 1972), chap. 25; Odette Hary-Hémery, "Rationalisation technique et rationalisation du travail à la compagnie des Mines d'Anzin (1927–1938)," *Le Mouvement social* 72 (July–September 1970): 3–48; Marie-Antoinette Boudet, *La Semaine de 40 heures* (Paris, 1935), pp. 85–88, 101–8; and Adolphe Hodée, *Les travailleurs devant la rationalisation* (Paris, 1934).

2. Michelle Collinet, *La Condition ouvrière* (Paris, 1951), chaps. 1 and 2. Examples of the reformist French disillusionment with rationalization include *Information sociale* (April 30, 1930); CGT, *Congrès national corporatif* (Paris, 1931), pp. 43–51; and *Le Peuple* (September 12 and 15, 1931). Communist views are summarized in CGTU, *Congrès national ordinaire* (Paris, 1931), pp. 39–40, 128–29, 153–58, 450, 458. British sentiments are expressed in the *Proceedings at a Meeting between Engineering and Allied Employers' National Federations and Various Trade Unions, 40 Hours Week* (London, February 1934), pp. 1–5, 8–9, 11–12; and International Association for Social Progress, *Inquiry into the Hours Problem* (London, 1933), pp. 48–51.

3. TUC, *Proceedings* (1933), pp. 71–72, 214; *Labour Magazine* (February 1933): 438–42; and PRO LAB 2 1008 IL 113/1933, undated report on the TUC; International Association for Social Progress, *Inquiry,* pp. 48–49.

4. *The Times* (October 27, 1932); and Josiah Stamp, *The Present Position of Rationalisation* (London, 1932).

5. See, for example, Charles Dukes of the General and Municipal Workers, *Labour Magazine* (January 1935): 112.

6. *Proceedings . . . between Engineering . . . and Various Trade Unions, 40 Hour Week*, p. 15; and TUC, *Proceedings* (1933), p. 71.

7. One of the few direct references to the benefits of the two-day weekend is the amusing pamphlet by the Communist Party of Great Britain, "Friday Night Till Monday Morning," which would allow the worker to "please the wife" and "treat . . . the kiddies now and then." The pamphlet featured a cartoon showing a man sleeping in on Saturday morning with the words of an old music hall song underneath, "S'nice to get up on Saturday morning, but s'nicer not to!"

8. Other good examples are William Sherwood, "Shipbuilding Industry: Application for the 40 Hour Week without Reduction in Pay" (Edinburgh, June 27, 1934), in TUC Archives, HD 9678, and the negotiations in the iron and steel industries, MRC ISTC, MSS 36 H29 and I30a between 1932 and 1937.

9. MCR EEF, H 11/3, National Confederation of Employers' Organisations, "The Unemployment Situation, Report Submitted to the Ministry of Labour" (December 6, 1933). See also Engineering and Allied Employers' National Federation, "40 Hours Week, Analysis by the Federation of the Case Presented by the Trade Unions," (London, February 15, 1934, and March 1934), in the LSE Pamphlet Collection.

10. International Association for Social Progress, *Inquiry,* pp. 3, 5–6, 14–17, and 21–24; C. A. Macartney (League of Nations Union Conference), *Hours of Work and Employment* (London, 1934), pp. 10–16, 26–27, 31–33, 38, 40–45, 51; M. Steward (New Fabian Research Board), *The 40 Hours Week* (London, 1937), esp. pp. 25–31; *Industrial Welfare* (October 1934): 42–43; Ernest Bevin, *My Plan for 2,000,000 Workless* (London, 1936); and H. M. Vernon, *The Shorter Working Week with Special Reference to the Two-Shift System* (London, 1934).

11. CGT, *Pourquoi la semaine de 40 heures* (Paris, 1933), pp. 7–15; CGT, *La Semaine de quarante heures* (Paris, 1932), pp. 22, 28, and 30; CGT, *Congrès Confédéral* (Paris, 1933), pp. 43–44; *Le Peuple* (June 10, 1933); *Voix du peuple* (January 1934): 36, (September 1934): 549–50, and (December 1934): 778; and M. Lescure, *Les Crises générales et périodiques de surproduction,* 3rd ed. (Paris, 1934). For the communist view, see Jacques Doriot, *Journée de sept heures avec salaire de huit heures* (Paris, 1932).

12. Jouhaux's speech at Lille on February 26, 1933, is cited in Boudet, *La Semaine,* p. 162. See also CGT, *La Semaine de quarante heures,* p. 4.

13. Boudet, *La Semaine,* p. 213; and Jean Duboin, *La Grande Relève des hommes par la machine* (Paris, 1935), pp. 341–54.

14. Pierre Collet, *La Semaine de quarante heures* (Paris, 1934), pp. 10–15, 33–39, 54–55, 150; M. Pinot, *La Semaine de 40 heures, le chômage et les prix*

(Paris, 1933), pp. 2–65, 39–121, 133; Georges Leduc, "La Semaine de quarante heures," *Revue d'économie politique* (September–October 1933): 1530; Eugène Combaz (Société pour la défense du commerce et de l'industrie de Marseille), *La Semaine de travail de 40 heures* (Marseille, 1932); and Boudet, *La Semaine,* pp. 114–15, 138, 155, 260–65.

15. For reports on the attitude of Catholic unions, see *Informations sociales* (June 19, 1933), p. 452; and Collet, *La Semaine,* pp. 44–45. The French branch of the International Association for Social Progress embraced the technological argument for unemployment in *Documents du Travail* (April 1933), as did Michael Scheler, "Technological Unemployment," *International Labour Review* 3 (1931): 24–26.

16. Benjamin Hunnicutt, "The New Deal: The Salvation of Work and the End of the Shorter Hour Movement," in *Worktime and Industrialization: An International History,* ed. Gary Cross (Philadelphia, 1988), pp. 217–43. For a full analysis, see Benjamin Hunnicutt, *Work without End: The Abandonment of Shorter Hours for the Right to Work* (Philadelphia, 1988). Note also Subcommittee on the Judiciary, U.S. Senate, *Hearings on The Thirty-Hour Work Week, January 1933* (Washington, D.C., 1933); Harold Moulton, *The 30-Hour Week* (Washington, D.C., 1935); and R. C. Wallhead, *A Six Hour Working Day* (London, 1933).

17. ILO, *Hours of Work and Unemployment Report to the Preparatory Conference* (Geneva, 1933), pp. 1–2, 8–9, 17–19, 28–29, 48–65. For additional background, see Lello Gangemi, *Il Problema della Durata del Lavoro* (Florence, 1929); Collet, *La Semaine,* pp. 16–24; and Boudet, *La Semaine,* chap. 1.

18. ILO, *Hours of Work and Unemployment Report of the Preparatory Conference, January 20 to 25, 1933* (Geneva, 1933), pp. 8–10, 12–13, 22–23; and PRO LAB 2 1008 IL 13/1933, reports on the ILO conference in January 1933, especially the report on Forbes-Watson (February 7, 1933).

19. In addition to the publication of the International Labour Conferences of 1933–1938, which are replete with hours matters, note, among the numerous documents dealing with the ILO forty-hour issue, PRO CAB 24/235, Labour Ministry memo (December 19, 1932); CAB 24/247, Ministry of Labour memos (February 6 and 7, 1934); CAB 24/255, Ministry of Labour memo (May 18, 1935); CAB 24/226, Ministry of Labour memo (December 13, 1935); PRO LAB 2 IR 409/1933, report on meeting of the Treasury concerning the forty-hour week (April 29, 1933); and LAB 2 10008 IL 173/2, Labour of Ministry memo (February 13, 1934). See also the thorough study of Boudet, *La Semaine,* pp. 275–76, 341.

20. The classic discussion of international economic policy in the depression is Charles Kindleberger, *World in Depression* (Berkeley, 1978).

21. TUC, *Proceedings* (1933), pp. 243–49, (1935), pp. 70–71, 138–42, 161–63, 171–74, 314–16, and (1936), pp. 71, 171–73, 341–44; PRO LAB 2 2047 IL 1935, Minister of Labour memo (July 27, 1933); and *Labour Maga-*

zine (March 1935): 159 and (August 1937): 294. See also nn. 8 and 9, this chapter.

22. *Labour Magazine* (November 1933): 70; Manchester City Council, "Reports of the Establishment Committee and the Finance Committee on the Financial Effect of the Establishment of a 40-Hour Week for All Manual Workers in The Employment of the Corporation" (Manchester, 1936), in the TUC Archive, HD 5165. See also Stephen Jones, "The Trade Union Movement and Work-Sharing Policies in Interwar Britain," *Industrial Relations Journal* 16 (1985): 57–69.

23. A summary is in CGT, *Congrès Confédéral* (1935), pp. 74–84, and (1938), pp. 65–66. See also *Voix du peuple* (June 1936): 65, 388. A fine recent analysis of the period is Julian Jackson, *The Politics of Depression in France* (New York, 1985).

24. René Belin, *La Semaine de quarante heures et la réduction du temps de travail* (Paris, 1937), pp. 1–14; and Jean-Charles Asselain, "Une Erreur de politique économique: La Loi de quarante heures de 1936," *Revue économique* 25 (1974): 690–91.

25. See chapter 9, nn. 10–11.

26. Belin, *La Semaine,* pp. 25–26.

27. Asselain, "Une Erreur," pp. 672–705; and Michael Seidman, "The Birth of the Weekend and the Revolts against Work during the Popular Front, 1936–1938," *French Historical Studies* 12 (Fall 1982): 249–76.

28. Note John Hobson's rejection of shorter hours and support instead for increased purchasing power through taxation and fiscal policy in *Rationalisation and Unemployment: An Economic Dilemma* (London, 1930), p. 123.

29. Charles Mills, *Vacations for Industrial Workers* (New York, 1927), pp. 149–210; Patrice Boussel, *Histoire des vacances* (Paris, 1961), pp. 27–161; Curtis et al. (Industrial Relations Staff), "Annual Paid Vacations for Workers in Countries Outside of the United States" (New York, December 1925), pp. 4–6, a copyrighted manuscript in the TUC Archive, HD 5106; Mass Observation Archive, "Worktown," Box 35/A, for clippings and notes on the survival of traditional wakes weeks in England in the mid-1930s; and House of Commons, *Minutes of Evidence Taken before the Committee on Holidays with Pay* (London, 1937), pp. 36–38. In 1912, British iron and steel trades demanded double time for work on holidays (MRC ISTC, MSS 36 H8).

30. John Beard and Alexander Dalgeish, *Out-of-Work Pay or Holidays with Pay: Which?* (Birmingham, 1926), pp. 1–15; TUC, *Proceedings* (1926), p. 433; *Labour Gazette* (August 1920): 230; Curtis et al., "Vacations," pp. i–iii, 5–8; Mills, *Vacations,* p. 308; and Miners' Federation of Great Britain, *Annual Volume* (1920), pp. 596–97, 682. See also TUC Archive HD5106 for various union vacation with pay proposals and agreements (1920–1924).

31. Georges Bachelier, *Les Congés payés à l'étranger du point de vue international* (Zurich, 1937), pp. 197–98; Roger Guerrand, *La Conquête des va-*

cances (Paris, 1963), p. 47; Conseil supérieur du travail, *Compte rendu* (1936): 156–64, 175; "Congés payés aux ouvriers," *Bulletin du Ministère du travail* (April–June 1929): 121–29; Curtis, "Vacations," p. 6; and Mills, *Vacations*, p. 307.

32. The 1931 bill provided that the vacation was to be extended slowly until reaching a maximum of fifteen days per year after fifty years of work. See Conseil supérieur du travail, *Compte rendu* (1935), pp. 129–40, 187–223, 228–32; and *Voix du Peuple* (November 1935): 893–94. See also A. Lorch, *Les Congés payés en France* (Paris, 1938); Nicole Odinet, *Les Congés annuels payés* (Paris, 1937); and Roger-Daniel Flament, *Les Congés payés* (Lille, 1938).

33. MRC EEF, H12/34, National Confederation of Employers' Organisations report on the Holiday with Pay Bill (1936), and EEF Circular (February 12, 1937); PRO CAB 24/257, Ministry of Labour memo (December 13, 1935); and Conseil supérieur du Travail, *Compte rendu* (1935), pp. 14–152.

34. Note, for example, the comments of employers in James Whittaker, *Holidays with Pay* (London, 1937), pp. 7–12.

35. See, for example, the following articles in *Industrial Welfare:* J. L. Hammond, "Industry and Leisure" (May 1934), p. 27; "Recreation Education" (May 1936), pp. 21–25; "Notes on Towns, Centres and Tours" (April 1937), pp. 27–31; and Kate Liepmann, "Journey to Work" (January 1938), pp. 7–10. See also Kate Liepmann, *The Journey to Work: Its Significance for Industrial and Community Life* (London, 1944).

36. *Labour Magazine* (October 1933): 45; (December 1933): 94. See also Stephen Jones, *Workers at Play: A Social and Economic History of Leisure, 1918–1939* (London, 1986), chap. 6.

37. Conseil supérieur du travail, *Compte rendu* (1935), pp. 226–27.

38. International Commission of Workers' Spare Time, *Official Bulletin* 1 (1938): 4–19, 48–49. See also Georges Mequet, "Spare Time in the Country, An English Experiment in Organisation," *International Labour Review* 9 (June 1924): 829; and idem, "Workers' Spare Time," *International Labour Review* 10 (November 1924): 555.

39. Again Britain refused to support the convention but was at least willing to agree to a "recommendation," a commitment that did not require legislation as did a convention. For details, see ILO, "Holidays with Pay, Report V," *International Labour Conference* (Geneva, 1935); and "Holidays with Pay, Report II," *International Labour Conference* (Geneva, 1936).

40. For example, the British economist Alfred Marshall, at the beginning of his career, had identified the ideal world as a place where "no one in it should have any occupation which tends to make him anything else than a gentleman"—a status that required freedom from work. Marshall advocated in his *Future of the Working Class* (London, 1873), pp. 9–12, two six-hour shifts and, for especially fatiguing work, three four-hour stints. Although from the 1880s he combated the job-sharing argument of short-hours advocates, in the fifth

edition of his *Principles of Economics* (London, 1920), pp. 693–98, he noted that "the coming generation is interested in the rescue of men, and still more women, from excessive work, at least as much as it is in handing down to it of a good stock of material wealth."

41. Among these cautionary reports about leisure (many by Americans) are George Cutten, *The Threat of Leisure* (New Haven, Conn., 1926); Constance Harris, *The Use of Leisure in Bethnal Green* (London, 1927); and Henry Durant, *The Problem of Leisure* (New York, 1938). More hopeful were Arthur Dahlberg, *Utopia through Capitalism: A Study of the Possibility of a Shorter Workday* (Madison, Wis., 1927); Clifford Furnas, *America's Tomorrow: An Informal Excursion into the Era of the Two-Hour Working Day* (New York, 1932); and Harry Overstreet, *A Guide to Civilized Loafing (Leisure)* (New York, 1934).

42. John Hammond, *The Growth of the Common Enjoyment* (London, 1933); C. Delisle Burns, *Leisure in the Modern World* (London, 1932), pp. 75–114, 234, 255–56; and Bertrand Russell, *In Praise of Idleness and Other Essays* (London, 1935), pp. 26–29. Compare William Pangburn, "The Workers' Leisure and His Individuality," *American Journal of Sociology* 27 (January 1922): 433–41.

43. House of Commons, *Evidence before the Committee on Holidays with Pay,* pp. 21–22, 27; TUC, *Holidays for All* (London, 1937), preface, pp. 3–20; TUC, *Proceedings* (1931), p. 334, and (1936), p. 174; *Labour Magazine* (August 1937): 279; and Whittaker, *Holidays,* pp. 12–20.

44. House of Commons, *Report on the Committee on Holidays with Pay* (Command Doc. 5724) (London, April 1938), pp. 5–7; PRO CAB 24/267, Ministry of Labour memo (January 28, 1937); CAB 24/276, Ministry of Labour memo (April 21, 1938); and CAB 24/277, Ministry of Labour memo (May 27, 1938). See also Stephen Jones, "Trade Union Policy between the Wars: The Case of Holidays with Pay," *International Review of Social History* 31 (1986): 40–67. See also n. 33.

45. House of Commons, *Report on the Committee on Holidays with Pay,* pp. 28–30; House of Commons, *Evidence before the Committee on Holidays with Pay,* pp. 135, 142, 153, 165, 171–73, 178–80, 189–90, 335–46; and John A. R. Pimlott, *The Englishman's Holiday* (London, 1948), pp. 215–41. See also Jones, *Workers at Play,* pp. 19–20.

46. House of Commons, *Report on the Committee on Holidays with Pay,* pp. 21–23.

47. Pay for holidays was often made conditional upon good attendance records and was sometimes reduced for single men and boys; holidays often required consecutive service to one employer for a year and were restricted to a July or August week when the plant or industrial district shut down. Some trades like printing, engineering, and transportation gave longer paid holidays (often up to fourteen days) for senior workers. Emile Brunner, *Holiday Making and the Holiday Trades* (London, 1945), pp. 3–4; Ministry of Labour, *Holidays*

with Pay: Collective Agreements between Organisations of Employers and Workpeople (London, 1939), pp. 7, 10; Miners' Federation of Great Britain, *Summary of the Provisions of the Holiday Schemes in Operation in the Districts* (London, 1938); MRC ISTC, MSS 36/H8, memo on holidays (September 29, 1938), and EEF, H12/34, holiday with pay memo (March 1938); PRO POWER 20/44, "Holiday with Pay in Mines, Summary Sheet" (December 1937–March 1938); and TUC and Labour Party, "Joint Research and Information on the Annual Holiday with Pay," no date, in TUC Archives, HC 5106.

48. Guerrand, *La Conquête,* pp. 48–57. A fine study of the role of the vacation in the ideology and policy of the Popular Front is Julian Jackson, "'Le Temps des Loisirs': Popular Tourism and Mass Leisure in the Front Populaire's Cultural-Political Vision," paper delivered at the conference, Front Populaire/Frente Popular: Comparative Perspectives on the Popular Front Experiences of France and Spain (1936–1986), University of Southampton, April 15–17, 1986.

49. Guerrand, *La Conquête,* pp. 48–50, and Jackson, "Le Temps," pp. 5–6. See also Gilbert Pouteau and Eugène Raude, *Le Message de Léo Legrange* (Lyon, 1950).

50. Jean Parant, *Le Problème du tourisme populaire* (Paris, 1939), pp. 79–180; Yves Becquet, *L'Organisation des loisirs des travailleurs* (Paris, 1939), pp. 227–28; and *Le Peuple* (April 11, 24, 19, 23, 24; May 5, 7, 11; July 13, and esp. August 4, 1937). Jackson, "Le Temps," pp. 6–12, is especially useful.

51. Raude, *Legrande,* cited in Jackson, "Le Temps," pp. 8–10, and *Le Peuple* (August 4, 1937). See also Gary Cross, "Vacations for All: The Leisure Question in the Era of the Popular Front," *Journal of Contemporary History* (in press).

52. Brunner, *Holiday Making,* pp. 5–10; Industrial Welfare Society, "Conference on Workers' Holidays" (London, November 30, 1938), and National Saving Holiday Clubs, "Holidays with Pay" (London, 1939), in the TUC Archive, HD 5106; MRC EEF, H12/39, Memo on National Savings Committee (September 17, 1937); TUC, *Proceedings* (1936), pp. 118–19; and PRO POWER 20/44, poster on Holiday Clubs (1938).

53. Workers' Travel Association, "Holidays with Pay Mean Hard Work for Somebody," *Labour Magazine* (August 1937): 282; and "The National Committee to Provide Holidays for Unemployed Workers in Distressed Areas" (London, 1938), in TUC Archive HD 5106. See also Colin Ward and Dennis Hardy, *Goodnight Campers! The History of the British Holiday Camp* (London, 1986), pp. 22–77.

54. See the local newspaper clippings (Spring 1982) in Mass Observation Archive, "Worktown," Box 31/D; MRC EEF, H12/34, Memos on holidays (February 28, 1936; November 12, 1938; and June 19, 1939); TUC, *Proceedings* (1938), p. 440; International Union of Food and Drink Workers, *Holidays with Pay in the Food and Drink Industry* (Zurich, 1938), p. 23; Louis Smith,

Holidays with Pay: A Plea for Voluntary Arrangements (Lincoln, 1939); and British Railway's Press Office, "Notes about Early Holidays" (London, 1938), in TUC Archive, HD 5106.

55. International Association for Workers' Spare Time, *Official Bulletin* 2 (1938): 15, 35–36. For the fascist equivalent, see International Central Bureau, *Joy and Work: Report of the World Congress for Leisure Time and Recreation, July 1936* (Berlin, 1937). Note also Victoria De Grazia, *The Culture of Consent: Mass Organization of Leisure in Fascist Italy* (New York, 1981); Victoria De Grazia, "La Politique sociale du loisir: 1900–1940," *Les Cahiers de la recherche architecturale* 15–17 (1985): 24–35; and Lebert H. Wier, *Europe at Play: A Study of Recreation and Leisure Time Activities* (New York, 1937).

56. Miners' Federation of Great Britain, *Annual Volume* (1938), pp. 18–22. Mass Observation Archive, "Worktown," Box 51, James Whittaker's essay contest entrants (September 1937).

57. See, for example, John Clarke, Chas Critcher, and Robert Johnson, *Working-Class Culture: Studies in History and Theory* (New York, 1979); Patrick Brantlinger, *Bread and Circuses: Theories of Mass Culture as Social Decay* (Ithaca, N.Y., 1983); J. Clarke and Chas Critcher, *The Devil Makes Work: Leisure in Capitalist Britain* (London, 1985); Cris Rojek, *Capitalism and Leisure Theory* (London, 1985); Tony Bennett, Colin Mercer, and Janet Woollacott, *Popular Culture and Social Relations* (Milton Keynes, England, 1986), for sources and recent discussion of this theme. A classic example of this theory of privatization and consumerism is Richard Hoggart, *The Uses of Literacy* (London, 1957).

58. Among the many sources available on the new short-hours movement, see especially Anne Lapping, *Working Time in Britain and West Germany: A Summary* (London, 1983); Sue Roger, *Vers une société du temps libre* (Paris, 1982); Yves Barou, *Les 35 heures et l'emploi* (Paris, 1983); Gert Hautsch, *Ziel: 35 Studen. Kampf um Arbeitszeitverkürzung* (Frankfurt, 1980); and Karl Hinrichs and Helmut Wiesenthal, "Arbeitswerte und Arbeitszeit: Zur Pluralierung von Wertmustern und Zeitverwendungswünschen in der modernen Industriegesellschaft," in *Arbeitszeitpolitik: Formen und Folgen einer Neuverteilung der Arbeitszeit,* ed. Claus Offe, Karl Hinrichs, and Helmut Wiesenthal (Frankfurt, 1982), pp. 116–36.

59. Hunnicutt, "The End of Short Hours." See also Reginald Carter, "The Myth of Increasing Nonwork Time vs. Work Activities," *Social Problems* 18 (1971): 52–66; and David Roediger and Phillip Foner, *Our Own Time: History of American Labor and the Working Day* (Westport, Conn., 1988).

60. George Orwell, *Road to Wigan Pier* (New York, 1962), p. 80.

61. Wassily Leontief, "The Distribution of Work and Income," *Scientific American* (September 1982): 100–13; W. Leontief and Faye Duchin, *The Future Impact of Automation on Workers* (New York, 1986); and Barry Jones, *Sleepers Wake! Technology and the Future of Work* (London, 1982), pp. 200–5. See also Ronald Ehrenberg, *Longer Hours or More Jobs* (Ithaca, N.Y., 1982).

62. Karl Hinrichs, Claus Offe, and Helmut Wiesenthal, "The Crisis of the Welfare State and Alternative Modes of Work Distribution," paper presented at the Conference on the Future of the Welfare State, European Centre for Work and Society, University of Limburg, December 1984. See also Echange et Projets, *La Révolution du temps choisi* (Paris, 1980).

63. Especially useful is Carmen Sirianni and Michele Eayrs, "Time, Work and Equality," unpublished paper (authors at Department of Sociology, Northeastern University, Boston).

64. See, for example, Fred Best, *Flexible Life Scheduling* (New York, 1980), and Carmen Sirianni, ed., *Worker Participation and the Politics of Reform* (Philadelphia, 1987).

Appendix

1. In the 1830s, Louis René Villermé found that daily hours in French textiles varied from ten to fifteen hours depending on region, character of production, and fabric. The lower hours were confined to the Midi and the higher to the Sedan. The most common schedule was the twelve- to fourteen-hour day. In comparison, the English standard was ten to twelve hours. Louis René Villermé, *Tableau de l'état physique et moral des ouvriers employés dans les manufactures de coton, de laine, et de soie* (Paris, 1840), pp. 83–85, 337. See also Ivy Pinchbeck and Margaret Hewitt, *Children in English Society* (London, 1979), 2: 395–98.

2. Charles Rist, "La Durée du travail dans l'industrie française," *Revue d'économie politique* (1897): 371, 390–91; and Georges Duveau, *La Vie ouvrière en France sous le Second Empire* (Paris, 1946), pp. 240–43.

3. See Charles Rist, *Réglementation légale de la journée de travail de l'ouvrier adulte en France* (Paris, 1898), pp. 182–92, for details of problems of comparing British and French worktime statistics.

4. Note, for example, the works by the French economist M. Spuller, "Commission d'enquête parlementaire sur la situation des ouvriers de l'industrie et de l'agriculture en France," France ChDoc Annex (1884), esp., pp. 209–11, and the English railroad developer Thomas Brassley, *Foreign Work and English Wages* (London, 1873), pp. 177–84.

5. Ministère du commerce, *Rapports sur l'application pendant l'année 1899 des lois réglementant la journée de travail de l'ouvrier adulte* (Paris, 1899), pp. 210–21, 509.

6. Rist, *Réglementation,* pp. 186–87; Armand Audiganne, *Les Populations ouvrières et les industries de la France* (Paris, 1860), 2: 87, 139; William Reddy, *The Rise of Market Culture: The Textile Trade and French Society, 1750–1900*

(New York, 1985), p. 238; and Frédéric Le Play, *Les Ouvriers européens: Etudes sur les travaux, la vie domestique, et la condition morale des populations ouvrières de l'Europe* (Paris, 1877–1879), 4: 308–10.

7. See Clive Behagg, "Controlling the Product," in *Worktime and Industrialization: An International History,* ed. Gary Cross (Philadelphia, 1989), pp. 41–58; Richard Whipp, "'A Time to Every Purpose,'" in *Historical Meanings of Work,* ed. Patrick Joyce (London, 1987), pp. 210–36; and Richard Whipp, "'The Art of Good Management': Managerial Control of Work in the British Pottery Industry, 1900–1925," *International Review of Social History* 29 (1984): 359–85.

8. Louis Blanc, *Le Socialisme* (Paris, 1948), p. 30; Ministère du travail, *Salaires et durée du travail en 1906* (Paris, 1907), pp. 242–65; Rist, *Réglementation,* pp. 200–3; and Roland Trempé, *Les Mineurs de Carmaux, 1848–1914* (Paris, 1971), pp. 192–98. Several very interesting studies of the formation of the French working class appear in *Working-Class Formation,* ed. Ira Katznelson and Aristide Zolberg (Princeton, 1986): William Sewell, "Artisans, Factory Workers, and the Formation of the French Working Class," pp. 45–71; Michelle Perrot, "On the Formation of the French Working Class," pp. 71–110; and Alain Cottereau, "The Distinctiveness of Working-Class Cultures, 1848–1900," pp. 111–156.

9. See especially the analysis and notes of G. Stedman Jones, *Outcast London* (London, 1971), chaps. 3 and 4; and Norman Dearle, *Problems of Unemployment in the London Building Trades* (London, 1908), pp. 26–45, 80–89.

Index

Compositor:	G & S Typesetters, Inc.
Text:	10/13 Galliard
Display:	Galliard
Printer:	Braun-Brumfield, Inc.
Binder:	Braun-Brumfield, Inc.